The Administration and Supervision of Special Programs in Education

MW00831624

Third Edition

Anita Pankake
University of Texas—Pan American

Mark Littleton
Tarleton State University

Kendall Hunt
publishing company

Cover image © Shutterstock, Inc.

Kendall Hunt
publishing company

Copyright © 2001, 2005, 2012 by Kendall/Hunt Publishing Company

ISBN 978-1-4652-0241-3

All rights reserved. No part of this publication may be reproduced, stored in a
retrieval system, or transmitted, in any form or by any means, electronic, mechanical,
photocopying, recording, or otherwise, without the prior written permission of the
copyright owner.

Printed in the United States of America
10 9 8 7 6 5 4 3 2

Contents

About the Authors and Contributors

Authors

Anita Pankake is Professor of Educational Leadership (retired) at The University of Texas – Pan American, Edinburg, Texas. Her e-mail address is: apankake@utpa.edu.

Mark Littleton is Professor of Educational Administration at Tarleton State University, Stephenville, Texas. His e-mail address is: Mlittleton@tarleton.edu.

Contributors

Jesus "Chuey" Abrego is Assistant Professor in the Department of Educational Psychology & Leadership at The University of Texas at Brownsville, Brownsville, Texas. E-mail: chuey.abrego@utb.edu

Michelle H. Abrego is Associate Professor in the Department of Educational Psychology & Leadership at The University of Texas at Brownsville, Brownsville, Texas. E-mail: michelle.abrego@utb.edu

Casey Graham Brown is Associate Professor, Director of the EDAD Doctoral Program and Co-director of the Meadows Principal Improvement Program in the Educational Leadership Department at Texas A & M University – Commerce, Commerce, Texas. E-mail: Casey_Brown@tamu-commerce.edu

Jennifer T. Butcher is Associate Professor in the Department of Educational Leadership at Lamar University, Beaumont, Texas. E-mail: jentbutcher@yahoo.com

Reba Criswell is Associate Professor and School Counseling Program Coordinator in the School of Education and Behavioral Sciences at Southeastern Oklahoma State University, Durant, Oklahoma. E-mail: rcriswell@se.edu

Stacey L. Edmonson is Chair and Professor in the Department of Educational Leadership and Counseling at Sam Houston State University in Huntsville, Texas. E-mail: edu_sle01@shsu.edu

Encarnación Garza, Jr. is Associate Professor in the Department of Educational Leadership & Policy Studies at The University of Texas at San Antonio, San Antonio, Texas. E-mail: ENCARNACION.GARZA@UTSA.EDU

María Luisa González is Associate Dean in the College of Education at The University of Texas at El Paso in El Paso, Texas. E-mail: mlgonzalez6@utep.edu

Diana K. Freeman is Director of Program Development at Ennis Independent School District, Ennis, Texas. E-mail: Diana.Freeman@Ennis.K12.TX.US

Richard Lampe is Professor in the Department of Counseling (retired) at Texas A & M University-Commerce, Commerce, Texas. E-mail: srlampe@embargmail.com

Velma D. Menchaca is Professor and Department Chair in the Department of Educational Leadership at The University of Texas – Pan American, Edinburg, Texas. E-mail: menchaca@utpa.edu

Rebecca Miller is Assistant Professor in the Department of Curriculum and Instruction at Tarleton State University, Stephenville, Texas. E-mail: rmiller@tarleton.edu

Shirley J. Mills is Assistant Professor in the Department of Educational Leadership at The University of Texas – Pan American, Edinburg, Texas. E-mail: millssj@utpa.edu

Ava J. Muñoz is Assistant Professor in the Department of Education Leadership and Policy Studies at the University of Texas – Arlington, Arlington, Texas. E-mail: avamunoz@uta.edu

Terry Overton is a Professor of Special Education at the University of Texas at Brownsville, Brownsville, Texas. E-mail: terry.overton@utb.edu

Mariela A. Rodríguez is Associate Professor in the Department of Educational Leadership & Policy Studies at the University of Texas at San Antonio, San Antonio, Texas. E-mail: MARIELA.RODRIGUEZ@UTSA.EDU

Alejo Salinas, Jr. is a Lecturer in the Department of Educational Leadership at The University of Texas – Pan American, Edinburg, Texas. E-mail: alejo3968@utpa.edu

Marie Simonsson is Associate Professor and Director of the Doctoral Program in the Department of Educational Leadership at The University of Texas – Pan American, Edinburg, Texas. E-mail: msimonsson@utpa.edu

Randy Tierce is Assistant Professor of Education, Liberty University Online. E-mail: krtierce@liberty.edu

Jerry Trusty is Professor in the Department of Educational Psychology, Counseling, & Special Education at Penn State University, University Park, Pennsylvania. E-mail: jgt3@psu.edu

Fernando Valle is Assistant Professor of Educational Leadership at Texas Tech University, Lubbock, Texas. E-mail: f.valle@ttu.edu

Karen M. Watt is Professor of Educational Leadership and the national Director for AVID Research at The University of Texas Pan American, Edinburg, Texas. E-mail: watt@utpa.edu

Mary Kay Zabel is Professor of Special Education (retired) at Kansas State University, Manhattan, Kansas E-mail: mkz@k-state.edu

Introduction

Schools of today are more sophisticated and offer an increasing array of programs than ever before. No one person is likely to possess a complete understanding of every program delivered in the typical public school. Consequently, this third edition of *The Administration and Supervision of Special Programs in Education* is designed to provide school personnel—particularly school administrators and teacher leaders—with the knowledge needed to successfully manage the various special instructional and support programs in schools. For some readers, this book will be their first contact with school programs such as Title I/NCLB, student activities, and migrant education. For others, this book will serve as an excellent resource to increase understanding of programs with which they already interact daily.

Each chapter of the book begins with a list of objectives and ends with thoughtful questions that highlight some of the important points of the chapter. Most all chapters include a history of the program and appropriate legislative and legal backgrounds for the program. Following the material presentation in each chapter is a case study; this scenario is intended to demonstrate the application of the chapter concepts in a school/district setting.

As was the case in both the first and second editions, the first chapter is focused on special education and the second on 504. Both present concise overviews of these programs, both of which affect all schools. While these chapters are not intended to replace a well-written text, treatise or basic introductory course on special education, they are designed to provide a concise, yet thorough understanding of special education and 504 issues and procedures. Prospective school administrators and teachers are well advised to carefully read the text regarding federal and state laws and regulations. Special education programs and 504 are very sophisticated and require a great deal of attention to detail. A section on school leaders' roles in special education/504 is included in each chapter to provide guidance to novice and experienced administrators alike.

The advent of the sweeping legislation commonly called No Child Left Behind (NCLB) required a complete rewrite of the Title I chapter found in the first edition. The chapter in this third edition offers readers an overview of this 2001 authorization of Title I and likely changes as they are currently known. The NCLB legislation is being implemented and interpreted; readers are encouraged to use this chapter as a place to begin their extensive study of these new federal requirements for schools. Readers are encouraged to watch information releases from state and federal entities to stay abreast of the changes in this legislation and its accompanying rules and regulations. With each reauthorization and each administration, educators can expect changes.

In this edition, we have a new chapter on student activities. Student activities are extremely important for the students, parents and often, the community at large. Student activities begin to appear in the elementary level and become major components of the student's curriculum and the administrator's responsibilities at the secondary level.

Another chapter added to this edition is the one on RTI (Response to Intervention). The focus of this chapter is on the interventions that can (must) be taken in attempting to address students' learning challenges at the classroom level. This is an important mindset for educators who seek to make quality classroom instruction inclusive for all learners. Closely associated with the concept of RTI is the chapter on *Academic Enhancement, Intervention and Preparation Programs.* The information in the chapter will help educators identify program options of various sorts that help students succeed in PK-12 and prepare them for postsecondary options.

Chapters focused on programs for migrant students, bilingual students, gifted and talented students and young children provide information to educators that include developmental stages and social and environmental perspectives influencing the children and families involved. The authors for each of these chapters have provided some practical instructional strategies and resources for immediate use. Information regarding the funding for each of these programs is crucial for school leaders to know. The complexity of funding for migrant and bilingual programs will need additional attention beyond what is shared in this book. Early childhood programs are funded differently depending on the population served, while most gifted and talented programs are dependent on local support. Knowing the source of funding and how the funds may be spent is crucial from an accounting point of view and from a program quality perspective.

The previously titled *Career and Technology* chapter has been renamed and refocused in this third edition. Career Readiness Education is the new title and with it a focus on not only career and technology program options, but also redesign issues for secondary schools intended to increase graduation rates and career readiness of high school students. The education programs have a rich history and new versions continue to be advocated throughout the country. This chapter may be of most interest to principals and teacher leaders in secondary schools; however, all educators can glean important information related to making schooling relevant to students and aligned with community needs.

The school counselor has become a necessary and vitally important member of the school community; consequently we include a revised chapter on what constitutes an effective counseling program. Few school administrators (and even fewer teachers) have a formal counseling background. Furthermore, the role of the counselor is not well-defined, generally with the job description varying from school to school.

We retained the chapters on teacher leaders and accessing central office resources. The topics of community/parent engagement and staff development have been dropped as specific chapters; authors of the included chapters were encouraged to embed these concepts as appropriate. Feedback on these and the other changes implemented in this edition will be welcomed. We are deeply indebted to those who spent many hours preparing their contributions to the book. The names of the contributors are listed at the beginning of each chapter, yet it is apropos to mention them once again. Our very special thanks to:

Casey Brown	Reba J. Criswell	Terry Overton
Jesus 'Chuey' Abrego	Diana Freeman	Rebecca Miller
Michelle H. Abrego	Randy Tierce	Marie Simonsson
Stacey Edmonson	Richard Lampe	Mariela Rodríguez
Velma Menchaca	Shirley Mills	Mary Kay Zabel
Ava Muñoz	María Luisa González	Alejo Salinas, Jr.
Jennifer Butcher	Jerry Trusty	Karen Watt
Fernando Valle	Encarnación Garza, Jr.	

Putting this book together has provided many challenges and opportunities. It is always a pleasure to work with outstanding colleagues such as those contributors to this edition, for that we are grateful. We are both pleased and proud as we survey this finished product. We certainly hope you find it helpful as your leadership journey continues to unfold.

Anita Pankake & Mark Littleton

Special Education

1

Stacey L. Edmonson

While the passage of EHA was a significant step toward the provision of educational guarantees for disabled children, history would show us that it was the Civil Rights case, *Brown v. Board of Education* (1954), that would become the basis for many of the improvements in the educational rights of special needs students.

—*Brenda R. Kallio & Richard T. Geisel*

Objectives[1]

1. Report the legislative history of special education
2. Discuss the social impetus behind the development of special education in public schools
3. Discuss the major educational components of the Individual with Disabilities Education Act
4. Discuss the referral and evaluation process for special education services
5. Outline yearly progress as it relates to special education students

[1]Adapted from Kallio, B.R., & Geisel, R.T. (2008). Special education. In Pankake, A., Schroth, G., & Littleton, M. (Eds.), *Administration and Supervision of Special Programs in Education*. Dubuque, IA: Kendall Hunt.

Introduction

Administrators play a critical role in securing a free and appropriate education (FAPE) for special needs students. Implementation of special education programs is not easy and may at times become a daunting task. To assist administrators in their quest to stay abreast of current special education practices, this chapter presents information on the history of special education legislation and discusses many of the principles fundamental to the Individuals with Disabilities Education Act (IDEA). (Note: This chapter is based on federal legislation and readers should be advised that individual state guidelines may differ slightly from federal law.)

History of Special Education

During this country's early years, disabled students were not entitled to public education. In fact, a Massachusetts court ruled that student misbehavior resulting from imbecility was grounds for expulsion (*Watson v. City of Cambridge, Massachusetts, 1893*). Likewise in 1919, a Wisconsin court ruled that a handicapped student could be excluded from regular public school classes because his handicap had "a depressing and nauseating effect on the teachers and school children" (*Beattie v. Board of Education, Wisconsin, 1919*). There were, however, areas of the country that recognized the educational needs of disabled students. For example, Hartford, Connecticut (1817) established the American Asylum for the Education of the Deaf and Dumb, and New York, New York (1818) established the Institution for the Education of the Deaf and Dumb (Alexander & Alexander, 2001). However, educational opportunities such as those offered in Hartford and New York were the exception and for much of U.S. history, a vast majority of disabled children were taught by parents in the privacy of their homes and/or lived out their lives secreted in basements and attics.

Although support for expanding the educational opportunities of special needs students was limited, The White House Conference on Children (1910) had as one of its primary goals the establishment of remedial programs for special needs children. Ultimately, the Conference hoped to move society away from the then prevalent philosophy of isolation (institutionalizing or ignoring disabled children) toward an attitude of segregation (separate classrooms within public schools). For several decades it appeared as though the Conference had been successful in altering society's views of education for disabled children, and between 1910 and 1930 the number of classes and support services for disabled children increased. However, the number of programs and services began decreasing during the 1930s. In part the decline was likely due to the Great Depression and its incumbent financial constraints. However, the decline was also attributed to large numbers of persons who professed that education, as a democratic ideal, required high educational standards . . . standards unattainable with the inclusion of disabled children (Yell, 1998).

Despite conferences espousing goals that recognize the educational rights of disabled children, the passage of various state compulsory education laws, and relatively obscure special education court cases, the educational rights of disabled children did not significantly change during the first 70 years of the 20th century. Schools continued to exclude students who were "feeble minded," "mentally deficient," or deemed unable to reap the benefits of education (*Department of Public Welfare v. Haas, 1958*).

The plight of disabled children began to change when, in 1970, Congress passed legislation that recognized the educational entitlements of special needs children. This 1970 legislation, the Education of the Handicapped Act (EHA), required, among other things, that states provide free and appropriate education to special needs students, provide appropriate assessment, and notify parents of their children's educational rights.

While the passage of EHA was a significant step toward the provision of educational guarantees for disabled children, it was the civil rights case *Brown v. Board of Education* (1954) that would become the basis for many of the improvements in educational rights of special needs students. While the U.S. Supreme Court's decision in *Brown* specifically addressed the issue of "separate but equal" (as defined in the Supreme Court's 1896 decision in *Plessy v. Ferguson,* 163 U.S. 537) as it pertained to racial minorities, parents and advocates for special needs children began asking the courts to apply *Brown's* doctrine, that separate is inherently unequal, to educational opportunities for disabled students. Thus, it was a racial antidiscrimination case that served as the guiding precedent for the 1972 benchmark special education decision in *Pennsylvania Association of Retarded Citizens v. Pennsylvania (PARC)*. In addition to requiring that a free education be provided to all mentally retarded children between the ages of 6 and 21, the ruling in *PARC* defined "education" as broader than pure academics. In addition, the Supreme Court ruled that mentally retarded children could benefit from schooling when education was defined in the proper context. The Court's *PARC* decision also included language promoting the education of mentally retarded children in the least restrictive environment.

In *Mills v. Board of Education* (1972) the Court's ruling extended the educational rights previously granted to mentally retarded students *(PARC)* to all disabled students. The *Mills* decision also outlined procedural safeguards for labeling, placement, and exclusion of students with disabilities. These safeguards included:

- the right to a hearing (with representation, a record, and an impartial hearing officer),
- the right to appeal,
- the right to access personal records,
- written notice at all stages of the process. (Yell, 1998, p. 60)

In addition to the rulings from *PARC* and *Mills,* federal legislation passed during the early to mid 1970s (i.e., the Americans with Disabilities Act and Section 504 of the Rehabilitation Act) prohibited discrimination against disabled persons and required employers to make reasonable accommodations if the person was qualified for the position. Initially, this legislation was designed to protect disabled veterans; however, the legislation was quickly applied to public education. In 1975, Congress passed legislation (Public Law [P.L.] 94–142) that mandated children with suspected disabilities must have access to nondiscriminatory testing and placement in the least restrictive environment (LRE). Other features of P.L. 94–142 included a more clearly outlined procedure for parental due process; guidelines for FAPE; and procedures for identification, evaluation, and placement of students with disabilities. P.L. 94–142 also expanded the age parameters set forth in *PARC* (6–21 years of age) to include children ages 3–6, allowed parents who sued for violations of P.L. 94–142, and won, to recover attorney fees and other legal costs, and intimated that federal funds would be made available to reduce state and local costs for special education programs.

The rights of disabled children continued to grow, and in 1986, P.L. 99–457 mandated that all states provide programs for disabled children beginning at birth. In 1990, Congress passed P.L. 101–476 which, in an attempt to make the terminology more politically correct, changed the name of the current disability legislation from the Education for All Handicapped Children Act (EAHCA) to the Individuals with Disabilities Education Act (IDEA). In addition to the name change, the 1990 version of IDEA required school districts to include transition plans in the Individualized Education Plans (IEPs) of all special needs children once the child became 16 years of age.

In 1997, Congress amended the special education legislation and the newly reauthorized special education legislation (P.L. 105–17) by emphatically stating that children with disabilities are to be full participants in school programming and that special education is a service and not a place (Council for Exceptional Children and National Association of Elementary School Principals, 2001, p. 5). Public Law 105–17 also mandated transition planning with interagency responsibility, placed greater emphasis on improving results, further delineated procedural safeguards, changed the composition of the IEP team and the content of the IEP document, established voluntary mediation, and added language regarding the discipline of students (e.g., manifestation determination).

Major Principles of IDEA

Over time, several components of the P.L. 94–142 reauthorizations have stood out as IDEA provisions that affect administrators on a regular basis. Therefore, the topics selected for discussion in the balance of this chapter have been chosen for their relevance to special education issues.

CHILD FIND

Under IDEA's child find requirements, states are required to locate, identify, and evaluate disabled children from birth to age 21. The process for locating disabled children is not specified at the federal level and states are allowed to establish individual plans as long as the plan identifies the agency responsible for the child find, outlines the child find procedures, and details the resources available to sustain the child find program. In most cases, public schools are assigned the task of locating all disabled children within their service area. Techniques for finding children include contacting nursery schools, pediatricians, and nearby medical facilities. Additionally, districts frequently post notices in public places such as grocery stores, run public service announcements with radio and TV stations, and place ads in newspapers. Each district is required to adopt board policy regarding compliance with child find requirements. Furthermore, failure of parents to identify their child as disabled does not relieve the district of its child find responsibilities [34 C.F.R. §300.125(a)(1)(i)].

CONFIDENTIALITY OF INFORMATION

Parents of special needs children are permitted to inspect their child's records and may seek to amend or remove documents they believe are inappropriate. If the parents request a change or removal from a document in the student's file and the district disagrees, the parents may write a letter stating why the document should be removed or amended and the district is obligated to include the letter in the student's file. Should the district and the parents agree on the removal or change in the contents of a special needs student's file, the district may destroy or adjust the documents accordingly.

Districts in the process of destroying old student records should consult state law for specifics on the manner of destruction, the length of time records must be retained (the length of retention may be longer for special needs children than for regular education students), and the specific rules for notifying specified persons that the records are to be destroyed.

DISABILITY CATEGORIES

Currently, there are 13 categories of disability protected by IDEA (see Table 1-1). Not all students with disabilities are protected under IDEA. The statute extends only to

Table 1-1	**Disability Categories According to 20 U.S.C. 1401(a)(1)(A)(i)**
• mental retardation	• hearing impairment
• speech or language impairment	• visual impairment
• deaf-blindness	• multiple disabilities
• emotional disturbance	• orthopedic impairment
• specific learning disability	• other health impaired
• autism	• traumatic brain injury (TBI)
• deafness	

students whose disability falls within the scope of the specified list of disabilities and only to those whose disability has an adverse impact on their education. For example, a student who exhibits inappropriate social behaviors would not be eligible for special education services unless the behaviors hindered the student's ability to make reasonable academic progress.

The original list of IDEA disability categories did not include autism, attention-deficit/hyperactivity disorder (ADHD), or traumatic brain injury. The categories of autism and traumatic brain injury were added with the 1990 version of IDEA; however ADHD was not given a separate category. Instead, the Department of Education has stated that children with ADHD may be granted special education status under the categories of specific learning disability, serious emotional disturbance, or other health impaired.

IDEA 2004

IDEA was reauthorized in 2004 and signed into law as the Individuals with Disabilities Education Improvement Act. A number of important changes took place with the reauthorization, each designed to improve the services provided to students with special education needs. A summary of these major changes includes:

Districts may use a response to intervention approach to identifying students with learning disabilities, rather than the method that required a severe discrepancy between academic achievement and IQ.

Reevaluations of students cannot take place more than one time per year and no less than once every 3 years.

The school district may not file a due process claim to require a parent to accept special education and related services. If a parent refuses services, the district is no longer obligated to offer FAPE to that student.

All special education services should be based on peer-reviewed research.

Short-term objectives are not required for IEPs.

Specific transition services must be initiated for students by age 16, rather than simply having a transition plan in place.

Members of the IEP team may choose not to attend if their area of expertise or service is not at issue and the district and parent agree. Alternative means of attending are also allowed, including videoconferencing or conference call.

Pilot programs for paperwork reduction and multiyear IEPs may be implemented in up to 15 states.

Parents now have 2 years to file a due process claim if their child's rights under IDEA were violated.

Schools can remove students for up to 45 school days for causing serious bodily injury; previously this provision was only available for drugs and weapons offenses.

The "stay put" provision that allowed a special education student to remain in his or her placement pending an appeal for disciplinary action has been removed from federal law. Students can now be placed in an interim setting, with a hearing required within 20 school days of the placement and a decision reached within 10 school days of the hearing.

DISCIPLINE

The U.S. General Accounting Office (GAO), at the request of Congress, conducted a study to determine whether the discipline sections of the 1997 IDEA affected the ability of schools to maintain a safe environment conducive to learning. As a part of their study, the GAO found more incidences of serious misconduct in non–special education student populations than among special education students. However, the rate (percentage) of serious misconduct was greater in the special education population (Markowitz, 2001).

When Markowitz focused on if and how administrators met the IDEA discipline requirements, he found that 86% of the principals surveyed in the GAO study reported their school district policies provided special education protections beyond what was required by IDEA. However, only 64% of administrators knew they were not allowed to suspend a special needs student for more than 10 cumulative school days during a school year for an incident related to the child's disability. For example, administrators may not suspend a special needs child for 4 days, then 3 days and then 4 days, as the cumulative total of days of suspension total more than 10 days. Only 24% of the administrators knew they were required to determine whether the student's misconduct was a manifestation of his/her disability whenever discipline was being considered (Markowitz, 2001). The numbers from the GAO study would indicate that not only were the administrators not *exceeding* the minimal discipline standards set forth in IDEA (as they had reported doing), but in fact, administrators were not even *meeting* IDEA expectations with regard to disciplining special education students.

Discipline, as a component of IDEA, has proven to be both complicated and controversial. Change of placement due to behavior, manifestation determination, the stay-put provision, and behavior intervention plans have shown to be some of the most controversial aspects of the statute and will be discussed in the sections that follow.

Change of Placement Due to Behavior

School personnel may suspend or otherwise change the placement of a special education student for 10 days providing the same change of placement would be applied to regular education children who break the same school rules. In addition, a disabled student may be placed in an interim alternative educational setting for a maximum of 45 days for weapon and/or drug offenses. A 45-day interim alternative placement must be determined by an IEP team, and special education students assigned to an alternative setting must continue to receive the services and modifications set forth in their IEP. According to the IDEA, a change in placement does not alter the services the student is to receive. Rather, it only changes the place where the student receives the services.

Prior to implementing disciplinary measures that involve a change in educational placement, the IEP team must determine whether there is a relationship between the student's disability and the misbehavior, and whether an inappropriate placement resulted in the misbehavior.

Manifestation Determination

To determine whether a child's behavior is related to his/her disability, the district is required to conduct a manifestation determination hearing. If it is decided the misconduct is not related to the disability, the child may be disciplined the same as a regular education student. Should the team find the misconduct is directly related to the child's disability, the child must receive special accommodations and the discipline adjusted according to the severity of the child's disability. Courts have upheld the manifestation determination provision of IDEA and continue to prohibit the unilateral exclusions of special education students from educational settings for behavior that manifests from the child's disability (*Honig v. Doe,* 1988).

If a manifestation determination is required, IEP teams will be in a better position to determine the relationship between the student's behavior and the disability if the team has laid an appropriate foundation at previous IEP meetings. IEP teams that have asked parents whether their child is able to follow the school rules as outlined in the school handbook, whether their child knows right from wrong, and whether their child exhibits discipline problems outside of the school environment have established baseline information that becomes invaluable should the team need to have a manifestation determination hearing for disciplinary decisions.

Stay-Put Provision

Until the reauthorization of IDEA in 2004, students with disabilities who were involved in disciplinary proceedings were protected by the "stay-put" provision. This meant that unless the school and the parent agree to a change of placement, a child involved in mediation or due process hearings must remain in his or her current educational placement (*Honig v. Doe,* 484 U.S. 385). If school personnel contended there was a danger the child would hurt himself or other children during the course of due process proceedings, the district could ask the court to sanction a temporary change of placement until a permanent change of placement is agreed upon [34 C.F.R. 330.526(c)(1)]. However, with the IDEA 2004 changes, the stay-put provision has been removed from federal law. Students can now be placed in an interim educational placement pending disciplinary procedures. A hearing is required within 20 school days of the placement, and a decision must be reached within 10 school days of the hearing.

Behavior Intervention Plans

In the case of children whose behavior impedes their learning or that of others, districts are required to address the child's behavior with the creation of or the adaptation of an existing Behavior Intervention Plan (BIP) [34 C.F.R. 300.346(a)(2)(i)]. A BIP should include services and modifications that address the student's behavior in a manner designed to extinguish the negative behaviors. Services and modifications that might be in a BIP include, but certainly are not limited to, seating arrangement, reduced or increased contact with other students, reward systems, and counseling with behavior specialists.

Response to Intervention

As a result of the reauthorization of IDEA in 2004, the term Response to Intervention (RtI) has become prevalent as a principle concept of serving students with disabilities. RtI is designed to provide early intervention learning assistance to students who are having academic difficulty and may be considered for referral to special education services. RtI is mentioned specifically in the 2004 reauthorization, and many proponents of RtI see it as an effective way for students with learning disabilities to qualify for special education services, even if they do not demonstrate a discrepancy between their intelligence and achievement. IDEA allows up to 15% of funds to be used for early identification procedures such as RtI. RtI also enables districts to identify students with learning disabilities other than through a statistical discrepancy between academic achievement and IQ, a method that sometimes made it difficult for districts to serve the special education needs of low ability, low achieving students (Fuchs & Fuchs, 2007).

Response to Intervention allows school personnel to document specific efforts and results that have been achieved for students who are not performing well academically, before these students are referred to special education or served under IDEA (National Association of State Directors of Special Education [NASDSE], 2005). According to the NASDSE (2005), RtI is based on a set of core assumptions: (1) the educational system is able to teach all students; (2) early intervention is an important part of helping prevent problems; (3) a multitiered service model for offering services is critical; (4) a multitiered model should involve problem solving; (5) interventions should be based on research; (6) monitoring of progress should inform instruction; and (7) decisions should be based on data.

Procedural Due Process

In addition to the requirement that disabled children are to receive a free and appropriate education, strong IDEA procedural guidelines have been established to ensure IDEA compliance. Within the three critical components of procedural due process (informing the person of the allegations against them; the opportunity for the accused to present a defense; and a fair, unbiased hearing), the courts have recognized that procedural due process is somewhat nebulous and that the amount of procedural due process owed to a person is dependent upon the magnitude of the substantive right to be taken away if the accused is found guilty. When comparing the amount of procedural due process owed a child who is about to lose a week's worth of recess to a student who is about to be expelled, it becomes easier to understand the court's rationale that not all situations require the same level of procedural due process.

As a result of current legislation and court cases, parents or other persons who have legal standing and who have exhausted their administrative remedies (e.g., the school board) may seek mediation. The purpose of mediation is to facilitate an agreement by the parents and the district on the issue at hand. Should the parties be unable to reach consensus during the mediation process, either party may request a due process hearing. While states have different titles for the hearing officers who preside over special education due process hearings, the ruling of the hearing officer is enforceable, just as a ruling by a judge would be. However, should either the parents or the district disagree with the ruling of the due process hearing officer, they may file suit in either a state or a federal trial court.

In a due process hearing, parents have the right to be accompanied by a lawyer or an individual with special knowledge of the problems of special needs children to present evidence, to confront and cross-examine witnesses, and to obtain a transcript of the hearing and the "judge's" written decision.

Some of the most highly contested issues regarding procedural due process include:

- failure to notify parents of a change in their child's placement,
- failure to provide explanations of documents,
- failure to provide information in primary language,
- lack of access to school records, and
- lack of compliance with stay-put provision during due process proceedings.

Free and Appropriate Public Education

IDEA requires that services delivered to special education students must be provided at public expense. Further, school districts may not refuse to furnish special education services due to district budget constraints. Lack of money is not an adequate reason for districts to limit or refuse needed services to special education students. While IDEA mandates that special education services are to be free of charge to students, districts are allowed to charge for incidentals such as art fees and field trips as long as the same fees are also charged to nondisabled children (OSEP Policy Letter, 1992).

Additionally, special education services must meet state education agency requirements in whatever ways required by individual states. However, state standards cannot provide less protection than those established by federal regulations. In other words, state standards can increase the services provided to students for special education, but they cannot be used to decrease the services required by IDEA.

In order to provide a truly free and appropriate public education (FAPE), IEPs must outline special education placement and related services. However, it should be noted that IEPs do not guarantee students will attain the goals stated in the document. The IEP document does commit the district to make a good faith effort to help the student reach the stated goals. In *Springdale School District v. Grace* (1981), the Eighth Circuit Court of Appeals determined that FAPE was more than the mere offering of special education services and that FAPE did not require the district to provide the best possible education. Similarly, in *Age v. Bullitt County Public Schools* (1982), the First Circuit Court of Appeals ruled that the existence of better programs did not make a school's proposed program inappropriate (as cited in Yell, 1998).

Referral and Placement

REFERRAL PROCESS

Federal regulations place an affirmative duty on public school districts to find those students in their district who have a disability and who may require special services (Nondiscrimination, 2003, 34 C.F.R. § 104.32). Frequently, school districts use free hearing and vision tests, letters to the community, preschool programs, advertisements, surveys, etc., to locate students who qualify for IDEA services. Students who are believed to be in need of services may be referred for evaluation by any person, including a parent/guardian, teacher, staff member, or even persons outside the school system (Puget Sound ESD, 2002, p. 10). Appendix A contains a chart showing the flow of the referral and placement process.

PROCEDURAL SAFEGUARDS

School districts must obtain parental permission to test a child with suspected disabilities. Should the parent(s) not consent to testing, schools may petition the courts for the necessary consent. In the event independent educational evaluations are required during the preplacement phase of the evaluation process, the district will most likely be required to pay. In the course of obtaining parental permission to test, school districts are required to provide parents/guardians with procedural safeguards such as notice, an opportunity to examine relevant records, information pertinent to requesting impartial hearings, and special education review procedures (Nondiscrimination, 2003, 34 C.F.R. § 104.369).

Subsequent to obtaining permission (parental or court mandated) to evaluate and after the parents or guardians have been duly notified of their rights, qualified persons may begin the evaluation process.

IDENTIFICATION AND EVALUATION

Evaluation of a special needs child must be full and individual. Evaluations must be conducted in all areas of suspected disability including health, vision, hearing, social and emotional status, general intelligence, academic performance, communicative status, and emotional disabilities [34 C.F.R. § 300.532(g)]. Also, evaluations must draw from a variety of sources and no single procedure or test may be used as the sole criterion for determining whether a child is a "child with a disability" [34 C.F.R. § 300.534(a)(1)]. Sources such as aptitude and achievement tests, parental input, teacher recommendation, physical condition, background, and adaptive behavior may be used to gather pertinent evaluation information. In addition to the use of multiple assessment techniques, the evaluations must be conducted in the child's primary (or native) language or using the child's primary mode of communication. The tests must be racially and culturally nondiscriminatory in both the way they are selected and the way they are administered. A final determination of special education identification must be made by a "panel of experts" (i.e., the IEP team).

INDIVIDUALIZED EDUCATION PLANS

Individualized education plans (IEP) are the cornerstone of IDEA. It is from these documents that parents, students, and school districts come to consensus on the educational placement and services that a student with disabilities will receive. Constructing an IEP can be complicated and stressful. However, when an IEP is constructed in a logical, linear manner, the outcome is a document designed to meet the needs of the child. Specifically, IDEA requires that an IEP must include

(II) a statement of measurable annual goals, including academic and functional goals, designed to—

(aa) meet the child's needs that result from the child's disability to enable the child to be involved in and make progress in the general education curriculum; and (bb) meet each of the child's other educational needs that result from the child's disability;

(III) a description of how the child's progress toward meeting the annual goals described in subclause (II) will be measured and when periodic reports on the progress the child is making toward meeting the annual goals (such as through the use of quarterly or other periodic reports, concurrent with the issuance of report card) will be provided; (NCSET, 2011)

The following steps can be used as a guideline in the development of an appropriate Individualized Education Plan for students with special needs.

1. Identify the category of disability most appropriate for the child based on the results of current educational assessment and evaluation.
2. Determine the areas of the general curriculum that will be adversely affected by the child's disability.
3. Determine how child's disability will adversely affect progress in those parts of the general curriculum.
4. Determine the student's current level of performance and establish how far he or she is expected to advance during the year.
5. Identify the tools, instruments, and methodologies that will be used to measure progress. (It is important to determine how progress will be measured early in the IEP development process.)

6. Decide where the team expects the student to be in one year. This is the annual goal and should be reasonable, observable, measurable, and achievable. On the other hand, the goals should have sufficient rigor that achievement of the annual goals will take more than minimal effort on the part of the school and/or the student.

7. Establish short term goals so that all parties involved will be able to see progress, even if the progress occurs in small steps.

8. Decide which special education instruction services the student will need to achieve the goals outlined in the IEP. Ask if adaptations to the content delivery, testing procedures, the physical classroom, etc. will be needed. (Remember, the team only needs to address those curricular areas outlined in step #2.)

9. Decide which related services will be needed to achieve the annual goals. Per federal law 20 U.S.C. 1401 (a)(17), qualifying related services include:
   - transportation
   - psychological services
   - speech/language pathology and audiology
   - physical and occupational therapy
   - recreation
   - early identification and assessment of disabilities
   - counseling, including rehabilitation counseling
   - orientation and mobility
   - medical services for diagnostic or evaluation purposes
   - school health services
   - social work services
   - parent training and parent counseling

10. Decide on the least restrictive environment. First write the IEP, then determine placement. Where is it most likely that the needs already spelled out in the IEP can be provided? The student's academic needs, goals, and objectives should drive his or her placement, not the other way around.

11. Determine what supplementary aids and services are necessary to help the student achieve the annual goals in the least restrictive environment. You should think in terms of needs of the student as well as the supports needed by the teacher(s). Supplementary aids and services are defined as "aids, services and other supports that are provided to enable children with disabilities to be educated with non-disabled children to the maximum extent appropriate" (34 C.F.R. 300.26).

12. Explain any exclusions from the regular classroom or from extracurricular activities due to the student's disability.

13. Be specific in outlining the involvement of the student in any classroom, state, or federally mandated testing program.

14. Identify when services begin and when they end. While this would seem obvious, write it down so there are no misunderstandings.

15. Identify how you will report on the student's progress. The law says that parents of special needs children are entitled to be informed of progress at least as often as parents of regular education students. Thus, if students who are in general education classes receive a report card every six weeks and a progress report every three weeks, then special education students should receive official reports of academic progress every three and six weeks as well. These students with special needs may receive progress reports more often, but not less often.

(adapted from J. Walsh, *Writing a Good IEP*, n.d.)

Yearly Evaluation

Districts are required to convene an IEP meeting for individual students at least once a calendar year. However, IEP teams are required to meet as frequently as necessary to assure the needs of the student are being met.

WHO IS REQUIRED TO BE IN ATTENDANCE AT IEP MEETINGS?

As a rule, an IEP meeting should consist of the following persons:

- Special education representative
- Regular education representative
- Administrator or designee who has the authority to commit district resources
- Assessment professional
- Parent or person with legal standing for the student
- Additional support staff (e.g., OT, PT, speech pathologist) as appropriate
- Student (if appropriate)
- Other persons as appropriate (e.g., lawyers, advocates)

In *Johnson v. Olathe Dist. Sch. Unified Sch. Dist No. 233* (2003), it was determined that a regular education teacher must be present at the IEP meetings only if the student will be participating in regular education programming and that a person with the designation of special education teacher does not need to be present at IEP meetings if there is a representative who is responsible for teaching and working directly with the child.

Minutes of IEP meetings are not required but are advisable. For IEP teams that create minutes, the minutes should be read back to the IEP team at the conclusion of each IEP meeting. Following the reading, persons present at the meeting should sign the signature page acknowledging the content of the minutes. Should a parent or other person disagree with the IEP document or the minutes of the IEP meeting, they may attach an addendum to the minutes.

Related Issues

PLACEMENT IN PRIVATE SCHOOLS

Under IDEA, public schools are required to provide a free and appropriate education (FAPE) to all qualifying students. Should a school district be unable to provide FAPE, and a private institution is able to provide the necessary services, the school district maintains responsibility for the services the student receives and is required to pay the educational costs (e.g., tuition and transportation) necessary for the child to attend the private school (*Florence County School Dist. Four v. Carter,* 1993). However, parents who unilaterally place their child in a private institution run the risk of bearing the burden of the tuition and other educational costs should it be determined that the public school district provided FAPE.

LEAST RESTRICTIVE ENVIRONMENT

Least restrictive environment (LRE) is a legal term found repeatedly throughout IDEA literature. When Congress included LRE in IDEA, the intent was to guarantee that handicapped children be educated with nonhandicapped children to the maximum extent appropriate. In recognizing students' varied levels of disability and need, legislators and the courts have acknowledged that LRE is a continuum, a range of programs with a variety of services with institutionalization on the more restrictive end and full inclusion in the regular classroom on the other. The IEP team is responsible for determining which program delivery style(s) and which services should be used to develop the least restrictive environment for each individual student. In fact, the words *mainstreaming* and *inclusion* are educational terms and represent possible points on the special education LRE continuum. (Mainstreaming and inclusion are not required under IDEA, but educating every child in the appropriate least restrictive environment is!) When determining LRE, IEP teams must factor in the opportunity for special needs children to socialize with nondisabled peers and whether provided services meet the portability test, meaning could these services be offered within a less restrictive environment (*Roncker v. Walters,* 1983).

ZERO REJECT

Under IDEA, all children are entitled to a free and appropriate education regardless of the severity of their disability. The concept of zero reject is based on the *PARC* (1972) ruling that education is more than academics, and therefore even the most severely disabled students are able to benefit from appropriately designed education. In a court case where the school district claimed a student was too severely disabled to benefit from education and moved to exclude the child from school, the First Circuit Court of Appeals upheld the concept of zero reject by ruling that all children are entitled to a public education, regardless of how severe the child's disability may be or how limited the educational benefit may seem that the child will receive from the school's services (*Timothy W. v. Rochester, New Hampshire, School District,* 1989).

Conclusion

The courts and society, as a whole, currently recognize that students with disabilities have a right to a free appropriate public education. While the right to an education may no longer be an issue, the specific issues of how to best serve the needs of special education students continues to offer a great number of challenges. Every year the courts at all levels hear a wide range of cases related to special education placements and services. With the reauthorization of IDEA in 2004, school leaders continue to work diligently to provide a free and appropriate educational environment for all students, including students with disabilities.

Applying Your Knowledge

Adam, a student at Utopia High School, has Down syndrome and is eligible for special education services. Adam is a junior who for the past 2 years has participated in the fine arts program as a special helper with the marching and symphonic bands. His duties are to help load and unload the large trucks that carry equipment and instruments. In the past, Adam has had adult chaperones assist him with his duties because his hyperactivity generally leads to inappropriate interactions between himself and the other band members.

Adam's parents are very active in his educational life and have made sure that his IEP includes participation in the extracurricular activities. While the IEP addresses the issue of participation, it does not require adult supervision.

Recently, the band announced its intention to travel on a 3-day, 2-night trip to Atlanta, Georgia, to participate in a contest. Adam would like to go on the trip. Adam's parents, who are refusing to go on the trip as chaperones, are adamant that this trip will be an important milestone in Adam's education and are requesting that he stay in a hotel room with other students who would be responsible for monitoring Adam's behavior. The band director is wary of having Adam on the trip without proper adult supervision and has asked for your thoughts.

QUESTIONS

1. Can the district deny Adam access to the field trip? Why or why not?
2. If the district allows Adam to travel without adult supervision, what is the extent of the district's liability if Adam creates a problem in Atlanta?
3. If Adam travels with the band and is housed in a room with regular education students, what responsibilities, if any, can the district impose on those students?
4. How does the wording in Adam's IEP affect the district's decision to allow or deny Adam's participation in the trip?

QUESTIONS FOR THOUGHT

1. Describe how society's view of persons with physical or mental disabilities has changed over time.
2. Why do you think the federal government felt it was necessary to mandate that individual school districts be held accountable for identifying handicapped children in their service areas (child find)?
3. Think about the children in your school who are identified as special needs and those who although are not identified may need special assistance. Are the 13 categories of disability sufficiently broad (or narrow) to meet the needs of all school-age children?
4. As an administrator, what steps can you take to ensure that teams make appropriate decisions at a manifestation determination meeting?
5. Describe the role related services play in the Individualized Education Plan (IEP) of a student with special needs.
6. Assume that because the district is unable to prove FAPE to a special needs child, the child is placed in a private institution. Conduct a financial comparison of the cost to educate the student at the private institution and in the public school. In addition to the financial ramifications, what other considerations might make placing a child in a private institution appropriate?
7. How has the reauthorization of IDEA in 2004 impacted special education services, particularly the identification of students with special needs?

References

Age v. Bullitt County Public Schools, 673 F.2d 141 (6th Cir. 1982).

Alexander, K., & Alexander, M. D. (2001).*American public school law.* Belmont, CA: Wadsworth/Thompson Learning.

Beattie v. Board of Education, Wisconsin, 172 N.W. 153 (Wis. 1919).

Brown v. Board of Education, 347 U.S. 483, 74 S.Ct. 686 (1954).

Council for Exceptional Children & National Association of Elementary School Principals. (2001).*IDEA: A guide for principals.* Alexandria, VA: Council for Exceptional Children.

Department of Public Welfare v. Haas, 154 N.E. 2d 265 (Ill.1958).

Florence County School Dist. Four v. Carter By and Through Carter, 510 U.S. 7 (1993).

Fuchs, D., & Fuchs, L. S. (2007). Introduction to Response to Intervention: What, why, and how valid is it? *Reading Research Quarterly, 41*(1), 93–100. doi:10.1598/RRQ.41.1.4.

Kallio, B. R., & Geisel, R. T. (2008). Special education. In Pankake, A., Schroth, G., &. & Littleton, M. (Eds.), *Administration and Supervision of Special Programs in Education.* Dubuque, IA: Kendall Hunt.

Honig v. Doe, 479 U.S. 1084 (1987).

Johnson v. Olathe Dist. Sch. Unified Sch. Dist No. 233, 316 F. Supp.2d 960 (D. Kan 2003).

Markowitz, J. (2001, April).*Synthesis brief: Student discipline and IDEA-Synthesis of GAO report.* Retrieved July 3, 2004, from http://www.nasdse.org/FORUM/PDF%20files/student_discipline_idea.PDF

Mills v. Board of Education of the District of Columbia, 348 F.Supp. 866 (D.D.C. 1972).

National Association of State Directors of Special Education. (2005). *Response to intervention: Policy considerations and implementation.* Alexandria, VA: NASDSE, Inc.

National Center on Secondary Education and Transition. (2011). Retrieved January 3, 2011 from http://www.ncset.org/publications/related/ideatransition.asp

OSEP Policy Letter, 20 IDELR 1155. (1992). Office of Special Education Programs.

Pennsylvania Association of Retarded Citizens (PARC) v. Commonwealth of Pennsylvania, 343 F.Supp. 279 (E.D. Pa. 1972).

Plessy v. Ferguson, 163 U.S. 537

Puget Sound ESD. (2002).*A parent & educator guide to free appropriate public education.* Retrieved July 6, 2004, from http://www.psesd.org/specialservices/pdfs/504manual.pdf

Roncker v. Walters, 700 F.2d 1058 (6th Cir. 1983).

Springdale School District v. Grace, 494 F.Supp. 266 (W.D. Ark 1980), aff'd, 656 F.2d 300 (8th Cir. 1981), vacated, 102 S.Ct. 3504 (1982), on remand, 693 F.2d 41 (8th Cir. 1982), cert. den. 461 U.S. 917 (1982).

Timothy W. v. Rochester, New Hampshire, School District, 875 F.2d 954 (1989).

Walsh, J. (n.d.).*Writing a good IEP.* Austin, TX: Walsh, Anderson, Brown, Schulze & Aldridge, P.C. (handout at presentation, no page number or date available).

Watson v. City of Cambridge, Massachusetts, 157 Mass. 561, 32 N.E. 864 (Mass. 1893).

Yell, M. (1998). *The law and special education.* Upper Saddle River, NJ: Merrill.

20 U.S.C. 1401(a)(1)(A)(i)

20 U.S.C. 1401 (a)(17)

34 C.F.R. § 104.32

34 C.F.R. § 104.369

34 C.F.R. § 300.125(a)(1)(i)

34 C.F.R. § 300.346(a)(2)(i)

34 C.F.R. § 300.532(g)

34 C.F.R. § 300.534(a)(1)

34 C.F.R. § 330.526(c)(1)

Appendix A

Referral and Placement for Special Education

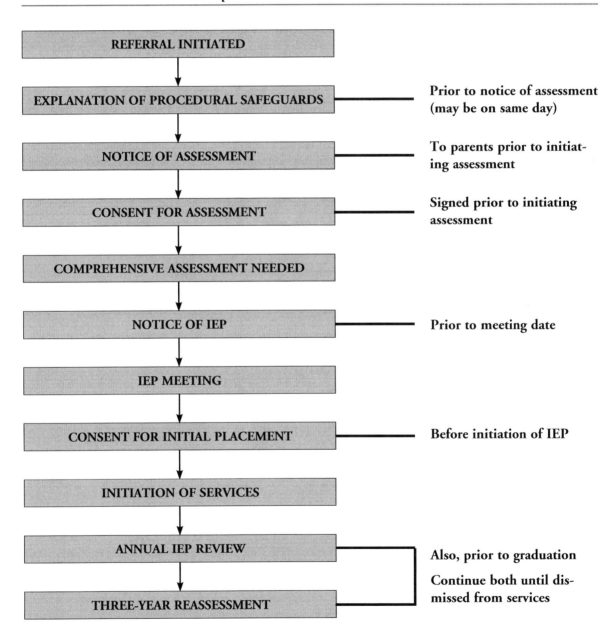

REFERRAL INITIATED	
EXPLANATION OF PROCEDURAL SAFEGUARDS	Prior to notice of assessment (may be on same day)
NOTICE OF ASSESSMENT	To parents prior to initiating assessment
CONSENT FOR ASSESSMENT	Signed prior to initiating assessment
COMPREHENSIVE ASSESSMENT NEEDED	
NOTICE OF IEP	Prior to meeting date
IEP MEETING	
CONSENT FOR INITIAL PLACEMENT	Before initiation of IEP
INITIATION OF SERVICES	
ANNUAL IEP REVIEW	Also, prior to graduation
THREE-YEAR REASSESSMENT	Continue both until dismissed from services

Schroth, G. and Littleton, M. (2001). *The Administration and Supervision of Special Programs in Education.* Dubuque, IA: Kendall/Hunt Publishing.

Section 504 of the Rehabilitation Act of 1973

2

Stacey L. Edmonson

". . . administrative competence and vigilance is necessary to ensure
that students with disabilities have the opportunity to receive
their federally granted right to a free and appropriate education."

—*Richard T. Geisel & Brenda R. Kallio*

Objectives[1]

1. Overview the history of Section 504 legislation
2. Describe eligibility for services, the identification process, and services delivery processes for Section 504
   - Discuss the administrator's roles in implementing Section 504
   - Compare and contrast major elements of Section 504 and IDEA
   - Provide sample forms for use in implementing Section 504

---

[1]This chapter was adapted from Geisel, R. T., & Kallio, B. R. (2008). Section 504 of the Rehabilitation Act of 1973. In Pankake, A., Schroth, G., & Littleton, M. (Eds.), *Administration and Supervision of Special Programs in Education*. Dubuque, IA: Kendall Hunt.

Introduction

In addition to the educational rights mandated by Individuals with Disabilities Education Act (IDEA), administrators are also bound by legislation emanating from Section 504 of the Rehabilitation Act of 1973 (hereinafter referred to as Section 504) in which Congress made a commitment to citizens that "to the maximum extent possible, [persons with disabilities] shall be fully integrated into American life." The combination of IDEA and Section 504 currently define the educational entitlements for children with disabilities. While IDEA and Section 504 appear to provide many of the same opportunities to persons with special needs, the two pieces of legislation are distinctly different. A comparison of major provisions of IDEA and Section 504 can be found in Appendix A. Additionally, Appendix B details the relationship between special education students (IDEA) and Section 504 students.

History of Section 504

Section 504 of the Rehabilitation Act of 1973 (2002) is a federal civil rights law that, among other things, prohibits organizations that receive federal funds from discriminating against individuals with disabilities. As a result, public elementary and secondary schools, as well as private schools accepting federal funds, must comply with the provisions of Section 504. In part, Section 504 provides that

> no otherwise qualified individual with a disability in the United States . . . shall, solely by reason of her or his disability, be excluded from the participation in, be denied the benefits of, or be subjected to discrimination under any program or activity receiving federal financial assistance.

The United States Department of Education has issued administrative regulations for the purposes of clarifying the educational applications of Section 504 and enforcing the nondiscrimination provisions of Section 504 (Nondiscrimination, 2003). These regulations make it clear that Section 504 applies "to preschool, elementary, secondary, and adult education programs or activities that receive federal financial assistance" (Nondiscrimination, 34 C.F.R. § 104.31). Consequently, school administrators must be alert to the affirmative obligations Section 504 imposes on their schools. However, unlike IDEA, Section 504 does not provide funding for services for eligible students. Additionally, IDEA funds cannot be used for services for Section 504 students.

Qualifying for Section 504

Section 504 is a legislative attempt to ensure that all students have the opportunity to receive a free and appropriate public education (FAPE), including students with disabilities. To comply with the provisions of Section 504, school administrators must know what qualifies as a legal disability. The federal regulations define a person with a Section 504 disability as one who "(i) has a physical or mental impairment which substantially limits one or more major life activities, (ii) has a record of such an impairment, or (iii) is regarded as having such an impairment" [Nondiscrimination, 2003, 34 C.F.R. § 104.3(j)]. While Section 504 requires that students have an impairment that limits one or more major life activities, it does not specifically require that the impairment impact students' ability to learn. Thus, students who have certain types of physical impairments may be eligible for services under Section 504 but not be eligible under IDEA.

DEFINING A "PHYSICAL OR MENTAL IMPAIRMENT"

A critical component of Section 504 is determining whether a student has a legally defined impairment. The regulations define a "physical or mental impairment" as any physiological disorder or condition, cosmetic disfigurement, or anatomical loss affecting one or more of the following body systems: neurological; musculoskeletal; special sense organs; respiratory, including speech organs; cardiovascular; reproductive, digestive, genitourinary; hemic and lymphatic; skin; and endocrine; or any mental or psychological disorder, such as mental retardation, organic brain syndrome, emotional or mental illness, and specific learning disabilities [Nondiscrimination, 2003, 34 C.F.R. § 104.3(j)(2)(i)].

A student who has an impairment that meets the above stated requirements, however, will not automatically qualify for Section 504 accommodations. Further investigation is required to determine whether the disability substantially limits one or more life activities.

In January 2009, the American with Disabilities Act Amendments of 2008 (ADAA) were officially implemented. The 2008 act expanded the definition and interpretation of disability and thus resulted in significant changes regarding eligibility for Section 504 services. Although the U.S. Department of Education has not yet submitted official guidelines for responding to these changes, the Office of Civil Rights has issued a document to help explain these differences (U.S. Department of Education, 2011).

SUBSTANTIAL LIMITATION OF A MAJOR LIFE ACTIVITY

Once it has been established that a student has a legal disability (or is regarded as having a disability or has a record of a disability as explained in the federal regulations), a determination must then be made as to whether disability substantially limits a major life activity (e.g., learning). A "major life activity" is defined as "functions such as caring for one's self, performing manual tasks, walking, seeing, hearing, speaking, breathing, learning, and working" [Nondiscrimination, 2003, 34 C.F.R. § 104.3(j)(2)(ii)].

Some students may have a legal disability that, nonetheless, does not substantially limit a major life activity. For example, attention-deficit disorder (ADD) or obsessive-compulsive disorder (OCD) can sometimes fall into this category. In *Bercovitch v. Baldwin School, Inc.* (1998) the parents of a student diagnosed with attention-deficit/hyperactivity disorder (ADHD) argued that their child should not have been suspended from school for behavioral problems because he was disabled based upon a doctor's diagnosis of ADHD. However, the First Circuit Court of Appeals noted that the student's academic achievement was not substantially below average (or below average at all) during his worst periods of misbehavior. Accordingly, the court refused to recognize the student's disability as a substantial impairment of his ability to learn.

Once a disability is confirmed, school administrators are required to determine whether the disability substantially limits a major life activity. Failure to go beyond simply establishing the existence of a disability could lead to the overidentification of Section 504 students, accompanied by unwarranted increases in the costs of providing special services.

The Process of Identification

Section 504 students are typically identified using a referral process similar to that used to identify students with IDEA disabilities. Section 504 students may be referred for evaluation by any person, including a parent/guardian, teacher, staff member, or person outside the school system (Puget Sound ESD, 2002, p. 10). Once a Section 504 referral is received, the building or district coordinator (in many districts, this coordinator is the special education director or a building principal) should assemble a review team to determine whether the child is eligible for Section 504 status. (Appendix C of this chapter contains an example of a Section 504 referral form.) Unlike IDEA referrals, evaluation and placement procedures for students served under Section 504 do not require parental consent. Instead, Section 504 requires only parental notice. Similar to IDEA, students evaluated for services under Section 504 should be evaluated according to a variety of documented sources using a team approach of persons who have informed knowledge of (a) the student's performance and ability, (b) the evaluative information on the student, and (c) the placements and services that are available to the student (U.S. Department of Education, 2011).

Procedural Safeguards

"Public elementary and secondary schools must employ procedural safeguards regarding the identification, evaluation, or educational placement of persons who, because of disability, need or are believed to need special instruction or related services" (Office of Civil Rights, n.d.). Upon receipt of a 504 referral, the school district must provide parents/guardians with procedural safeguards that include parental notice before any formal identification, evaluation, or placement action takes place (Yell, 1998, p. 112). "Section 504 requires districts to provide notice to parents explaining any evaluation and placement decisions affecting their children and explaining the parents' right to review educational records and appeal any decision regarding evaluation and placement through an impartial hearing officer" (Office of Civil Rights, n.d.). Unlike IDEA, Section 504 does not require parental consent for students to be identified or served; rather, school districts must simply provide notice to parents. (See Appendix D for a sample notice of rights under Section 504.) However, a school district must secure parental permission prior to conducting an evaluation of eligibility under Section 504.

Evaluation for Section 504 Eligibility

Once the evaluation is complete, the 504 team meets to consider the results and to make a determination as to whether the student qualifies for Section 504 services. The 504 team must base its determination of eligibility or noneligibility upon information gathered from several different sources, including input submitted by the child's parents/guardians (Puget Sound ESD, 2002, p. 10). Based upon the information gathered, the 504 team must determine whether the student has a physical or mental impairment that substantially limits a major life activity. Once the 504 team has made its determination, the child's parents/guardians should be notified of the team's decision and, once again, be provided a copy of their rights under Section 504. (See Appendix E for a sample determination of Section 504 eligibility.)

The Accommodation Plan

If the 504 team has determined that a student is eligible for Section 504 services or accommodation, the next step is for the team to develop the student's 504 accommodation plan. (See Appendix F for an example of a Section 504 individualized accommodation plan.) Accommodation plans should be designed to provide students access to a free and appropriate public education in spite of their disability. The Section 504 federal regulations state that public schools "shall provide a free appropriate public education to each qualified handicapped person who is in the recipient's jurisdiction, regardless of the nature or severity of the person's handicap" [Nondiscrimination, 2002, 34 C.F.R. § 104.33(a)]. Accordingly, the 504 individual accommodation plan must provide "regular or special education and related aids and services that are designed to meet individual educational needs of handicapped persons as adequately as the needs of non-handicapped persons are met" [Nondiscrimination, 34 C.F.R. § 104.33(b)]. Once the 504 team has developed an appropriate accommodation plan to address the student's disability, the plan must be submitted to the child's parents/guardians for their approval and consent (Puget Sound ESD, 2002, p. 11). Note, students identified under IDEA are required to have an Individual Education Plan (IEP). However, students identified under Section 504 are not required to have an IEP. The district may choose to develop an individual accommodation plan instead. Examples of accommodations that could be provided to students under Section 504 include repeated instructions, calculators, textbooks on tape, extended time on exams, oral testing, or behavior management strategies; however, the types of accommodations available under Section 504 can be as varied as the students' needs and the schools' resources (U.S. Department of Education, 2011).

The Role of the Building Administrator

To stay in compliance with Section 504, the 504 coordinator will need to: (1) make sure staff understand the essence of Section 504 and the importance of adhering to a student's 504 accommodation plan; (2) hold the staff accountable for using and following the terms of a student's 504 accommodation plan; (3) facilitate the 504 identification, evaluation and accommodation process in a timely manner; (4) provide parents/guardians with required notices in a timely manner; and (5) make sure to reevaluate students, "periodically" such as when there is a change in placement (e.g., elementary to middle school), when a parent requests it, or when conditions appear to warrant it (e.g., the accommodation plan is not working effectively or there has not been a reevaluation for 3 years).

Enforcement of Section 504

The federal regulations for Section 504 require that each public school district create

> a system of procedural safeguards that includes notice, an opportunity for the parents or guardian of the person to examine relevant records, an impartial hearing with opportunity for participation by the person's parents or guardian and representation by counsel, and a review procedure. [Nondiscrimination, 34 C.F.R. § 104.36]

If a parent/guardian has exhausted the school district's "review procedure" and is still convinced the school district is failing to provide a free and appropriate public education to their disabled child, the parent has two options. First, the parent/guardian can file a complaint with the Office of Civil Rights (OCR), which is the agency charged with the responsibility of enforcing Section 504. Generally, the OCR supports the use of informal negotiations and voluntary action to bring school districts into compliance with Section 504. However, federal funds may be terminated for a district that fails to correct its discriminatory practices (Cambron-McCabe, McCarthy, & Thomas, 2004, p. 191). The second option available to parents or guardians is to file a lawsuit in federal court (Office of Civil Rights, n.d.). However, in order to recover damages and attorney fees, a plaintiff must show gross misjudgment or bad faith on the part of school officials (*Smith v. Special Sch. Dist. No. 1,* 1999).

Conclusion

Both the IDEA and Section 504 were created to guarantee students with disabilities a free and appropriate public education. The similarities and subtle differences between the two laws can be confusing for even the most seasoned administrator. For example, not all students who qualify for Section 504 services qualify under IDEA; however, all students who qualify for services under IDEA qualify under Section 504. It is imperative that administrators understand how students with disabilities are appropriately identified, referred, evaluated, and placed. Additionally, administrators must hold teachers accountable for implementing the IEP or the 504 Accommodation Plan and must ensure that those plans are revisited and revised when it becomes apparent a change is required. In short, administrative competence and vigilance is necessary to ensure that students with disabilities have the opportunity to receive their federally granted right to a free and appropriate education.

Applying Your Knowledge

LeeAnna experienced a severe injury to her arm as the result of a fall from a swingset. She was in a cast for a period of time following some surgery to assist with bone placement and mending. This incident occurred nearly 6 years ago, when LeeAnna was still in elementary school. It appeared that the bones had healed and LeeAnna was doing well as she completed elementary school and junior high. However, about midway through her freshman year in high school, LeeAnna began to experience severe joint pain in the arm she had broken 6 years earlier. LeeAnna's parents took her to the doctor, but no apparent cause could be diagnosed at the time. The pain continued in the arm but also began to spread to other parts of LeeAnna's body (feet, legs, shoulders); all of the pain was only on the side of LeeAnna's body on which the arm had been broken. Additional problems such as extreme cold on the one side of LeeAnna's body, hypersensitivity of her skin, and painful leg aches began to occur and did not subside over time. Finally, a diagnosis was made of a rare joint disease resulting from the trauma experienced during the injury 6 years ago. Though some medications provided temporary relief, this condition would be chronic and increase and decrease in pain at different times. The strain of walking from one class to another in a large, comprehensive high school seemed to increase LeeAnna's leg pain; additionally, being in the halls during the passing periods with 2,300 other students assured that she would be bumped by others. When her hypersensitivity of the skin was occurring, the pain from these unavoidable contacts drove LeeAnna to tears. As the freshman year came to a close, LeeAnna begged her parents not to make her go back to school in the fall—it hurt too much.

QUESTIONS

1. Based on the information presented in this scenario is LeeAnna eligible for Section 504 accommodations? Why or why not?
2. Who should make the referral?
3. What might be some accommodations that would allow LeeAnna to remain in school without suffering?
4. Do you think LeeAnna should be referred for special education services? Why or why not?

QUESTIONS FOR THOUGHT

1. What is meant by the statement, "All special education students qualify as Section 504, but not all Section 504 students qualify for special education"?
2. Why does "substantial limitation of a major life activity" play a critical role in determining whether a student qualifies as Section 504?
3. What are the distinctions between IDEA and Section 504? Why is it important to understand these distinctions?
4. What are some ways in which classroom teachers can be helped to understand their roles and responsibilities for 504 accommodations?
5. Is it important that noncertified staff understand Section 504? Why or why not?
6. Who has the responsibility for 504 referrals? As the building principal, how would you make sure that referrals are done?
7. When disciplining a child who receives Section 504 services, is that child entitled to the same considerations and procedures as students covered by IEPs? Why or why not?

For Additional Information Online

Federal Regulations for Section 504, http://www.ed.gov/policy/rights/reg/ocr/edlite-34cfr104.html#D

Frequently Asked Questions about Section 504 and the Education of Children with Disabilities published by the Office of Civil Rights, http://www.ed.gov/about/offices/list/ocr/504faq.html

A Parent & Educator Guide to Free Appropriate Public Education published by the Puget Sound ESD, http://www.psesd.org/specialservices/pdfs/504manual.pdf

Meeting the Needs of All Students published by The Teacher's Guide, http://www.theteachersguide.com/504.html

504 Resources published by the Council of Educators for Students with Disabilities, Inc., http://www.504idea.org/504resources.html

Understanding and Working with the Office for Civil Rights (OCR) prepared by David M. Richards & Jose Martín, Attorneys at Law with Richards, Lindsay & Martin, L.L.P., http://www.504idea.org/OCR.pdf

References

Bercovitch v. Baldwin School, Inc., 133 F.3d 141 (1st Cir. 1998).

Cambron-McCabe, N. H., McCarthy, M. M., & Thomas, S. B. (2004). *Legal rights of teachers and students* (5th ed.). Needham Heights, MA: Allyn and Bacon.

Geisel, R. T., & Kallio, B. R. (2008). Section 503 of the Rehabilitation Act of 1973. In Pankake, A., Schroth, G., & Littleton, M. (Eds.), *Administration and Supervision of Special Programs in Education*. Dubuque, IA: Kendall Hunt.

Nondiscrimination on the Basis of Handicap in Programs or Activities Receiving Federal Financial Assistance, 34 C.F.R. § 104 (2003).

Office of Civil Rights. (n.d.). *Frequently asked questions about Section 504 and the education of children with disabilities.* Retrieved from http://www.ed.gov/about/offices/list/ocr/504faq.html

Puget Sound ESD. (2002). *A parent & educator guide to free appropriate public education.* Retrieved July 6, 2004, from http://www.psesd.org/specialservices/pdfs/504manual.pdf

Rehabilitation Act of 1973, 29 U.S.C. § 794 (2002).

Smith v. Special Sch. Dist. No. 1, 184 F.3d 764 (8th Cir. 1999).

United States Department of Education. (2011). Protecting students with disabilities. Retrieved from http://www2.ed.gov/about/offices/list/ocr/504faq.html

Yell, M. (1998). *The law and special education.* Upper Saddle River, NJ: Merrill.

Appendix A

A Comparison Chart: IDEA and Section 504

	IDEA	*Section 504*
Purpose	To ensure that all children with disabilities have available to them a free, appropriate public education.	To prohibit discrimination on the basis of disability in any program receiving federal funds.
Who Is Protected	Students who are eligible under the 13 categories of qualifying conditions.	Much broader. A student is eligible if s/he meets the definition of "qualified handicapped person," i.e., has or has had a physical or mental impairment that substantially limits a major life activity, has a record of or is regarded as disabled by others. Parents are also protected.
Duty to Provide a Free Appropriate Education	Both require the provision of a free appropriate education, including individually designed instruction, to students who qualify.	
	Requires the district to provide an individualized education program. "Appropriate education" means a program designed to provide "educational benefit."	"Appropriate" means an education comparable to the education provided to students without disabilities.
Special Education vs. Regular Education	A student is eligible to receive special education services only if a multidisciplinary team determines that the student has one of the handicapping conditions and needs special education.	A student is eligible if s/he meets the definition of "qualified handicapped person," i.e., has or has had a physical or mental impairment that substantially limits a major life activity, or is regarded as disabled by others. The student is not required to need special education in order to be protected.
Funding	YES	NO

	IDEA	*Section 504*
Accessibility	Not specifically mentioned although if modifications must be made to provide a free appropriate education to a student, IDEA requires it.	Detailed regulations regarding building and program accessibility.
General Notice	Require child find activities	Require child find activities
	Requires notification of parental rights.	Districts must include notice of nondiscrimination in its employee, parent, and student handbooks and, if the district has more than 15 employees, must specify the district's 504 coordinator(s).
Notice and Consent	Both require specific notice to the parent or guardian about identification, evaluation, and placement.	
	Requires written notice. Notice requirements are more comprehensive and specify what the notice must provide.	Requires notice. (A district would be wise to give notice in writing.)
	Written notice is required before any change in placement.	Requires notice before a "significant change in placement."
	Requires consent for initial evaluation placement.	Consent not required, but if a handicapping condition under IDEA is suspected, those regulations must be followed.
Evaluations	The regulations are similar.	
	Requires consent before an initial evaluation is conducted.	Requires notice, not consent.
	Reevaluations must be conducted at least every 3 years.	Requires "periodic" reevaluations.
	No provisions.	Requires a reevaluation before a significant change in placement.
	Provides for independent evaluations.	No provisions.
Determinations of Eligibility, Program, and Placement	Done by admission, review, and dismissal committee. Parent is a member of the committee.	Done by a group of persons knowledgeable about the child, the evaluation data, and placement options. While parental participation is not mentioned in the regulations, parental notice is required.

	IDEA	*Section 504*
Grievance Procedures	IDEA does not require a grievance procedure or a compliance officer.	Districts with more than 15 employees must designate an employee to be responsible for assuring district compliance with Section 504 and provide a grievance procedure (an informal hearing before a district staff member) for parents, students, and employees.
Due Process	Both require districts to provide impartial hearings for parents or guardians who disagree with the identification, evaluation, or placement of a student with disabilities.	
	Hearings conducted by a state hearing officer (who is an attorney). Decisions may be appealed to court.	Hearings conducted at the local level by an impartial person not connected with the school district. Person need not be an attorney. Decisions may be appealed to courts.
Enforcement	Compliance is monitored by the state's Education Agency which also receives and resolves complaints regarding IDEA. Office for Civil Rights does not enforce.	Enforced by the Office for Civil Rights by comprehensive investigation and monitoring activities.
Employment	No provisions.	Employment of persons with disabilities . . .

Appendix B

Serving Students with Needs

504

ADD
Dyslexia
Substance Abuse
Depression

504

ADHD
Conduct Disorder
Identity Disorder
Alcoholism

I
D
E
A

Autism
Mental Retardation
Visual Impairments
Hearing Impairments
Other Health Impairments
Emotional Disturbance
Speech or Language Impairments
A Specific Learning Disability
Orthopedic Impairments
Traumatic Brain Injury
Multiple Disabilities
Deaf-Blindness
Deafness

Suicidal
Encopresis
Enuresis
AIDS/HIV

TB
Asthma
Dystmia
Diabetes

Reprinted with permission from G. Schroth & M. Littleton, *The Administration and Supervision of Special Programs in Education,* p. 16, Dubuque, IA: Kendall/Hunt (2001).

Appendix C

Referral for Section 504

Student: _____ Birthdate: ____/____/____ Grade: _____
       Last Name   First Name

Parent/Guardian: _____

  Work Phone: _____

  Home Phone: _____

Address: _____
    Street Number   Street Name   City   Zip Code

Today's Date: _____ Person Making Referral: _____

Date of Receipt of Request ____/____/____

Signature: _____

Reason(s) for Referral (list specific concerns/behaviors): _____

_____

_____

To date, what accommodations or special provisions have been made to assist the student? _____

_____

_____

Is the student currently receiving special education or other services? Yes ☐ No ☐

If yes, what services is the student currently receiving? _____

_____

_____

Please submit completed referral to the building principal or Section 504 building coordinator.

Reprinted with permission from *A Parent & Educator Guide to Free Appropriate Public Education,* Puget Sound ESD, Office of Special Services, November 2002.

Appendix D

Section 504 Notice of Parent/Guardian and Student Rights

This is a notice of your rights under Section 504. These rights are designed to keep you fully informed about the district's decisions about your child and to inform you of your rights if you disagree with any of the district's decisions.

You have the right to:

1. Have your child participate in and benefit from the district's education program without discrimination based on disability.
2. An explanation of your and your child's rights under Section 504.
3. Receive notice before the district takes any action regarding the identification, evaluation, or placement of your child.
4. Refuse consent for the initial evaluation and initial placement of your child.
5. Have your child receive a free appropriate public education. This includes your child's right to be educated with non-disabled students to the maximum extent appropriate. It also includes the right to have the district provide related aids and services to allow your child an equal opportunity to participate in school activities.
6. Have your child educated in facilities and receive services comparable to those provided to non-disabled students.
7. Have your child receive special education services if she/he needs such services.
8. Have evaluation, educational, and placement decisions for your child based upon information from a variety of sources, by a group of persons who know your child, your child's evaluation data, and placement options.
9. Have your child be provided an equal opportunity to participate in non-academic and extracurricular activities offered by the district.
10. Have educational and related aids and services provided to your child without cost except for those fees imposed on the parents/guardian of non-disabled children.
11. Examine your child's education records and obtain a copy of such records at a reasonable cost unless the fee would effectively deny you access to the records.
12. A response to your reasonable requests for explanations and interpretations of your child's education records.
13. Request the district to amend your child's education records if you believe that they are inaccurate, misleading, or otherwise in violation of the privacy rights of your child. If the district refuses this request, you have the right to challenge such refusal.
14. Request mediation or an impartial due process hearing to challenge actions regarding your child's identification, evaluation, or placement. You and your child may take part in the hearing and have an attorney represent you.
    Hearing requests can be made to the district's Section 504 coordinator.
15. Ask for payment of reasonable attorney fees if you are successful on your claim.
16. File a local grievance or complaint with the U.S. Department of Education Office [for] Civil Rights.

The person in this district who is responsible for ensuring that the district complies with Section 504 is:

Reprinted with permission from *A Parent & Educator Guide to Free Appropriate Public Education,* Puget Sound ESD, Office of Special Services, November 2002.

Appendix E

Section 504 Student Eligibility Determination Form

Name: _____ Date of Meeting: _____

D.O.B. _____ School: _____ Grade: _____

1. Describe the nature of the concern:
_____
_____
_____

2. What is the student's mental or physical disability?
_____
_____
_____

3. Describe the basis for the determination of disability:
_____
_____
_____

4. Describe the educational impact of the disability on the student's learning:
_____
_____
_____

5. The student is eligible under Section 504: Yes: _____ No _____
   - If no, team recommendations:
   _____
   _____
   _____

   - If yes, recommended accommodations/services:
   _____
   _____
   _____

Participants' Names	Title	Date

Reprinted with permission from *A Parent & Educator Guide to Free Appropriate Public Education,*
   Puget Sound ESD, Office of Special Services, November 2002.

Appendix F

Section 504 Plan Accommodation Form

Student's Name: _____ Date: _____

Disability: _____ D.O.B. _____

School: _____ Grade: _____

Describe the educational and related aids and services that the student needs to receive a free appropriate public education.

Instructional:

_____
_____
_____

Environmental/Accessibility:

_____
_____
_____

Behavioral/Social:

_____
_____
_____

Assessment/Testing:

_____
_____
_____

Other:

_____
_____
_____

Implementation Date: _____ Review Date: _____

Participant/Title   Title   Date

_____
_____
_____
_____

Attach: Notice of Action/Consent and Notice of Parent/Guardian/Student Rights

Reprinted with permission from *A Parent & Educator Guide to Free Appropriate Public Education,* Puget Sound ESD, Office of Special Services, November 2002.

Title I and No Child Left Behind Act

3

Mark Littleton
Randy Tierce

Federal funding of Title I programs represents the largest single investment in public education by the federal government. Beginning with President Johnson's War on Poverty in 1965, Title I has reached millions of students in thousands of classrooms across the nation. Since the advent of the reauthorization of Title I with the No Child Left Behind Act, the law has become a powerful tool, raising standards for all children.

—Mark Littleton

Objectives

1. Describe the role of the federal government as it pertains to compensatory programs
2. Explain the evolution of the Elementary and Secondary Education Act to the No Child Left Behind Act and anticipated reauthorization of the ESEA
3. Identify the critical components of the No Child Left Behind Act
4. Illustrate the different Title I program designs and delivery options available to schools
5. Describe how current issues related to the No Child Left Behind Act affect the operation of public school campuses

Introduction

The U.S. Constitution is silent on public education. Rather, the legal development for public schools, and the subsequent funding of the schools, is left to the individual states (Alexander & Alexander, 2001). Given these circumstances, one would assume that federal involvement is minimal, at best. Yet, the federal government has been engaged in subsidizing various aspects of public education since the 19th century, and the federal government's role in public education was substantially shaped in the mid–1960s by the Elementary and Secondary Education Act (ESEA) (Finn, 1995). Within the 1965 ESEA, Title I was enacted to assist in America's war on poverty by directing federal funds to assist students from low-income families. Now authorized under the No Child Left Behind Act (NCLB) of 2001, Title I provides $13 billion in federal funds to education (U.S. Department of Education, 2009a). These funds target schools in which the student population is "disproportionately poor" (Puma & Drury, 2000, p. 2).

NCLB was bipartisan legislation that incorporated four key principles: (1) accountability for results, (2) flexibility in the use of funds, (3) greater parental choice, and (4) an emphasis on scientifically-based teaching methods (U.S. Department of Education, 2004). However, what began as a show of legislative solidarity to improve a failing educational system, NCLB became a hotbed of political debate (Mizell, 2003). Some early detractors characterized the law as being "in serious disrepair" (Cuban, 2004, p. 1). Still others who "applauded" the passage of NCLB initially have since changed their opinion because they believe the "philosophy of NCLB…uses accountability as a stick to threaten schools" (Ravitch, 2010, p. 20).

Although it is more of a federal subsidy than a program in the strictest sense (Puma & Drury, 2000), the success of Title I is open to debate (Fashola & Slavin, 1998; Jendryka, 1993; Le Tendre, 1999; Puma & Drury, 2000; Ravitch, 1997). Federal data indicate more than 17 million public school students nationwide receive Title I services (U.S. Department of Education, 2009a). However, detractors argue that standardized test scores for targeted students show no improvement and Title I schools deliver a curriculum that lacks challenge (Puma & Drury, 2000). In fact, NCLB proponents justified the massive overhaul of Title I in 2001 as a mechanism to fix a seriously troubled educational system (Mizell, 2003). Interestingly, those calling for the reauthorization of ESEA and attendant Title I makeover are motivated by similar concerns a decade after the most recent reauthorization (CCSSO, n.d.; Education Commission of the States, n.d.; Jennings, 2011).

Regardless, Title I funds affect over 50,000 schools (U.S. Department of Education, 2009a), and remain a substantial portion of the budget for many of these campuses. It would be prudent of school leaders to understand the mechanism for funding Title I programs and to know what practices enhance the success of those programs at the campus level.

History

If only in a political sense, the federal government has been reluctant to become directly involved in public education. Congress specifically prohibits intrusion into public education.

> No provision of any applicable program shall be construed to authorize any department, agency, officer, or employee of the United States to exercise any direction, supervision, or control over the curriculum, program of instruction, administration, or personnel of any educational institution, school, or school system. (20 U.S.C. Section 1232a)

However, the federal government has retained a strong interest in education. At the onset, the federal government took an indirect role in public education choosing to affect policy with subsidy. (Refer to Table 3-1 for a summary of legislation affecting education.) This indirect control was performed in two ways. First, grants were offered to states with the stated intent of supporting the common good for the general public. Second, grants with conditions (or strings) were offered to help subsidize special programs. Until the mid-1960s, federal funding focused on issues of national interests such as land grants and national defense projects (Alexander & Alexander, 2001). Eventually, federal funds were directed toward specific educational programs. Although there had been several previous attempts to provide subsidies for general education programs, the passage of ESEA was a significant policy statement showing the federal government's interest in education (Cross, 2004).

According to Spring (2005), it was a stroke of political genius that President Johnson directly addressed religious squabbles and concerns of educational lobbyists with a single piece of legislation. Proponents of federal aid to education wanted to pass a

Table 3-1 Federal Legislation Assisting Education Selected from the National Center for Education Statistics, 2009

Morrill Act of 1862—provided land grants for colleges specializing in the agricultural and mechanical arts.

Smith-Hughes Act of 1917—federal aid for vocational programs in public schools below the college level.

Lanham Act of 1940—federal aid to local governments for the construction of facilities, including schools.

National Defense Education Act (NDEA) of 1958—provided federal funds to promote scholarship in the sciences.

Economic Opportunity Act of 1964—provided federal funds for the War on Poverty, including Head Start.

Elementary and Secondary Education Act of 1965—authorized grants for elementary and secondary school programs for children of low-income families.

Education Consolidation and Improvement Act (ECIA) of 1981—consolidated 42 federal programs to be funded under the ESEA block grant authority.

Augustus F. Hawkins-Robert T. Stafford Elementary and Secondary Improvement Amendments of 1988—reauthorized ESEA and other programs through 1993.

Goals 2000: Educate America Act of 1994—formalized education goals and established a National Education Standards and Improvement Council providing for voluntary national board certification.

Improving America's School Act of 1994—Reauthorized ESEA.

Education Flexibility Partnership Act of 1999—allows states to participate in the Education Flexibility Partnership program.

No Child Left Behind Act of 2002—comprehensive reauthorization of ESEA and adding specific proposals related to accountability, assessment, and parental choice.

Student Grant Hurricane and Disaster Relief Act of 2005—authorized waivers of certain loan repayment requirements for students impacted by natural disasters.

Public Law 109-211 of 2006—reauthorized the Education Flexibility Partnership Act of 1999.

American Recovery and Reinvestment Act of 2009—provided $100 billion to states for economic stimulation and certain education programs, including Title I.

Table 3-2   **Elementary and Secondary Education Act of 1965**

Title I	Educationally deprived children
Title II	Libraries and textbooks
Title III	Supplementary education
Title IV	Cooperative research
Title V	State education departments
Title VI	Handicapped children
Title VII	Bilingual education
Title VIII	Dropout prevention & Adult education

general aid to education bill, but ESEA, with its more narrow focus of alleviating economic imbalances, survived the legislative process (Roeber, 1999). The act focused on providing aid to children of poor families instead of general aid to public and private schools (Spring, 2005). Contrary to popular opinion, ESEA was not designed to target "low-income students per se, but to all students, regardless of income, who suffered from poverty's deleterious effects upon their schooling" (Zamora, 2003, p. 419).

Of the eight titles in ESEA (see Table 3-2), the most significant piece is Title I, a section of law designed to assist educationally and economically deprived children. It is interesting to note the clarity of purpose of Title I as stated in Section 201 of ESEA. The initial purpose of the law was to address the special educational needs of low-income families, and to improve the instructional programs affecting schools impacted by low-income families.

Title I quickly became a popular federal subsidy with near-unanimous approval upon each reauthorization (Jendryka, 1993). As often happens with federal subsidy programs, federal controls increased with each reauthorization (Fowler, 2000). Elmore and McLaughlin (1982) note that these escalating compliance requirements were to amplify the federal government's presence in defining "certain specific responses at the local level" (p. 165). Sometimes called "a skillfully constructed package of compliance and assistance measures" (Elmore & McLaughlin, 1982, p. 162), procedural requirements and fiscal accountability increased dramatically during the first 15 years of Title I's existence. Designed to assist with reading and mathematics instruction, federal regulations required that Title I funds be used to supplement, not supplant, state, and local funds (Puma & Drury, 2000).

Yudof, Kirp, Levin, and Moran (1992) note that ESEA "exhibited the difficulties as well as the potential of federal involvement in education" (p. 743). Congress commissioned a study of ESEA in the 1974 reauthorization. Because of the perceived intrusion into public education by the federal government, program evaluation was a critical component of Title I (Fowler, 2009). In the extensive review, the National Institute of Education was very critical of the implementation of Title I at the federal and state levels. Apparently, the "federal preoccupation with compliance objectives" had occupied so much of state administrators' time that little attention was given to assistance (Elmore & McLaughlin, 1982, p. 168). Subsequent legislation reflected the concern with compliance requirements by providing options for schools with Title I and non-Title I programs.

The increased emphasis on fiscal accountability led schools to focus on a particular curriculum option called "pull out." (Program design options will be discussed in more detail later in the chapter.) Puma and Drury (2000) note that "pull outs came under increasing fire for their lack of coordination with regular classroom instruction and, in 1978, the 'schoolwide' option was introduced" (p. 3).

The size of Title I along with its complex set of regulations, "made it a prime target for the Reagan administration, which hoped to eliminate the program entirely" (Yudof et al., 2002, p. 743). Congress resisted the temptation to eliminate Title I, but then provided for fewer federal restrictions in the 1981 Education Consolidation and Improvement Act (ECIA). In the ECIA, Title I was renamed Chapter 1, a name that remained until the 1994 reauthorization (Elmore & Rothman, 1999; Goldberg, 1987).

The Hawkins-Stafford amendment to the ESEA in 1988 required that federally funded programs be gauged by *opportunity to learn* measures. These measures were designed to describe the educational process. Each district receiving Chapter 1 funds was to use the indicators to assess the quality of the program. The Hawkins-Stafford amendment signaled the return of administrative guidance as well as the beginning of parental involvement (Schwartz, 1995).

The 1994 reauthorization of Title I in the Improving America's Schools Act (IASA) represented a significant shift in the compensatory program. Although the most significant change (again renamed Title I) was the increase in parental involvement (Yudof et al., 2002), IASA required states to establish identical challenging standards and benchmarks for Title I and non-Title I students (Elmore & Rothman, 1999). Congress recognized that

> Although the achievement gap between disadvantaged children and other children has been reduced . . . the most urgent need for educational improvement is in schools with a high concentration of children from low-income families and achieving the National Education Goals will not be possible without substantial improvement . . . [and] educational needs are particularly great for low-achieving children in our Nation's highest-poverty schools . . . (20 U.S.C.S. 6301[1–3])

IASA attempted to align federal policies with state and local policies (Wirt & Kirst, 1997). According to Puma and Drury (2000), three programmatic themes emerged during this alignment. Under the umbrella of a standards-based reform theme, IASA required states to develop "challenging standards of performance and assessments that measure student performance against the standards" (Elmore & Rothman, 1999, p. 9). Upon identifying the struggling schools, states were then to provide additional assistance to the schools.

The second programmatic theme signaled a significant operational shift. Prior to 1978, Title I provided for targeted assistance programs that addressed the needs of individually identified students. In 1978 an additional program design was offered (Wang, Wong, & Kim, 1999). Schools were allowed the option of the school-wide design provided that the district matched federal funds with their own funds. Few schools opted for the school-wide design due to the matching funds requirement until the passage of the 1988 Hawkins-Stafford amendment eliminated this barrier. Schools in which at least 75% of the student population were identified as low-income qualified for the school-wide design. This design let the school co-mingle federal, state, and local funds to provide a comprehensive, coherent program of instruction. Under the IASA, the poverty-rate for the funding of school-wide programs was adjusted from 75% to 50%, allowing a considerably larger number of schools the freedom to combine funding sources (Puma & Drury, 2000).

Finally, IASA provided for more program management flexibility than previous reauthorizations of ESEA. In the Education Flexibility Partnership Act of 1999 (Ed Flex) federal and state officials were given authority to waive some federal requirements if those requirements were viewed as inhibiting school improvement (Puma & Drury,

2000; U.S. Department of Education, 2001). Prior to IASA, a large number of public schools received Title I funds—approximately 70% of elementary schools. Although IASA, through its funding provisions, reduced the percentage of schools receiving aid, there was "a precipitous increase in the percentage of high-poverty secondary schools receiving funding"—61% to 93% (Puma & Drury, 2000, p. 6).

Many of the provisions in IASA set the stage for dramatic changes with the No Child Left Behind (NCLB) Act. On January 8, 2002, President George W. Bush signed into law the NCLB Act, a bipartisan reauthorization of ESEA. NCLB symbolizes an historic extension of the federal government in public education (Wenkart, 2003). Based upon the four principles of accountability, local control, parental choice, and scientifically-based teaching (Sclafani, 2003), the major provisions of NCLB include (a) state accountability systems, (b) adequate yearly progress of schools, (c) local district and school improvement, (d) increased emphasis on school-wide programs, (e) teacher and paraprofessional qualifications, and (f) participation of eligible children in private schools (U.S. Department of Education, 2002). Former U.S. Secretary of Education Rod Paige noted the country's commitment, through NCLB, to "educate every child, regardless of skin color, spoken accent or zip code" (Paige, 2004).

Legislative plans to rewrite the Elementary and Secondary Schools Act will likely focus on the far-reaching amendments added to the ESEA in 2002 by NCLB. Some think that in addition to substantive revisions to the policies of NCLB, a change of name is almost certain (Jennings, 2011). However, skepticism has emerged over whether mere changes in nomenclature or "rebranding" of NCLB will result in meaningful changes in policy (Noguera, 2010). Consequently, the flurry of discussion over renaming of NCLB has led to characterizing the pending renewal as simply "an image makeover" (Garrett, 2011).

In 2010, U.S. Secretary of Education Arne Duncan disputed the idea of the ESEA renewal as mere window-dressing by noting the ESEA/NCLB rewrite will drop the "utopian" (as cited in Garrett, 2011, p.1) NCLB goal of student proficiency by 2014 in favor of new proficiency measures, included in the "Blueprint for Reform" ("Federal education budget project," n.d.; U.S. Department of Education, 2010a). The Blueprint ostensibly will focus on student readiness for college and career (see Table 3-3). Included in the Blueprint are proposed revisions to a variety of key policy elements, including accountability measures, academic standards, school improvement, teacher evaluation, funding schema, and the federal role in education (Jennings, 2011).

Table 3-3   NCLB vs. Blueprint

Category	NCLB	Blueprint
Goal	"Proficient" by 2014	"On-track" or graduating by 2020
Teachers	Must be "highly qualified"	"Effective" teachers identified
Standards	Established by states	Adoption of common core
Improvement	Range of improvement options	More specific options
Meet AYP	All students, even subgroups	Making progress vs. consistent fail
Not Meet AYP	School choice or tutoring	Flexibility
Performance	Cohort "Status Models"	Individual "Growth Models"
The Gap	No rewards	Flexibility and monetary rewards
Accountability	Reading and math	Other subjects can be used
Testing	Grades 3-8; high school	Same as NCLB
Student Data	Ethnicity and special subpopulations	Same as NCLB

It is worth noting that groups such as the Council of Chief State School Officers (2010) have urgently called for a congressional re-envisioning and reauthorization of ESEA; others see no need for revamping the law other than to refine the 2014 deadline and requirement for achieving 100% proficiency (Russo, 2011). Because NCLB is a massive nascent law, primarily the highlights of current NCLB as it pertains to the operation of Title I in the public schools will be presented in this chapter.

FEDERAL COMPENSATORY GUIDELINES

As has already been mentioned, federal guidelines for Title I are complex. Covering the minutia of program guidelines is beyond the scope of this book. However, an understanding of some of the broad fiscal and procedural guidelines may assist in effective program implementation and supervision.

Fiscal Guidelines

In the $13 billion Title I program, federal funds are distributed to the state education agencies (SEAs). The SEAs then distribute the funds to the qualifying local districts. According to Puma and Drury (1999), "Title I funds are distributed to counties, districts, and schools—generally in proportion to the number of poor school-age children in those jurisdictions" (p. 5).

In targeted assistance programs, Title I funds may be used only to supplement state and local resources (20 U.S.C. Section 6321(b)(1)). There is no single definition of "supplement, not supplant." However, the supplement not supplant standard usually applies if school personnel can show that the program would continue with local funds in the event that federal funds were to cease.

Funds for schoolwide programs may be used in combination with other federal, state, and local funds. Supplement not supplant applies to schoolwide programs, as well, but the determination of use is made at the school level instead of the program level. The funds must be used to support activities identified by a comprehensive school reform plan, which is developed with the involvement of community and school personnel. Although the Title I funds may be co-mingled, schools are admonished to maintain an accurate record of how Title I funds are distributed.[1]

Response to Intervention (RtI) is an instructional technique endorsed by the federal government with the reauthorization of IDEA in 2004 that is designed to assist students who are struggling academically and to mitigate overidentification of learning-disabled children (U.S. Department of Education, 2007b; "What Is RtI?", n.d.). Although not a Title I program issue per se, utilizing Title I funds within an RtI model presents unique challenges for school leaders. The primary obstacle centers on the requisite Title I stipulation of "supplement not supplant" attached to the funds (U.S. Department of Education, 2009b). Avoiding conflict between RtI and Title I in a schoolwide model is essentially straightforward. However, incorporating Title I dollars into a targeted assistance program can be problematic because every student that is identified for RtI does not automatically meet the eligibility requirements of Title I (Hicks, 2008; Texas Education Agency, 2008).

Funding of the provisions added by NCLB created considerable discontent between state and federal officials and members of the Bush administration. In January, 2004, 10 U.S. Senators sent a letter to U.S. Secretary of Education, Rod Paige, blasting the

---

[1]See, for example, Under Secretary Hickok's letter to the Honorable Sandy Garrett, Superintendent of the Oklahoma Department of Education, March 6, 2003.

administration for, among other things, underfunding NCLB (Kennedy et al., January 8, 2004). Eight states seriously considered "opting-out" of NCLB, but very few bar state funding of NCLB (Education Funding Research Council, 2004). Choosing to opt-out is attractive to some states primarily because the amount of state and local funds needed to comply with NCLB requirements can be more than the state receives in federal assistance (Tirozzi & Ferrandino, 2004). In response, federal government officials warn state officials of the dangers of opting-out, which may include funding losses in programs other than those funded through NCLB (Education Funding Research Council, 2004).

Subsequently, a plan was introduced to Congress in 2007 that would allow states to opt out of conforming to many of the NCLB mandates. The opt-out provisions allowed states to use federal funding at will as long as prescribed levels of transparency in state-level testing and dissemination of public information were maintained (Lips, 2007). In 2011, the first federal waiver from the achievement requirements of NCLB was awarded to a school district in McPherson, Kansas. Although third- through fifth-grade students in the district must still take the statewide math and reading assessments for AYP purposes, the waiver allows the Kansas district to use a test for sixth- through twelfth-grade students patterned after the American College Testing (ACT) exam (Deines, 2011).

More recently, Title I programs have benefited from the massive inflow of cash through the federal economic stimulus plans. According to the U.S. Department of Education (2010b), the American Recovery and Reinvestment Act (ARRA) of 2009 provided $97 billion in emergency funding to the States in response to budget shortfalls. Additionally, almost $40 billion of the State Fiscal Stabilization Fund (SFSF) (U.S. Department of Education, 2009c), a one-time infusion of almost $54 billion administered under the ARRA, was allocated for education reforms. On top of the original ARRA dispensation for education and the additional SFSF funds, another $10 billion in supplemental funding was distributed in the form of ESEA Title I Grants (U.S. Department of Education, 2009c). Critics of the ARRA and SFSF note that although the stimulus money effectively doubled Title I funding, the structural changes required to dispense the money failed to help disadvantaged students in a sufficient manner and "will have [negative] consequences long after the money runs out" (McNeil, 2010).

PROCEDURAL GUIDELINES

Although the fiscal structure of the distribution of Title I funds varies from state to state and the federal guidelines often are complex, the goal of Title I remains the same. In a 2001 report published by the U.S. Department of Education, the Planning and Evaluation Service noted that

> The primary purpose of the program has not changed since the time when it first became law—to ensure equal educational opportunity for all children regardless of socioeconomic background and to close the achievement gap between poor and affluent children, by providing additional resources for schools serving disadvantaged students. (p. 2)

Yet, NCLB has taken the purpose of Title I a step further. Section 6301 of the Act provides that

> The purpose of [Title I] is to ensure that all children have a fair, equal, and significant opportunity to obtain a high-quality education and reach, at a minimum, proficiency on challenging state academic achievement standards and state academic assessments. This purpose can be accomplished by:
> 1. Ensuring that high-quality academic assessments, accountability systems, teacher preparation and training, curriculum, and instructional materials are aligned with challenging state academic standards so that students, teachers, parents, and

administrators can measure progress against common expectations for student academic achievement;

2. Meeting the educational needs of low-achieving children in our nation's highest-poverty schools, limited-English proficient children, migratory children, children with disabilities, Indian children, neglected or delinquent children, and young children in need of reading assistance;

3. Closing the achievement gap between high- and low-performing children, especially the achievement gaps between minority and nonminority students, and between disadvantaged children and their more advantaged peers;

4. Holding schools, local educational agencies, and states accountable for improving the academic achievement of all students, and identifying and turning around low-performing schools that have failed to provide a high-quality education to their students, while providing alternatives to students in such schools to enable the students to receive a high-quality education;

5. Distributing and targeting resources sufficiently to make a difference to local educational agencies and schools where needs are greatest;

6. Improving and strengthening accountability, teaching, and learning by using state assessment systems designed to ensure that students are meeting challenging state academic achievement and content standards and increasing achievement overall, but especially for the disadvantaged;

7. Providing greater decisionmaking authority and flexibility to schools and teachers in exchange for greater responsibility for student performance;

8. Providing children an enriched and accelerated educational program, including the use of schoolwide programs or additional services that increase the amount and quality of instructional time;

9. Promoting schoolwide reform and ensuring the access of children to effective, scientifically based instructional strategies and challenging academic content;

10. Significantly elevating the quality of instruction by providing staff in participating schools with substantial opportunities for professional development;

11. Coordinating services under all parts of this subchapter with each other, with other educational services, and, to the extent feasible, with other agencies providing services to youth, children, and families; and

12. Affording parents substantial and meaningful opportunities to participate in the education of their children. (20 U.S.C. Section 6301)

PARENT INVOLVEMENT

Parent involvement is key to an effective Title I program. Section 6318 of NCLB specifies the parameters of parent involvement for the participating school districts. These guidelines require that each school served by NCLB funds establish a policy that involves parents in the planning, development, implementation, and evaluation of the Title I program. In the spirit of local control, NCLB does not mandate how parent involvement will be achieved, but school personnel would be well-advised to heed subparagraph (e)(3) of section 6318 which states that each participating school district

> shall educate teachers, pupil services personnel, principals, and other staff, with the assistance of parents, in the value and utility of contributions of parents, and in how to reach out to, communicate with, and work with parents as equal partners, implement and coordinate parent programs, and build ties between parents and the school.

Due, in part, to the fact that quality parental involvement has not been achieved in most Title I schools (Wang et al., 1999), section 6316 of NCLB provides a "choice plan" for school districts. The U.S. Department of Education (2001) notes that the lack of parent involvement is particularly noticeable from poor families. Previous reauthorizations of Title I strengthened the "emphasis on school/family community partnerships by: (1) specifying partnerships . . . linked to student learning; (2) asking schools to develop . . . a 'compact' . . .; and (3) allowing funds to be commingled to create unified programs that serve all parents" (Puma & Drury, 1999, p. 27). However, NCLB's choice option sends a clear signal to participating schools of the necessity to involve parents to the greatest extent.

Contemporary Issues

Regardless of its bipartisan beginnings, the implementation of NCLB and the anticipated reauthorization of ESEA have contributed to a steady stream of debate and controversy. For some states, the cost of implementing the law is more than the federal subsidy they would receive through the program. However, the detrimental effects of opting-out of the program may be too severe. The reauthorization of the ESEA purportedly will mitigate or eliminate some of the most controversial issues related to NCLB, including accountability, student testing, adequate yearly progress, and high-quality teachers (Duncan, 2010; Education Commission of the States, n.d.; Garrett, 2010; Jennings, 2010; Russo, 2011).

ACCOUNTABILITY

Each state must develop a single accountability system based on the state's academic standards, and include a system of punishments and rewards to hold each public school accountable for the performance of all students (34 C.F.R. Section 200.12).[2] Although accountability may be the most controversial provision in NCLB (Price, 2003), there are those who view it as "among the most race-conscious legislative remedies to racial inequity in K–12 education" (Losen, 2004, p. 246). NCLB requires each participating state to disaggregate student scores by gender, racial and ethnic group, English proficiency status, migrant status, students with disabilities, and economically disadvantaged (34 C.F.R. Section 200.2). This provision is a far-cry from previous testing programs that reflect a school, district, or state average. Sclafani (2003) notes that under NCLB, "it will not be enough to raise the average score by raising the performance of the best students even higher" (p. 46).

Proponents argue that accountability systems are necessary to obtain improvement. Additionally, accountability empowers parents and policymakers with the ability to ensure that schools provide a quality education. Furthermore, the disaggregation of the testing data will force schools to address the issues of the *neediest* of students. Opponents of accountability programs contend that poor and inadequate accountability systems will fail to accurately assess schools, and redirect valuable resources from necessary programs (Kucerik, 2002). While the accountability measures of NCLB require schools to show that every student, even those in major subpopulations, meet AYP each year, the revamping of NCLB will likely draw a clearer distinction (see Table 3-3) between schools exhibiting progress and those that consistently fail ("side-by-side", n.d.; U.S. Department of Education, 2010a).

STUDENT TESTING

Sclafani (2003) commented that "assessment is critical to making schools accountable and to identifying practices that make schools and teachers successful" (p. 45). Federal regulations require each state receiving funds to implement a system of

---

[2]U.S.C. is an acronym for United States Code, the actual law passed by Congress. C.F.R. is an acronym for Code of Federal Regulations, the U.S. Department of Education's rules for implementing the law.

student assessment in mathematics, reading/language arts, and science. The assessments must be aligned with state standards, and must provide for the assessment of all students, including limited English proficient students and students with disabilities (34 C.F.R. Section 200.2). The assessment results must be made available to parents (34 C.F.R. Section 200.8), and the results must be disaggregated by gender, racial and ethnic group, English proficiency status, migrant status, students with disabilities, and economically disadvantaged (34 C.F.R. Section 200.2).

Controversy regarding this aspect of the law stems from (a) inclusion of all students, even those students not served by federal funds, and (b) the arguable bias of standardized tests (Price, 2003)—that is, testing opponents contend that standardized testing does not adequately measure a student's or school's achievement level or progress (Kucerik, 2002). Testing is an expensive activity, and testing programs that involve every child are costly, in terms of time and money. Additionally, testing of limited English-proficient students and students with disabilities can adversely affect a school's adequate yearly progress. (Of course, the counterargument and a crucial component of NCLB is that all children should be tested so that none are "left behind.") The reauthorization of the ESEA is anticipated to allow testing in subjects other than those under NCLB, such as history and foreign language (National Federation of Republican Women, n.d.; "side-by-side", n.d.; U.S. Department of Education, 2010a).

ADEQUATE YEARLY PROGRESS

The backbone of the accountability system is adequate yearly progress (AYP). AYP is defined by the state, but must include a student assessment system that considers all public school students, and specific data on economically disadvantaged students, students from major racial and ethnic groups, limited English-proficient students, and students with disabilities (34 C.F.R. Section 200.13). In addition, graduation rates must be used to determine AYP. The states may use retention rates, attendance rates, and participation in academically-advanced programs (e.g., gifted-talented, advanced placement, and college preparatory) (34 CFR Section 200.19).

Controversy stems from the fact that some school districts report strong student performance on the assessment, but fail to have an adequate number of students to meet AYP (Robelen, 2004). Following the enactment of NCLB in 2002, polls indicated that the law's definition of AYP created discontent with the general public (Robelen, 2004). Former secretary Paige noted that for a school to be considered making AYP, the school must assess 95% of its students and students in each subgroup (Paige, 2002). For example, an ethnically and socially homogeneous school might need to meet student performance requirements based on the totality of the student population because the subgroups do not apply. On the other hand, an ethnically and socially diverse school will need to meet performance requirements of the total student population and the applicable subgroups of race, ethnicity, and limited English proficiency. In contrast, the proposal contained in the Blueprint for Reform (U.S. Department of Education, 2010a) distinguishes between the two scenarios. For example, a different set of interventions would be prescribed for persistently low-achieving schools as compared to those that miss academic targets because of one or two student subgroups.

In 2005 an attempt to bolster the validity of AYP determinations resulted in the Growth Model Pilot Project (GMPP). The GMPP allowed states to give credit to schools for students who were making significant growth. By making experimental adjustments to NCLB requirements, students who typically would not have been counted as proficient for the purpose of AYP determinations (U.S. Department of Education, 2009a) were deemed to be on the right track and therefore counted favorably toward AYP. In 2008, the GMPP resulted in more than 1,200 additional schools making AYP than in the previous year.

HIGHLY QUALIFIED TEACHERS

NCLB originally required that all participating states have *highly qualified* teachers in the core academic subject areas by the end of the 2005-06 school year (34 C.F.R. Section 200.57). The U.S. Department of Education defines a highly qualified teacher as one who has a bachelor's degree, state certification, and who has demonstrated competency in a core academic area (34 C.F.R. Section 200.56). In schoolwide programs, all teachers teaching one or more academic subjects must be highly qualified. In targeted assistance programs, any teacher whose salary is partially or fully paid by Title I funds must be highly qualified (Texas Education Agency, 2003).

Many schools found it difficult to meet this demanding standard. As a result, the U.S. Department of Education provided local districts with some flexibility in meeting the highly qualified teacher standard (Texas Education Agency, 2003). For example, federal policy changes made it easier for rural school districts and for science teachers to meet the highly qualified mandate (*Changing the Rules,* 2004).

The federal policy changes that made the certification of teachers highly qualified more accessible to states have come under closer scrutiny and met legal obstacles. In *Renee v. Duncan* (2009) parents and advocates of children with disabilities in California filed suit against the U.S. Department of Education challenging the NCLB ruling that allows teachers or interns in the process of acquiring certification to be counted as highly qualified. In late 2010, the Ninth Circuit Court dismissed the NCLB regulation, siding with the parents and advocates. A few months later Congress introduced an appropriations bill that essentially reversed the Ninth Circuit's ruling, further angering those supporting disabled and minority children and teachers. Due to the large number of special education teachers predicted to retire by 2015, and the anticipated lack of a sufficient number of highly qualified teachers, ripples from this recent wave of legal action are likely to become larger (Shah, 2011).

Program Design and Delivery Options

TARGETED ASSISTANCE

Implementation of Title I programs takes one of two different designs. The predominant pattern has been the targeted assistance plan which are "pull-out programs that deliver supplementary instruction to low-achieving students during the time they would have spent in their regular classes" (Puma & Drury, 2000, p. 7). In-class instruction is another aspect of the targeted assistance design. The in-class model allows for isolated groups within the academic classroom. Often the in-class model was little more than the pull-out model located within the academic classroom. As mentioned earlier, the targeted assistance model was the exclusive design until 1978.

One state agency directs districts to develop targeted assistance programs that

1. help students meet the state's performance standards,
2. are based on improving student achievement,
3. incorporate a plan considering the needs of the students served,
4. utilize effective instructional strategies,
5. support the regular instructional program,
6. provide for a well qualified staff, supported by professional development, and
7. increase parental involvement. (Texas Education Agency, 2001)

Targeted assistance programs have been a "target" for many Title I critics. Anstrom (1995) warns that "curricular fragmentation resulting from Chapter 1 [now Title I] students missing out on core academic instruction while attending remedial reading and math classes has been a frequently occurring side effect" (p. 3).

SCHOOLWIDE PROGRAMS

Prior to NCLB, schoolwide programs required that 50% of the student population qualify as low income. Wang et al. (1999) note that "although Title I legislation has permitted school-wide programs since 1978, these programs were rarely implemented prior to the passage of the IASA, partly due to the requirement that school districts match federal grants with their own funds" (p. 5). IASA further encouraged the schoolwide program by reducing the low-income student population requirement to 50% (from 75%). As a result the number of schools moving to the schoolwide design increased. Under NCLB, the required low-income student population requirement was reduced to 40%, providing opportunities for additional schools to operate on a schoolwide basis.

The core elements of a schoolwide program include a comprehensive needs assessment based upon the achievement of the children on the state assessment. From that needs assessment, reform strategies for the school must (a) provide opportunities for all children (not only Title I identified students) to meet proficient levels on the state assessment, (b) use effective instructional methods that strengthen the core academic areas and increase the amount of instructional time, and (c) provide for the needs of low-achieving children through counseling services, college and career awareness, and integration of vocational and technical education programs (20 U.S.C. Section 6314).[3]

Regardless of whether a schoolwide or targeted assistance Title I plan is implemented, as noted previously the incorporation of Response to Intervention creates a need for increased circumspection on the part of the school when utilizing the federal funds (Hicks, 2008; Texas Education Agency, 2008; U.S. Department of Education, 2007b, 2009b).

Private School Participation

As originally passed, the Elementary and Secondary Education Act of 1965 was designed to benefit children from low-income families. It was designed to improve instruction for *all* children. In all reauthorizations, as with the original bill, private school children are included under the provision of helping all children. However, the federal government does not send federal funds directly to private schools. As the funds are granted to the local educational agencies (school districts), the agencies become responsible for serving eligible students within the boundaries of their district. Often, private school administrators and public school officials work closely to generate requests for federal funds. After consultation with private school administrators, public school officials must provide for equitable participation in the Title I program for eligible private school students (20 U.S.C. Section 6320).

In 2005, almost 200,000 private school students nationwide benefited from Title I funds. Typically private school students receive Title I services from teachers sent from the public schools (U.S. Department of Education, 2007a). There has been considerable discussion and some litigation regarding the use of public funds to assist private schools. However, the courts have determined that Title I funds can be used to assist eligible students in private schools. Anyone interested in further discussion is encouraged to investigate the cases of *Agostini v. Felton* (1997) and *Mitchell v. Helms* (2000).

---

[3]See 34 C.F.R. Section 200.26 et seq. for additional, specific information from the U.S. Department of Education. Additionally, state-specific information can be obtained from each state agency of the participating states.

VOUCHERS

In 1999, Rosenthal noted the federal government's desire to provide greater flexibility in the Title I program. Combining the large ESEA monies (of which Title I is the largest portion) into block grants was one way to do this. Under the voucher concept, the federal government would provide parents of Title I eligible students with vouchers. These vouchers would be taken to the school of parental choice (private or public). The school, in turn, would send the voucher to the state for reimbursement for educating the child. However, such a move makes it difficult to ensure that low-income students benefit from Title I funds. The use of vouchers in the Title I program has already prompted political debates, and is sure to generate court challenges. For example, the U.S. Supreme Court upheld an Ohio law that provided tuition vouchers for students in poor performing schools to attend public or private schools of their choice (*Zelman v. Simmons-Harris,* 2002). Regardless of the federal constitutionality of such programs, state constitutional provisions may be more restrictive.

Supervision

As with many federal programs, Title I is reauthorized periodically. As a result, rules and policies change regularly. Fowler (2009) notes that these important policy updates should be followed closely. Astute supervisors will follow the changes closely to ensure that their school is not in danger of losing funds.

Supervisors also need to know what works. Fortunately, Title I programs have been thoroughly researched, and there is ample information concerning indicators of a successful program. Wang et al. (1999) suggest that schoolwide programs are more effective than targeted assistance designs. Also, U.S. Department of Education (2001, p. 35) research suggests that when teaching reading, teachers should:

- give children access to a variety of reading and writing materials,
- present explicit instruction for reading and writing, both in the context of authentic and isolated practice,
- create multiple opportunities for sustained reading practice in a variety of settings,
- carefully choose instructional-level text from a variety of materials, and
- adjust the grouping and explicitness of instruction to meet the needs of individual students.

The same study (U.S. Department of Education, 2001, p. 36) suggests that effective teaching of mathematics include the following methodology:

- Focusing on problem solving. Students need conceptual understanding to deal with novel problems and settings and to become autonomous learners. Instruction should encourage multiple solutions to problems.
- Defining basic skills to involve more than computation.
- Emphasizing reasoning and thinking skills, concept development, communicating mathematically, and applying mathematics. Students must learn mathematics with understanding, building new knowledge from experience and prior knowledge.
- Presenting content in a logical progression with an increasing emphasis on higher-order thinking skills, such as problem-solving and mathematical reasoning, and mathematical communication.
- Integrating topics of numeration, patterns and relations, geometry, measurement, probability and statistics, algebra, and algorithmic thinking. Instruction should

broaden the range of mathematical content studied, an aspect of teaching in which low-income children are often short-changed.

● Taking advantage of calculators and computers to extend students' mathematical reach.

Understanding the research regarding effective reading and mathematics instruction is not sufficient. The instructional staff (teachers, teacher's aides, etc.) need continual development and training to hone their instructional skills and to stay abreast of current effective instructional methodology (Puma & Drury, 1999; U.S. Department of Education, 2001). Teachers are, after all, the most effective resource in improving student achievement (Darling-Hammond, 2000; Greenwald, Hedges, & Laine, 1996). Quality professional development programs for Title I teachers will be strong in content, be distributed over an extended period of time in which teachers are actively engaged, utilize study groups and mentoring, and be aligned with the standards and assessment instruments used to measure student progress (U.S. Department of Education, 2001).

Conclusion

Federal funding of Title I programs represents the largest single investment in public education by the federal government. Beginning with President Johnson's War on Poverty in 1965, Title I has reached millions of students in thousands of classrooms across the nation. Since the advent of the reauthorization of Title I with the No Child Left Behind Act, the law has become a powerful tool, raising standards for all children.

However, the best of tools will not work if they are not used properly. There is evidence to suggest that Title I programs operate best on a schoolwide basis, particularly when class sizes are reduced and quality instruction is implemented. All children, those receiving Title I services included, should be held to high standards of performance, and taught by a qualified staff who engage in appropriate professional development activities. Teachers should utilize instructional strategies known to be effective and focus on improving student performance. Last, but certainly not least, parents need to be involved in every phase of the process. Parental involvement is often the key to student engagement and, consequently, student learning.

The shrewd supervisor is not only knowledgeable of effective programs and instructional practices, but she or he is cognizant of the rules and regulations associated with implementing a Title I program. As a result, professional development is important for the supervisor as well as the teacher. Only when supervisors are aware of effective program designs, instructional practices, and program requirements and limitations can they ensure that the Title I program supports the entire instructional program of the school.

The impending reauthorization of ESEA will inevitably retool many of the policies of NCLB. Therefore, school leaders must also remain vigilant regarding the evolving standards based reform landscape by wisely sifting through the policies and inevitable politics of the renewal in order to discover the most salient details of the ESEA reauthorization (Jennings, 2010).

Applying Your Knowledge

A bedroom community is located in a suburb of a large metropolitan area. The district is located conveniently near the headquarters of several large corporations, but it is rapidly becoming an industrial center. The elementary school has a student population of 610. The demographics of the school are quite interesting. Approximately 15% of the students live in homes where the household income exceeds $200,000. These students live in a neighborhood that is stable, where the parents drive to manage major divisions of large corporations. The data reveal that students from the high-income households are the top students and have instructional needs addressed through honors and gifted programs. Interestingly, during the previous school year, 48% of the students at the elementary school were from low-income households. However, due to the rapid immigration of low-income families to the industrial region, the projected low-income population is expected to reach 53%. Student scores are declining as the number of students from low-income households increases.

QUESTIONS

1. What is the best program design for the campus? Why?
2. What can the campus principal do to ensure that the school maintains adequate yearly progress?
3. What should the campus principal do to attain participation from both low-income and high-income parents?

QUESTIONS FOR THOUGHT

1. How has federal involvement in education changed from the enactment of ESEA to NCLB?
2. What are the major differences between targeted assistance programs and school-wide programs?
3. Do you view vouchers as deleterious to the public school system? Why or why not?
4. What are the positive and negative aspects to standardized testing programs for students?
5. How can schools involve parents in a significant way?

For Additional Information Online

Council of Chief State School Officers (CCSSO)—http://www.ccsso.org/

Education Commission of the States (ECS)—http://www.ecs.org/

Internet Education Exchange—http://www.iedx.org/

National Center for Education Statistics—http://www.nces.ed.gov/

Texas Education Agency—http://www.tea.state.tx.us

U.S. Department of Education—http://www.ed.gov

References

STATUTES

Title I, Improving the Academic Achievement of the Disadvantaged, 34 Code of Federal Regulations (C.F.R.), Part 200.

Helping Disadvantaged Children Meet High Standards, 20 United States Code (U.S.C.), Chapter 70, Subchapter I, Section 6301 et seq.

Elementary and Secondary Education Act, Public Law 89-10 (April 11, 1965).

Fiscal Requirements, 20 U.S.C. Chapter 70, Subchapter I, Section 6321.

Parental Involvement, 20 U.S.C. Chapter 70, Subchapter I, Section 6318.

Participation of Children Enrolled in Private Schools, 20 U.S.C. Chapter 70, Subchapter I, Section 6320.

Prohibition Against Federal Control of Education, 20 U.S.C. Section 1232(a).

Statement of Purpose, U.S.C. Chapter 70, Subchapter I, Section 6301.

Strengthening and Improvement of Elementary and Secondary Schools Helping Disadvantaged Children Meet High Standards, 20 United States Code (U.S.C.), Chapter 31, Section 1232a.

COURT CASES

Agostini v. Felton, 521 U.S. 203; 117 S.Ct. 1997 (1997).

Mitchell v. Helms, 530 U.S. 793; 120 S.Ct. 2530 (2000).

Renee v. Duncan, 623 F.3d 787 (2010).

Zelman v. Simmons-Harris, 536 U.S. 639; 122 S.Ct. 2460 (2002).

OTHER

Alexander, K., & Alexander, M. D. (2001). *American public school law* (5th ed.). Belmont, CA: West/Thomson Learning.

Anstrom, K. (1995). New directions for Chapter 1/Title I. *Directions in Language and Education, 1.* National Clearinghouse for Bilingual Education. Retrieved September 23, 2000 from http://128.164.90.197/ncbepubs/directions

Changing the rules. (2004, April 7). *Education Week* on the Web. [On-line Serial]. Available at http://www.edweek.org

Council of Chief School State School Officers. (n.d.). *Letter to Congress calling for ESEA reauthorization.* Retrieved on March 26, 2011 from http://www.ccsso.org/News_and_Events/Current_News/CCSSO_Sends_ESEA_Leadership_Letter_to_Congress.html

Cross, C. (2004). *Political education.* New York: Teachers College Press.

Cuban, L. (2004, March 17). The contentious 'No Child' law: Who will fix it? And how? *Education Week on the Web.* Retrieved March 22, 2004 from http://www.edweek.org

Darling-Hammond, L. (2000, January 1). Teacher quality and student achievement: A review of state policy evidence. *Education Policy Analysis Archives* [On-line Serial], *8,* Available at http://olam.ed.asu.edu/epaa

Deines, A. (2011, March). McPherson school officials answer questions. *The Capital-Journal.* Retrieved on March 26, 2011 from http://cjonline.com/news/education/2011-03-08/mcpherson-school-officials-answer-questions

Duncan, A. (2010). *Education: We have to change the rules, eliminate the excuses and hold ourselves accountable.* Speech presented to the National Press Club in Washington, D.C. Retrieved on March 25, 2011 from http://www.ed.gov/news/speeches/quiet-revolution-secretary-arne-duncans-remarks-national-press-club

Education Commission of the States. (n.d.). No Child Left Behind. Retrieved on March 25, 2011 from http://www.ecs.org/ecsmain.asp?page=/html/newsMedia/ECSNewsroom.asp

Education Funding Research Council. (2004, March). *Title I Monitor, 9* (3).

Elmore, R. F., & Rothman, R (Eds.). (1999). *Testing, teaching, and learning: A guide for states and school districts* (National Research Council). Washington, DC: National Academy Press.

Elmore, R. F. & McLaughlin, M. W. (1982). In A. Lieberman & M. W. McLaughlin (Eds.), *Policy Making in Education: Eighty-first Yearbook of the National Society for the Study of Education.* Chicago: The University of Chicago Press. pp. 159–194.

Fashola, O. S., & Slavin, R. E. (1998, January). Schoolwide reform models, *Phi Delta Kappan, 79,* 370–380.

Federal Education Budget Project. (n.d.). *New America Foundation.* Retrieved on March 25, 2011 from http://edmoney.newamerica.net/sites/newamerica.net/files/articles/Comparing_NCLB_and_Obama_Blueprint.pdf

Finn, C. (1995). Towards excellence in education. *Public Interest, 120,* 41–54.

First, P. F. (1992). *Educational policy for school administrators.* Boston: Allyn and Bacon.

Fowler, F. C. (2009). *Policy studies for educational leaders* (3rd ed.). Columbus, OH: Merrill.

Garrett, R. (2010). NCLB reauthorization: The new blueprint. Retrieved on March 25, 2011 from http://www.education.com/magazine/article/new-nclb-blueprint/ved

Goldberg, K. (1987, December 9). Lawsuit challenges Chapter 1 and 2 aid to church schools. *Education Week on the Web.* [On-line serial]. Available at http://www.edweek.org

Greenwald, R., Hedges, L., & Laine, R. (1996). The effect of school resources on student achievement. *Review of Educational Research, 66,* 361–396.

Hicks, T. (2008). Using Title I funds for RTI will be a challenge. Retrieved on March 25, 2011 from http://www.wrightslaw.com/news/08/rti.fund.constraints.01.08.htm

Jendryka, B. (1993). Failing grade for federal aid. *Policy Review, 66,* 77–81.

Jennings, J. (2010, December). The policy and politics of rewriting the nation's main education law. *Phi Delta Kappan, 92*(4), 44–49. Retrieved on March 27, 2011 from http://www.kappanmagazine.org/content/92/4/44.abstract

Kennedy, E., Dodd, C., Harkin, T., Mikulski, B., Bingaman, J., Murray, P., Reed, J., Edwards, J., Clinton, H. R., & Miller, G. (2004, January 8). *Letter to Secretary Paige on the Bush administration's failure to properly implement No Child Left Behind Act.* Retrieved on February 25, 2004 from http://edworkforce.house.gov/democrats/paigenclbletter.html

Kucerik, E. (2002). The No Child Left Behind Act of 2001: Will it live up to its promise? *Georgetown Journal on Poverty Law and Policy, 9,* 479–487.

Le Tendre, M. J. (1999). *Title I must be #1 now!* Speech presented at the National Association of State Title I Directors in New Orleans, LA. Retrieved August 31, 2000 from http://www.ed.gov/offices/OESE/CEP/neworlea2.html

Lips, D. (2007). Saving accountability and transparency in public education. *The Heritage Foundation.* Retrieved March 25, 2011 from http://www.heritage.org/Research/Education-Notebook/Saving-Accountability-and-Transparency-in-Public-Educationnbsp

Losen, D. (2004). Challenging racial disparities: The promise and pitfalls of the No Child Left Behind Act's race-conscious accountability. *Howard Law Journal, 47,* 243–298.

McNeil, M. (2010). Red flags raised over inequities as consequence of stimulus aid. *Education Week, 29*(22), 16–18. Retrieved March 25, 2011 from EBSCO host.

Mizell, H. (2003, July). *NCLB: Conspiracy, compliance or creativity.* Paper presented at the "Learn and Lead" Week of the National Staff Development Council, St. Louis, MO.

National Federation of Republican Women. (n.d.). *No Child Left Behind vs. Blueprint for Reform.* Retrieved March 25, 2011 from http://www.nfrw.org/documents/literacy/nclb.pdf

Noguera, P. (2010, June 14). A new vision for school reform. *The Nation.* Retrieved on March 27, 2011 from http://www.thenation.com/article/156807/reframing-education-debate

Paige, R. (2002, July 24). *Letter from the Secretary on Adequate Yearly Progress.* Retrieved April 8, 2004 from http://www.ed.gov/policy/elsec/guid/secletter/020724.html

Paige, R. (2004, March 11). *Memo to editorial writers.* Retrieved March 22, 2004 from http://www.ed.gov/news/opeds/edit/edit/2004/03112004.html

Price, D. (2003). Outcome-based tyranny: Teaching competency while testing like a state. *Anthropological Quarterly, 76*(4), 715–729.

Puma, M. J., & Drury, D. W. (2000). *Exploring new directions: Title I in the year 2000.* Alexandria, VA: National School Board Association.

Ravitch, D. (2010, June). Why I changed my mind. *The Nation.* Retrieved on March 27, 2011 from http://www.thenation.com/article/why-i-changed-my-mind

Ravitch, D. (1997, June 2). Success in Brooklyn, but not in D.C. *Forbes, 159,* 90.

Robelen, E. W. (2004, September 1). Poll: Public still on learning curve for Federal school law. *Education Week on the Web.* [On-line serial]. Available at http://www.edweek.org

Roeber, E. D. (1999). Standards initiatives and American educational reform. In G. J. Cizek (Ed.), *Handbook of Educational Policy,* pp. 151–181. Boston: Academic Press.

Rosenthal, I. (1999). ESEA debate heats up. *Technology and Learning, 20,* 43.

Russo, A. (2011). NCLB: The case against reauthorization. Retrieved March 25, 2011 from http://scholasticadministrator.typepad.com/thisweekineducation/nclb_news/

Schwartz, W. (1995). Opportunity to learn standards: Their impact on urban students. *ERIC Clearinghouse on Urban Education.* New York. (ERIC Document Reproduction No. ED 389 816).

Sclafani, S. (2003). No Child Left Behind, *Issues in Science and Technology, 19,* 2.

Shah, N. (2011). Are teachers in training good enough for special ed.? *Education Week on the Web.* Retrieved March 25, 2011 from http://blogs.edweek.org/edweek/speced/2011/02/are_teachers_in_training_good.html

Side-by-side guide to reauthorization. (n.d.). *Education Week.* Retrieved on March 27, 2011 from http://www.edweek.org/media/esea-c1.pdf

Spring, J. (2005). *Conflicts of interests: The politics of American education* (5th ed.). Boston: McGraw-Hill.

Texas Education Agency, Division of NCLB Program Coordination. (2008). Preliminary guidance for the implementation of coordinating NCLB funds in an RtI model. Retrieved on March 27, 2011 from http://www.tea.state.tx.us/index4.aspx?id=4478&menu_id=798

Texas Education Agency. (2003). *NCLB Bulletin, 1* (1). Retrieved April 8, 2004 from http://www.tea.state.tx.us/nclb/bulletin.html

Texas Education Agency. (2001). Division of Student Support Programs. Retrieved on February 7, 2001 from http://www.tea.state.tx.us/support/titleia

Tirozzi, G., & Ferrandino, V. (2004, March 31). *Improving NCLB.* Message posted to Principals.org, archived at http://www.principals.org/advocacy/views/ImprovingNCLB.cfm

Troller, S. (2011, March 5). Once staunch proponent of No Child Left Behind has moved on. *The Cap Times.* Retrieved on March 27, 2011 from http://host.madison.com/ct/news/local/education/article_68986ba0-45d0-11e0-be47-001cc4c002e0.html

U.S. Department of Education, Office of Planning, Evaluation and Policy Development. (2010a). A Blueprint for Reform: The reauthorization of the Elementary and Secondary Education Act. Retrieved on March 27, 2011 from http://www2.ed.gov/policy/elsec/leg/blueprint/blueprint.pdf

U.S. Department of Education (2010b). *FY 2011 budget summary.* Retrieved on March 26, 2011 from http://www2.ed.gov/about/overview/budget/budget11/summary/edlite-section2.html

U.S. Department of Education, National Center for Educational Statistics. (2009a). *Digest of education statistics* [Data file]. Retrieved March 25, 2011from http://nces.ed.gov/programs/digest/d09/ch_4.asp

U.S. Department of Education. (2009b). Implementing RTI using Title I, Title III, and CEIS funds: Key issues for decision-makers. Retrieved on March 27, 2011 from http://www2.ed.gov/programs/titleiparta/rti.html

U.S. Department of Education. (2009c). *State fiscal stabilization fund.* Retrieved on March 26, 2011 from http://stimulusschools.org/SFSF_funds.pdf

U.S. Department of Education. (2007). *Final report on the national assessment of Title I: Summary of key findings.* Washington, DC: Institute of Education Services. Retrieved on March 26, 2011 from http://ies.ed.gov/ncee/pdf/20084014_rev.pdf

U.S. Department of Education. (2007). *Questions and answers on Response to Intervention (RTI) and Early Intervening Services (EIS).* Retrieved March 27, 2011 from http://idea.ed.gov/explore/view/p/,root,dynamic,QaCorner

U.S. Department of Education. (2004). Retrieved on April 5, 2004 from http://www.ed.gov/nclb/

U.S. Department of Education. (2002). *The No Child Left Behind Act: Summary of final regulations.* Retrieved February 12, 2004 from http://www.No ChildLeftBehind.gov

U.S. Department of Education, Planning and Evaluation Service. (2001). *High standards for all students: A report from the national assessment of Title I on progress and challenges since the 1994 reauthorization.* Washington, DC: 2001. Doc. No. 2001–16.

Wang, M. C., Wong, K. K., & Kim, J. R. (1999). *A national study of Title I school-wide programs: A synopsis of interim findings.* A research report supported by the Office of Educational Research and Improvement, U.S. Department of Education, and the Laboratory for Student Success, Temple University Center for Research in Human Development and Education. (ERIC Document Reproduction Service No. 436 596).

Wenkart, R. (2003, July). *Contracting for supplemental educational services under the No Child Left Behind Act.* Paper presented at the Tenth Annual Education Law Conference, Portland, ME.

What Is RTI? (n.d.). National Center on Response to Intervention. Retrieved March 25, 2011 from http://www .rti4success.org/

Wirt, F. M., & Kirst, M. W. (1997). *The political dynamics of American education.* Berkely, CA: McCutchan Publishing Corp.

Yudof, M. G., Kirp, D. L., Levin, B., & Moran, R. F. (2002). *Educational policy and the law* (4th ed.). St. Paul, MN: West Publishing Company.

Zamora, P. (2003). In recognition of the special educational needs of low-income families: Ideological discord and its effects upon Title I of the Elementary and Secondary Education Acts of 1965 and 2001. *Georgetown Journal on Poverty Law and Policy, 10,* 413–447.

Ensuring Success for Migrant Students

Velma D. Menchaca
Alejo Salinas, Jr.
Encarnación Garza, Jr.

It is important that teachers create a positive classroom environment for migrant students. Migrant students often find themselves in new classrooms. The challenges of adjusting to strange, new learning and home environments often contribute to feelings of isolation and loneliness.

—*Velma Menchaca & Alejo Salinas Jr.*

Objectives

1. Present demographics of the migrant population in the United States
2. Describe some of the unique educational experiences of migrant students
3. Discuss the issue of culturally relevant teaching as it relates to migrant students
4. Describe involvement of parents of migrant students
5. Discuss how schools can assist and support migrant students to succeed

Introduction

There are approximately 3.5 million migrant and seasonal farmworkers in the United States—men, women, and children who work in all 50 states during peak periods of agriculture. A migrant farmworker is an individual who moves from a permanent place of residence for the purpose of obtaining employment in agricultural work. Each year their lives revolve around working and moving from one harvest to another with the hope of improving their finances (Kugel & Zuroweste, 2002).

Migrants in the United States are extremely diverse. Approximately 92% of all migrants are culturally and linguistically diverse, with 85% being Hispanic. Of the Hispanic migrant population, 60% are Mexican American and are the largest subgroup followed by Puerto Ricans, Cubans, and Central and South Americans (Kissam, 1993). While White Americans make up 8% of the migrant population, the remaining 7% is comprised of Black Americans, Jamaicans, Haitians, Laotians, Thais, and other racial and ethnic minorities (National Center for Farmworker Health, 2001).

Migrants who have immigrated to the United States from Mexico and parts of Central America primarily harvest fruits and vegetables (Fix & Passel, 1994; Oliveira, Effland, & Hamm, 1993). In the summers, they may harvest tomatoes or broccoli in Texas or apricots, peaches, or grapes in California. They tend to migrate up and down along three known geographic routes: the East Coast stream, the midcontinent stream, and the West Coast stream following seasonal crops.

Educating migrant students is one of the solutions to changing their lives in a positive manner. Whether a family decides to continue with yearly migration or relocates permanently in proximity to their seasonal work, the task of educating the migrant student remains of paramount importance. The dynamics, which shape the migrant students' environment, provides parameters for understanding the migrant educational context.

This chapter is organized around several broad categories: educational experiences of migrant students, culturally relevant teaching, migrant parental involvement, and the challenges for secondary schools. An array of information on the lives of migrant children, and hardships they encounter in the fields is provided. Also discussed are the challenges migrants encounter in schools because of their mobile lifestyles, the obstacles that keep them from graduating, and the hurdles they must successfully jump to get into college. Additionally, instructional strategies that have been successful with migrant students and strategies for educational leaders to incorporate to ensure positive parental involvement, the involvement of migrant parents in the schools, and diversification of the curriculum by implementing culturally relevant content are addressed. Finally, the authors have provided several lessons with examples relevant to the lives of migrant students.

PROFILE OF THE MIGRANT FAMILY

Over 80% of migrants and seasonal farmworkers are U.S. citizens or are legally in the United States (Fix & Passel, 1994). Approximately 50% of all farmworkers earn less than $7,500 per year, while about 50% of all farmworker families earn less than $11,000 per year, far below the federal poverty level (U.S. Department of Labor, Office of the Assistant Secretary for Policy, Office of Program Economics, 2000). The work of migrant farmworkers tends to be seasonal and often very inconsistent. The number of farmworkers needing housing exceeds the number of available substandard housing units (National Center for Farmworker Health, 2001). Therefore, farmworkers, particularly migrants, face obstacles in obtaining housing. Agricultural employers recognize that lack of adequate housing is a serious challenge. They resort to temporary housing such as labor camps; however, construction and maintenance of these labor camps can be expensive, especially since labor camps are only occupied during harvest season. The housing that is readily available for most migrant families may not meet the minimum inspection standards, posing a national health problem. Migrant families tend to live without adequate restroom facilities and clean drinking water in substandard houses, which are usually barrack-like structures, run-down farmhouses, trailer homes, or small shacks (Shotland, 1989). Some migrants may be forced to sleep in tents, cars, or even ditches when housing is not available.

Many migrant families suffer occupation-related health problems such as risk of injury from farm machinery and equipment and from pesticide poisoning (Menchaca & Ruiz-Escalante, 1995). Respiratory problems caused by pesticide poisoning, natural fungi, and dusts are common. Lack of safe drinking water contributes to dehydration, heat strokes, and heat exhaustion. Dermatitis, a skin rash, is often intensified because of the sun, sweat, and lack of sanitary facilities. Other health concerns are attributed to poor sanitation and poverty. Thus, the intensity of health problems for migrant farmworkers is greater than for the general population (National Center for Farmworker Health, 2001).

About two-thirds of migrant families and about 70% of migrant children live below the federal poverty line (National Farm Worker Ministry, 2009). Some commonly reported health problems among migrant children include lower height and weight, respiratory diseases, parasitic conditions, chronic diarrhea, and congenital and developmental problems, to name a few. Poverty, hunger, fear, and uncertainty fill the lives of migrant children.

Educational Experiences of Migrant Students

Children of migrant farmworkers have not been academically successful in public schools. Poverty and migration make it difficult for migrant children to create a different life and future than that of their parents. Their schooling may be interrupted several times throughout one school year; a high mobility rate places an enormous stress on migrant children and on the schools. The challenges they confront as they progress through the grades eventually can multiply. These challenges must be addressed in order for students to fully develop their intellectual potentials. For example, their educational needs vary considerably; some lack literacy skills in Spanish while English language abilities are limited for others. The quality of instruction for migrant students may be hampered if the curriculum does not adequately address their needs or provide supplemental instructional services to overcome academic difficulties that result from frequent educational disruptions. Most school personnel are not prepared to adequately serve the academic needs of Hispanic students, in general, nor migrant students in particular (Menchaca, 1996).

Migrant students have the lowest graduation rate of any population group in the U.S. public schools (Johnson, Levy, Morales, Morse, & Prokop, 1986). The dropout rate among children of migrant farmworkers is almost twice that of children from nonmigrant families. This rate is conservatively estimated at 45%, well above the national average of 25% (National Program for Secondary Credit Exchange and Accrual, 1994). Data from other studies show that the dropout rates for migrant students range from 45% to 65% (Levy, 1987; Vamos Inc., 1992). These longitudinal studies focused on Hispanic students identified while they were in sixth grade; however, these students were not tracked for long because of a high disappearance rate. They either moved, disappeared, dropped out, or no longer qualified for services.

Approximately 50% of migrant students are one or more years below grade level. Thus, half of all migrants could be at risk of dropping out of school (Migrant Education

Secondary Assistance Project, 1989). Research indicates that several factors influence the students to leave school before graduating. Living in poverty leads to dropping out of school; the addition of family member contributing to the household income is welcomed. Students also tend to drop out of school if they are not proficient in English; yet, learning English for all migrants is an economic asset. These students generally have suffered academically due to their mobile lifestyles, dislike for school, little participation in school activities, lack of a home base, economic disadvantage, low motivation, and low persistence (Rasmussen, 1988). Some teachers become disinterested in migrant students due to their diverse academic, social, and economic needs; consequently, the students leave school.

In a study conducted by the Migrant Youth Program (1985), some students indicated school personnel were not meeting their needs, although teachers and counselors believed the students' needs were met. Martinez (1994) reported that according to principals and teachers, factors that influence the school performance of migrant children are (a) social prejudice, (b) lack of communication, (c) mobility, (d) no educational continuity, (e) education not valued, (f) inappropriate home environment, and (g) lack of knowledge of how educational systems operate. Yet, migrant advocates such as mentors, counselors, or advisors had a more holistic perspective on reasons migrant students leave school. Many of them indicated that poverty contributed to school absences because these students needed to work; also, they often had to care for younger siblings or stay home due to illnesses (Martinez & Cranston-Grigras, 1996; Martinez, Scott, Cranston-Grigras, & Platt, 1994).

Migrant Student Information Exchange Initiative

The U.S. Department of Education was mandated by Congress, in Section 1308 (b) of the Elementary and Secondary Education Act, as amended by the No Child Left Behind Act of 2001 (NCLB), to assist states in developing effective methods for the electronic transfer of student records and in determining the number of migratory children in each state. This was to ensure a system to link migrant student records. In accordance with the mandate, the USDE has implemented the Migrant Student Information Exchange Initiative whose primary mission is to ensure the appropriate enrollment, placement, and accrual of credits for migrant children. The Migrant Student Information Exchange (MSIX) is the technology that allows states to share educational and health information on migrant children who travel from state to state and who, as a result, have student records in multiple states' information systems. MSIX works in concern with the existing migrant student information systems that states currently use to manage their migrant data to fulfill its mission to ensure the appropriate enrollment, placement, and accrual of credits for migrant children (U.S. Department of Education, 2007).

The primary goals of the MSIX are to:

Goal 1: Create an electronic exchange for the transfer of migrant student education and health data amongst the states.

Goal 2: Promote the use of MSIX.

Goal 3: Ensure the use of the consolidated migrant student record for the purposes of enrollment, placement, and accrual of credit of migrant students in school and migrant education projects.

Goal 4: Produce national data on the migrant population. (U.S. Department of Education, 2007)

Migrant children transfer to several schools during the span of their education, sometimes as often as three times a year. The implementation of the MSIX will ensure the appropriate enrollment and placement for migrant children especially because these experiences are not pleasant, and at times can be uncomfortable. Migrant children must be assisted in adjusting to new environments because many times they do not feel grounded or as if they truly belong to any one school.

When some students do feel a sense of belonging or have made friends, they are soon uprooted to go to the next harvest site. What may compound the situation more is that these children may not be proficient in English; therefore, they may not be accepted by some of their classmates (Dyson, 1983). These children tend to withdraw, are not noticed, and thus are overlooked. They experience isolation for not being accepted for who they are, intensifying their sense of low self-esteem. Consequently, educators would be wise to provide an environment for migrant students that aids rapid adjustment. For example, the Jackson County Migrant Education Program (1981) in Medford, Oregon, produced a handbook titled *Migrant Education—Harvest of Hope.* This handbook covers several topics including knowledge of children for whom English is a second language (ESL). The handbook also addresses how migrant students relate to teachers, and provides suggestions for meeting the needs of ESL students. Most important is the message that the migrant students need the teachers to care, respect, understand, and encourage them.

Another site that provides migrant children rich learning experiences is Waitz Elementary in Mission, Texas, located in the southern-most part of Texas about 6 miles north of the Texas-Mexico border. Approximately 30% of the children at Waitz Elementary are from migrant families who live in tarpaper shacks or in trailer homes along dirt roads. With a 99% Mexican-American student population, Waitz Elementary annually rates among the top 10% of all Texas schools in reading and mathematics achievement. The school "defies predictions of low achievement by a sustained focus on multiple factors" (Cawelti, 1999, p. 1) that remarkably improve student performance. The principal and teachers are committed to high expectations and make every effort to ensure high student achievement. They are committed to quality implementation of multiple changes that contribute to student achievement. Teachers use bilingual education approaches with students who enter with limited English skills. The teachers focus on making sure that all students pass the state-mandated assessment. The school strongly emphasizes regular attendance and recognizes classrooms with all children present; good citizenship is recognized and rewarded.

DEBUNKING DEFICIT THINKING

It is ironic that a lifestyle that deems us as "culturally disadvantaged and severely at-risk" and bestows upon us the low expectations of a deficit thinking society, is also the lifestyle that enabled us to become resilient and invulnerable (Garza, 1998).

The migrant lifestyle is often blamed for the academic failures of migrant children, but it must also be given credit for their successes. Many children of migrant farm workers have overcome the negative effects of the stress factors associated with the migrant lifestyle. They "beat the system" precisely because of (not in spite of) lessons learned as members of a migrant farm worker family. The migrant lifestyle provides them with the basic lesson for survival. These experiences helped them develop the qualities and attributes of resiliency. The migrant lifestyle was a natural setting that served to develop social competence, problem-solving skills, autonomy, and a sense of purpose and hope (Garza, Reyes, & Trueba, 2004).

Garza (1998) found that migrant students were "successful" and took advantage of the opportunities to learn from the real-life situations they encountered as a result of their lifestyles. They grew up in families that taught them respect and pride, and gave them a sense of hope. Migrant parents modeled a strong work ethic as they worked in the fields without complaining day in and day out. Though resources were limited, there was always enough to provide for a family's basic needs. They worked together in the fields for one common cause and purpose. They could make concrete connections between hard work and food on their tables. Migrants knew where their food, clothing, and shelter came from. Though they were poor, there was always a sense of pride. They learned to respect others, but especially themselves. This sense of pride helped them cope with the pain of cruelty when others made fun of the way they dressed, their language, and their family. Their parents had little formal schooling, yet they valued education highly. They encouraged them to break away from their way of living without making them feel ashamed. Parents were proud of who they were, but they had high expectations for all their children. There was never a doubt that they were expected to graduate from high school and go to college. A strong sense of family support kept them from falling through the cracks while they established a support system within the schools. This gave them time to learn the rules of the game they were expected to follow. In the process, migrant students found caring teachers that encouraged them to "break the cycle of migrancy" without making them feel inferior about their way of making a living. Teachers validated their lifestyle while they were living it and raised their sense of self-worth (Garza, 1998).

Culturally Relevant Teaching

Culturally relevant teaching (Ladson-Billings, 1990, 1995) is a pedagogy that empowers students intellectually, socially, emotionally, and politically to examine critically educational content and processes. It uses the students' home culture to help create meaning and understanding of the children's world. The culturally relevant teacher emphasizes, not only academic success, but also social and cultural successes (Ladson-Billings, 1992, 2009). Migrant students can be empowered through the school curricula if they see connections between their home culture and their school, thus encouraging pride in who they are.

Culturally relevant teaching rests on three criteria: (1) academic success, (2) cultural competence, and (3) cultural consciousness (Ladson-Billings, 1995). Teachers must direct, reinforce, and cultivate academic success and excellence in their migrant students. They must attend to students' academic needs, not just make them feel good. Teachers who use culturally relevant strategies believe that academic success is possible for all students when they help them make connections with their community. Making this connection allows migrant students to learn from a familiar cultural base which acknowledges their ancestors and develops understanding in their culture, thus empowering them to build on their personal backgrounds (Gay, 2002; Grant & Sleeter, 2007; Ladson-Billings, 2009; Menchaca, 2000). Teachers who use culturally relevant teaching believe that migrant students have special strengths that need to be explored and utilized in the classroom.

Teachers who embrace culturally different strategies utilize the migrant students' culture as the vehicle for learning. Historically, textbooks have failed to address the cultures of Hispanic students in general, and Hispanic migrant students in particular. Consequently, Hispanic students encounter concepts taught in culturally unfamiliar fashions (Carrillo, 2009; Gay, 2002; Grant & Sleeter, 2007; Ladson-Billings, 2009; Nieto, 2004). Thus, many students never acquired the desired level of understanding. Teachers using culturally relevant strategies encourage migrant students to use their home language while they acquire the second language, English.

Culturally relevant teaching allows students to develop a "sociopolitical cultural consciousness that allows them to critique the cultural norms, values, mores, and institutions that produce and maintain social inequalities" (Ladson-Billings, 1995, p. 162). They must have opportunities to make decisions and to take actions related to the topic, issue, or problem they are studying. Students can gather data, analyze their values and beliefs, synthesize their knowledge and values, identify alternative courses of action, and decide what actions need to be taken, if any. Students are taught thinking and decision-making skills that empower them and provide a sense of political efficacy. In other words, when students identify a problem and are given the freedom to make decisions on what action needs to be taken to remedy the problem, they will gain a sense of pride and satisfaction. It is important for teachers to communicate to students that they are being successful.

Integrating Relevance for Migrant Students

Teachers validate the cultures of students by integrating culturally relevant content into the curriculum (Gay, 2002; Gonzáles, 1991; Ladson-Billings, 1995, 2009; Nieto, 2004; Menchaca, 2000). Teachers legitimize Hispanic migrant students' real-life experiences as part of the formal curriculum. In a science lesson, for example, the use of culturally familiar plants, flowers, and fruits prevalent to the Hispanic culture could be presented along with the content in the textbook. Studying the production of plants, fruits, and vegetables gives teachers an excellent opportunity to introduce the mobile lifestyle of migrant students. Because of their mobile lifestyles, migrant students bring rich experiences to the classroom. Teachers can build on students' strengths by embracing and incorporating their experiences in the lessons. When studying the food pyramid in a health lesson, the use of culturally familiar foods and examples of diseases that are prevalent in migrant family households will enhance concept acquisition (Marines & Ortiz de Montellano, 1993).

In a language arts lesson, teachers can incorporate a variety of Hispanic children's books. Much of the Hispanic literature focuses on the life and experiences of migrant students. Teachers can encourage positive ethnic affiliation for migrant students. Nurturing ethnic affiliation helps migrant students learn about and respect other cultural groups' heritage and histories while retaining the value of their own culture instilled in their hearts and minds. There are many young children's books that can easily be incorporated in language arts or history classes. Some examples of these books are *What Can You Do with a Paléta?* (Tafolla, 2009), *René Has Two Last Names–René Tiene Dos Apellidos* (Laínez, 2009), *No Time for Monsters–No Hay Tíempo para Monstruos* (Rivas, 2010), and *The Bakery Lady–La Señora de la Panaderia* (Mora, 2001).

The following adolescent novels can be used at the middle schools or high schools with migrant students: *A So-Called Bacation* (Gonzáles, 2009), *Por Unos Elotes–Harvest of Redemption* (Howell, 2006), *He Forgot to Say Goodbye* (Sáenz, 2008), and *The Case of the Pen Gone Missing* (Saldaña, 2009). These novels explore conflict, friendships, loyalties, racial identities, death, and Hispanic traditions. Other novels such as *Ya Será Hora?—Is It Time?* and *Qué Será? What Is It?* (Salinas, 1999, 2004) depict the successes of Mexican American families. With humor and sensitivity, the authors shed light on the lives of middle school and high school Hispanic adolescents. Migrant students can read about their own life experiences as they read the mysteries, challenges, dreams, and conflicts of other young Hispanic adolescents. Teachers can incorporate both their own personal experiences and the experiences of migrant students in the lessons. Teachers can personalize the curriculum by using the foods, places, locations, and names familiar to these students. It is always important that teachers build on the richness of all students' experiences and culture to make learning more meaningful. For example, it is important for White students to read about the successes, challenges, and dreams of Hispanic students or of Black students, to view the various ethnic perspectives, and to understand the ways in which the histories and cultures of our nation are inextricably bound.

Hispanic students, and migrants in particular, possess a source of emotional, physical, moral, and spiritual strength. While they travel to different parts of the country during the harvest seasons, they ameliorate differing cultural values. What they lack is a consistent base of role models who project success. The literature and curricula have omitted meaningful Mexican American figures as a source of inspiration and motivation for success. Instead, textbooks have given token attention to the Hispanic culture (Carilla, 2009; Sleeter & Grant, 2007; Nieto, 2004). Historically, textbooks have presented foreign-born Hispanics as role models or heroes instead of native-born Hispanic role models like Jamie Escalante, a Bolivian born Hispanic teacher from East Los Angeles who had a movie made about him because of his success with Latino students. There are many native-born Hispanic role models, like Federico Peña, a Mexican American from Brownsville, Texas, who was elected mayor of Denver and eventually appointed by President Clinton as U.S. secretary of transportation; or Ellen Ochoa, a Latina astronaut born in Los Angeles who has logged over 978 hours in space and has flown on four NASA space shuttle missions. A very prominent role model for migrant students that has been obviously from the school curriculum is César Chávez. Chávez is considered to be the champion for the rights of migrant farmworkers. Chávez was a farmworker, labor leaders, and civil right activist who co-founded the United Farm Workers (UFW) with Dolores Huerta. Escamilla (1996) investigated the cultural exclusion of Mexican Americans in the school curricula. She concluded that neither Mexican American students nor students of other ethnic groups had a thorough understanding of the history, culture, or contributions of Mexican Americans.

The lack of recognizable role models at the national level is limited and oftentimes overlooked in the schools. Migrant students of Hispanic origin would benefit from recognizing their unsung heroes. Their foundations, trials, tribulations, and success stories should be included as part of the school curriculum. Students tend to be motivated by persons they recognize, who live within their midst, and who are successful local products of their communities.

Instructional Strategies for Migrant Students

Instructional strategies, such as cooperative learning, developing metacognitive skills, enhancing self-concept, creating a positive environment, building on migrant students' strengths, and personalized lessons with migrant students' experiences, are recommended to help teachers understand migrant students. Migrant students do well in cooperative learning settings because they sense other students are encouraging and supporting their efforts to achieve. Cooperative learning lowers anxiety levels and strengthens motivation, self-esteem, and empowerment by using students as instructional agents for migrant students (Platt, Cranston-Gingras, & Scott, 1991). Students take responsibility for both their own learning and the learning of their peers. By becoming active group participants, they gain equal access to learning opportunities.

Metacognitive skills help students become independent learners by helping them comprehend concepts, monitor their success, and make the necessary adjustments when they have difficulty understanding concepts. Students learn to recognize when they are approaching an obstacle, make necessary corrections, and proceed. Teachers instruct students to employ alternative strategies once they have recognized and determined a breakdown in comprehension. For example, if a student is reading and has difficulty understanding the text, he or she could apply some "fix-it" strategies (Baker & Brown, 1984), such as ignore and read on, anticipate the problem to be resolved by future information, make an educated guess based on prior knowledge, reflect on what has already been read, refocus on the current sentence or paragraph, and consult the glossary, encyclopedia, or teacher.

It is important that teachers create a positive classroom environment for migrant students. Migrant students often find themselves in new classrooms several times in a single school year. The challenges of adjusting to strange, new learning and home environments often contribute to feelings of isolation and loneliness. Teachers can help students overcome these feelings by modeling respect and eliminating any form of threat or ridicule. Teachers can further foster a sense of safety and trust by sharing some of their own experiences, and by assigning older students to act as mentors or buddies to new immigrant students when appropriate. When students have faith in their own abilities, they are more likely to persist and succeed despite the many obstacles they encounter in schools. When necessary, teachers can modify assignments to allow for success in meaningful activities that are valued by the migrant student and by others, such as family and friends.

Teachers reach out to migrant students when they build on their strengths. Most migrant students have lived, traveled, and studied in several states. Teachers can incorporate into lessons these diverse experiences and the richness of students' cultures and languages. Examples include recognizing migrant children for their travel experiences, their knowledge of geography, and their ability to overcome crisis situations. Building on these experiences and capabilities serves to validate students' knowledge, which in turn, enhances students' self-images and sense of self-worth (Gonzáles, 1991). Drawing from students' home and work experiences in lessons helps students understand ideas and transfer them to other content. To find out about students' experiences, teachers can have them write or tell about their migrant trajectory and experiences. Later, teachers can incorporate both their own experiences and those of the children into content lessons such as language arts, social studies, and science. Teachers can personalize content by using familiar places and names in addition to using analogies to connect new concepts to students' experiences.

Padrón and Waxman (1999) proposed five effective instructional practices to support students' language acquisition, development, and knowledge. These practices are culturally responsive teaching, cooperative learning, instructional conversation, cognitively guided instruction, and technology-enriched instruction. These practices were proposed for bilingual learners, yet so many of migrant students are in bilingual education or ESL programs that these practices would be very appropriate for them as well.

Culturally responsive teaching was discussed earlier as culturally relevant teaching. The terms tend to be used interchangeably. Cooperative learning and cognitively guided instruction, which fosters the students' metacognitive skills, were also discussed earlier in this section. Instructional conversation is an extension of a dialog on the lesson between the students and the teacher. This extended dialog is about the instruction being used. The conversation is benefitting the students as they are "reorganizing" the previous content connecting new vocabulary to that content. Web-based instruction, multimedia, networks, and telecommunications derived via the Internet give students access to information. Technology-enriched instruction is another effective instructional practice that connects the migrant students' home life to classroom learning.

Extracurricular Activities

Since schooling for migrant students is interrupted with each move, most are not in-volved in any form of extracurricular activity. Many migrant children do not participate in after-school activities because they lack transportation to and from, have after-school responsibilities, or their parents are not aware of the extracurricular activities available. Yet, participating in extracurricular activities can provide enriched learning experiences. These experiences provide migrant students opportunities to develop social skills, tal-ents, and promote positive attitudes about themselves and their schools. Some of these challenges can be overcome by providing transportation since many school-sponsored sports and activities are held after classes are over and by informing parents of all before- and after-school activities. In some communities, clubs, organizations, or local parks and recreation departments sponsor after-school recreation programs. In Florida, the Dade County Park and Recreation Department has activities specifically designed for migrant students since the enrollment of these students has increased dramatically in that area (Dyson, 1983). The facility, located close to a migrant camp, offers adult supervision and activity coordination including bilingual explanations for games and planned activities. The goal of this facility is to contribute to the total well-being of children regardless of language or ethnicity.

The possibilities of migrant students participating in organized sports such as foot-ball, baseball, basketball, or golf are limited by their constant mobility. Their brief atten-dance at various schools, or lack thereof, precludes participation. Recognition of athletic abilities is partly attributed to engagement in local sports and school team sports. Because migrant students arrive late and leave early during the school year, their competitive at-tributes in the sports realm are usually overlooked. In isolated cases, coaches attempt to persuade parents to allow the student to enroll at the beginning of the school year or remain until the spring sports are concluded. Most of the parents refuse these requests because they value their family work over a sports program. Leaving their children be-hind with relatives to participate in sports while parents migrate for work is considered an undue burden for all involved. Students that are exempted from the migrant stream rituals of late arrivals and early withdrawals prove to be outstanding athletes.

Extracurricular participation in academic areas, such as spelling bees, University Interscholastic League, and literary competition, are more accessible to migrant stu-dents. The periods of competition are usually held in the early spring and allow more opportunities for migrant students to participate. Late enrollment is compensated by longer practice sessions and preparation time. Such activities provide migrant students recognition for their academic capabilities and success; these activities serve to further motivate academic challenges. Success is for all students and migrant students are en-titled to their share.

Migrant Parental Involvement

Educating students is not the sole responsibility of the schools. Parents play an im-portant role in the education of their children. Yet, schools are not always clear about developing or defining their expectations for parental involvement. However, educa-tors can understand how migrant parents define schooling and education and their perceptions of how schools operate (Martinez & Velasquez, 2000). Historically, school districts have lacked coherent policies or practices for attending to parental needs, specifically those of migrant parents. On the other hand, parents are often preoccupied with other concerns and do not become actively involved in their children's schools unless the activity satisfies a particular personal interest. The hardships migrant parents confront are much greater than those of most parents. Their lives revolve around work and moving from place to place, making it difficult to be involved in their children's education.

Often schools limit parental involvement to attending open house, parent-teacher conferences, monitoring children's homework, and reinforcing school discipline policies. These traditional approaches are one-way communications from school to home, rather than respecting the home situation and recognizing that all parents have something valuable to contribute. Migrant parents tend to be intimidated and not responsive if they did not have positive school experiences as youngsters. A directed, authority-based form of communication that lacks a sense of closeness and mutual interest intensifies feelings of nonparticipation. Many migrant parents have not been sure how best to be involved in schools, nor the degree of involvement that is appropriate. These parents know they do not possess the skills necessary for successful participation. Moreover, the language used in educational settings is not always clear to them. Quite often, they struggle to understand education jargon. Migrant parents have not played an active role in the school system in the past, but educators could increase their involvement by taking the initiative to ensure that migrant parents feel safe and welcome.

While many intervention programs tend to be "prescriptive" instead of real and inclusive (Valdes, 1996), the following parent involvement strategies can be adopted and incorporated to develop strong relationships between the school and community (Ruiz-Escalante & Menchaca, 1999). This type of partnership can support and empower migrant parents to become more involved in schools. Schools at all grade levels should:

- rethink how to attract language minority parents and migrant parents to their campuses,
- provide training in the language which parents understand and speak,
- train parents to explore the processes of decision making,
- help parents improve their parenting skills and provide them the necessary tools to assist their children with homework,
- inform parents of trainings through communication in their home language,
- train parents to work within the system to bring about positive change,
- identify what support services are offered for children of different cultures or different languages,
- design in-service training to learn how to empathize with parents and recognize their strengths while making the most of parent-teacher conferences, and
- respond to the multicultural needs of parents and the community to effectively facilitate this relationship.

Developing a variety of strategies to contact and reach out to migrant parents can be helpful. Educators who continuously make connections with parents can positively affect the children's academic performance. Sometimes, someone other than parents, such as teachers or counselors, can inspire students to complete school and graduate. Some migrant parents believe it is the sole responsibility of the school to educate children (Chavkin, 1991), and believe their involvement in the schools might be construed as interference. The following are parent involvement strategies that can help dispel such myths and foster healthy relationships between the school and community (Ruiz-Escalante & Menchaca, 1999). These strategies usually require a moderator or central person such as a community or church official to lead the charge by:

- inviting educators to community centers or church meetings,
- sharing the social and cultural dimensions of the migrant community with educators,

- inviting educators to the community to talk about the school's goals or answer parents' questions,
- exploring ways parents can become volunteers in schools, and
- working actively with the school system to bring about positive change.

The Challenges for Public Schools

High dropout rates, low achievement test scores, poor attendance, and over-aged students in classes are problems common to migrant students (Salerno, 1991). High mobility, cultural differences, and limited proficiency in English are also challenges migrant students encounter. From the school's standpoint these challenges can be overwhelming. Most teachers have not been trained to teach the culturally or linguistically diverse student, the migrant student, and/or the limited-English speaking student. Thus, schools must hire, train, and retain competent staff to provide appropriate instruction to migrant students.

Schools have begun to seek assistance from external entities to respond to the needs of migrant students by establishing, for example, bilingual or dual-language programs in elementary schools and ESL programs. Instruction in bilingual programs is in the native language and instruction in dual-language programs is in English and Spanish. In most bilingual programs, students are transitioned to English usually by third grade; in dual-language programs, students continue to learn in both languages each year as they advance in grade level. ESL classes are typically found in secondary schools and instruction is in English. In some programs, migrant students receive additional help when needed. For example, some ESL classes have a teacher aide or a tutor to assist with the instruction because ESL classes enroll students whose native languages vary greatly. Flexible instructional programs and support programs are needed to facilitate their schooling through reading and writing and critical thinking skills. Such support programs include tutorial services, counseling services, enrichment activities, career awareness, health services, and medical referrals. Intervention must be provided to these highly mobile students. There must be an emphasis on high expectations and excellence. Placing migrant students in small classrooms, where instruction is more personalized, is also important. When teachers make an effort to have personal contacts with students, the students tend to become more confident and responsible. Since many migrant students enter school after the school year has begun, teachers may have preconceived notions about their inabilities to be successful. Therefore, having a staff that sets high expectations for all students is necessary. Assigning classroom buddies for late-enrolling migrant students gives them a warm and receptive welcome.

Migrant high school seniors' needs are numerous in nature, and schools must plan solutions for their success. There are more Hispanic seniors in vocational or general education programs than in the college preparation programs. There are fewer numbers of Hispanic seniors in courses such as trigonometry, calculus, physics, chemistry, or English. Fewer Hispanics take the Scholastic Aptitude Test (SAT) and the American College Test (ACT) which are examinations used for college admissions. These deficits exclude Hispanics and more specifically, Hispanic migrant students, from opportunities for admission into colleges. Public schools need to nurture a supportive environment in with expressed expectations by staff that migrant students will attend college and be successful. Schools should provide academic opportunities for making up credits, tutoring, taking appropriate courses, and test-taking skill development. School counselors should assist migrants in applying to and preparing for college. This type of involvement increases college attendance rates (Horn & Chen, 1998). Other forms of support services could be in the form of (a) early identification of college-bound students which enhances the chances for better preparation, (b) transition services that provide migrants with study skills for taking the SAT and ACT, (c) tutorials for academic courses, (d) a system to alert students about visits from college recruiters, test deadlines, college fairs, scholarship deadlines, etc., and (e) information related to college admission and financial aid.

Other more personal services that schools can provide migrant students are academic assistance such as counseling, extended day/week/year programs, and special summer schools. Career awareness about work experiences and vocational education has also been successful with migrant students. Even successful migrant students are at-risk in high school. For this reason, the following programs have been designed for continued support (Rasmussen, 1988).

- The College Assistance Migrant Program (CAMP) is a title IV program that provides tutoring, orientations, and counseling for migrants planning to enter college. CAMPs are found on many university campuses and have been successful for migrant students. They have lowered freshmen dropout rates by offering academic support work options to students during their first year of college (National Commission on Migrant Education, 1992).
- The College Bound program is a summer program for seniors to assist them in the transition from high school into college. Students work, study, and receive assistance and counseling at a college campus; approximately 90% of College Bound students enroll in colleges the following semester.

Graduation rates of migrant students have risen from 10% to more than 40%. This increase is attributed to the U.S. Department of Education's Migrant Education Program, which has for more than 20 years worked with states to prepare migrant students for a successful transition to postsecondary education or employment (Morse & Hammer, 1998). Admission into college requires migrant students to have completed high school with the appropriate courses for postsecondary education, knowledge of application requirements and financial aid deadlines, and strategies and skills to progress through a system that was not created for migrant students. Factors that have contributed and facilitated migrant students' college attendance are access to counseling centers that offer an array of options; exercise of their personal motivation and sense of self-efficacy; access to financial aid and scholarships, loans, and work-study programs; support from family, friends, and educational personnel; and parental involvement in decisions about their children's education. Thus, schools can take an active role in ensuring that migrant students receive assistance in preparing and applying for college by providing opportunities for migrants to make up credit, being receptive of work transferred from other schools, providing assistance through tutoring, and helping students develop study skills and test-taking skills (Morse & Hammer, 1998).

The Principal's Role

The principal's role in migrant education has changed from the inception of the program. Principals were responsible for implementing a program designed by central office staff with built-in assurances. The principal provided campus monitoring to ensure that only migrant students were served with designated funds. The migrant program, in essence, was a duplicate of the regular program in a segregated setting. The ultimate goal was compliance with the migrant application guidelines and to avoid supplanting programs.

At the present time, district personnel responsible for migrant education guide principals. In identification and recruitment, the principal may select an enrollment day for migrant parents and students. This can be done prior to the start of the school or on any given date during the school year. Recruitment of migrant students can also take place at community-based sites. House-to-house recruitment is also available.

Assisting the principals in many school districts are cadres of federally funded clerks who go house to house in an effort to identify students. Migrants who leave the migrant stream may not realize that services and help are available for 3 years after the last migration. It is also of paramount importance to school districts to identify and increase numbers of students in order to generate needed funds for services.

Because the principal is on the frontline of recruitment and services for migrant students, every effort must be made to provide instructional services to students. Students who do not qualify for school-related programs can be referred to programs such as Head Start, Even Start, or State Migrant Head Start. A home-based program can be provided to 3- and 4-year-olds not enrolled in an early childhood program. Student development is a priority for principals once migrant identification has occurred.

The principal must also ensure that the campus is providing culturally, developmentally, and linguistically appropriate programs and materials. The promotion of research-based programs and curricula that are culturally appropriate is also part of a principal's responsibility. The principal is also involved in adequate staff development that emphasizes training on culturally and linguistically appropriate practices.

Coordination of information is a crucial job. The principal must communicate with other administrators, counselors, teachers, and parents concerning interpretation of progress reports and test data utilized to assess student needs. Compliance with opportunities for students to participate in extracurricular activities is also important. The principal serves as an advocate for migrant students and their families by promoting the evaluation and modification of instructional programs to meet student needs.

Secondary school principals have additional responsibilities; they must inform students, parents, and staff about local and state requirements for promotion and graduation as well as prerequisites for postsecondary education. Adequate placement of students and documentation of local and out-of-district credit completion are ultimate responsibilities of the principal. The principal also plays a significant role in ensuring that students have an opportunity to complete their credits or make up work. Besides focusing on students graduating under the Recommended or Distinguished Achievement Plan (in applicable states), the principal also refers students for advanced placement courses, bilingual/ESL, gifted and talented, magnet programs, special education and Title I programs.

The principal is involved in numerous migrant-related activities to ensure student success. Ultimately, the graduation rate, test data, and postsecondary attendance serve as gauges indicative of the combined efforts of numerous persons to transform the education of migrant students into a positive and productive experience.

Conclusion

This chapter has provided information on the lives of migrant children. These students encounter hardships in the fields, including health aliments they suffer because of the serious type of work they and their families undertake. The poverty that surrounds the lives of these students is a way of life. Also, migrant students encounter many challenges, generally due to their mobile lifestyles. Consequently, many migrant students fail to graduate. A supportive school environment can serve to overcome some of the barriers migrant students encounter.

This chapter also provided information on how schools can nurture a positive environment for parental involvement. Several examples of lessons, diversified with culturally relevant content, were discussed. Examples of instructional strategies that have been successful for migrant students were also presented.

The authors ask that all educators keep one thing in mind: migrant students dream of being successful and of not having the same lifestyles as their families. Many want to work hard, graduate, and be successful. They, often more than other students, know about work ethics. Educators have the power to help make their dreams come true. This can be done by training teachers to set high expectations for students, being sensitive to their needs, and providing opportunities for them to be successful.

It is always a challenge for educators to advocate for migrant children without making them feel that their lifestyle is not worthy. There is a fine line between sympathy and empathy. Sympathy enables children whereas empathy empowers them. Sympathy lowers expectations whereas empathy validates their strengths. The last thing migrant children need from teachers is pity or sympathy. We call this the *pobrecito* (poor little thing) syndrome and others call it the "missionary" attitude. Children who feel that they are being helped because they are *pobrecitos* begin to believe that they are indeed incapable of caring for themselves. They develop low self-concepts because they begin to believe that they do not have control of their own destiny. They have an excuse to fail. It is the self-fulfilling prophecy at its best.

Teachers must be aware of that fine line to avoid feeling sorry for these children and their migrant lifestyle. Teachers want migrant children to be successful in school, but they must also find ways to dignify and honor their success in life while they are still in the midst of the migrant way of life. Teachers must encourage migrant children to break the cycle without making them feel shame for the way they live.

Applying Your Knowledge

You are the principal of Ochoa Elementary School. A parent informs you that her child, Teresa, feels uncomfortable in Ms. Henry's fifth-grade class. You begin to question the parent and as the dialog continues, you realize that Teresa was asked several questions about her experience picking apricots when she returned to school in late September. The parent reports that this had also happened to three other students in Teresa's class. The children were embarrassed by the approach Ms. Henry used to have these migrant students share their summer experiences with the rest of the students. The other students were surprised that Teresa and the three other migrant students actually worked to help support their families or took care of their younger siblings while both parents worked in the fields. You decide to meet with Ms. Henry to discuss how the migrant students felt while they were asked to discuss some very private experiences. Ms. Henry stated that she was trying to empower the migrant students by portraying them as heroes to the rest of the class. Not realizing what she was doing, Ms. Henry had been singling out or profiling the migrant students.

QUESTIONS

1. Why did the migrant students feel different from the rest of the students?
2. As the principal, what would you tell Ms. Henry?
3. As the principal, what approaches would you suggest to Ms. Henry?
4. How can Ms. Henry better understand migrant students?

QUESTIONS FOR THOUGHT

1. How can principals ensure that the educational experiences of migrant students will be more positive on their campuses?
2. How can migrant students overcome the challenges they encounter in schools because of their mobile lifestyles?
3. Explain why principals must support culturally relevant teaching for all students.
4. Discuss how the hardships migrant families encounter in the fields can be detrimental to their children's success in school.
5. What are the obstacles that often keep migrant students from graduating?
6. What approaches can principals implement so migrant parents feel more welcomed on their campuses?

For Additional Information

Migrant Education Program, U.S. Department of Education, www.ed.gov/programs/mep/index.html

Office of Elementary and Secondary Education, U. S. Department of Education, www.edlgov/about/offices/list/oese/ome/index.html

Resources for Migrant Education, AEL, Inc., www.ael.org

The Best Migrant Education Resources, www.lone-eagles.com/migrant.html

References

Baker, L., & Brown, A. (1984). Metacognitive skills and reading. In P. D. Pearson, R. Barr, M. L. Kamil, & P. Mosenthal, (Eds.), *Handbook of reading research* (vol. I, pp. 353–394). New York: Longman.

Carrillo, A. L. (2009). The cost of success: Mexican American identity performance within culturally coded classrooms and educational achievement. Review of Law and Social Justice, 18(3), 641–676.

Cawelti, G. (1999). Improving achievement. *American School Board Journal, 186,* 34–37.

Chavkin, N. F. (1991). *Family lives and parental involvement in migrant students' education.* Washington, DC: U.S. Department of Education, Office of Educational Research and Improvement. (ERIC Document Reproduction Service No. ED335174).

Dyson, D. S. (1983). *Utilizing local resources at the local level.* Fact Sheet. Las Cruces, NM: ERIC Clearinghouse on Rural Education and Small Schools. (ERIC Document Reproduction Service No. ED286702).

Escamilla, K. (1996). *Do they really know their culture?* Paper presented at the annual conference of the Arizona Association for Bilingual Education. Flagstaff, Arizona, February.

Fix, M., & Passel, J. S. (1994). *Immigration and immigrants: Setting the record straight.* Washington, DC: The Urban Institute.

Garza, E. (1998). *Life histories of academically successful migrant students.* (Doctoral dissertation, University of Texas at Austin, 1998). UMI Dissertation Services.

Garza, E., Reyes, P., & Trueba, E. T. (2004). *Resiliency and success: Migrant children in the United States.* Boston: Paradigm Publishers.

Gay, G. (2002). Culturally responsive teaching in special education for ethnically diverse students: Setting the stage. *Qualitative Studies in Education, 15*(6), 613–629.

Gonzáles, F. (1991). *Validating the students' culture in the classroom.* San Antonio, TX: Intercultural Development Research Association.

González, G. (2009). *A so-called vacation.* Houston, TX: Arte Público Press.

Grant, C. A., & Sleeter, C. E. (2007). *Turning on learning: Five approaches for multicultural teaching plans for race, gender, and disability* (4th ed.). Hoboken, NJ: John Wiley & Sons, Inc.

Horn, L. J., & Chen, X. (1998). *Toward resiliency: At risk students who make it to college.* Washington, DC: U.S. Department of Education Office of Educational Research and Improvement.

Howell, E. (2006). Por unos elotes—Harvest of redemption. Bloomington, IN: AuthorHouse.

Jackson County Migrant Education. *Migrant education—harvest of hope.* Medford, OR: Jackson County Educational Service District, 1981. (ERIC Document Reproduction Service No. ED212441).

Johnson, F. C., Levy, R. H., Morales, J. A., Morse, S. C., & Prokop, M. K. (1986). *Migrant students at the secondary level: Issues and opportunities for change.* Las Cruces, NM: ERIC Clearinghouse on Rural Education and Small Schools. (ERIC Document Reproduction Service No. ED270242).

Kissam, E. (1993). Formal characteristics of the farm labor market: Implications for farm labor policy in the 1990s. In *Migrant Farmworkers in the United States.* Briefing of the Commission on Security and Cooperation in Europe, Washington, DC: U.S. Government Printing Office.

Kugel, C., & Zuroweste, E. L. (2002). Migrant workers. In Lester Breslow, MD (Ed.), Gale Encyclopedia of Public Health (vol. 4). New York: Macmillan Reference USA.

Ladson-Billings, G. (1990). Like lightning in a bottle: Attempting to capture the pedagogical excellence of successful teachers of Black students. International Journal of Qualitative Studies in Education, 3(4), 335–344.

Ladson-Billings, G. (1992). Liberatory consequences of literacy: A case of culturally relevant instruction for African American students. *Journal of Negro Education, 61*(3), 378–391.

Ladson-Billings, G. (1995). But that's just good teaching! The case for culturally relevant pedagogy. *Theory into Practice, 34*(3), 159–165.

Ladson-Billings, G. (2009). *The dream-keepers: Successful teachers of African American children.* San Francisco: John Wiley & Sons, Inc.

Laínez, R. C. (2009). *René has two last names—René tiene dos apellidos.* Houston: Arte Público Press.

Levy, R. (1987). *Migrant attrition project.* Oneonta, NY: Eastern Stream Center on Resources and Training.

Marines, D., & Ortiz de Montellano, B. (1993). *Multiculturalism in science: Why and how?* Presented at National Science Teacher Association Conference, Oaxpec, Mexico.

Martinez, Y. G. (1994). Narratives of survival: Life histories of Mexican American youth from migrant and seasonal farmworkers who have graduated from High School Equivalency Program. Unpublished. University of South Florida.

Martinez, Y. G., Scott, J., Cranston-Gingras, A., & Platt, J. S. (1994). Voices from the field: Interviews with students from migrant farmworker families. *Journal of Educational Issues of Language Minority Students, 10,* 333–348.

Martinez, Y. G., & Cranston-Gingras, A. (1996). Migrant farmworker students and the educational process: Barriers to high school completion. *The High School Journal, 80*(1), 28–38.

Martinez, Y. G., & Velazquez, J. A. (2000). *Involving migrant families in education.* Charleston, WV: ERIC Clearinghouse on Rural Education and Small Schools. (ERIC Document Reproduction Service No. ED448010).

Menchaca, V. D. (1996). The missing link in teacher preparation programs. *Journal of Educational Issues of Language Minority Students, 17,* 1–9.

Menchaca, V. D. (2000). Culturally relevant curriculum for limited-English proficient students. *The Journal of the Texas Association for Bilingual Education, 5*(1), 55–59.

Menchaca, V. D., & Ruiz-Escalante, J. A. (1995). *Instructional strategies for migrant students.* Charleston, WV: Appalachia Educational Laboratory, ERIC Clearinghouse on Rural Education and Small Schools. (ERIC Document Reproduction Service No. ED388491).

Migrant Education Secondary Assistance Project. (1989). *MESA National MSRTS Executive Summary.* Geneseo, NY: BOCES Geneseo Migrant Center.

Migrant Youth Program. (1985). *Perceptions of why migrant students drop out of school and what can be done to encourage them to graduate.* Albany, NY: Upstate Regional Offices and Migrant Unit, State Education Department.

Mora, P. (2001). *The bakery lady—La señora de la panadería.* Houston: Arte Público Press.

Morse, S., & Hammer, P. C. (1998). *Migrant students attending college: Facilitating their success.* Charleston, WV: ERIC Clearinghouse on Rural Education and Small Schools. (ERIC Document Reproduction Service No. ED423097).

National Center for Farmworker Health. (2001). *About America's farmworkers.* Available at http://www.ncth.org/abouttws.htm

National Commission on Migrant Education. (1992). *Invisible children: A portrait of migrant children in the United States.* Final Report. Washington, DC: U.S. Department of Education. (ERIC Document Reproduction Service No. ED348206).

National Farm Workers Ministry. (2009). Below-poverty wages, malnutrition and hunger. Retrieved from http://www.nfwm.org/content/below-poverty-wages-malnutrition-and-hunger

National Program for Secondary Credit Exchange and Accrual. (1994). Options and resources for achieving credit accrual for secondary-aged migrant youth. Washington, DC: U.S. Department of Education. Office of Migrant Education.

Nieto, S. (2004). *Affirming diversity: The sociopolitical context of multicultural education* (4th ed.). Boston, MA: Allyn & Bacon.

Oliveira, V., Effland, J. R., & Hamm, S. (1993). *Hired farm labor use of fruit, vegetable, and horticultural specialty farms.* Washington, DC: U.S. Department of Agriculture.

Padrón, Y. N., & Waxman, H. C. (1999). Effective instructional practices for English-language learners. In H. C. Waxman and H. J. Walberg (Eds.), *New directions for teaching, practice, and research* (pp. 171–203). Berkeley, CA: McCutchan.

Platt, J. S., Cranston-Gingras, A., & Scott, J. (1991). Understanding and educating migrant students. *Preventing School Failure, 36*(1), 41–46.

Rasmussen, L. (1988). *Migrant students at the secondary level: Issues and opportunities for change.* Las Cruces, NM: ERIC Clearinghouse on Rural Education and Small Schools. (ERIC Document Reproduction Service No. ED296814).

Rivas, S. (2010). *No time for monsters—No hay tíempo para monstruos.* Houston: Arte Público Press.

Ruiz-Escalante, J. A., & Menchaca, V. D. (1999). Creating school-community partnerships for minority parents. *Texas Teacher Education Forum, 24,* 45–49.

Salerno, A. (1991). *Migrant students who leave school early: Strategies for retrieval.* Geneseo, NY: BOCES Geneseo Migrant Center. (Eric Document 335 179).

Sáenz, B. A. (2008).*He forgot to say goodbye.* New York: Simon & Schuster Books.

Saldáña, R. (2009).*The case of the pen gone missing.* Houston: Arte Público Press.

Salínas, A. (1999). *Ya será hora?—Is it time?* Hidalgo, TX: Hidalgo ISD Permanent Scholarship Foundation.

Salínas, A. (2004). *Qué será, será!—Whatever will be will be!* Hidalgo, TX: Hidalgo ISD Permanent Scholarship Foundation.

Shotland, J. (1989). *Full fields, empty cupboard: The nutritional status of migrant farmworkers in America.* Washington, DC: Public Voice for Food and Health Policy. (ERIC Document Reproduction Service No. ED323076).

Sleeter, C. A., & Grant, C. (2007). *Making choices for multicultural education; Five approaches to race, class, and gender* (5th ed.). Hoboken, NJ: John Wiley & Sons, Inc.

Tafolla, C. (2009). *What can you do with a paléta?* Berkeley, CA: Tricycle Book Press.

U. S. Department of Education. (1994). Improving America's Schools Act, 103-382 statute, Title 1, part C, (Migrant Education) Program Purpose, Section 1301-(4). Washington, DC: Office of Educational Research and Improvement.

U. S. Department of Education. (2007). Migrant Student Records Exchange Initiative, (Migrant Education) Student Records Exchange. Washington, DC: Office of Educational Research and Improvement. Available at http://www2.ed.gov/admins/lead/account/recordstransfer.html

U.S. Department of Labor, Office of the Assistant Secretary for Policy, Office of Program Economics. (2000). Findings from the national agriculture workers survey 1997-1998: A demographic and employment profile of U.S. farmworkers (Research Report No. 8). Washington, DC: US Department of Labor, Office of the Assistant Secretary for Policy, Office of Program Economics.

Valdes, G. (1996). *Con respeto: Bridging the distance between culturally diverse families and schools: An enthno-graphic portrait.* New York: Teachers College Press.

Vamos, Inc. (1992). *National migrant student graduation rate formula, for the national program for secondary credit exchange and accrual.* Geneseo, NY: BOCES Geneseo Migrant Center.

Academic Preparation, Enhancement, and Intervention Programs

Karen M. Watt

Fernando Valle

"Today's high school diploma qualifies students only for jobs that do not require what we like to think of as a high school education . . . *college and career readiness* is the level of preparation a student needs in order to enroll and succeed—without remediation—in a credit-bearing course at a postsecondary institution that offers a baccalaureate degree or transfer to a baccalaureate program, or in a high-quality certificate program that enables students to enter a career pathway with potential future advancement"

—*David Conley, 2010.*

Objectives

1. Provide a historical background of events that led to the creation of academic preparation, enhancement, and intervention programs in the United States
2. Discuss basic components of selected academic preparation, enhancement, and intervention programs
3. Highlight similarities and differences between programs
4. Explain the outcomes of each program
5. Examine how school personnel can contribute to the success of these programs

Introduction and Background

Of the billions of dollars spent to ensure educational opportunity for America's children, very little is spent on programs that encourage students to prepare for, enter, and graduate from college. Many programs focus on dropout prevention, remediation, and after-school academic support activities. This chapter highlights programs that address the large gaps in academic performance and disparity in college enrollment rates between students from economically disadvantaged families and more advantaged students. One of the goals of early intervention programs is to provide at-risk student groups with the college preparation skills and knowledge needed to enter and succeed in college (Perna & Swail, 2001). While existing preparatory programs offer a variety of services, those that have the potential to increase the number of underrepresented students who enroll and succeed in college offer high-quality instruction, special services such as tutoring, or a redesigned curriculum that better suits the students' needs (Gandara & Bial, 2001; Gandara & Moreno, 2002).

In 1954, the Supreme Court's ruling in *Brown v. Board of Education* recognized the urgency for equitable educational opportunities for all students. For disadvantaged students a college education remained unattainable because of academic, economic, cultural, and social barriers (Moore, 1997). By the early 1960s Congress realized that the nation's commitment to economic circumstances extended beyond high school. In support of the commitment, Congress established a series of programs to help low-income Americans enter college, graduate, and move on to participate more fully in America's economic and social life (Upward Bound, 1999, as cited in Schroth, 2001).

Johnson's War on Poverty spurred the passing of the Economic Opportunity Act of 1964, legislation that increased attention to the country's large disadvantaged population and raised an awareness of the social and economic advantages of educating all children. Johnson's legislation provided funds for a number of programs, several of which provided funds for the pursuit of postsecondary degrees. Out of this legislation, Upward Bound and Talent Search were born (Schroth, 2001).

In 1968, the Special Services for Disadvantaged Students Program was created and later termed Student Support Services (SSS). Authorized by the Higher Education Amendments, SSS became the third in the series of educational opportunity programs. SSS programs provide disadvantaged college students with academic and motivational support to enable them to complete their postsecondary education and pursue graduate studies. These three initiatives, Upward Bound, Talent Search, and SSS, became known as the TRIO Programs (Federal TRIO Programs, 2000, as cited in Schroth, 2001). TRIO programs help low-income Americans enter college, graduate, and move on to participate more fully in America's economic and social life (Hooker & Brand, 2009).

Recently, the Office of Postsecondary Education that houses federal TRIO programs, developed educational opportunity centers (EOCs). These centers provide counseling and information on college admissions to qualified adults who want to enter or continue a program of postsecondary education. The goal of EOCs is to increase the number of adult participants who enroll in postsecondary education institutions by providing financial-aid counseling and assisting in the application process. Some of the services provided by the program include academic advice, career workshops, information on financial assistance, and tutoring and mentoring (Federal TRIO Programs, 2011).

Since the birth of TRIO, several other programs have been designed to increase college attendance and success rates of students from underrepresented groups. These include SCORE, Project GRAD, Career Academies, Communities in Schools, Early College High Schools, GEAR UP, and AVID. These programs are "distinctive in their focus on ensuring that promising Latino and other minority students do what is necessary to attend college" (Slavin & Calderon, 2001, p. 79). In a recent review of over 20 intervention, preparation, and enhancement programs, Hooker and Brand (2009) found several common elements of success. These programmatic elements of success included rigor and academic support, relationships, college knowledge and access, and effective instruction, among others. The structural elements of success they identified included partnerships and cross-systems collaboration, strategic use of time, leadership and autonomy, and effective use of data (Hooker & Brand, 2009). These program initiatives will be discussed in this chapter.

Upward Bound

Upward Bound (UB) is one of largest federally funded college access programs that provides low-income students with extra instruction, study skills, and tutorials. UB was the first of the TRIO programs established by the Higher Education Act of 1965, and supports high school students from underrepresented groups by providing college preparatory academic and nonacademic enrichment courses, along with guidance in the college search and application process. Many UB projects are hosted by 4-year colleges and universities and offer summer academic programs held on the college campus, along with courses provided outside of regular school hours during the school year; these program elements support the theory that rigorous coursework and exposure to a college environment help prepare students for the demands of higher education (Cahalan, 2009; Knapp, Heur, & Mason, 2008; Seftor, Mamun, & Schirm, 2009).

Upward Bound represented the largest federal intervention aimed at helping students attain a postsecondary education until GEAR UP grants were established as part of the Higher Education Amendments of 1998 (Myers & Schirm, 1999). In 1966, $2 million was allocated to support 42 Upward Bound projects, and in 1989-90, $426.1 million were awarded to support 177 projects around the country (Hexter, 1990, as cited in Schroth, 2001).

All Upward Bound projects must provide the following services:

- instruction in reading, writing, study skills, and other subjects necessary for success in education beyond high school,
- academic, financial, or personal counseling,
- exposure to academic programs and cultural events,
- tutorial services for Upward Bound classes as well as those taken in the student's local school,
- mentoring programs (students are closely monitored so staff can intervene should the students experience problems),
- information on postsecondary education opportunities,
- assistance in completing college entrance and financial aid applications,
- assistance in preparing for college entrance examinations, and
- work study positions to expose participants to careers requiring a postsecondary degree. (Upward Bound, 2000, as cited in Schroth, 2001)

Myers and Schirm (1999) found that Upward Bound students received more academic credits in math and social studies than did a comparison group. Natriello, McDill, and Pallas (1990) concluded that Upward Bound is successful in getting students to graduate from high school and enter college, but it does not necessarily demonstrate that students who enter college will persist toward attaining a college degree. This lack of encouragement for student persistence is attributed to too little time devoted to academic instruction during high school, and no definite strategy for intervention once an Upward Bound student enters college (U.S. Department of Education, 1991).

At the high school level, UB has had a small, positive impact on credit accumulation, and a larger, statistically significant effect on high school credits earned by students with lower initial academic expectations and those at greater levels of academic risk. The longer a student participates in UB and completes the UB program, the more likely s/he was to enroll in a 4-year institution and earn a bachelor's degree. UB also has positive impacts on postsecondary enrollment and college completion rates for certain subgroups, such as students who start school with lower academic expectations and those not initially on track with college preparatory coursework in the ninth grade (Cahalan, 2009; Knapp, Heur, & Mason, 2008; Seftor, Mamun, & Schirm, 2009).

Other research on UB programs suggest that exposure to rigorous courses, college knowledge, and extra supports may boost the confidence and academic performance necessary for underprepared and first-generation students to recognize their potential for college success and pursue postsecondary education (Cahalan, 2009; Knapp, Heur, & Mason, 2008; Seftor, Mamun, & Schirm, 2009). As of 2010, there were 64,391 participants in 953 Upward Bound programs being served (U.S. Department of Education, 2010).

Talent Search

Talent Search (TS) is another one of the federal TRIO programs designed to increase low-income, first-generation college students' rates of high school graduation, college preparation, and college access. A 1968 amendment to Title IV of the Higher Education Act of 1965 that created Talent Search stipulated that participants must have "exceptional potential" for postsecondary education (Hexter, 1990). TS aims to improve the college enrollment of these populations through offering counseling, including guidance on college preparatory course enrollment, and assistance with the financial aid application process (Cahalan, Silva et al., 2004; U.S. Department of Education, Office of Postsecondary Education, 2008).

TS assumes that small interventions at crucial points along the pathway to college can be critically important for underserved students. TS projects are usually organized by a host college or university (either a 2- or 4-year program) that works with a target group of middle and high schools. Most TS services are provided within the target schools (Cahalan, Silva et al., 2004; U.S. Department of Education, Office of Postsecondary Education. 2008).

Rosenbaum (1992) summarized the three major goals of Talent Search:

1. Identifying youth of extreme financial and cultural need with an exceptional potential for postsecondary education and encouraging them to complete secondary school and undertake further education
2. Publicizing existing forms of student financial aid, including aid furnished under the Higher Education Act
3. Encouraging secondary school or college dropouts of demonstrated aptitude to reenter educational programs (Schroth, 2001, p. 4)

Agencies receiving TS dollars may also provide the following services:

1. academic, financial, career, or personal counseling including advice on entry or reentry to secondary or postsecondary programs,
2. career exploration and aptitude assessments,
3. tutorial services to help students achieve in their academic classes,
4. information on postsecondary education,
5. information on student financial assistance,

6. assistance in completing college admissions and financial aid applications,
7. assistance in preparing for college entrance exam,
8. mentoring programs to give students personal attention when problems arise,
9. special activities for sixth through eighth graders, and
10. workshops for the families of participants (Talent Search, 1999, as cited in Schroth, 2001).

By providing this wide array of services, Talent Search is able to increase the student's chances for entering and completing college. One drawback is that TS directors often attempt to provide interventions with a limited number of program staff (Hexter, 1990, as cited in Schroth, 2001).

A study conducted across three different states found that TS participants were more likely to have applied for federal financial aid and to have enrolled in a public college or university than non-TS participants. TS participation was found to be associated with increased enrollment at 2-year colleges, and participants were more likely to enroll in the type of institution that hosted their TS project (2-year versus 4-year colleges) (Cahalan, Silva et al., 2004; U.S. Department of Education, Office of Postsecondary Education, 2008).

As of 2010, there were 359,740 participants in 463 TS projects served (U.S. Department of Education, 2010).

Student Support Services

The third of the group of TRIO programs is Student Support Services (SSS), which center on students while they are in college or other postsecondary educational programs. The goals of SSS are to increase the college retention and graduation rates of its participants and to facilitate the transition of students from one level of higher education to the next (SSS, 1999, as cited in Schroth, 2001).

The government requires that SSS provide students with:

1. instruction in basic study skills,
2. tutorial services,
3. scademic, financial, or personal counseling,
4. assistance in securing admission and financial aid for enrollment in 4-year institutions,
5. assistance in securing admission and financial aid for enrollment in graduate and professional programs,
6. information about career options, and
7. special services for students with limited English proficiency. (U.S. Department of Education, 1994, as cited in Schroth, 2001)

The SSS projects may also provide students with:

1. individualized counseling for personal, career, and academic information, activities, and instruction designed to acquaint students with career options;
2. exposure to cultural events and academic programs not usually available;
3. mentoring programs; and
4. providing housing during breaks homeless students and foster care students. (Federal TRIO Programs, 2011)

Only institutions of higher education may sponsor SSS programs and must ensure that SSS participants are offered financial aid packages to meet their full financial needs. In 2000, there were 796 colleges and universities nationwide hosting SSS programs (U.S. Department of Education, 1994, as cited in Schroth, 2001).

The U.S. Department of Education evaluates all TRIO programs and has found that SSS projects impacted student persistence, graduation and transfer rates, and other measures:

- The overall persistence rate (81%) for those projects exceeded the Department of Education's goal of 73%. Overall, the rate of persistence at 4-year institutions was identical to that of 2-year institutions—that is, 81%.
- The overall grantee-level 6-year graduation rate (32.3%) for those projects exceeded the Department of Education's goal (29%).
- Over half (58%) of all SSS projects for which a rate was calculated had graduation rates of 29% or higher (i.e., at or above the Education Department's targeted goal).
- The overall grantee-level 3-year graduation rate (28%) for those projects exceeded the Education Department's goal (27.5%).
- Forty-six percent of all SSS projects for which a rate was calculated had graduation/transfer rates of 27.5% or higher (i.e., at or above the Education Department's targeted goal).
- Overall, the cost per successful outcome (efficiency measure) at 2-year institutions was more than double that at 4-year institutions, $271 vs. $127, respectively. [TRIO Student Support Services (SSS), 2007–2008]

Score

Score for College, or SCORE (Johnson, 1983, as cited in Fashola & Slavin, 1998) is a dropout prevention/college preparatory program that was developed in partnership with the Orange County Department of Education and the University of California, Irvine. The program staff conducted a comprehensive, ongoing formative evaluation during the first 3 years of operation (1979–1982). Data gathered in the formative phase of the program was used to make programmatic changes to more effectively accomplish the goals and objectives of the program (U.S. Department of Education, 2008).

The program targets at-risk students in grades 9 through 12 whose likelihood of graduating from high school or enrolling in college is perceived to be low by their teachers. Students receive career counseling, tutoring, opportunities to join clubs, and a summer academic program focusing on college preparatory courses. SCORE also focuses on moving students out of ESL classes and into the mainstream (Fashola & Slavin, 1998).

In several case studies conducted on SCORE schools, findings revealed that the number of Latino students enrolled in algebra, chemistry, and physics increased, as well as participation in SAT taking (Wells, 1981). University of California eligibility rates of the first group of SCORE students were compared to a random sample of high school African American and Latino graduates. Eligibility rates of SCORE students were 40% as compared to the random sample's 5.2%; SCORE students also enrolled in 4-year colleges at a higher rate (41%) than the other group (11%) (Wells, 1981, as cited in Fashola & Slavin, 1998).

SCORE was awarded the Elementary and Secondary Education Act (ESEA), Title IV-C Exemplary Status in 1982 based on a comprehensive summative evaluation conducted by an outside evaluator. The comprehensive evaluation yielded statistically significant data (p < .001) in all major areas (U.S. Department of Education, 2008). The comprehensive evaluation revealed that all major program goals and objectives were met or exceeded, in addition to the following:

1. Of the first SCORE class in 1981, 40% were eligible to attend the University of California by having completed the A-F course requirements with a high enough

combination of grade point average and test score. This finding was statistically significant ($p < .001$).

2. Of this same senior class, 40.8% enrolled in a 4-year college or university. This finding was statistically significant ($p < .001$).

3. Of those students who participated in a summer residential program and received school year assistance through the guidance, tutoring, motivation, and parent programs, 56% enrolled in a 4-year college or university. This finding was statistically significant ($p < .001$).

By the end of the third year, 100% of SCORE students were enrolled in two or more college preparatory courses at their local high schools as compared to 52% at a comparison high school (U.S. Department of Education, 2008).

In 1986, SCORE staff conducted an informal survey of the 17 students who were enrolled at UC Irvine in 1982. Of those, 15 were still enrolled, 9 were candidates for graduation in only 4 years (average at UC is 5.5 years), and their cumulative average college GPA was 2.7.

In 1994, SCORE was awarded validation as a National Exemplary Education model by the U.S. Department of Education. This distinction makes SCORE a member of a National Diffusion Network (NDN), which promotes the sharing of exemplary educational programs, and practices throughout the United States. SCORE's validation as a U.S. Department of Education model program was based on five claims:

1. High-risk students who participate in SCORE are successfully up-placed into a rich common core college preparatory curriculum.

2. SCORE high-risk students enroll in colleges and universities at rates higher than their peers.

3. Students involved in SCORE test out of limited English proficient (LEP) programs at rates higher than their peers.

4. SCORE schools decrease remedial course offerings and increase college preparatory curriculum.

5. Schools that implement an effective SCORE program increase graduation rates. (Success in a Rich Core Curriculum for Everyone, 2011)

In 1995, SCORE received the Parade of Excellence Award from the National Council of States for the outstanding contribution it is making nationally to professional development and to educational excellence. SCORE became a private educational agency in order to better position itself for national dissemination in 1997 (Success in a Rich Core Curriculum for Everyone, 2011).

In 2009, SCORE merged with KAPLAN Test Centers, due to loss of revenue. At the end of March 2009, the Washington Post Company approved a plan to offer tutoring services, previously provided at SCORE, in Kaplan test prep centers. In conjunction with this plan, 14 existing SCORE centers will be converted into Kaplan test prep centers and the remaining 64 SCORE centers will be closed (The Washington Post Company, 2009).

Project GRAD

Project GRAD (Graduation Really Achieves Dreams) began in the feeder middle schools for Jefferson Davis High School in Houston, Texas, in 1993–1994 to address the chronic underperformance and high rates of suspensions and expulsions. Collaboration efforts between the business community, led by Tenneco Corporation, The University of Houston, and the school district date back to the early 1980s, when corporate partners began funding scholarships to address the problems of underperforming schools.

In 1998, Project GRAD was scaled up to other districts nationwide, and has often been combined with other reform initiatives (Snipes, Holton, Doolittle, & Sztejnberg, 2006).

GRAD provides scholarship incentives for students who graduate on time with at least a 2.5 GPA. This comprehensive school reform model targets "feeder systems" of elementary, middle, and high schools, with the goal of increasing low-income students' academic achievement, high school graduation, and college attendance. A main goal of GRAD is to instill a college-going culture at all levels of school and into the first year of college, with a strong emphasis on family and community involvement. Project GRAD maintains that schools operate in the context of communities, and that key stakeholders—especially parents—must take ownership of school reform (Snipes, Holton, Doolittle, & Sztejnberg, 2006).

Project GRAD implements a series of interventions to assist a school in preparing more students to graduate from high school to enter postsecondary educational institutions. First, Project GRAD uses Consistency Management and Cooperative Discipline to facilitate classroom management and student–teacher cooperation. Second, Project GRAD implements educational initiatives to supplement basic elementary and middle school reading and math curricula. Third, the initiative works through Communities in Schools to improve the quality and level of parental and community support for school activities. Finally Project GRAD implements a comprehensive outreach program which includes a community-wide Walk for Success to recruit students and their parents (Watt & Reyes, 2005).

One of Project GRAD's primary goals is to raise the college enrollment rates of graduates from its high schools. In addition, Project GRAD provides scholarships to students who graduate on time, take a minimum of 3 years of mathematics, maintain a 2.5 grade point average, and complete a minimum of two summer institutes provided by local universities (Opuni, 1999). At the younger grades, the model consists of curricular reforms and teacher professional development in reading and mathematics. Students and families even learn about the scholarship opportunity as early as elementary school (Snipes, Holton, Doolittle, & Sztejnberg, 2006).

The effectiveness of this program was demonstrated in one study that showed the percentage of students graduating (50%) and attending college (10%) rose to 78% and 60%, respectively (Ketelsen, 1994; McAdoo, 1998). Other positive findings included increased numbers of credits earned, increased performance on standardized tests, and improved attendance and on-time promotion rates. These results were not statistically significant (Snipes, Holton, Doolittle, & Sztejnberg, 2006).

Project GRAD currently serves over 121,000 students in 205 of the nation's most disadvantaged schools in nine states (Project GRAD USA, 2011).

Gear Up

The programs Gaining Early Awareness and Readiness for Undergraduate Programs (GEAR UP) was established under the Higher Education Amendments of 1998 to support programs which provide information on early college awareness, academic support, and financial assistance to disadvantaged students to encourage them to enter and succeed in postsecondary education. The awards are competitive for up to 6 years in duration, and the grants are available to states and partnerships between middle schools, high schools, colleges and universities, community organizations, and businesses. The intent is to positively impact low-performing schools serving low-income and minority students. The uniqueness of the program is it serves entire cohorts of low-income students, starting in seventh grade, rather than those chosen based on predetermined criteria. The grant stipulates that at least 50% of the participants must be eligible for free or reduced lunch or rank at 150% of the poverty level (GEAR UP, 2011).

The GEAR UP model relies upon partnerships between local school districts, institutions of higher education (IHEs), and at least two other organizations, often community-based or nonprofits. Program activities may include tutoring, mentoring, college counseling, college field trip, financial aid assistance, and other college awareness activities. These activities begin in middle school and are believed to increase the aspirations, college awareness, and engagement of students, families, and schools, which will ultimately lead to increased postsecondary enrollment. By serving entire grade cohorts in high-poverty schools, the GEAR UP model posits that a college-going culture will be developed and reenforced. It also allows services to be integrated into regular educational offerings during the school day (Yampolskaya, Massey, & Greenbaum, 2006).

GEAR UP differs from other programs in that it is a working partnership between public and private entities engaged in a common purpose: to significantly increase the number of low-income students prepared to enter and succeed in postsecondary education. Schools, universities, community colleges, and business and community partners share in this responsibility. More importantly, the program focuses on local and sustainable initiatives that will continue to prepare new cohorts of students as they reach middle school (National Council for Community and Education Partnerships, 2004).

The GEAR UP initiative provides support for schools to develop a college-going culture through engagement in systemic reform that provides all students, not just a select few, an opportunity to prepare for college. Reform initiatives may include aligning of the K–16 curriculum, eliminating academic tracking, and implementing professional development models that prepare teachers to integrate technology and other innovations into the instructional program.

Comprehensive services offered to students such as mentoring, tutoring, and counseling are designed to raise students' educational aspirations and prepare them academically for success in college. Other services such as preparation for college admissions tests, dissemination of information concerning the college application process, and financial aid counseling, all serve to further increase college awareness and preparation. To demystify the college experience, students also participate in tours and engage in summer activities on college campuses.

Since parental expectations influence and are predictive of the educational aspirations of children (Looker & Pineo, 1983; Mau, 1995), GEAR UP focuses on providing parents with information in an effort to raise awareness of college entrance requirements and their very important role in their children's preparation for postsecondary education. Financial constraints often present themselves as barriers to a postsecondary education for low-income parents; therefore, every GEAR UP student receives the 21st Century Scholars Certificate indicating notification of eligibility for financial aid. Some programs also offer a scholarship component to provide college financial assistance to its participating students (Cunningham, Redmond, & Merisotis, 2003).

The program is currently implemented in 47 states and serves approximately 1.2 million students. Since its inception, funding has reached almost 1.2 billion which supports 280 partnerships and 36 state grants (GEAR UP, 2011).

In recent studies, GEAR UP improved middle school students' and parents' knowledge of the college admission process, and increased parental involvement in education. GEAR UP students were more likely to take advanced science courses in the middle grades than their non-GEAR UP peers, and increases in the overall rate of enrollment in advanced courses for African American students were found. Overall, African American students in GEAR UP took more high-level courses than did their peers in non–GEAR UP schools. GEAR UP did not have a significant effect on students' GPA, grades in core subjects, attendance, or educational expectations. A previous study of GEAR UP in one Florida high school (Yampolskaya, Massey, & Greenbaum, 2006) found that the higher levels of participation in GEAR UP academic and behavior-related services were associated with improvements in GPAs and reductions in disciplinary referrals (U.S. Department of Education, 2008).

GEAR UP serves 747,260 students in 42 state and 167 partnership grants (Washington GEAR UP, Program Update, 2009–2010).

Avid

Advancement via Individual Determination (AVID) is a college preparatory program established in 1980 in one English teacher's classroom as a means to serve students who were recently bussed to a newly desegregated suburban high school. Mary Catherine Swanson began a social and academic support elective class called AVID to assist this group of students in their rigorous courses in which they were recently enrolled. Mrs. Swanson believed her students could succeed in the most rigorous curriculum, such as Advancement Placement classes, but only needed extra support provided by the AVID elective. Of the 30 students who began AVID in 1980, 28 went to college (Mehan, Villanueva, Hubbard, & Lintz, 1996).

AVID has since spread to many states, and in some cases, such as Texas, has been used as a school reform model (Watt, Yanez, & Cossio, 2002). The Obey-Porter Comprehensive School Reform Demonstration (CSRD) program legislation includes nine components that schools must use in order to implement a reform model. These nine components have been aligned with the AVID essentials that were developed by Swanson in 1980.

AVID has established indicators by which to measure the success of the program in middle schools and high schools. Schools that implement AVID must successfully implement 11 essentials to be certified as an AVID school. The 11 AVID essentials include:

1. student recruitment and selection requirements,
2. voluntary participation agreements from student, staff, and parents,
3. integration of the AVID elective class within the regular school day,
4. enrollment in rigorous curriculum that satisfies college requirements,
5. introduction of a strong writing and reading curriculum,
6. introduction of inquiry for critical thinking skills,
7. emphasis on collaborative instruction,
8. academic assistance through tutoring with trained college tutors,
9. evaluation of program implementation through data collection and analysis,
10. district/school commitment to AVID funding appropriations and compliance, and
11. interdisciplinary site team collaboration. (Swanson, 2000)

Implementation of the AVID essentials ensures a school environment conducive to empowering students to become more responsible for their learning, and thus increases their college preparation and educational expectations to pursue a college degree. AVID can be adapted to serve grades 4–12, and has recently been implemented at the postsecondary level.

The significance of AVID in schools has been documented in studies conducted within the California school system. Students enrolled in AVID on a continuous basis demonstrated a greater propensity toward attempting and completing college-level courses, thereby producing a larger number of AVID students enrolling in colleges or universities than AVID student dropouts or students with no AVID background (Slavin & Calderon, 2001, p. 86). AVID's reputation for improving college rates and academic success in underserved minorities assisted in increasing its implementation in over 700 U.S. schools and its overseas implementation in U.S. government-sponsored schools in Europe and Asia, subsequently earning an international status (Slavin & Calderon, 2001, p. 88).

The AVID Center's mission is to "close the achievement gap by preparing all students for college readiness and success in a global society" (AVID Center Mission, 2011). The AVID program is based on the theory that all students can succeed in a rigorous curriculum if they are given extensive academic and social support. By raising the number of students who complete college entrance course requirements, AVID aims to increase the enrollment of underserved students in higher education (Hooker & Brand, 2009). AVID professional development is provided to teachers across disciplines, allowing educators to reinforce the same strategies in all classrooms, thereby taking AVID "schoolwide" (Hooker & Brand, 2009; Watt, Powell, Mendiola, & Cossio, 2006; Watt, Huerta, & Mills, 2010).

AVID has been shown to increase the overall proportion of students enrolled in advanced courses by encouraging students with average academic performance to enroll in at least one AP, IB, honors, or dual enrollment course each year. Other than academic preparation and readiness, AVID provides students with the time management, study skills, organizational skills, and personal support needed for the success of first-generation college-goers in postsecondary education. Increased participation in advanced placement (AP) courses, particularly among African American and Hispanic students, has been found in AVID schools (Watt, Powell, Mendiola, & Cossio, 2006), as well as increased college preparedness and aspirations for Hispanic students (Mendiola, Watt, & Huerta, 2010; Lozano, Watt, & Huerta, 2009).

AVID serves students in 47 states as well as 16 countries and territories, many through the Department of Defense Dependent Schools and Canada. As of 2008–2009, AVID served students in more than 4,500 schools in 898 districts. More than 220,000 students have graduated from AVID programs (AVID Postsecondary, 2011).

Early College High School

Early college high schools are small schools designed so that students can earn both a high school diploma and an associate's degree or up to 2 years of credit toward a bachelor's degree (Hoffman & Vargas, 2005). Early college high schools strive to improve graduation rates and better prepare students for high-skilled careers by engaging them in a rigorous, college preparatory curriculum and decreasing the number of years they have to spend earning a college degree (Hoffman & Vargas, 2005). The Early College High School Initiative (ECHSI) effectively and efficiently blends secondary and postsecondary education.

Webb (2004) states that the early college concept provides personalized, coherent education and meaningful credentials that set young people on a path to success in work, college, and life. The early college initiative ambitiously attempts to integrate high school and community college, as it allows students to complete their high school coursework and earn an associate's degree or 2 years of college credit within 4 to 5 years (Kisker, 2006).

Early colleges are designed for students traditionally underrepresented in higher education as well as those who have not had access to the academic preparation necessary to succeed in college (Kisker, 2006). Early college academies, which each serve about 400 students, eliminate the physical transition between high school and college and provide students with a personalized learning environment through mastery of subject matter rather than matriculation through grade levels (Jobs for the Future, 2004).

The focus of early college high schools is to develop "college going aspirations" in their students and a "college-going culture" in the school (Webb, 2004).

By minimizing the physical transition between high school and college, and allowing students to move ahead in subjects as they demonstrate success, early colleges enable students to earn a high school diploma and complete 2 years of college credit (or an associate's degree) within 4 to 5 years of entering ninth grade (Jobs for the Future, 2004). The initiative is based upon a "theory of change": by changing the structure of the high school years, compressing the number of years to a college degree, and removing financial and other barriers to college, early college high schools have the potential to improve high school and college graduation rates and better prepare traditionally underserved students for family-supporting careers.

Through the ECHSI, partnering organizations and various initiative sponsors have created or redesigned more than 250 small schools that blend high school and college. For public school leaders who are pursuing this initiative, the innovative paradigm of dividing costs and sharing revenues between secondary and postsecondary schools should be weighed, researched, and discussed. Jobs for the Future continues to coordinate and supports the partners and the effort as a whole. The ECHSI is sponsored by The Bill & Melinda Gates Foundation in partnership with Carnegie Corporation of New York, The Ford Foundation, The W.K. Kellogg Foundation Initiative, and other local foundations.

As of 2008–2009, the ECHSI has started or redesigned 197 schools in 24 states and the District of Columbia. The initiative plans to have approximately 250 schools in operation by 2011 (Early College High School Initiative, 2011).

Career Academies

Career academies have existed in high schools for over 40 years, providing a systematic approach to addressing the challenges young people face as they confront the demands of high school and prepare for postsecondary education and the workforce. Changing perspectives on career and technical education (CTE) in the late 1980s brought an increased emphasis on career academies as a vehicle for both college preparation and career awareness, rather than direct job skill training: and the target population has also expanded to include all students.

Typically career academies serve between 150 and 200 students from grades 9 or 10 through grade 12 and are defined by three distinguishing features:

1. They are organized as small learning communities to create a more supportive, personalized learning environment.
2. They combine academic and career and technical curricula around a career theme to enrich teaching and learning.
3. They establish partnerships with local employers to provide career awareness and work-based learning opportunities for students.

There are estimated to be more than 2,500 career academies across the country, operating either as a single program or as multiple programs within a larger high school (Kemple, 2008).

Operating as schools within schools and typically enrolling 30 to 60 students per grade, career academies are organized around such themes as health, business and finance, computer technology, and the like. Academy students take classes together, remain with the same group of teachers over time, follow a curriculum that includes both academic and career-oriented courses, and participate in work internships and other career-related experiences outside the classroom. Over time, improving the rigor of academic and career-related curricula has become an increasingly prominent part of the career academy agenda (Kemple, 2008).

A career academy is a smaller learning community (SLC) organized around a career theme, usually existing within a larger high school. These academies integrate academic and vocational curricula using the context of the career theme and usually provide work-based learning opportunities with employers and community partners (Hooker & Brand, 2009).

The three main structural features of a career academy include employer partnerships, SLCs, and combined academic and vocational curricula, and are designed to enhance the rigor and relevance of the high school curriculum by providing enriched learning, career awareness, and interpersonal supports. At the high school level, career academies have been shown to increase all students' likelihood of completing the required credits for graduation and increased high-risk students' likelihood of staying in school and completing a core academic curriculum; however, they did not ultimately impact high school graduation or dropout rates (Kemple, 2008).

At the postsecondary level, career academies produced a significant, sustained increase in former participants' earnings and overall months and hours of employment. These labor market impacts were particularly concentrated among young men and youth who had been in the high-risk subgroup. The former academy participants also had higher rates of family formation and living independently, as opposed to with parents, by 8 years after their expected high school graduation. Career academies are found in 40 states and in over 4,800 high schools (MDRC, 2011).

Communities in Schools

Communities in Schools (CIS) is an integrated student services model featuring partnerships between public schools and local, community-based organizations. CIS addresses students' multiple psychosocial, health-related, and academic needs. "CIS is best described as a ëprocess' of engaging schools and students, and filling gaps in need" (ICF International, 2008, as cited in Hooker & Brand, 2009, p. 58). CIS targets the whole school community and individual students by both bringing nonprofit organizations onto the school campus and collaborating with outside partners. CIS strives to "help young people successfully learn, stay in school, and prepare for life" (Hooker & Brand, 2009, p. 58).

CIS is guided by five basic essentials called the "Five Basics" that every child needs to succeed. These include:

1. A one-on-one relationship with a caring adult. Nearly 90% of CIS affiliates provide mentoring for students by connecting them with positive role models who offer encouragement and academic support.
2. A safe place to learn and grow. CIS is dedicated to ensuring that all students have a safe, appropriate environment in which to learn through after-school and/or nontraditional educational settings.
3. A healthy start and a healthy future. Access to basic health and dental care for students is provided.
4. A marketable skill to use upon graduation. Students develop career readiness and are provided pathways to access postsecondary education.
5. A chance to give back to peers and community. CIS works with students to develop their leadership skills and strengthen their involvement in community service and service-learning initiatives (Communities in Schools Annual Report, 2009).

CIS sites have made progress in reducing dropout rates and raising on-time graduation and attendance rates than comparison schools. The schools implementing the most CIS components increased academic performance in math and had the greatest improvements in graduation rates. The positive impact on graduation and attendance rates was most pronounced in urban schools serving communities of color, in particular, Latino students had the greatest gains in academic achievement (Hooker & Brand, 2009).

The CIS network includes approximately 3,300 schools in 27 states and the District of Columbia, and serves 1.3 million students (Communities in Schools, 2011).

Administrator's Role

For a high school or middle school principal, choosing an intervention program can be daunting. There are many opportunities available for principals seeking to decrease their dropout rates and increase the college-going rates of their students. Finding the best fit for an administrator's campus is the challenge.

Considerations administrators need to make when selecting a program for implementation include funding, technical assistance, links to other programs, sustainability, and evaluation. Typically the administrator seeks out programs that are supported by a funding source so that technical support is available in the first 2 to 3 years. Throughout the first 3 years of implementation, administrators should work with staff members to develop a sustainability plan for when the initial funding source comes to an end.

In a recent study of AVID, Watt, Huerta, and Cossio (2004) found that the campus leaders had a direct impact on program implementation. Major findings included the need for the campus administrators to attend implementation training along with their teachers, as well as the need for administrators to provide ideological and financial support for the program. Shared responsibility, low teacher turnover, appropriate staff development, and appropriate resource allocation are critical to the success of any implemented program.

Summary

In summary, many models have been developed over the years that address issues of access and equity for students underrepresented in higher education. Most of these models have been developed because of federal legislation resulting in the allocation of millions of dollars for college preparation and career guidance and training. Though not all programs have resulted in the preparation of large numbers of students for college (Project GRAD, AVID), some have been used for school reform models (AVID) and for supplemental resources (GEAR UP, TRIO). Recently, college and career readiness have been emphasized in new and existing programs to ensure that all students are prepared for higher education and the workforce. Table 5-1 shows various characteristics of each model discussed in this chapter

Table 5-1   **Intervention Models**

	Year	Funding Source	Purpose	Main Services Provided
Upward Bound	1966	U.S. Department of Education–Amendment to Higher Education Act	Aimed at helping students attain a postsecondary education	• Instruction • Counseling • Tutoring • Mentoring • Assistance in applying to college and completing financial aid forms
Talent Search	1968	U.S. Department of Education–Amendment to Higher Education Act	Encourage economically disadvantaged youth to complete secondary school and undertake further education. Encourage secondary school or college dropouts of demonstrated aptitude to reenter educational programs.	• Academic, financial career, or personal counseling • Career exploration and aptitude assessments • Tutorial services • Assistance in completing college admissions and financial aid applications • Mentoring programs • Family workshops
SSS	1968	U.S. Department of Education–Amendment to Higher Education Act	Increase the college retention and graduation rates and facilitate the transition of students from one level of higher education to the next.	• Study skills • Tutorial services • Academic, financial, or personal counseling • Assistance in securing admission and financial aid for enrollment in 4-year institutions • Information about career options • Mentoring • Special services for LEP students

	Year	*Funding Source*	*Purpose*	*Main Services Provided*
Career Academies	First partnership in 1969 with Philadelphia Electric Co. In the 1980s, academies spread to California and New York, and the National Academy Foundation (NAF) formed.	Various Funding Sources: Community Partnerships, Public Agencies, Chamber of Commerce, Private Funding, & United Way	A "schools-within-schools" concept offers structured, personalized learning through rigorous academics and career-related classes with focus on technical skills for a chosen industry. Succeed academically and gain valuable knowledge toward a lifetime career.	• Small learning communities • College prep curriculum with career theme • Partnering with community, employers, and higher education • Internships, job shadowing, targeted field trips, industry mentors, and professional certifications
Communities in Schools	1977	Various local, state, and federal funding sources; corporate and individual family foundations	Largest dropout prevention program in the country. Surround students with a community of support, empowering them to stay in school and achieve in life.	• A school-based coordinator, builds a team and strategically aligns and delivers needed resources • Tutors • Service learning • College visits • Job shadowing • Health and family issues • Mentors
SCORE	1979	Orange County Department of Education and University of California at Irvine	Dropout prevention/college preparatory program	• Career counseling • Tutoring • Opportunities in join clubs • Summer academic program focusing on college preparatory courses • Moves students out of ESL classes and into the mainstream
AVID	1981	Private, nonprofit organization; various funding sources: grants, local and state funding	To restructure the teaching methods of an entire school and to open access to the curricula that will ensure 4-year college eligibility to almost all students	• AVID elective class • Professional development • Enrollment of students in rigorous curriculum • Strong writing and reading curriculum

				Services
				• Inquiry for critical thinking skills • Collaborative instruction • Tutoring with trained college tutors
Project GRAD	1989	Tenneco and University of Houston; now private, nonprofit organization	Dropout prevention/college preparation program. Series of interventions to assist a school and enter postsecondary educational institutions	• Provides scholarship incentives for students who graduate on time with at least a 2.5 GPA • Consistency management and cooperative discipline • Supplement basic elementary and middle school reading and math curricula • Improve the quality and level of parental and community support
GEAR UP	1998	U.S. Department of Education	To provide information on early college awareness, academic support, and financial assistance to disadvantaged students to encourage them to enter and succeed in postsecondary education.	• Mentoring • Tutoring • Counseling • Preparation for college admissions tests • Dissemination of information concerning the college application process • Financial aid counseling
Early College High School	2003–2004 school year	Bill & Melinda Gates Foundation and private funding; various funding sources; state and local district funding	Initiative to serve low-income, first-generation college goers, English language learners, and students of color, and transition them into postsecondary education. Earn up to 2 years of transferable college credit while in high school or an associate's degree.	• Personalization and student supports • Power of place • Small size • Academic and social supports • Opportunity to earn an associate's degree • Eliminate physical transition between high school and college

Applying Your Knowledge

You are the principal of a high school that has a diverse student body. The ethnic makeup is 70% Hispanic, 25% African American, and 5% White and Asian. Over 60% of the student body qualifies for free and reduced lunch and 25% are limited English proficient. Though your students have always done well on state-mandated tests resulting in high accountability rating, only 3% are enrolled in AP classes and only 17% attend 4-year colleges or universities. Your freshman class typically has 800 students enrolled, and most of your students are still graduating without being college and career ready.

QUESTIONS

1. What are some steps you as the campus instructional leader will take to address the issue of low enrollment in AP and low college-going rates?
2. Which intervention programs discussed in this chapter would be appropriate to implement to increase the number of students who graduate from college and are career ready? How will you find out about these programs, and how are they funded?
3. Which intervention programs discussed in this chapter could be implemented to assist students in acquiring financial aid for college?
4. Describe your role as campus leaders in the implementation of the intervention program(s) you choose to address the issues stated above.

QUESTIONS FOR THOUGHT

1. What are the major advantages and disadvantages of each of the intervention programs discussed in this chapter?
2. What are the criteria for selecting students for each of the following programs: AVID, GEAR UP, career academies, and early college high school?
3. Should administrators rely on the government to offer funding for intervention programs? What are some alternatives for funding intervention programs?
4. How are the intervention programs sustained, and is sustainability an important consideration?
5. Which intervention programs are supported by research? Why is it important to consider only programs that have a research base for implementation?

Additional Information

www.avidonline.org

www.ed.gov/gearup

www.projectgrad.org

www.score.org

www.trioprograms.org

References

AVID Center Mission. (2011). Retrieved from http://www.avid.org/abo_mission.html

AVID Postsecondary. (2011). Retrieved from http://www.avid.org/sta_avidpostsecondary.html

Cahalan, M. (2009). *Do the Conclusions Change? Addressing Study Error in the Random Assignment National Evaluation of Upward Bound.* Washington, DC: Council for Opportunity in Education.

Cahalan, M., Silva, T., Humphrey, J., Thomas, M., & Cunningham, K. (2004). *Implementation of the Talent Search Program, Past and Present: Final Report from Phase I of the National Evaluation.* Washington, DC: Mathematica Policy Research, Inc., U.S. Department of Education Doc 2004-4.

Communities in Schools (CIS) Annual Report. (2009). *Empowering students to achieve.* Retrieved from http://www.communitiesinschools.org/static/media/uploads/attachments/Annual_Report_209.pdf

Conley, D. T. (2010). *College and career ready: Helping all students succeed beyond high school.* San Francisco: Jossey-Bass.

Cunningham, A., Redmond, C., & Merisotis, J. (2003). *Investing early. Intervention programs in selected U.S. states.* Montreal, Canada: Institute for Higher Education Policy.

Early College High School Initiative. Retrieved February 16, 2011 from http://www.earlycolleges.org/overview.html#basics1

Fashola, O. S., & Slavin, R. E. (1998). Promising programs for elementary and middle schools: Evidence of effectiveness and replicability. *Journal of Education for Students Placed at Risk, 2,* 251–307.

Federal TRIO Programs. U.S. Department of Education. Retrieved February 21, 2011 from http://www2.ed.gov/about/offices/list/ope/trio/index.html

Gaining Early Awareness and Readiness for Undergraduate Programs (Gear Up). Retrieved from http://www.ed.gov/offices/OPE/gearup

Gandara, P., & Bial, D. (2001). *Paving the way to postsecondary education: K-12 intervention programs for underrepresented youth.* Washington, DC: U. S. Department of Education, National Center for Educational Statistics.

Gandara, P., & Moreno, J. F. (2002). Introduction: The Puente Project: Issues and perspectives on preparing Latino youth for higher education. *Educational Policy, 16*(4), 463–473.

Hexter, H. (1990). *A description of federal information and outreach programs and selected state, institutional and community models.* Background paper 3. Washington, DC: Advisory Committee on Student Financial Assistance. (ERIC Document Reproduction Service No. ED 357 686).

Hoffman, N., & Vargas, J. (2005). *Integrating grades 9 through 14: State policies to support and sustain early college high schools.* Early College High School Publications and Other Resources. Retrieved February 20, 2011 from http://www.earlycolleges.org/publications.html

Hooker, S., & Brand, B. (2009). *Success at every step: How 23 programs support youth on the path to college and beyond.* Washington, DC: American Youth Policy Forum.

Jobs for the Future. (2004). *The early college high school initiative at a glance.* Boston: Author. Retrieved from http://www.earlycolleges.org/Downloads/ECHSIAtAGlance120204.pdf

Kemble, J. J. (2008). *Career academies: Long-term impacts on labor market outcomes, educational attainment, and transitions to adulthood.* New York: MDRC.

Ketelsen, J. L. (1994). Jefferson Davis feeder school project. Houston, TX: Tenneco Corporation Project GRAD.

Kisker, C. (2006). Integrating high school and the community college previous efforts and current possibilities. *Community College Review, 34*(1), 68–86.

Knapp, L. G., Heuer, R. E., & Mason, M. (2008). *Upward Bound and Upward Bound math-science program outcomes for participants expected to graduate high school in 2004–06, with supportive data from 2005–06.* Washington, DC: RTI International.

Looker, E. D., & Pineo, P. C. (1983). Social psychological variables and their relevance to the status attainment of teenagers. *American Journal of Sociology, 88,* 1195–1219.

Lozano, A., Watt, K. M., & Huerta, J. (2009). A comparison study of 12th grade Hispanic students' college anticipations, aspirations, and college preparatory measures. *American Secondary Education, 38*(1), 92–110.

Mau, W. (1995). Educational planning and academic achievement of middle school students: A racial and culture comparison. *Journal of Counseling and Development, 73*(5), 518–526.

McAdoo, M. (1998). Project GRAD's strength is in the sum of its parts. *Ford Foundation Report, 29*(2), 8–11.

MDRC. (2011). *Career academies.* Retrieved February 16, 2011 from http://www.mdrc.org/project_29_1.html

Mehan, H., Villanueva, I., & Lintz, A. (1996). *Constructing school success: The consequences of untracking low-achieving students.* Cambridge, UK: Cambridge University Press.

Mendiola, I. D., Watt, K. M., & Huerta, J. (2010). The impact of Advancement Via Individual Determination (AVID) on Mexican American students enrolled in a four-year university. *Journal of Hispanic Higher Education, 9*(3), 209–220.

Moore, M. T. (1997). *A 1990's view of Upward Bound: Programs offered, students served, and operational issues.* Washington, DC: U.S. Department of Education.

Myers, D. E., & Shirm, A. L. (1999). *The national evaluation of Upward Bound. The short-term impact of Upward Bound: An interim report.* Washington, DC: U.S. Department of Education.

National Council for Community and Education Partnerships. (2004). GEAR UP in the United States: Scope, design/impact, efficiencies, and alignment. Retrieved February 23, 2011 from http://www.edpartnerships.org

Natriello, G., McDill, E., & Pallas, A. (1990). *Schooling disadvantaged children: Racing against catastrophe.* New York: Teachers College Press.

Opuni, K. A. (1999). *Project GRAD: Program evaluation report, 1998-99.* Houston, TX: The University of Houston.

Perna, L., & Swail, W. (2001). Pre-college outreach and early intervention. *Thought & Action, 17*(1), 99–110.

Project GRAD USA. Retrieved February 17, 2011 from http://www.projectgrad.org/site/pp.asp?c=fuLTJeMUKrH&b=365959

Rosenbaum, J. E. (1992). *Review of two studies of talent search.* U.S. Department of Education Office of Policy and Planning's Design Conference for the Evaluation of the Talent Search Program (pp. 103–132). Washington, DC: U.S. Government Printing Office.

Schroth, G. (2001). Upward Bound and other TRIO programs. In G. Schroth and M. Littleton (Eds.), *The Administration & Supervision of Special Programs in Education* (pp. 55–66). Dubuque, IA: Kendall/Hunt.

Seftor, N. S., Mamun, A., & Schirm, A. (2009). *The impacts of regular Upward Bound on postsecondary outcomes 7-9 years after scheduled high school graduation.* Submitted by Mathematica Policy Research to the U.S. Department of Education, Policy and Program Studies Service.

Slavin, R. E., & Calderon, M. (2001). *Effective programs for Latino students.* Mahwah, NJ: Lawrence Erlbaum Associates, Inc.

Snipes, J. C., Holton, G. I., Doolittle, F., & Sztejnberg, L. (2006). *Striving for student success: The effect of Project GRAD on high school student outcomes in three urban school districts.* New York: MDRC.

Student Support Services. 34 Code of Federal Regulations 646 (U. S. Government Printing Office, 1999).

Success in a Rich Core Curriculum for Everyone. Retrieved February 20, 2011 from http://www.score-ed.com/index.php?app=ccp0&ns=display&ref=record

Swanson, M. C. (2000). Rigor with support: Lessons from AVID. *Leadership, 30*(2), 26–29.

Talent Search. 34 Code of Federal Regulations 646 (U. S. Government Printing Office, 1999).

TRIO Student Support Service (SSS), Performance & Efficiency Measure Results. (2007–2008). Retrieved from http://www2.ed.gov/programs/triostudsupp/efficiencyintro2007-08.html

Upward Bound. 34 Code of Federal Regulations 645 (U. S. Government Printing Office, 1999).

Upward Bound Math/Science Program. (2000). U.S. Department of Education. Retrieved from http://www.trioprograms.org

U.S. Department of Education. (1991). *Evaluation of Upward Bound: The basic approach.* Report prepared for the Office of Planning and Evaluation. Washington, DC: Author.

U.S. Department of Education. (1994). *Federal TRIO programs and the school, college, and university partnership program.* Washington, DC: U.S. Government Printing Office.

U.S. Department of Education. (2008). *Early outcomes of the GEAR UP program: Final report.* Retrieved February 20, 2011 from http://www2.ed.gov/rschstat/eval/highered/gearup/earlyoutcomes.pdf

U.S. Department of Education. (2010a). *Talent search program. 2010-11 grantees talent search program.* Retrieved February 18 from http://www2.ed.gov/programs/triotalent/awards.html

U.S. Department of Education. (2010b). *Upward Bound program. 2010-11 grantees regular Upward Bound program.* Retrieved February 18 from http://www2.ed.gov/programs/trioupbound/ubgrantees2010.pdf

U.S. Department of Education, Office of Postsecondary Education. (2008). *A profile of the federal TRIO programs and child care access means parents in school program.* Washington, DC: Author.

Washington GEAR UP: Program Update. (2009–2010). GEAR UP Washington State/Washington Higher Education Coordinating Board, Olympia, WA.

Washington Post Company. (2009). Press release: The Washington Post company reports first quarter earnings. Retrieved February 17, 2011 from http://phx.corporateir.net/External.File?item=UGFyZW50SUQ9NDEwMXxDaGlsZElEPS0xfFR5cGU9Mw==&=1

Watt, K. M., Huerta, J., & Cossio, G. (2004). Leadership and AVID implementation levels in four south Texas border schools. *Catalyst for Change, 33*(2), 10–14.

Watt, K. M., Huerta, J. J., & Mills, S. J. (2010). The impact of AVID professional development on teacher perceptions of school culture and climate in the United States. *International Journal of Educational Reform, 19*(3), 172–184.

Watt, K. M., Powell, C. A., Mendiola, I. D., & Cossio, G. (2006). School-wide impact and AVID: How have selected Texas high schools addressed the new accountability measures? *Journal of Education for Students Placed At Risk, 11*(1), 57–74.

Watt, K. M., & Reyes, M. A. (2005). Academic enhancement, intervention, and preparation programs. In A. Pankake (Ed.), *The Administration of Special Programs in Education* (2nd ed., chap. 4). Dubuque, IA: Kendall/Hunt.

Watt, K. M., Yanez, D., & Cossio, G. (2002). AVID: A comprehensive school reform model for Texas. *National Forum of Educational Administration and Supervision Journal, 19*(3), 43–59.

Webb, M. (2004). What is the cost of planning and implementing early college high school? Retrieved from http://www.earlycolleges.org/Downloads/FinanceReport.pdf

Wells, J. (1981). *SCORE. Final report for ESEA Title IVC.* Sacramento, CA: California Department of Education.

Yampolskaya, S., Massey, O., & Greenbaum, P. (2006, September). At-risk high school students in the "gaining early awareness and readiness program (GEAR UP)": Academic and behavioral outcomes. *Journal of Primary Preventions, 27*(5).

Career Readiness Education

6

Karen M. Watt
Terry Overton

The Carl D. Perkins Act has the ability to stimulate "educators to rethink what they have been doing for so many years, discover new ways to design more relevant curricula and provide more meaningful integrated and articulated instruction"

—*Finch, 1999, p. 201.*

Objectives

1. Discuss the history and legislation related to career and technology education (CATE)
2. Discuss the phases of vocational education reform
3. Discuss technical preparation (Tech Prep), programs of study (POS), and career clusters™
4. Explain the relationship between early college high school and CATE
5. Identify the role of the administrator in the integration in CATE reform

Introduction

The Carl D. Perkins Career and Technical Education Act of 2006 (Public Law 109-270) requires states to offer programs of study (POS), which local education agencies and postsecondary institutions may adopt as an option for student participating in career and technical education (CTE). This reauthorization of the Perkins act was the third of its kind since the original act in 1984. Also known as Perkins IV, the act provides states with the flexibility to establish their own criteria for approving CTE programs that qualify for federal Perkins funding support and was intended to strengthen the focus on responsiveness to the economy as well as to integrate academics and technical standards (Threeton, 2007).

This chapter will focus on Perkins IV, but will also provide a historical context of career and technology education in the United States, discuss vocational reform and technical preparation, introduce new career readiness initiatives, and explain the school leader's role in implementation of career and technology programs.

Historical Perspective

Social, economic, and political forces led to the development of this country's vocational education through the *Smith-Hughes Act of 1917* for the purpose of preparing youth for jobs resulting from the industrial revolution. In 1914, the Commission on National Aid to Vocational Education's (CNAVE) investigation on the national need for vocational education yielded recommendations that led to this act. The act provided an alternative form of curriculum that would better meet the needs of the working class children, who, for the first time in history, were attending high school but were not headed for professional careers (Gray, 1991). "Thus, the earliest vocational programs were grounded primarily in the need to prepare more blue-collar-type students with practical skills for the nation's farms, factories, and homes" (Lynch, 2000, p. 2).

This system of vocational education continued for the next seven decades. Enrollment in high school vocational programs continued to increase until the early 1980s when a decline in enrollment began. A few reasons blamed for the decline in vocational education enrollment included perceptions that the programs did not meet the needs of students, employers, and the community; programs competed against other curricular programs such as college preparatory; programs had an image of a dumbed-down curriculum; programs targeted primarily to educationally disadvantaged students; and that vocational programs inhibit rather than enhance youth's future career and educational choices (Lynch, 2000). Around this same era was when curriculum differentiation in the form of "tracking" came under fire. Scholars such as Rosenbaum (1976), Bowles and Gintis (1976), Goodlad (1984), and Oakes (1985) criticized tracking for reproducing and exacerbating social inequalities. They pointed out that poor, non-English speaking, and minority youngsters were disproportionately assigned to low tracks (including the "vocational track") and wealthier, white students to high tracks. Oakes's book helped ignite a firestorm of antitracking activity. This trend gained popularity in the late 1980s and managed to ignite a growing public demand for excellence in the public schools.

Vocational Education Reform

The U.S. government has been aggressively involved in vocational education reform during the last 20 years. The 1983 report, *A Nation at Risk* (National Commission on

Excellence in Education) addressed the threat of potential economic catastrophe that could occur in the absence of major elementary and secondary educational reform.

Policymakers and educators were made aware of the numbers of students emerging from high school without the skills to enter college or succeed in the world of work. The threat of technology replacing traditional jobs with new jobs that demanded higher skill and knowledge challenged U.S. communities to reevaluate the existing educational system.

A public document prepared by the National Commission on Secondary Vocational Education (1984), titled *The Unfinished Agenda,* introduced Tech Prep as an innovative concept for educational improvement. This commission recommended that the Tech Prep students' preparedness for college and the workforce be accomplished through improved coordination between secondary and postsecondary education, integrated applied academics and technical studies, and assisted transition into 2-year postsecondary education.

The Commission on the Skills of the American Workforce (1990) produced a report, *America's Choice: High Skills or Low Wages,* calling for reform in workforce preparation that centered on skill standards and the attainment of a certificate of mastery. The report mentioned the exportation of American low-skill jobs to workers in developing countries, where wages were 3 to 10 times lower. The report stressed the importance of developing high skills in U.S. workers in order to obtain and keep higher paying jobs. The report created the challenge for U.S. policymakers and educators to prepare students for higher skill, higher wage careers.

This urgent call for educational reform led to the first significant legislative act, the Carl D. Perkins Vocational and Applied Technology Education Act of 1990 (U.S. Congress, 1990). This act focused on vocational-technical education reform efforts by (a) promoting integrated vocational and academic curricula and instruction; (b) developing technical preparation education (Tech Prep) programs; (c) promoting participation of special populations, especially the economically disadvantaged; (d) developing state systems of performance standards and measures; and (e) incorporating "all aspects of industry" into curricula and instruction.

Tech Prep initiatives were specified under Titles II and IIIE of Public Law 101-392 of the Perkins act. Tech Prep was defined as a combined secondary and postsecondary education program that focused on:

- an associate degree or 2-year certificate,
- technical preparation in at least one field of engineering technology, applied science, mechanical, industrial, or practical art or trade, or agriculture, health, or business,
- student competence in mathematics, science, and communication (including applied academics) through sequential courses of study, and
- placement in employment. (U.S. Congress, P.L. 101-392, 1990)

The federal government funded a study to identify the skills considered essential to building a high-performance economy characterized by high-skill, high-wage employment (The Secretary's Commission on Achieving Necessary Skills, 1991). This report stressed the need for a high-performance workplace with workers demonstrating solid foundation in basic literacy and computational skills, thinking skills, and personal qualities that make workers dedicated and trustworthy. Effective workers were also characterized as possessing interpersonal skills and the ability to manage resources, information, technology, and systems. Policymakers and educators were now encouraged to integrate skill standards such as the SCANS competencies into the curriculum.

A second critical legislative reform effort in vocational-technical education was the Goals 2000: Educate America Act of 1994 (U.S. Congress, P.L. 103-227, 1994a). Goals

2000 centered on the adoption of content and student performance standards in elementary and secondary education. The National Skill Standards Board (NSSB) was created under Goals 2000 to identify occupational clusters; establish a system of voluntary partnerships to develop standards; conduct research, disseminate and coordinate strategies; and endorse the skill standards systems. Goals 2000 refocused the Perkins established performance systems of career awareness and occupational skill development to student performance and emphasized accountability and reform.

A third piece of federal legislation, the School-to-Work Act of 1994 (U.S. Congress, P.L. 103-239, 1994b), was established to help states develop programs that broaden students' career options, make learning more relevant, and promote successful transition to college. According to Warnat (1997):

> The School-to-Work Act represents a significant philosophical shift in the focus of federal legislation that prepares young people for work. First of all, it focuses on all students, breaking down the tradition of individuals choosing either the college track or the vocational track. Secondly, it concentrates on preparing young people for both college and careers, so that they can choose which education-career path to take and when. No one is excluded from the opportunity to continue with further education. Third, education is no longer the sole domain of schools . . . workplaces are seen as education learning environments along with secondary and post-secondary schools (p. 34).

The School-to-Work Act introduced the concept of career majors/pathways and encouraged early career exploration as school-based learning components. Workplace mentoring and a coherent sequence of courses focusing on the development of workplace competencies addressed the work-based learning component. Connecting activities were encouraged such as employer incentives to participate in school-based and work-based learning programs. School-to-Work expanded the Perkins's innovations, reinforced Goals 2000's standards framework, and added the work-based learning component.

Reauthorization of Perkins (1998)

Legislative action resulting in educational reform in the late 1990s was the reauthorization of Carl D. Perkins Vocational and Technical Education Act of 1998 (U.S. Congress, P.L. 105-332, 1998). This act has often been referred to as Perkins III and was primarily focused on restructuring and reform of programs from the 1990 Perkins Act. Perkins III supports state and local educational reform that creates seamless education and workforce development systems. It also emphasized the development of quality vocational and technical programs with academic integration. Perkins III reauthorized Tech Prep and promoted the use of work-based learning and new technologies in Tech Prep programs. Partnership development was encouraged between Tech Prep programs and business, labor organizations, and postsecondary institutions that award baccalaureate degrees. Perkins III also attempted to align vocational and technical education program reform with state and local reform efforts intended to improve student achievement, prepare students for postsecondary education, and result in smooth transition to the workplace. This act clarified the common goals and objectives of vocational-technical education and the Tech Prep reform initiative.

Perkins III supported the Workforce Investment Act of 1998, which restructures employment training, adult education, and vocational rehabilitation programs by promoting the development of integrated, one-stop education and workforce development systems for adults and youth. The restructured Perkins III sets out a new vision of student academic and technical achievement in postsecondary education and opportunities in high-skill, high-wage careers.

Tech Prep

States are responsible for interpreting the Perkins Act and developing consistent and concrete definitions of a Tech Prep participant and program. Defining and describing local Tech Prep programs and participants has generated ongoing concerns since the implementation of this reform initiative. Opposing views of what a Tech Prep program should consist of or exactly who should be considered a Tech Prep participant has led to different state (or even consortia within a state) definitions.

Some consortia believe Tech Prep should not be considered a distinct program because it will lead inevitably to the stigma associated with "tracking," particularly of vocational students. Consortia following this approach may not differentiate students in Tech Prep from the general student population or may count students as in Tech Prep if they happen to take any of the courses considered fundamental to the Tech Prep initiative (e.g., articulated vocational courses). Students, however, are unaware of their participation in a "program." On the other hand, some consortia view Tech Prep as a true program; students apply for admission, enroll, and participate in a defined set of activities that set them apart from other students. These consortia often consider a cohesive Tech Prep program to have the added benefit of allowing students to feel that they are part of something special, and sometimes encourage students to wear Tech Prep logos or take the students on special field trips to reinforce this attitude (Silverberg & Hershey, 1995, p. 10).

Despite the fact that identification of Tech Prep students differs among consortia, most Tech Prep students meet common criteria. Tech Prep students identify and select a career pathway of interest; participate in the development of a 4- or 6-year educational plan leading toward that career pathway; enroll in vocational courses in the selected career pathway; and participate in applied academic classes that reinforce real-world skills (Silverberg & Hershey, 1995, sec. V, p. 10). The two most common elements of the definition of a Tech Prep student include participation in vocational or career and technology education (CATE) and applied academic coursework.

Parnell (1993, p. 7) suggests that the most successful Tech Prep programs typically contain the following characteristics:

1. a structural and substance-rich applied academic curriculum that provides opportunities for all students to understand the relationship between academic subject matter and real-life application;
2. high standards for achievement, as well as thorough assessment policies;
3. learning and guidance strategies that allow all students to acquire positive attitudes toward life skills, lifelong learning, and family-wage career opportunities;
4. teacher-counselor preservice and inservice programs about Tech Prep;
5. collaboration among high school, college, and employer representatives; and
6. strategies aimed at changing attitudes about vocational-technical education community and technical college "bridge" programs that prepare adult students who have missed the high school portion of the sequence to move into and succeed in the Tech Prep program.

Even though Tech Prep has been popular with businesspersons and educators, Lynch (2000) believes that no direct cause-and-effect quantifiable data are available on the effectiveness of Tech Prep. Lynch suggests that a major problem in assessing Tech Prep's impact on measured student achievement is the varied definition it has developed by state consortia throughout the nation.

Assessing the effectiveness of nationwide Tech Prep programs is complicated and multidimensional due to diverse and unique characteristics of local consortia. The U.S.

Department of Education intentionally allowed states considerable freedom to design Tech Prep systems to be responsive to local conditions and constraints (American Vocational Association, 1992). Due to the diversity of local Tech Prep programs, researchers have struggled to find consistent and clearly defined measurable outcomes on Tech Prep programs and participant achievement necessary in documenting systemic change.

Hershey, Silverberg, Owens, and Hulsey (1998) state in *Focus for the Future: The Final Report of the National Tech Prep Evaluation* that the creation of Tech Prep consortia has strengthened local collaboration among educators, increased career guidance, emphasized applied academics, and increased employer involvement with schools. Since federal legislation specified the components of Tech Prep with local consortia discretion on implementation, Tech Prep has taken diverse forms emphasizing individual components. This study found that most consortia have not brought these individual aspects of Tech Prep together in a structured, challenging program of study that substantially change students' educational experience.

Research on the Effectiveness of Tech Prep Programs

By promoting articulation agreements between high schools and community colleges, Tech Prep programs have been shown to ease the transition into college for many high school students. Cellini (2006) found that Tech Prep programs help participants complete high school and encourage enrollment in 2-year colleges. Because of the increased enrollment in 2-year colleges, it is suggested that Tech Prep programs may divert students from 4-year to 2-year colleges in the years immediately following high school. Although Tech Prep programs appear to increase educational attainment, they do not necessarily promote college enrollment among the middle majority (Cellini, 2005).

Recent evidence on the effectiveness of Tech Prep initiatives implies that they had minimal impact upon postsecondary educational outcomes (Lewis, 2008). Stone and Aliaga (2003) found no significant relationship between Tech Prep participation and GPA. Bragg et al. (2002) conducted a longitudinal study to assess the effects of participating in Tech Prep and found that students, both Tech Prep and nonparticipants, enrolled in college-level classes but few earned sufficient credits to obtain a certificate or degree. They also found that 40% to 80% of Tech Prep participants in their study took some college-level coursework, compared to nearly 30% to 76% among nonparticipants. The range of college completers was 8.5% to 19.0% for both Tech Prep and non–Tech Prep students, and many had to take developmental coursework once enrolled in college.

A congressionally mandated evaluation of Tech Prep (Hershey, Silverberg, Owens, & Hulsey, 1998) included case studies of 10 consortia and interviews with 486 former Tech Prep students conducted approximately 18 months after they graduated from high school. Enrollment in postsecondary education or other types of formal occupational preparation from these 10 consortia was 61%, but only 15% reported that their programs awarded credits for the articulated courses they had taken in high school. Over one-third (37%) of those attending community colleges had not started programs leading to degrees, but instead was taking developmental and general education courses.

Reauthorization of Perkins (2006) and Programs of Study

The Carl D. Perkins Career and Technical Education Act of 2006(Public Law 109-270 or Perkins IV) calls for states to offer programs of study (POS), which local educational agencies and postsecondary institutions may adopt for students participating in career and technical education (CTE). Each local recipient of Perkins IVfunds must offer at least one POS that, at a minimum:

- incorporates and aligns secondary and postsecondary education elements;
- includes academic and CTE content in a coordinated, nonduplicative progression of courses;
- offers the opportunity, where appropriate, for secondary students to acquire post-secondary credits; and
- leads to an industry-recognized credential or certificate at the postsecondary level, or an associate or baccalaureate degree. (Office of Vocational and Adult Education, 2010)

The Program of Study Design Framework (Perkins Collaborative Resource Network, 2010) is shown below.

PROGRAM OF STUDY DESIGN FRAMEWORK

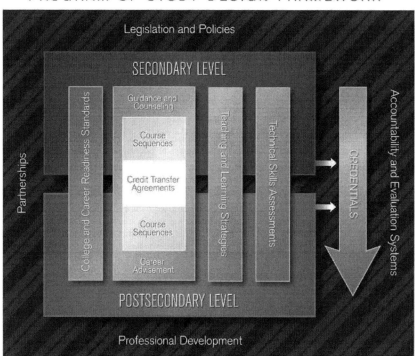

School districts typically submit evidence to the state that illustrates sufficient size, scope, and quality of their CTE program to be eligible for Perkins funding. Current program approval processes may need to be modified or enhanced for state staff to ensure local POSs are sufficiently meeting Perkins IVrequirements. As specified by the act, the following four statutory requirements define a program of study.

1. **Incorporate and align secondary and postsecondary education elements.** For generations, two separate education systems have existed in the United States and have been relatively isolated from one another. The country's P–12 and postsecondary systems have different cultures, governance, finance, and accountability. This historic lack of alignment has caused many students—especially those who are low income, minority, and underserved—to "fall between the cracks at different stages along the educational pipeline" (Pathways to College Network, 2007). Of the 70% of students who finish high school only about half go directly on to college, and just over one-third of those earn a degree (Mortenson, 2004–2006).

As 21st-century jobs increasingly require postsecondary education, alignment of the two divergent educational systems is necessary so that students' post-secondary aspirations can become realistic and attainable. P–16 alignment seeks to bridge the P–12 and postsecondary educational sectors in three critical areas:

- academic standards and curriculum expectations,
- testing and assessment, and
- early college opportunities. (Pathways to College Network, 2007)

When submitting a program of study, local educational entities must submit a single proposal that spans both secondary and postsecondary entities. This evidence must reflect deliberate planning and alignment between the secondary and postsecondary levels, such as a POS that illustrates how the secondary CTE program sequence aligns with the postsecondary credential, certificate, or degree program.

2. **Include academic and CTE content in a coordinated, nonduplicative progression of courses.** Historically many school districts have provided opportunities for students to enroll in and complete college credit–bearing courses while still in high school. In order to meet the standards of the POS, school districts must provide evidence that these courses will count toward a degree or certificate program without having to be duplicated once a student enters higher education.

   Concurrent enrollment has often been termed "dual credit," "dual enrollment," or "college in the high schools." Each of these terms describes a different model of accelerated learning; however, the National Alliance for Concurrent Enrollment Partnerships (NACEP) defines a concurrent enrollment program as one that offers college courses to high school students:

   - in the high school,
   - during the regular school day, and
   - taught by high school teachers. (National Alliance of Concurrent Enrollment Partnerships, 2010)

   Other programs that provide a direct connection between secondary and post-secondary institutions and an opportunity for collegial collaboration include:

   - programs in which the high school student travels to a college campus to take courses prior to graduating from high school, and
   - programs where college faculty travel to the high school to teach courses.

   The College Board Advanced Placement Program and the International Baccalaureate Program offer standardized tests to assess students' knowledge of a curriculum developed by a committee consisting of both college and high school faculty (National Alliance of Concurrent Enrollment Partnerships, 2010).

   Traditionally, dual enrollment programs have focused on high-achieving students, but recently perceptions toward these programs have changed. Dual enrollment has been shown to be as beneficial in promoting academic rigor and easing the high school to college transition for average students seeking technical careers.

   Karp, Calcagno, Hughes, Jeong, and Bailey (2007) tracked high school and college outcomes for dual enrollment participants pursuing career and technical education. The researchers found that dual enrollment is positively associated with the likelihood that students will earn a high school diploma, initially enroll in a 4-year institution, enroll full time, and persist in college to a second semester. Students who participated in dual enrollment in high school had significantly higher cumulative college grade point averages 3 years after high school graduation than did their peers who did not participate in dual enrollment programs. Dual enrollment participants also earned more college credits than nonparticipating peers.

The study finds conflicting evidence on the question of whether the intensity of dual enrollment participation has an effect on outcomes. In Florida, researchers found that the outcomes remain relatively constant whether high school students take one college course or more than five, while in New York City, the positive effect on GPA occurs only after students take two or more college courses.

"The big conclusion is that we have some real evidence now that this is an effective strategy for helping students make a better transition to college and persist in college once they're there . . . We see that as being particularly effective for lower-income students and for males and if you're looking at lower-income students, states and policymakers are weighing how to invest their money" (Karp et al., 2007, p. 79).

Documentation must illustrate how a planned sequence of coursework will not result in any duplication for a student participating in a POS. For example, a single POS template could satisfy documentation for both the alignment of the secondary and postsecondary sectors and illustrate the coordinated, nonduplicative progression of courses.

3. **Offer the opportunity, where appropriate, for secondary students to acquire postsecondary credits.** As mentioned, one of the important implications of implementation of the Perkins act is the requirement that programs align secondary and postsecondary programs so that they result in a sequence leading to a postsecondary credential. For example, early college high schools offer high school students the opportunity to complete their high school years on a college or university campus while earning high school and college credits. This delivery system is targeted especially to include individuals who are first-generation college students and who are also likely from low socioeconomic backgrounds and who are culturally or ethnically diverse (Edmunds et al., 2010). The early college high school programs accelerate the path from high school to credentialing and improve academic achievement (Kuo, 2010). Students attending these institutions have been found to achieve higher on language and math proficiency assessments than students from traditional high school settings (Berger, Adelman, & Cole, 2010).

Programs offering dual enrollment are required to have articulated agreements between the secondary schools and the local colleges or community colleges about the courses offered and how they fit into an official postsecondary POS. In addition to meeting the requirements of obtaining college-level credit, dual enrollment programs must maintain state requirements that include ensuring that the courses students take meet higher education requirements such as those required in general education courses within degree or credential programs. These programs then are meeting Perkins requirements, local degree requirements, and state requirements for both public schools and state higher education regulatory boards.

Articulated agreements necessitate that the curriculum be aligned within the programs of study. Alignment of curriculum assists students in many ways. Attending a high school in which the curriculum is aligned with the local college, community college, or technical school decreases the likelihood that students will take unnecessary courses, unrelated courses, or will complete a degree lacking courses required for their field of study.

To assist high schools and postsecondary institutions in the alignment of curriculum, the National Association of State Directors of Career and Technical Education Consortium (NASDCTEc, 2008) designed a common conceptual framework of career clusters™. The States' Career clusters™ Initiative (SCCI) provides critical components of the schools, as presented here. NASDCTEc (2010) reported that 68% of the states have adopted the 15 critical components of the career clusters™ and an additional 21% modified them.

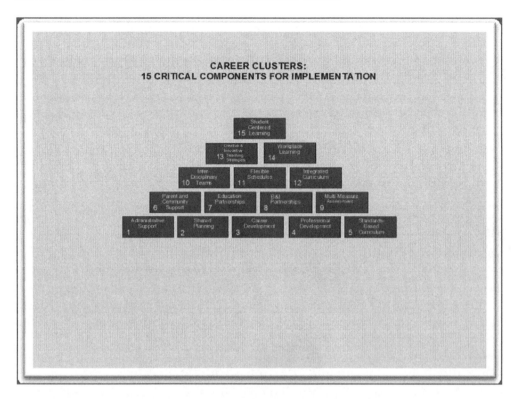

Programs of study for high school students include courses for meeting the expectations of college and technical careers. The combination of coursework that is designed for college preparatory skills and technical skills during high school has been found to increase math skills and knowledge (DeLuca, Plank, & Estacion, 2006).

4. **Lead to an industry-recognized credential or certificate at the postsecondary level, or an associate or baccalaureate degree.** Perkins IV requires that programs of study result in the attainment of a credential with the overarching goal of acquiring skills and knowledge that will lead to employability. This means that the POS would be designed to lead to the credentials expected in specific career fields. In an industrial technology field area, for example, the credential might be a certificate or associate 2-year degree or a 4-year degree, dependent upon the student's desired occupation. To be employed in the field of health care, a student may acquire a certificate, an associate degree, a bachelor's degree, or a graduate degree. The POS within the high school career pathway must prepare the student for the knowledge and skills expected so that the student can decide which career and credential is the ultimate goal. The focus is on development of the requisite skills to be able to acquire the final credential.

Requiring that programs result in a credential that will increase employability is underscored throughout the regulations. There has been significant research indicating that too many students were completing their education without employable credentials (Deil-Amen & DeLuca, 2010). The traditional high school preparation pathways were divided between the college preparatory and technical or career tracks. This division of curriculum resulted in divided opportunities and discrepancies in knowledge and skills between students completing the two tracks. Thus, the Perkins regulations seek to allow students to obtain common skills and knowledge that ultimately result in specific credentials as required by the job market.

CAREER CLUSTERS™

According to Perkins IV guidelines, states may develop and implement career and technical programs of study in one or more of 16 career clusters™ that are recognized by the Office of Vocational and Adult Education (OVAE) and NASDCTEc. These clusters are occupational categories with industry-validated knowledge and skills statements that define what students need to know and be able to do in order to be career-ready in a chosen field. Within each of the clusters, programs of study (also called "career pathways") outline sequences of academic, career, and technical courses and training that begin as early as ninth grade and lead to progressively higher levels of education and higher-skilled positions in specific industries or occupations. The 16 career clusters™ are as follows:

- Agriculture, Food, and Natural Resources
- Architecture and Construction
- Arts, A/V and Communications
- Business, Management, and Administration
- Education and Training
- Finance
- Government and Public Administration
- Health Science
- Hospitality and Tourism
- Human Services
- Information Technology
- Law, Public Safety, Corrections, and Security
- Manufacturing
- Marketing, Sales, and Service
- Science, Technology, Engineering, and Mathematics
- Transportation, Distribution and Logistics (National Association of State Directors of Career Technical Education Consortium, 2011)

As stated above, career clusters™ have 15 critical components that are explained in the table below.

Career clusters™:
15 Critical Components For Implementation
CRITICAL COMPONENT DESCRIPTIONS:

Critical Component #1: Administrative Support
The superintendent, principal, and school board members are informed and understand the concept of the career emphasis/focus (cluster) process and its components.

Critical Component #2: Shared Planning Time
The teaching team has a schedule that allows for weekly, shared program planning, curriculum design, and other career cluster™–related activities.

Critical Component #3: Career Development
Parents are included in the career planning sessions to increase ownership of the career-education plan.

Critical Component #4: Professional Development

All members of the cluster team will attend professional development activities related to one or more of the 15 critical components to successfully implement the program.

Critical Component #5: Standards-Based Curriculum

Curriculum is designed to include both the career cluster™ foundation standards and appropriate academic standards. Curriculum enhances and reinforces academic content and, as a result, improves both career content and academic achievement.

Critical Component #6: Parent and Community Support

Parents/guardians are informed of the program content, participate in the career decision-making process, and support the program in various settings. Community groups offer program support through sponsorships and marketing. They assist with identifying workplace learning sites and building industry partnerships.

Critical Component #7: Education Partnerships

Educational partnerships will be formalized within the region to establish an articulated continuum of learning for the career cluster™ program.

Critical Component #8: Business and Industry Partnerships

Industry partners are representative of the entire spectrum of the career cluster™ delivery represented in the community.

Critical Component #9: Multi-Measure Assessment

Assessment includes both cumulative and on-demand measures and meets criteria for multiple disciplines.

Component #10: Interdisciplinary Teams

The cluster team works collaboratively to offer the curriculum in an interdisciplinary approach. The content is typically designed around a common theme or project with a culminating activity, product, or service, as a result of the instruction.

Critical Component #11: Flexible Schedules

School schedules are flexible and allow for interdisciplinary team-managed blocks of time, as needed, for projects, labs, and other action-based activities.

Critical Component #12: Integrated Curriculum

The curriculum is developed and taught by the cluster team. The content is multidisciplinary and based on academic and career cluster™ foundation standards and taught in the context of the industry. Career cluster™ content is strengthened by the integration of academic concepts.

Critical Component #13: Creative and Innovative Teaching Strategies

Team building, critical thinking, and problem-solving activities are incorporated into the program. All content is reinforced through application and practice.

Critical Component #14: Workplace Learning

All students participate in workplace learning experiences that are in alignment with their career goals.

Critical Component #15: Student-Centered Learning

Students are involved in the design and development of their coursework, based on their interests, career goals, and what is consistent with the standards to be met.

From Implementing Career Clusters and Pathways by the National Association of State Directors of Career Technical Education Consortium (NASDCTEc). Copyright NASDCTEc. Reprinted by permission.

EARLY COLLEGE HIGH SCHOOL INITIATIVE

As mentioned in another chapter of this book, the Early College High School Initiative has assisted students in preparing for college and careers since 2002. This initiative was designed so that first-generation college-goers and other student groups underrepresented in higher education can earn a high school diploma and an associate's degree or up to 2 years of credit toward a bachelor's degree tuition free while still in high school. The Bill & Melinda Gates Foundation, the Carnegie Corporation of New York, the Ford Foundation, the W.K. Kellogg Foundation, and other local foundations fund this initiative (Early College High School Initiative, 2007).

The Early College High School Initiative involves small schools developed with the intent of improving graduation rates and better preparing students for entry into high-skilled careers by engaging all students in a rigorous, college preparatory curriculum. In addition, by participating in the early college initiative, students decrease the number of years it takes to complete a college degree (Hoffman & Vargas, 2005).

The early college initiative is an attempt to integrate high school and community college, as it allows students to complete their high school coursework and earn an associate's degree or 2 years of college credit within 4 to 5 years. Early college academies, each of which serve approximately 400 students when fully enrolled, help ease the transition between high school and college by providing students with a personalized learning environment where mastery of subject matter, rather than matriculation through grade levels, is the goal (Jobs for the Future, 2004).

The objective of the Early College High School Initiative is to provide underrepresented students in higher education opportunities to not only navigate but successfully complete the journey through the rigors of higher education. Historically these students have not had access to the academic preparation needed to meet college readiness standards and come from low-income families where the cost of college is prohibitive. The early college high school aims to develop "college-going aspirations" in their students and a "college-going culture" in the school (Webb, 2004). Early college high schools reach out to middle schools to provide extensive support to ensure that all students are ready for college-level courses in high school (Jobs for the Future, 2004).

CAREER AND TECHNICAL STUDENT ORGANIZATIONS

The Office of Vocational and Adult Education identifies several CTE student organizations. The U.S. Department of Education has endorsed career and technology student organizations (CTSOs) as a critical component of an effective CTE program. The responsibility for CTE instructional programs and related activities, including CTSOs, rests with state and local education agencies. The Department of Education allows states to use federal Perkins funds to provide leadership and support for the CTE student organizations (SEC 124) (Ullrich, Pavelock, Fazarro, & Shaw, 2007). These student organizations are as follows:

Business Professionals of America is a student organization that contributes to the preparation of a world-class workforce through the advancement of leadership, citizenship, academic, and technological skills for students at the secondary and postsecondary levels. Business Professionals of America members compete in demonstrations of their business technology skills, develop their professional and leadership skills, network with one another and professionals across the nation, and get involved in the betterment of their community through good works projects.

Distributive Education Clubs of America (DECA), a national association of marketing education students, provides teachers and members with educational and leadership development activities to merge with the education classroom instructional program.

Future Business Leaders of America - Phi Beta Lambda (FBLA-PBL) is an organization of young people preparing for success as leaders in our businesses, government, and communities. The organization's website was created to help current and prospective FBLA-PBL members find information about the association, its programs and services, and its members.

Future Educators Association (FEA), sponsored by Phi Delta Kappa International, is a student organization that provides students interested in education-related careers with activities and materials that help them explore the teaching profession in a variety of ways. FEA helps students develop the skills and strong leadership traits that are found in high-quality educators and significantly contributes to the development of the next generation of great educators.

Family, Career and Community Leaders of America (FCCLA) offers members the opportunity to expand their leadership potential and develop skills for life—planning, goal setting, problem solving, decision making, and interpersonal communication—necessary in the home and workplace. Since 1945, FCCLA members have been making a difference in their families, careers, and communities by addressing important personal, work, and societal issues through family and consumer sciences education. Today over 227,000 members are active in a network of associations in 50 states as well as in the District of Columbia, the Virgin Islands, and Puerto Rico.

Health Occupations Students of America (HOSA) is a national vocational student organization endorsed by the U.S. Department of Education and the Health Occupations Education Division of the American Vocational Association. HOSA's twofold mission is to promote career opportunities in the health care industry and to enhance the delivery of quality health care to all people. HOSA's goal is to encourage all health occupations instructors and students to join and be actively involved in the HOE-HOSA Partnership.

National Future Farmers of America (FFA) makes a positive difference in the lives of students by developing their potential for premier leadership, personal growth, and career success through agricultural education.

National Postsecondary Agricultural Student Organization (PAS) is an organization associated with agriculture/agribusiness and natural resources offerings in approved postsecondary institutions offering associate degrees or vocational diplomas and/or certificates.

National Young Farmer Educational Association is the official adult student organization for agricultural education as recognized by the U.S. Department of Education. With the goal of being America's Association for Educating Agricultural Leaders, the association features leadership training, agricultural career education, and community service opportunities.

Skills USA is a national organization serving high school and college students and professional members who are enrolled in technical, skilled, and service occupations, including health occupations.

Technology Student Association (TSA) is the only student organization devoted exclusively to the needs of technology education students who are presently enrolled in, or have completed, technology education courses.

Ullrich and colleagues (2007) found that school administrators perceived CTSOs as being very effective at meeting students' needs. Overall, these administrators indicated that the FFA was the most effective or second most effective in teaching leadership skills, keeping students engaged in school, improving technical skills, and improving academic achievement. HOSA and Skills USA also were highly rated for providing one of the four characteristics.

The Principal's Role

Critical to the success of the Tech Prep reform movement and POS is the school administrator. Craig (1998) believes that the success of Tech Prep programs depends on the involvement of key administrators such as the superintendent, high school principal, and vocational director. These administrators' responsibilities include the development of a district Tech Prep philosophy and policy, promotion of the Tech Prep concept within the school and community, curriculum restructuring and reform, providing necessary staff training, and development of school planning teams.

Another critical administrative responsibility is the development and support of a clear plan for integrating the Tech Prep reform initiative into existing academic and vocational programs. According to Hull (2000),

> The old voc-ed courses won't work anymore; they were designed to support the workforce of a past generation, which did not require strong academic foundations. Today, these courses won't open minds and doors to lifelong careers with multiple options of achievement and responsibility (p. 35).

The primary responsibility of reforming existing CATE programs to the Tech Prep system falls mainly on the administrators overseeing these programs, the high school principal, and the vocational director. A critical component includes the integration of academic and CATE programs, which requires collaboration between the two disciplines. However, in the age of academic accountability, many principals focus the majority of their time and effort on academic reform and are reluctant to share limited staff development opportunities toward collaborative integrated training among academic and CATE staff.

School principals are challenged to understand the role CATE and Tech Prep play in preparing students for transition into the real world. An effective principal empowers staff members to implement the Tech Prep reform strategies into existing CATE programs and encourages integration activities between academic and CATE staff. The principal also promotes the development of active partnerships with community businesses and postsecondary institutions that result in articulation agreements, internships, and other work-based learning experiences for students and staff.

Applying Your Knowledge

You are the principal of a large urban high school that has implemented Tech Prep for the past several years. Enrollment in the Tech Prep courses has been increasing, but the percentage of graduates attending college has not increased. With the new Perkins IV legislation, you are now under pressure to development a POS.

QUESTIONS

1. What data would you use to determine how to go about developing a program of study? Who would you involve in the process?
2. How could you enhance your current Tech Prep program to ensure that more students are prepared for 2-year and 4-year colleges?
3. What steps would you take to evaluate your current CTE program?
4. What types of college credit–bearing courses would you put in place and why?

QUESTIONS FOR THOUGHT

1. How do current career and technology programs differ from vocational programs in the 1960s, 1970s, and 1980s?
2. What is Tech Prep and what are some advantages to belonging to a Tech Prep consortium?
3. What are career clusters™?
4. What are some examples of career and technology student leadership opportunities?
5. How are career and technology programs funded?
6. What are programs of study and their required elements?

References

American Vocational Association. (1992). *The Carl D. Perkins vocational and applied technology education act of 1990: The final regulations.* Alexandria, VA: Author.

Berger, A., Adelman, N., & Cole, S. (2010). The early college high school initiative: An overview of five evaluation years. *Peabody Journal of Education: Issues of Leadership, Policy, and Organizations, 85*(3), 333–347.

Bowles, S., & Gintis, H. (1976). *Schooling in capitalist America: Education reform and the contradictions of economic life.* New York: Basic Books Inc.

Bragg, D. D., Loeb, J. W., Gong, Y., Deng, C.-P., Yoo, J.-s., & Hill, J. L. (2002). *Transition from high school to college and work for Tech Prep participants in eight selected consortia.* St. Paul, MN: National Research Center for Career and Technical Education.

Cellini, S. R. (2006). Smoothing the transition to college? The effect of Tech-Prep programs on educational attainment. *Economics of Education Review, 25,* 394–411.

Commission on the Skills of the American Workforce. (1990). *America's choice: High skills or low wages!* Rochester, NY: National Center on Education and the Economy.

Craig, R. M. (1998). Attitudes of Ohio school administrators toward tech prep. *Dissertation Abstracts International* (Digital Dissertation No. AAT 9842102).

Deil-Amen, R., & DeLuca, S. (2010). The underserved third: How our educational structures populate an educational underclass. *Journal of Education for Students Placed at Risk, 15*(1/2), 27–50. DOI: 10.1080/10824661003634948

DeLuca, S., Plank, S., & Estacion, A. (2006) *Does career and technical education affect college enrollment? National Research Center for Career and Technical Education.* St. Paul: University of Minnesota. Retrieved from http://inpathways.net/cteandenrollment.pdf

Early College High School Initiative. (2007). Retrieved from http://www.earlycolleges.org/overview.html

Edmunds, J. A., Bernstein, L., Glennie, E., Willse, J., Arhavsky, N., Unlu, F., Bartz, D., Silberman, T., Scales, W. D., & Dallas, A. (2010). Preparing students for college: The implementation and impact of the early college high school model. *Peabody Journal of Education, 85*(3), 348-364. DOI: 10.1080/0161956X.2010.491702

Finch, C. R. (1999). Using professional development to meet teachers' changing needs: What we have learned. *CenterPoint Series.* ED428259.

Goodlad, J. I. (1984). *A place called school.* New York: McGraw-Hill. ED236137

Gray, K. (1991). Vocational education in high school: A modern Phoenix? *Phi Delta Kappan, 71*(6), 437–445.

Hershey, A., Silverberg, M., Owens, T., & Husley, L. (1998). *Focus for the future: The final report of the national tech-prep evaluation.* Princeton, NJ: Mathematical Policy Research, Inc.

Hoffman, N., & Vargas, J. (2005). *Integrating grades 9 through 14: State policies to support and sustain early college high schools.* Retrieved from http://www.earlycolleges.org/publications.html

Hull, D. M. (2000). *Education and career preparation for the new millennium: A vision for systemic change.* Waco, TX: Center for Occupational Research & Development.

Jobs for the Future. (2004). *The early college high school initiative at a glance.* Boston: Author. Retrieved fromhttp://www.earlycolleges.org/Downloads/ECHSIAtAGlance120204.pdf

Karp, M. M., Calcagno, J. C., Hughes, K. L., Jeong, D. W., & Bailey, T. R. (2007). *The postsecondary achievement of participants in dual enrollment: An analysis of student outcomes in two states.* Community College Research Center, Teachers College, Columbia University.

Kuo, V. (2010). Transforming American high schools: Possibilities for the next phase of high school reform. *Peabody Journal of Education, 85*(3), 389–401. DOI: 10.1080/0161956X.2010.491709.

Lewis, M. V. (2008). Effectiveness of previous initiatives similar to programs of study: Tech prep, career pathways, and youth apprenticeships.*Career and Technical Education Research, 33*(3), 165–188.

Lynch, R. L. (2000). High school career and technology education for the first decade of the 21st century. *The Journal of Vocational Education Research, 25*(2), [On-line], March 4, 2002. Available from http://scholar.lib.vt.edu/ejournois/JVER/v25n2/lynch.html

Mortenson, T. (2004–2006). Projections of high school graduates by race/ethnicity and state to 2018. *Postsecondary Education Opportunity, 146.* College continuation rates for recent high school graduates 1955 to 2005. *Postsecondary Education Opportunity, 166.* College graduation rates, 1947 to 2006. *Postsecondary Education Opportunity, 173.*

National Alliance of Concurrent Enrollment Partnerships. (2010). An organization for education professionals administering or participating in concurrent enrollment partnerships. Retrieved from http://nacep.org/

National Association of State Directors of Career and Technical Education Consortium. (2010). A look inside: A synopsis of CTE trends. Retrieved from http://www.fortbend.k12.tx.us/administration/CATE/TexasCareerClusters.pdf

National Association of State Directors of Career Technical Education Consortium. (2011). *Career clusters™.* Retrieved from http://www.careerclusters.org

National Commission on Excellence in Education. (1983). *A nation at risk: The imperative for educational reform.* Washington, DC: U.S. Government Printing Office.

National Commission on Secondary Vocational Education. (1984). *The unfinished agenda.* Columbus: National Center for Research in Vocational Education, Ohio State University.

Oakes, J. (1985). *Keeping track: How schools structure inequality.* New Haven, CT: Yale University Press.

Office of Vocational and Adult Education. (2010). Retrieved from http://www2.ed.gov/about/offices/list/ovae/index.html

Parnell, D. (1993). What is the tech prep/associate degree program? *The Balance Sheet, 75*(2),6–8.

Pathways to College Network. (2007). *Academic rigor at the heart of college access and success.* Boston: Pathways to College Network.

Perkins Collaborative Resource Network. (2010). *Programs of study.* Washington, DC: U.S. Department of Education, Office of Vocational and Adult Education. Retrieved from http://cte.ed.gov/nationalinitiatives/rposdesignframework.cfm

Secretary's Commission on Achieving Necessary Skills (SCANS). (1991). *What work requires of schools.* Washington, DC: U.S. Department of Labor.

Silverberg, M. K., & Hershey, A. M. (1995). *The emergence of tech-prep at the state and local levels.* Report submitted to the U.S. Department of Education. Princeton, NJ: Mathematical Policy Research, Inc.

States Career clusters™ Initiative. (n.d.) *Career clusters™: 15 critical components for implementation.* Retrieved from http://www.careerclusters.org/resources/implementation/CriticalComponent.pdf

Stone, J. R., III., & Aliaga, O. A. (2003). *Career and technical education, career pathways and work-based learning: Changes in participation 1997-1999.* St. Paul, MN: National Center for Career and Technical Education.

Tech-Prep Texas. (2001). *Closing the gaps: How tech-prep programs have increased participation and success in Texas schools, a five-year study.* Tech-Prep Evaluation, Region 5 Education Service Center, Beaumont, TX.

Threeton, M. D. (2007). The Carl D. Perkins Career and Technical Education (CTE) Act of 2006 and the roles and responsibilities of CTE teachers and faculty members. *Journal of Industrial Teacher Education, 44*(1). Available from http://scholar.lib.vt.edu/ejournals/JITE/v44n1/threeton.html

Ullrich, D. R., Pavelock, D., Fazarro, D., & Shaw, B. (2007). Effectiveness of career and technology student organizations (CTSOS) in Texas. *Online Journal of Workforce Education and Development, 2*(4).

U.S. Congress, P.L. 101-392, 1990.

U.S. Congress. (1994a). *Goals 2000: Educate America Act.* Public Law 103-227. Washington, DC: U.S. Government Printing Office.

U.S. Congress. (1994b). *School-to-work opportunities act of 1994.* Washington, DC: U.S. Government Printing Office. Public Law 103-239.

U.S. Congress. (1998). *Carl D. Perkins vocational and technical education act of 1998.* Public Law 105-332. Washington, DC: U.S. Government Printing Office.

U.S. Department of Labor, The Secretary's Commission on Achieving Necessary Skills. (1991).*Skills and tasks for job: A SCANS report for America 2000.* Washington, DC: U.S. Government Printing Office.

Warnat, W. I. (1997). Building a school-to-work system in the United States. In L. McFarland (Ed), *New Visions: Education and training for an innovative workforce* (pp. 12-43). Berkley: National Center for Research in Vocational Education, University of California.

Webb, M. (2004). *What is the cost of planning and implementing early college high schools?* Boston: Jobs for the Future.

Achieving Equity through Enrichment: Bilingual Education

7

Mariela A. Rodríguez
María Luisa González

Teachers and administrators must understand the nature
of bilingualism and the importance of advocacy for all students.
In this manner educators can collectively make decisions
that will benefit students in bilingual programs.

—*Rodriguez & González*

Objectives

1. Discuss language attitudes, beliefs about bilingual education programs, and the way federal legislation has impacted the education of English language learners
2. Describe the difference between enrichment and remedial models of bilingual education
3. Discuss the important role that school leaders and teachers play in supporting bilingual education programs

Introduction

What's in a name? The term *bilingual education* conjures up a myriad of perceptions. It has its advocates and those who oppose it. Each belief system stems from epistemological views held by individuals. Some of these views are political while others are influenced by society at large. Various stigmas are often associated with participation in bilingual education programs. In the recent past a label, limited English proficient (LEP), was assigned to students in public schools who did not speak English well. This label in itself demonstrates a deficit attitude toward such students. The label reinforces what these students lack, rather than the strengths they bring to school. Their native language is a strength that is often not capitalized within classroom instruction.

In a rush to help students acquire English without an adequate foundation in their native language, these students often struggle academically. Rather than focus on limitations, a new term has emerged that highlights the strengths of students—that is, English language learner (ELL). This new term signals a move to counter the stigma for students participating in these programs. We prefer the use of ELL; however, other terms are in use and will be seen in this chapter, especially when other works are being cited. This chapter will review federal legislation that has impacted bilingual education programs and then the different models of bilingual education. The chapter will conclude with the important role of school leaders in supporting bilingual programs.

Demographics

The National Clearinghouse on English Language Acquisition (NCELA) maintains data regarding student enrollment in U.S. public schools. In the section labeled "LEP Enrollment Growth," the state of Texas experienced an increase in LEP student enrollment of almost 40% between the 1997–1998 and 2006–2007 school years—that is, over 600,000 students. A percentage increase of almost 40% in 10 years is sizable and resulted in the state of Texas becoming a majority-minority state in 2005. Latinos are the largest minority in Texas. Georgia experienced an increase of over 400% in the enrollment of ELLs between 1997–1998 and 2007–2008. An even larger increase in ELLs occurred in South Carolina; the Palmetto State experienced an ELL enrollment increase of over 800% in the same time span. These increases in the enrollment of students who are learning English have implications for educators in these schools and districts. Changes in practices and policies will be needed for educators to be effectively prepared to meet the needs of culturally and linguistically diverse (CLD) students.

The National Center for Education Statistics' Condition of Education reported that the number of school-age children who spoke a language other than English reached over 10 million in 2004 (Aud et al., 2010). Shin and Kominski (2010) referenced the American Community Surveys (2007) reported by the U.S. Census Bureau as identifying Spanish as the most commonly spoken language other than English. Through this same report, they also learned that Spanish-speakers who self-identified as speaking English less than "very well" had the highest percentage of having less than a high school education and the lowest percentage of having earned a bachelor's degree or higher. The national population of ELLs is almost 10 million; Spanish is the most common of over 400 different languages spoken by these students (Center on Instruction, 2006). Given these statistics and national projections, it is imperative that teachers and school leaders be prepared to work effectively with second language learners.

Language Attitudes

Language attitudes in the United States stem from years of discrimination and persistent misconceptions about second language learners. The attitudes in the country today toward languages other than English are ambivalent, at best. Some persons for whom English is a second language face prejudices in schools, workplaces, and communities; those on the receiving end of these prejudices are often immigrants and second language learners. A major misconception is that these people are not as intelligent as their English-speaking counterparts. This misconception is often due to an assumption that individuals whose native language is not English or who speak English with an accent are not academically successful. This deficit perspective perpetuates negative attitudes toward ELLs. Sadly this perspective is pervasive in the public school system, higher education, and work environments. The language attitudes of all persons can be influenced through education about the benefits of bilingualism and meaningful reflection and experiences.

Background

The Office for Civil Rights (OCR) enforces Title VI of the Civil Rights Act of 1964. The OCR plays a critical role in bilingual education. First, OCR ensures that students who are learning English are not discriminated against in schools. As second critical role of OCR is to ensure that the bilingual education programs are in place and meet three principles.

> The first principle is the rationale for selecting an educational approach. School districts must select sound, research-based educational strategies for bilingual education programs.

> The second principle focuses on the implementation of the selected educational approach. This implementation involves the school district providing the resources that will help execute the approach effectively.

> The third principle involves an annual program evaluation that yields information regarding student progress. Program evaluation is key in determining whether or not the selected educational approach meets student academic needs. This process allows district educators to acknowledge which aspects of the program are successful and which need to be modified.

From *Lau v. Nichols* to NCLB

Bilingual education has been shaped by key legislation. A landmark case that put bilingual education on the map was the 1970 U.S. Supreme Court case *Lau v. Nichols*. The case centered on a lawsuit brought forth by parents of Chinese students against the school district of San Francisco alleging that the district's practices violated their equal rights. In the end, the Supreme Court ruled against the school district. Justice Douglas wrote:

> Under these state-imposed standards there is no equality of treatment merely by providing students with the same facilities, textbooks, teachers, and curriculum; for students who do not understand English are effectively foreclosed from any meaningful education. Basic English skills are at the very core of what these public schools teach. Imposition of a requirement that, before a child can effectively participate in the educational program, he must already have acquired those basic skills is to make a *mockery of public education*

(emphasis authors'). We know that those who do not understand English are certain to find their classroom experiences wholly incomprehensible and in no way meaningful *(Lau v. Nichols, 1974).*

Table 7-1 offers a quick review of the various court cases (at all levels of the judicial system) that have influenced bilingual education in some way. Complete citations for each of the cases listed is offered in the reference section at the end of this chapter for those interested in delving more deeply into the details of the litigation aspects of ELLs.

Title VII of the Elementary and Secondary Education Act (ESEA) of 1968 focused on educating students who were learning English as a second language. This section of the legislation provided funding for school districts that were providing bilingual programs for students. Title VII required that programs be offered when at least 25 students of the same language group are identified. Almost 20 years later, the Bilingual Education Act of 1984 gave state education agencies and local education agencies more flexibility regarding the models of bilingual education utilized.

In 2004, ESEA was reauthorized under the title of the No Child Left Behind (NCLB) Act. This legislation markedly impacted bilingual education. By removing the term "bilingual education" from the legislation, NCLB's Title III: Language Instruction for Limited English Proficient and Immigrant Students focuses on funding programs that

Table 7-1   Court Cases Impacting Bilingual Education*

Case and Court	Result
Serna v. Portales Municipal Schools (1974) 9th Circuit Court of Appeals	Appeal courts ruled that students have a right to bilingual education.
Aspira of New York, Inc. v. Board of Education of the City of New York (1977) Federal Court New York City	No court decision, but parties agreed to a consent decree. The school district agreed to follow Lau. The district also agreed not to use submersion to teach non-English-speaking students.
Rios v. Reed (1978) District Court, New York	Non-English-speaking students have a right to quality bilingual education.
Otero v. Mesa County Valley School District No. 51 (1972)	Court rejected the right to a specific bilingual education program.
Keyes v. School District No. 1, Denver, Colorado (1975) 10th Circuit Court of Appeals	Court ruled that it was not up to the courts to mandate specific programs.
Guadalupe Organization, Inc. v. Tempe Elementary School District No. 3 (1978)	Bureau of Indian Affairs was not required to offer bilingual education programs.
Idaho Migrant Council v. Board of Education (1981) 9th Circuit Court of Appeals	State agencies have the power and responsibility to supervise bilingual education programs in public schools.
Gomez v. Illinois State Board of Education (1987) 7th Circuit Court of Appeals	State boards of education have the responsibility to supervise educational programs for English language learners.
California Teachers Association v. State Board of Education (2001)	Court ruled that Proposition 227 did not have a "chilling effect" on freedom of speech.

*Adapted from Gómez, L., & J. A. Ruiz-Escalante. (2005). Achieving equity through enrichment bilingual education. In A. Pankake, M. Littleton, & G. Schroth, *The Administration & Supervision of Special Programs in Education* (2nd ed., pp. 95–112). Dubuque, IA: Kendall/Hunt.

promote English language acquisition. This refocus of purpose makes the priority transitioning students from their native language to English as efficiently as possible rather than maintenance of the student's native language.

Beginning in the late 1990s, voters in the states of California, Arizona, and Massachusetts passed legislation that replaced bilingual education with English immersion. These decisions impacted thousands of ELLs. While research studies differ on the impact English immersion programs have on the academic achievement of second language learners, the use of English immersion substantially limits bilingual education strategies that support ELLs.

Actions, such as dropping bilingual programs and offering only English immersion, perpetuate the attitude that the English language is better than other languages. A shift in language attitudes can only occur when the public understands the value of learning more than one language. Being multilingual benefits the educational system, the workforce, and the economy. By being able to communicate with a variety of entities, the person who speaks more than one language plays a more active role in a global society.

Assessment and Accountability

Another significant impact on the education of ELLs from the No Child Left Behind Act is the structured accountability mandates that have been placed on them. Students must meet annual targets on specified measures in order attain adequate yearly progress (AYP). Academic indicators identified as annual measurable achievement objectives (AMAOs) are the benchmarks that students must meet. Such objectives are determined by school districts which confirm students are making progress toward English language acquisition. ELLs must demonstrate English proficiency in speaking, listening, reading, and writing. Each state determines how progress in each of these areas will be measured. In Texas, for example, the Texas English Language Proficiency Assessment System (TELPAS) serves as the assessment system that helps identify student progress in the four required areas for ELLs.

Basis of Second Language Learning

English language learners traditionally have a foundation in their native language (L1). It is important to have such a foundation so that students can then transition more effectively to English (L2). Language researcher Jim Cummins (1986) identified two dimensions of language that students must meet on their way to language proficiency. The first dimension is Basic Interpersonal Communication Skills (BICS). When operating in this dimension, students build on oral language development through social communication. This could take place in and out of classrooms through formal and informal settings. It is important for students to progress through BICS as they approach Cognitive Academic Language Proficiency (CALP). CALP is academic English that students must master to be successful in content areas at advanced levels. Other researchers, such as Thomas and Collier (1997), identified that learning a second language takes about 5 to 7 years. When considering such information in the context of the accountability demands, it is important for educators to understand how these are in conflict. Since students vary in the time it takes them to progress through stages of language development, pushing them to acquire English before they are ready can mean that they miss important steps. Locating, adopting, and implementing a model of bilingual education that fits within the dimensions of second language learning are imperative if long-term student success is of primary concern.

Models of Bilingual Education

There are two types of bilingual education models. The first type is remedial. The models within remedial bilingual education focus on accelerating ELLs toward the acquisition of English. Since the purpose of these models is not necessarily the maintenance of a student's native language while acquiring English, the model is often referred to by experts in the field as subtractive. Remedial or subtractive models are built on the perspective that the non-English language is a deficit or a problem that must be corrected. Depending on the specific model, little or no attention is devoted to fully developing the L1 of the students enrolled. Some of these models include submersion, English as a second language (ESL), and transitional bilingual education (TBE). These models attempt to expedite students' acquisition of English; some students, however, may not be prepared to meet the rapid transition expectations of such programs.

Other models fall into the type categorized as enrichment or additive bilingual education. These models assume that the student's non-English language is positive, not a negative. Enrichment or additive models seek to maintain a student's native language while they are learning English. Every effort is made to fully develop the student's native language and use it as a resource for English acquisition. The most popular enrichment model is dual language education. According to the Center for Applied Linguistics (CAL), as of 2011, there are almost 200 dual language education programs in 100 school districts in 19 states. Dual language education is a model of bilingual education for native English speakers and native speakers of another language, with the goal of promoting high academic achievement, development of both languages, and a cross-cultural experience for all students involved (Howard & Sugarman, 2007).

Dual language models vary based on the proportion of instruction in one language or the other. Some dual language models include a 50/50 balance of instruction in both languages A less balanced model is the 90/10 language model with the vast majority of instruction in only one of the languages (Soltero, 2004). According to Thomas and Collier (2003), the benefits of learning two languages supports student's future academic success as longitudinal research has demonstrated. Through their research, Collier and Thomas (2009) determined that students who participated in a dual language education program showed higher normal curve equivalent scores than students in other models of bilingual education. As the evidence for the benefits for dual language education continues to emerge, ensuring that teachers and administrators understand the school-wide efforts that must be in place to maintain program fidelity will be imperative. These efforts include (a) pedagogical equity in both languages of instruction, (b) supporting effective bilingual teachers, (c) getting parents involved with program development, and (d) continuity of school leaders who understand the importance of bilingualism and biliteracy (Alanís & Rodríguez, 2008).

Gomez and Ruiz-Escalante (2005) developed Table 7-2 as a quick reference regarding various models for bilingual education. All of the models presented earlier are included here and a few that were not a part of the earlier discussion. A variety of models are available for consideration; in every instance, however, the local needs of students and the state and federal regulations should take priority in decision making.

School-Based Indicators

There are several indicators that must be present in schools for ELLs to flourish in bilingual education programs (Rodríguez, 2008). Teachers and administrators must understand the nature of bilingualism and the importance of advocacy for all students. In this

Table 7-2   **Remedial versus Enrichment Models for Educating Language Minority Students***

Model or Program	Description	Linguistic/Academic and Cultural Goal
Remedial and Subtractive Models of Bilingual Education		
Sub-mersion	Academic instruction in L2 only for language minority students. No instructional support is provided by a trained specialist. This model fails to meet the guidelines set forth in the Supreme Court decision in *Lau v. Nichols*.	Monolingualism and full assimilation
Language-based ESL	Language instruction in L2 only for language minority students. Typically, L2 language instruction, taught by second language specialists, is sequenced and grammatically based.	Monolingualism and full assimilation
Content-based ESL	Academic instruction in L2 only for language minority students. L2 instruction is taught via a content-area by second language specialists. L1 used for concept clarification.	Monolingualism and full assimilation
Early-exit transitional bilingual education	Academic instruction in both L1 and L2 for language minority students only, with minimal emphasis on the L1. Typically implemented PK–3. Continuous emphasis on L2.	Minimal bilingualism and full assimilation
Late-exit transitional bilingual education	Academic instruction in both L1 and L2 for language minority students only, with emphasis on the L2. Typically implemented PK–5.	Moderate bilingualism and assimilation
Enrichment and Additive Models of Bilingual Education		
Immersion education	Academic instruction through both L1 and L2 for K–12. Originally developed for language majority students in Canada.	Biliteracy pluralism
Dual language education	Academic instruction in both L1 and L2 for either language minority or majority students or both together (two way). Percentage of language instruction varies in 90–10 and 50–50 models.	Biliteracy pluralism
Mainten-ance bilingual education	Academic instruction in both L1 and L2 for language minority students only with emphasis on the L1. Typically implemented PK–6.	Biliteracy pluralism

*Adapted from Gómez, L., & J. A. Ruiz-Escalante. (2005). Achieving equity through enrichment bilingual education. In A. Pankake, M. Littleton, & G. Schroth, *The Administration & Supervision of Special Programs in Education* (2nd ed., pp. 95–112). Dubuque, IA: Kendall/Hunt.

manner educators can collectively make decisions that will benefit students in bilingual programs. Additionally, educators can maintain constant communication regarding student achievement and program effectiveness among stakeholders. Teachers should be caring individuals who hold high expectations of students. Additionally, principals should make a concerted effort to remain current about effective teaching practices for bilingual students. These campus leaders must frequently observe classroom instruction to make sure that best practices that support language learning are being used regularly. Instructional leaders must demonstrate a combination of skills and knowledge to successfully lead a school in providing quality education for ELLs (González, 1998). ELL students need advocates who can empower stakeholders through a supportive network that is student-centered; communication and collaboration are key to this process. Through a shared commitment by the principal, teachers, staff, parents, students, and community, the school will be able to sustain a program of enriched language learning. Teachers and school leaders who understand the value of building on a child's native language will advocate for the adoption of dual language models as the norm. They will present this model as a teaching tool in oral and written language development that will enhance learning opportunities for students in two or even more languages.

Conclusion

There are several indicators that must be present in schools for ELLs to flourish in bilingual education programs (Rodríguez, 2008). Teachers and administrators must understand the nature of bilingualism and the importance of advocacy for all students. In this manner educators can collectively make decisions that will benefit students in bilingual programs. Additionally, educators can maintain constant communication regarding student achievement and program effectiveness among stakeholders. Teachers should be caring individuals who hold high expectations of students. Additionally, principals should make a concerted effort to remain current about effective teaching practices for bilingual students. These campus leaders must frequently observe classroom instruction to make sure that best practices that support language learning are being used regularly. Instructional leaders must demonstrate a combination of skills and knowledge to successfully lead a school in providing quality education for ELLs (González, 1998). ELL students need advocates who can empower stakeholders through a supportive network that is student-centered; communication and collaboration are key to this process.

Applying Your Knowledge

You are the bilingual coordinator for a school district enrolling approximately 20,000 students in grades PK–12. The district has provided a bilingual program for students over the last 25 years; until recently that program served the large non-English population of Latin American immigrants. Now because of some economic changes, including new industries, there is need to provide bilingual services for recently arrived Korean students. You have been charged by the superintendent of schools to bring together a team that represents the various district internal and external stakeholders to (a) determine the effectiveness of current bilingual program models used in the district; (b) identify what changes, if any, are needed to serve the needs of all English language learners in the district; and (c) recommend budgetary and staffing plans to align with the findings of the team.

QUESTIONS

1. Who would you invite to serve on the team? Why?
2. How would you go about determining the program effectiveness of current programs? Who should be involved in this assessment of these programs? Why?
3. As you understand the various bilingual instructional models, what would you recommend as the best model to address the needs of the growing populations of Korean ELLs? Should the model used for the Korean ELLs be the same as the one used for the Hispanic ELLs? Why or why not?
4. What are the various things you and your team need to include in your budgetary and staffing recommendations?

QUESTIONS FOR THOUGHT

1. Who are the ELLs identified in your school district and campus? Which languages do they speak? How are their linguistic needs being served?
2. In which ways do the language attitudes of teachers affect their relationship with students in the classroom? What could be done to influence teacher attitudes toward ELLs?
3. If enrichment bilingual models such as dual language education offer more benefits than other types of programs, why aren't more schools adopting this model?
4. What are some ways in which school principals can demonstrate their advocacy for ELLs?

For Additional Information Online

National Association for Bilingual Education (NABE), http://www.nabe.org/

Texas Education Agency Bilingual Education, http://www.tea.state.tx.us/

Public Broadcasting System (PBS), http://www.pbs.org/kcet/publicschool/roots_in_history/bilingual.html/

Texas Association for Bilingual Education (TABE), http://www.tabe.org/

Rethinking Schools – Special Reports – Bilingual Education Resources, http://www.rethinkingschools.org/special_reports/bilingual/resources.shtml

Bilingual Education: An Overview, http://www.policyalmanac.org/education/archive/bilingual.pdf

Center on Instruction English Language Learners Strand, Texas Institute for Measurement, Evaluation, and Statistics University of Houston, www.centeroninstruction.org

References

Alanís, I., & Rodríguez, M. A. (2008). Sustaining a two-way immersion program: Features of success. *Journal of Latinos and Education, 7*(4), 305–319.

Aspira of New York, Inc. v. Board of Education of the City of New York, 394 F. Supp. 1161 (S.D. N.Y 1973).

Aud, S., Hussar, W., Planty, M., Snyder, T., Bianco, K., Fox, M., Frohlich, L., Kemp, J., & Drake, L. (2010). *The condition of education 2010* (NCES 2010-028). Washington, DC: National Center for Education Statistics, Institute of Education Sciences, U.S. Department of Education. *California Teachers Association v. State Board of Education,* 263 F. 3rd 888 (9th Cir 2001). Center for Applied Linguistics. (2011). *Directory of two-way bilingual immersion programs in the U.S.* Available from http://www.cal.org/twi/

Center on Instruction. (2006). Practical guidelines for the education of English language learners: Research-based recommendations for instruction and academic interventions. Available at: http://www.centeroninstruction.org/practical-guidelines for-education-of-english-language-learners-research-based-recommendation.

Collier, V. P., & Thomas, W. P. (2009). Educating English learners for a transformed world. Albuquerque, NM: Dual Language Education of New Mexico and Fuente Press.

Cummins, J. (1986). Empowering minority students: A framework for intervention. *Harvard Education Review, 56*(1), 18–36.

Gómez, L., & Ruiz-Escalante, J. A. (2005). Achieving equity through enrichment bilingual education. In A. Pankake, M. Littleton, & G. Schroth (Eds.), *The Administration & Supervision of Special Programs in Education* (2nd ed., pp. 95–112). Dubuque, IA: Kendall/Hunt.

Gomez v. Illinois Board of Education, 811 F. 2nd 1030 (7th Cir. 1987).

González, M. L. (1998). Successfully educating Latinos: The pivotal role of the principal. In M. L. González, A. Huerta-Macías, & J. Villamil Tinajero (Eds.), *Successfully educating Latino students: A guide to successful practice* (pp. 3–28). Lancaster, PA: Technomic Publishing Co., Inc.

Guadalupe Organization, Inc. v. Tempe, 587 F. 2d 1022 (Circuit, 1978).

Howard, E. R., & Sugarman, J. (2007). *Realizing the vision of two-way immersion: Fostering effective programs and classrooms.* Washington, DC: Center for Applied Linguistics.

Idaho Migrant Council v. Board of Education, 647 F. 2d 69 (10th Cir. 1981).

Keyes v. School District No. 1, Denver, Colorado, 521 F. 2d 465 (10th Cir. 1975).

Lau v. Nichols, 414 U.S. 563 (1974).

Otero v. Mesa County Valley School District No. 51, 408 F. Supp. 162 (D.C. Colo. 1972).

Rios v. Reed, 480 F. Supp. 14 (U.S. D.C. E.D.N.Y. 1978).

Rodríguez, M. A. (2008). Program quality indicators. In J. M. González (Ed.), *Encyclopedia of Bilingual Education* (pp. 682–684). Thousand Oaks, CA: Sage.

Serna v. Portales Municipal Schools, 351 G. Supp. 1279 (N.D. N. Mex. 1972).

Shin, H. B., & Kominski, R. A. (2010). Language use in the United States: 2007, American Community Survey Reports, ACS 12. Washington, DC: U.S. Census Bureau.

Soltero, S. W. (2004). *Dual language: Teaching and learning in two languages.* Boston: Pearson.

Thomas, W. P., & Collier, V. (1997). *School effectiveness for language minority students.* Report disseminated by the National Clearinghouse for Bilingual Education.

Thomas, W. P., & Collier, V. P. (2003). The multiple benefits of dual language. *Educational Leadership, 61*(2), 61–64.

Early Childhood/Early Childhood Special Education

8

Mary Kay Zabel

Since the National Association for the Education of
Young Children (NAEYC) defines "early childhood"
as the ages of birth through eight years (www.naeyc.org),
it is clear that any elementary school contains
a number of ECE programs and classrooms.

—Mary Kay Zabel

Objectives

1. Understand the principles of developmentally appropriate practice and their application to programs for all young children
2. Discuss the principles and methods of appropriate assessment for young children with disabilities and their typical peers
3. Identify the continuum of programs and intervention practices that should be available for infants and young children with and without disabilities, and the role of families in these programs
4. Apply this knowledge by assessing programs for young children in a particular school or district

Historical/Legislative Background

National and legislative interest in the care and education of young children began to surface in the United States in the early 1900s. At this time, daycare centers were operated selectively and were a part of the social welfare system, designed for "pathological" families (Howard, Williams, Port, & Lepper, 2001). The Great Depression and the Works Progress Administration (WPA) furthered the notion that young children could benefit from group care by establishing 1,900 WPA daycare centers serving 40,000 children by 1937 (Howard et al., 2001). As World War II took its toll on the families of the world, Europe and the United States increased the numbers and types of childcare available to parents and children.

In the 1950s, investigations into the effect of poverty on children and families became a policy initiative, culminating in the passage of the Economic Opportunity Act of 1964. This legislation eventually resulted in the creation of the Head Start program—a program which "recognized the linkage between children's health and development, the importance of local community-based control, the emphasis on supporting parents in their decision making, and the need to be able to thoughtfully coordinate the many needed services from different domains . . ." (Guralnick, 1997, p. 4). Very soon after the establishment of Project Head Start (1965), the Handicapped Children's Early Education Program was created (1968) to fund model preschool programs for children with disabilities. The continued progress and development of both these strands of early childhood education have been closely linked from that point. In 1972, Congress required Head Start to reserve 10% of its enrollment for children with disabilities, and in 1975, PL 94-142, the Education for All Handicapped Children Act (EAHCA), provided incentive funding for programs serving children ages 3–5 who had disabilities. Each subsequent amendment of EAHCA has provided for more services for young children with disabilities, and programs serving these children are now required of all schools by the Individuals with Disabilities Education Act (IDEA).

Many states now endorse or certify teachers of young children with a "blended" or "integrated" license. Such an endorsement credential often combines early childhood education and early childhood special education in one license, rather than having separate licensure for each. In addition, programs for infants and toddlers (birth to age 3) are often a part of this mix. While programs for children 3 years of age and older are clearly a part of each school district's responsibility, the supervision of programs for infants and toddlers varies from state to state. Each state identifies a lead agency to oversee these programs, which can vary with the decision of the state agencies. Approximately equal numbers of states selected their Department of Education or their Department of Health to administer this part of IDEA, while remaining states and territories designated other agencies such as Mental Health, Mental Retardation, or Human Resources as their lead agencies (Howard et al., 2001). (In Texas, the Health and Human Services Commission, Department of Assistive and Rehabilitative Services Division, or HHSC-DARS, is responsible for serving children birth to age 3 with special needs.)

Program Description

Two of the major themes in early childhood education and early childhood special education are developmentally appropriate practice and natural environments. Developmentally appropriate practice (DAP) is the title given to the widely researched and accepted outline of factors necessary for high-quality care and education of young children. It is promoted and disseminated by the National Association for the Education of Young Children (NAEYC) and forms the bedrock for many of the decisions made by teachers and administrators every day. According to Bredekamp and Copple (1997, pp. 10–15), 12 principles delineate DAP:

1. Domains of children's development—physical, social, emotional, and cognitive—are closely related. Development in one domain influences and is influenced by development in other domains.
2. Development occurs in a relatively orderly sequence, with later abilities, skills, and knowledge building on those already acquired.
3. Development proceeds at varying rates from child to child as well as unevenly within different areas of each child's functioning.
4. Early experiences have both cumulative and delayed effects on individual children's development; optimal periods exist for certain types of development and learning.
5. Development proceeds in predictable directions toward greater complexity, organization, and internalization.
6. Development and learning occur in, and are influenced by, multiple social and cultural contexts.
7. Children are active learners, drawing on direct physical and social experience as well as culturally transmitted knowledge to construct their own understandings of the world around them.
8. Development and learning result from interaction of biological maturation and the environment, which includes both the physical and social worlds that children live in.
9. Play is an important vehicle for children's social, emotional, and cognitive development, as well as a reflection of their development.
10. Development advances when children have opportunities to practice newly acquired skills as well as when they experience a challenge just beyond the level of their present mastery.
11. Children demonstrate different modes of knowing and learning, and different ways of representing what they know.
12. Children develop and learn best in the context of a community where they are safe and valued, their physical needs are met and they feel psychologically secure. (Also available on NAEYC website, www.naeyc.org)

While all of these principles are important for administrators and school leaders in constructing quality programs for young children, one of the most critical is number nine—the importance of play. In this era of high stakes testing, quality performance assessments, and outcomes-based learning, it is critical for school leaders to understand the vital nature of play in the development of cognitive, social, motor, and language skills in the young child. As Lamb stated (2001), "Creating a learning environment based on play activities requires considerable time, commitment, and resources" (p. 100). Both children with disabilities and their typically developing peers learn and expand their horizons through play activities. Their interactions with each other, their observation of peers using materials in various ways, and their exposure to various play environments are crucial to the acquisition of skills that will allow them to be successful students in the upper grades.

Identification and Assessment

Children under age 5 are identified for inclusion in early childhood education (ECE) and early childhood special education (ECSE) programs in a variety of ways. Children entering Head Start programs must meet income guidelines based on the

Department of Health and Human Services poverty level delineations for the current year. As stated previously, 10% of the enrollment of Head Start classes is reserved for students with disabilities; these disabilities can be in any area of development, including speech and language. For example, in Texas, in order for a child to be counted as part of the 10% with disabilities for Head Start, the child must meet the eligibility guidelines for special education or early childhood intervention (IDEA Part B for 3–5 and IDEA Part C for birth–3). In other words, Head Start does not have its own guidelines for determining disability. Young children who might need services provided in ECSE programs for 3- to 5-year-olds can be referred by parents who have concerns about the development of their children, physicians who have similar concerns, or the children may be identified in a district-wide screening open to all families residing in the district. These screenings, usually staffed by district personnel, have as their sole purpose the identification of children who might benefit from further assessment. No diagnostic, programmatic, or referral decisions should be made on the basis of a screening test, as these are only designed to note the need for further information.

Once children in the 3–5 age range have been referred by a parent or other interested party, or have been identified as needing further assessment by a screening, assessment procedures similar to those for older children with disabilities are considered. All the procedural safeguards, notification requirements, and parental permissions required for any child under IDEA are also required for young children (in this book, see Chapter 1 Special Education). In addition, the Division for Early Childhood, a division of the Council for Exceptional Children, suggested the following recommended practices designed to fully include families in the assessment procedure, to see that assessment is individualized and appropriate, and to ensure that assessment provides useful information for intervention. These practices are for families with children in the infant toddler range as well as the 3–5 age group (Sandall, McLean, & Smith, 2000, p. 23). Some of the recommended practices for including families are:

1. Professionals provide families with easy access by phone or other means for arranging initial screening and other activities.
2. Professionals ensure a single point of contact for families throughout the assessment process.
3. Families receive a written statement of program philosophy regarding family participation in assessment planning and activities.

Recommended practices for ensuring individualized and appropriate assessment for the child and family include (Sandall et al., 2000, p. 24):

1. Professionals use multiple measures to assess child status, progress, and program impact and outcomes (e.g., developmental observations, criterion/curriculum-based interviews, informed clinical opinion, and curriculum-compatible norm-referenced scales).
2. Professionals choose materials and procedures that accommodate the child's sensory, physical, responsive, and temperamental differences.
3. Professionals rely on materials that capture the child's authentic behaviors in routine circumstances.
4. Professionals seek information directly from families and other regular caregivers, using materials and procedures that the families themselves can manage, to design Individual Family Service Plan/Individual Education Plan (IFSP/IEP) goals and activities.
5. Professionals assess children in contexts that are familiar to the child.

Practices ensuring that assessment provides useful information for intervention include (Sandall et al., 2000, p. 25):

1. Families and professionals assess the presence and extent of atypical child behavior that may be a barrier to intervention and progress.
2. Professionals use functional behavioral analysis to assess the form and function of challenging behaviors.
3. Program supervisors, in concert with the ECE/ECSE team, use only those measures that have high treatment validity (i.e., that link assessment, individual program planning, and progress evaluation).
4. Professionals appraise the level of support that a child requires in order to perform a task.
5. Professionals report assessment results in a manner that is immediately useful for planning program goals and objectives.

While even these abbreviated lists (for full lists see Sandall et al., 2000) seem daunting in their length and detail, such attention to the procedure and content of assessment practices is necessary when working with children where diagnostic labels may be difficult or impossible to apply, and where the full participation of the family is critical.

Most programs for children 3 to 5 years of age who have disabilities also include typically developing peers. This program model has become the most popular way of serving the educational needs of young children with disabilities because of its emphasis on the development of typical behaviors and skills.

Deciding on the method of choosing typical peers is an important part of the ECE/ECSE team's (including the principal or other designated school leader) program design. Some school districts accept applications and place typical peers on a first come, first served basis, while others review the applications and try to balance the class in terms of age and gender. An approach used by some school districts gives the preschool-age children of teachers in the district first chance at these typical peer slots. That procedure often increases the likelihood that the typical peers will have good language, cognitive, and social skills—in addition to providing a nice perk to teachers. Whatever the method used, care should be taken to ensure that the typical peers do, in fact, exhibit development appropriate to their age. It is tempting to utilize peer spaces to serve children who do not meet the requirements for special education service, but would nonetheless benefit from such help. While this is a laudable intention, it does defeat the purpose of having typical peers for the children with disabilities and can substantially add to the ECE/ECSE teacher's actual caseload, without increasing resources.

Program Models

There are many different models of service provision in this area of education/special education. For the purposes of clarity, they will be discussed under three broad headings: infant/toddler programs (children with disabilities only); early childhood/early childhood special education integrated programs; and separate early childhood and early childhood special education programs.

INFANT/TODDLER PROGRAMS

As discussed earlier in this chapter, these programs may come under the lead of many different state agencies, but no matter which lead agency is chosen (education, health, mental retardation, developmental disabilities), the school district is inevitably part of the plan. District involvement can vary from state to state as well as one program model to another. For example, in Texas, if children have an identified vision or hearing problem, special education teachers from the school district will generally be part of the plan for services. Likewise, if parents want transition to the school district at age 3, the transition outcomes in the plan will address the school district. But in many cases, in the Texas ECI program, the school district and its services are not a part of the child's plan until the child is nearly 3 years old. Most first contacts for families seeking services for their infant or toddler whom they suspect may have developmental delays are either members of the medical community or the school. Because of the frequent involvement of schools, it is critical that a first contact person be clearly designated by the school district, and such information publicized where parents can find it. Information on screening, referral processes, and information sources should be provided to physicians' offices, public health departments, social services offices, churches, schools, and other places where parents of young children might be found. Once families in need of services have been identified, the above assessment practices should be put into place and assessment conducted in the areas of specific needs.

After the assessment process has been concluded, an Individual Family Service Plan (IFSP) is written for the child and his or her family. This plan is similar to an IEP, but has some important differences. First of all, the inclusion of the word "family" in the title is no accident. While the IEP focuses on the needs of the child, the IFSP focuses on family needs. The infant or toddler is always viewed in the context of his or her family. IFSPs seek to strengthen the family's ability to enhance the child's development, and this is done through a series of outcomes and activities, not the goals and objectives and/or benchmarks found in the IEP. The IFSP resembles the IEP, however, in that it is written in full collaboration with parents and team members; that the team sees all outcomes and activities as essential to the child's optimal development; and that transitions to other levels of service (center-based programs, for example) are a part of the plan.

If the infant or toddler qualifies for services, the next decision centers on what services should be provided. The recommended practice is that infant/toddler services—whether provided by a speech/language therapist, an occupational/physical therapist, an early intervention teacher (ECSE), an early intervention specialist (EIS), or a combination of these and other professionals—should be in the "natural environment" where "natural routines" can be a part of the process (Raver, 1999). The natural environment for most infants is, of course, the home. Services may be provided in the child's home, the home of another caregiver (e.g., relative, daycare provider), or some other environment that is a part of the child's natural routine. Clearly, the purpose of such placement of services is designed to help parents integrate exercises, activities, learning strategies, and language experiences into the daily fabric of their lives with their children. Activities and experiences that can be integrated into meal times, bath times, diaper changing times—any aspect of the family's routine—is the goal for interventionists at this level. Learning experiences integrated in this way are much more likely to be repeated, reinforced, and made a part of what happens in this family on a daily basis.

EARLY CHILDHOOD EDUCATION/EARLY CHILDHOOD SPECIAL EDUCATION INTEGRATED PROGRAM

Programs for 3- to 5-year-olds with and without disabilities are based on two models. They may be *inclusive* (the main focus of the program is on typically developing young children, but children who have disabilities are welcomed, included, and curriculum and activities are adapted for their needs—Head Start is an example); or *integrated* (class sizes are smaller, program focus is on both children with disabilities and typically developing peers, and the ratio of children with disabilities to typical peers tends to be larger than in inclusive programs). In both types of programs, early childhood special education teachers, speech/language therapists, occupational/physical therapists, and other specialists may provide services in the classroom or other appropriate places.

Curriculum areas in the EC/ECSE classroom may include many different types of learning and exploration. This age group includes major goals such as helping children learn problem-solving skills, make choices, and engage in active exploration of the environment and materials. Teachers strive to provide engaging and stimulating settings, to promote a supportive classroom environment, and—perhaps most importantly—to create a language-rich environment (Dunlap, 1997). Acquiring a useful language system, whether it is spoken word, sign language, a picture exchange program, or a language system supported by assistive technology, is a critical task for the preschool years. Teachers of students with special needs as well as those of typically developing children emphasize, elaborate, generate, modify, and support all types of language use in the EC/ECSE classroom.

Teachers also provide dramatic play areas, where socialization skills may be learned and practiced, and children have an opportunity to work through areas in their lives where such play may help them sort out feelings and behavior. A reading or library center is an essential part of the EC/ECSE classroom where a comfortable environment and a wealth of interesting, engaging books encourage children to explore literature alone or with peers and teachers. An area with blocks for building, supporting math concepts, fine motor abilities, cooperative play, and problem solving is also an integral part of such a program (Lamb, 2001). Science and math materials, puzzles and games, an art activity center, and tables for sensory exploration, perhaps containing sand, water, or other materials, also aid in learning for all children (Lamb, 2001). Technology in the early childhood classroom is a current and controversial topic; NAEYC has a draft position statement on the topic. This will be an issue worth monitoring by school and classroom leaders.

Classroom assessment is a large part of any program serving young children, although such assessment may not resemble techniques used by teachers of children in upper grades. Children who have IEPs are, of course, continually assessed based on the goals, objectives, and benchmarks written by the IEP team to guide and evaluate their progress. Assessment in this area will largely rely on daily teacher observation and recording of data, and a clipboard or file system for each child is often utilized for this purpose. Also, teachers may use computers or other devices (e.g., PDAs or IPads) to document child progress on a daily basis. Other assessment systems, such as the Work Sampling System, are available for assessing progress for all children (Dichtelmiller, Jablon, Marsden, & Meisels, 2001). This system, available for preschool (age 3) through fifth grade, provides specific, measurable developmentally appropriate guidelines to "enhance the process of observation and to ensure the reliability and consistency of teachers' observations" (Dichtelmiller et al., 2001, p. vii). The guidelines are drawn from many local, state, and national standards supporting curriculum development. While this system incorporates standards from these various agencies, they do not form an external template designed to fit every child. As Meisels says, "[The Work Sampling System] does not stand on its own: it comes to life only in the hands of a teacher. Like a car it needs a driver, like a book it requires a reader, like a musical composition it calls for a performer" (Dichtelmiller et al., 2001, p. xiv). There are also curriculum planning programs, such as the Activity-Based Approach to Early Intervention, that integrate assessment, planning, and evaluation from the beginning, thus providing a linked system that supports positive outcomes for children (Bricker, Pretti-Frontczak, & McComas, 1998).

EARLY CHILDHOOD SPECIAL EDUCATION PROGRAMS

While the majority of school or center-based programs serving young children with special needs follow the integrated or inclusive models discussed above, there are programs where all the children enrolled have specific disabilities. These programs are sometimes associated with schools for older children serving that disability (e.g., state or regional schools for the blind or for the deaf), programs that serve low-incidence disabilities (e.g., deaf/blind) or programs that may be associated with public or private facilities (psychiatric centers or hospitals) (Handleman & Harris, 2001). These programs often make efforts to see that the children spend time in some way with typically developing peers. Peer interaction at any age, but particularly as children are acquiring and refining group social interaction skills, should be an essential part of any program.

EARLY CHILDHOOD PROGRAMS

Since the National Association for the Education of Young Children (NAEYC) defines "early childhood" as the ages of birth through 8 years (www.naeyc.org), it is clear that any elementary school contains a number of ECE programs and classrooms. Reconciling the growing demands for high stakes content testing at younger ages with the demonstrated and research-based needs for developmentally appropriate learning environments for young children is a major task for teachers and administrators. The goals of both are similar—at least in intent: to provide the best possible educational experience for children. Many teachers, however, focus on this task from an input perspective. They are most concerned with how the children acquire knowledge and skills, many employing a constructivist approach (leaning heavily on the work of Piaget) that emphasizes children being involved in authentic tasks, and working on projects that require active learning. The teachers' skills are utilized to integrate such learning into themes, set up opportunities for the learning to take place, and guide children on their own process of discovery (Branscombe, Castle, Dorsey, Surbeck, & Taylor, 2003). The focus of many governing bodies is on outcomes. The only questions being asked involve how well children have learned specific concepts and mastered specific skills.

While this may be something of an oversimplification of the issues, this is a debate that is going on in literally every state and locale in the nation. Our ability to resolve these competing agendas will be critical in the effort to provide a truly appropriate education to all children over the coming years. Issues such as content testing in Head Start, prekindergarten programs in all schools, and full day kindergarten are some of the points where these camps are engaging one another. Such dialogue is good if it eventually results in compromise that is beneficial. As Lamb (2001) points out, "Some communities feel the need for full-day rather than half-day kindergarten. Research has not shown that academic test scores increase when kindergarten is conducted for a full day; however, test scores in these early years are not accurate indicators of the long-term effects of early education on academic achievement, particularly if individual needs are met the first years of school" (p. 105). She goes on to point out that it *is* clear that for many children (particularly ELL students), kindergarten does provide a language-rich environment and a great opportunity for growth. She concludes, "The real question is whether or not a truly rich kindergarten program can be achieved in a 3- to 4-hour program. In kindergarten if children spend time in each learning center, engage in outdoor play, enjoy music and art, and are involved in large group activities, a half-day program may not suffice" (p. 106). This illustrates the task that is really before early childhood educators and administrators. The key is in asking the right questions: What constitutes a rich and responsive learning environment for young children? And how can we use and devise appropriate measures to demonstrate that it is effective? Our decisions must be based on what we know and what we continue to learn about quality programs for young children, and our commitment must be to see that they are implemented for all.

Assessing the Situation

Using the Administrator's Essentials Checklist for EC/ECSE, evaluate an early childhood program with which you are familiar. Are there aspects of the program that need immediate attention? Whose responsibility is it to see that these recommendations for appropriate practice are in place? Do you see areas where knowledge and skills may be at an awareness level, but need more resources? More focus? More administrative attention? What would the next steps be?

Administrator's Essentials Checklist for EC/ECSE

I. Administrators, other professionals, and families shape policy at the national, state, and local levels that promote the use of recommended practices in EC/ECSE.
Examples/Notes:

Is this practice evident in policy/procedure? ❑ *Yes* ❑ *Emerging* ❑ *No*

II. Administrators ensure that they and their staff have the knowledge, training, and credentials necessary to implement the recommended practices in EC/ECSE.

A. Program coordinators/supervisors have training in EC/ECSE, intervention, and supervision.
Examples/Notes:

Is this practice evident in policy/procedure? ❑ *Yes* ❑ *Emerging* ❑ *No*

B. Administrators are affiliated with professional EC/ECSE organizations and encourage staff to maintain their affiliations. Continuing education such as attendance at meetings and conferences to enhance professional growth is supported.
Examples/Notes:

Is this practice evident in policy/procedure? ❑ *Yes* ❑ *Emerging* ❑ *No*

1. Program policies provide clear job descriptions and provide for personnel competencies and on-going staff development, technical assistance, supervision, and evaluation to inform and improve the skills of practitioners and administrators.
Examples/Notes:

Is this practice evident in policy/procedure?   ❑ *Yes*   ❑ *Emerging*   ❑ *No*

III.   Program policies and administration promote families as partners in the planning and delivery of services, supports, and resources.

A. When creating program policies and procedures, strategies are employed to capture family and community voices and to support the active and meaningful participation of families and community groups including those that are traditionally underrepresented.
Examples/Notes:

Is this practice evident in policy/procedure?   ❑ *Yes*   ❑ *Emerging*   ❑ *No*

B. Program policies create a participatory decision-making process of all stakeholders including individuals with disabilities. Training in teaming is provided as needed.
Examples/Notes:

Is this practice evident in policy/procedure?   ❑ *Yes*   ❑ *Emerging*   ❑ *No*

C. Program policies ensure that families understand their rights including conflict resolution, confidentiality, and other matters.
Examples/Notes:

Is this practice evident in policy/procedure?   ❑ *Yes*   ❑ *Emerging*   ❑ *No*

D. Program policies are examined and revised as needed to ensure that they reflect and respect the diversity of children, families, and personnel.
Examples/Notes:

Is this practice evident in policy/procedure?   ❑ *Yes*   ❑ *Emerging*   ❑ *No*

E. Program policies are provided in sufficient detail and formats so that all stakeholders understand what the policy means.
Examples/Notes:

Is this practice evident in policy/procedure? ❑ *Yes* ❑ *Emerging* ❑ *No*

F. Program policies require a family-centered approach in all decisions and phases of service delivery (system entry, assessment procedures, IFSP/IEP, intervention, transition, etc.) including presenting families with flexible and individualized options for the location, timing, and types of services, supports, and resources that are not disruptive of family life.
Examples/Notes:

Is this practice evident in policy/procedure? ❑ *Yes* ❑ *Emerging* ❑ *No*

G. Program policies provide for the dissemination of information about program initiative and outcomes to stakeholders.
Examples/Notes:

Is this practice evident in policy/procedure? ❑ *Yes* ❑ *Emerging* ❑ *No*

IV. Program policies and administration promote the use of recommended practices.

A. Program policies reflect recommended practices including personnel standards, child-staff ratios, group size, caseloads, safety, assistive technology, and EC/ECSE service and practices. Incentives, training, and technical assistance to promote the use of recommended practices in all settings are provided.
Examples/Notes:

Is this practice evident in policy/procedure? ❑ *Yes* ❑ *Emerging* ❑ *No*

B. Program policies establish accountability systems that provide resources, supports, and clear action steps to ensure compliance with regulations and ensure that recommended practices are adopted, utilized, maintained, and evaluated resulting in high-quality services.
Examples/Notes:

Is this practice evident in policy/procedure? ❑ *Yes* ❑ *Emerging* ❑ *No*

C. Program policies support the provision of services in inclusive or natural learning environments (places in which typical children participate such as the home or community settings, public and private preschools, childcare, recreation groups, etc.). Strategies are used to overcome challenges to inclusion.
Examples/Notes:

Is this practice evident in policy/procedure? ❏ *Yes* ❏ *Emerging* ❏ *No*

D. Program policies ensure that the IFSP/IEP is used on a regular and frequent basis to determine the type and amounts of services, the location of services, and desired outcomes.
Examples/Notes:

Is this practice evident in policy/procedure? ❏ *Yes* ❏ *Emerging* ❏ *No*

E. Program policies ensure that family supports, service coordination, transitions, and other practices occur in response to the child and family needs rather than being determined by the age of the child.
Examples/Notes:

Is this practice evident in policy/procedure? ❏ *Yes* ❏ *Emerging* ❏ *No*

F. Program policies ensure that multiple instructional models are available to meet the individual needs of children (e.g., less structure–more structure; child-driven to teacher-driven; peer-mediated to teacher-mediated).
Examples/Notes:

Is this practice evident in policy/procedure? ❏ *Yes* ❏ *Emerging* ❏ *No*

G. Administrators provide for a supportive work environment (e.g., hiring and retention policies, compensation and benefits, safety, workspace).
Examples/Notes:

Is this practice evident in policy/procedure? ❏ *Yes* ❏ *Emerging* ❏ *No*

V. Program policies and administration promote interagency and interdisciplinary collaboration.

A. Program policies include structures and mechanisms such as job descriptions, planning time, training, and resources for teaming resulting in meaningful participation for ongoing coordination among professionals, families, and programs related to service delivery, including transition.
Examples/Notes:

Is this practice evident in policy/procedure? ❏ *Yes* ❏ *Emerging* ❏ *No*

B. Program policies facilitate and provide for comprehensive and coordinated systems of services through interagency collaboration by clearly delineating the components, activities, and responsibilities of all agencies.
Examples/Notes:

Is this practice evident in policy/procedure? ❏ *Yes* ❏ *Emerging* ❏ *No*

C. Program policies result in families and professionals from different disciplines working as a team developing and implementing IFSPs/IEPS that integrate their expertise into common goals.
Examples/Notes:

Is this practice evident in policy/procedure? ❏ *Yes* ❏ *Emerging* ❏ *No*

VI. Program policies, administration, and leadership promote program evaluation and systems change efforts at the community level.

A. A shared vision (of all stakeholders), clear values/beliefs, and an understanding of the culture and context to be changed guide efforts to restructure and reform systems. Decisions about what to change result from regu lar analysis and evaluation of discrepancies among the vision, beliefs, knowledge, and current practices.
Examples/Notes:

Is this practice evident in policy/procedure? ❏ *Yes* ❏ *Emerging* ❏ *No*

B. Assessment of the interests, issues, and priorities of constituent groups guides the selection and direction of leadership and systems change strategies.
Examples/Notes:

Is this practice evident in policy/procedure?   ❏ *Yes*   ❏ *Emerging*   ❏ *No*

C. Leadership and systems change efforts produce positive outcomes for children, families, and communities that are responsive to their needs. Evaluation data are used to ensure: (a) service utilization, (b) more efficient and effective supports for children, families, and staff, and (c) appropriate systems change leadership and strategies.
Examples/Notes:

Is this practice evident in policy/procedure?   ❏ *Yes*   ❏ *Emerging*   ❏ *No*

D. Leadership capacity, risk taking, and shared decision making among professionals and families at all levels of the organization are cultivated.
Examples/Notes:

Is this practice evident in policy/procedure?   ❏ *Yes*   ❏ *Emerging*   ❏ *No*

E. Leadership and systems change efforts include attention to: timely job-embedded professional development, funding, program evaluation, accountability, governance, program accreditation, curriculum and naturalistic instruction/supports.
Examples/Notes:

Is this practice evident in policy/procedure?   ❏ *Yes*   ❏ *Emerging*   ❏ *No*

F. Leadership and systems change efforts rely on strong relationships and collaboration within and across systems: between consumer and system, across systems that deal with children and families, among components within a system, and among professionals from diverse disciplines.
Examples/Notes:

Is this practice evident in policy/procedure?   ❏ *Yes*   ❏ *Emerging*   ❏ *No*

G. Leadership is committed and willing to change organizational structures (staffing, schedules, teaming) to be responsive to individual needs.

Examples/Notes:

Is this practice evident in policy/procedure? ❏ *Yes* ❏ *Emerging* ❏ *No*

H. Change is institutionalized through the development of coordinated management and accountability systems.

Examples/Notes:

Is this practice evident in policy/procedure? ❏ *Yes* ❏ *Emerging* ❏ *No*

I. Resources are provided for program evaluation that occurs along established time points, incorporating appropriate measurable indicators of progress including child and family outcomes and preferences.

Examples/Notes:

Is this practice evident in policy/procedure? ❏ *Yes* ❏ *Emerging* ❏ *No*

J. Program evaluation is comprehensive, is multidimensional, and incorporates a variety of methods for assessing the progress and outcomes of change. Evaluation efforts take into account differing cultural, contextual, demographic, and experiential perspectives including those of parents and of individuals with disabilities.

Examples/Notes:

Is this practice evident in policy/procedure? ❏ *Yes* ❏ *Emerging* ❏ *No*

K. Program policies delineate all components of service delivery and provide for tracking and evaluation of all components, including child and family outcomes, to ensure that recommended practices are implemented as intended.

Examples/Notes:

Is this practice evident in policy/procedure? ❏ *Yes* ❏ *Emerging* ❏ *No*

Adapted from Smith, B. J. (2000). Administrator's essentials: Creating policies and procedures that support recommended practices in early intervention/early childhood special education. In Sandall, S., McLean, M. E., & Smith, B. J. (Eds.), *DEC recommended practices in early intervention/early childhood special education.* Reston, VA: Division for Early Childhood, Council for Exceptional Children.

Applying Your Knowledge

In Monday morning's mail, you find this letter from the parent of one of the children in the ECSE classroom. The teacher in this classroom is experienced and skilled as an ECSE teacher and uses play as the major method of instruction for students in her classroom. Mrs. Smith has exhibited concern on a previous occasion, stating that Anwar is not "catching up" to the other children she knows. Since Anwar has Down syndrome and a fairly substantial hearing loss, "catching up" is probably an appropriate goal at this time.

Dear Ms. Alessjandro:

I am writing this letter to you because I am afraid if I come to talk to you after school, I will not remember all the things I want to say. I am really concerned about Anwar's learning and I am considering asking that he be placed in another ECSE classroom.

Please do not think that I dislike his teacher, or that Anwar is unhappy . . . that is not the problem. He loves to go to school and he loves being in the class and playing with the other children. I guess that is part of the problem. I am afraid that Anwar needs more than playing, and that is all he does in Ms. Finch's room.

As you know, Anwar's Down syndrome and hearing problems make it very difficult for him to learn, and I am afraid that without some very specific learning, he will not be able to succeed in the world at all. I know that he has disabilities, but he is almost four and a half years old, and most people still cannot understand him when he talks to them. He does know several signs, and that is helpful at home, but I think he needs to have more specific time in learning to speak and learning to do the things other children his age do.

This last weekend, my sister and her family were at our house, and I was amazed to see all the things her three year old could do! She listened to stories and said some of the words with her mother, she built things with blocks, she counted 'one, two' and she could sit for a long time to play with her toys. Anwar does none of these things.

Like I said, he really likes to come to his program, but I am afraid he is falling farther and farther behind the other children, because all he does is play. I know you and Ms. Finch have told us parents that you teach through play, but I don't see that Anwar is learning much. Soon he will be in school with bigger children, and he won't be able to do any of the things that are required in the classroom. I don't feel that I can let this situation continue. I am sorry to have to say these things, because I know you are a caring person and you have been very kind to Anwar. But I must look out for his future.

Thank you for your time.

Sincerely,

Mrs. Antelia Smith (Anwar's mother)

QUESTIONS

1. How will you structure your discussion with Mrs. Smith—what questions will you ask? Who will you ask to be present?
2. Assuming that you believe this program to be the most appropriate one for Anwar, how will you help Mrs. Smith to see that his needs are being met?
3. What actions, other than your conversation with Mrs. Smith, will you suggest to address her concerns?

QUESTIONS FOR THOUGHT

1. What would be some questions that you would ask of applicants for an early childhood teaching position in your school to ensure that the individual understands and advocates developmentally appropriate practice (DAP)?
2. If you were charged with organizing a workshop for principals on understanding and supporting quality early childhood/early childhood special education programs, what would your content be and what are some activities you might use in delivering the identified content?
3. Are you an advocate of using standardized achievement tests with your children? Explain your position.
4. How do program issues in EC/ECSE link to other special instructional programs (e.g., migrant education, bilingual education, gifted/talented)?
5. How do IEPs and IFSPs differ? Why are IFSPs especially important for work with young children?
6. How would you go about organizing a quality child find effort? Explain what you would do, who you would involve, and why?

For Additional Information Online

National Association for the Education of Young Children: www.naeyc.org

The Children's Defense Fund: www.childrensdefense.org

Council for Exceptional Children (link to Division of Early Childhood): www.cec.org

Early Childhood Research Institute: www.clas.uiuc.edu

Assistive Technology and Communication for Early Childhood: www.uchsc.edu/library

National Early Childhood Technical Assistance Center: www.nectac.org

References

Branscombe, N. A., Castle, K., Dorsey, A. G., Surbeck, E., & Taylor, J. B. (2003). *Early childhood curriculum: A constructivist perspective.* Boston: Houghton Mifflin.

Bredekamp, S., & Copple, C. (Eds.). (1997). *Developmentally appropriate practice in early childhood programs.* Washington, DC: National Association for the Education of Young Children.

Bricker, D., Pretti-Frontczak, K., & McComas, N. (1998). *An activity-based approach to early intervention* (2nd ed.). Baltimore, MD: Paul H. Brookes.

Dichtelmiller, M. L., Jablon, J. R., Dorfman, A. B., Marsden, D. B., & Meisels, S. (2001). *Work sampling in the classroom: A teacher's manual* (3rd ed.). New York: Pearson Education.

Dichtelmiller, M. L., Jablon, J. R., Marsden, D. B., & Meisels, S. (2001). *The work sampling system: Preschool through third grade, omnibus guidelines* (4th ed.). New York: Pearson.

Dunlap, L. L. (1997). *An introduction to early childhood special education.* Boston: Allyn and Bacon.

Guralnick, M. J. (1997). *The effectiveness of early intervention.* Baltimore, MD: Paul H. Brookes.

Handleman, J. S., & Harris, S. L. (Eds.). (2001). *Preschool education programs for children with autism.* Austin, TX: ProEd.

Howard, V. F., Williams, B. F., Port, P. D., & Lepper, C. (2001). *Very young children with special needs: A formative approach for the 21st century* (2nd ed.). Upper Saddle River, NJ: Merrill/Prentice-Hall.

Lamb, H. (2001). Early childhood education. In G. Schroth and M. Littleton (Eds.), *The administration and supervision of special programs in education.* Dubuque, IA: Kendall/Hunt.

Raver, S. A. (1999). *Intervention strategies for infants and toddlers with special needs: A team approach* (2nd ed.). Upper Saddle River, NJ: Merrill/Prentice-Hall.

Sandall, S. M., McLean, M. E., & Smith, B. J. (Eds.). (2000). *DEC recommended practices in early intervention/early childhood special education.* Reston, VA: Council for Exceptional Children.

Programs for Gifted and Talented Students[1]

Rebecca Miller

Marie Simonsson

Although gifted students can and do emerge from all
varieties of home environments, many parents of
gifted students require a high level of involvement
in the education of their child. In most cases,
the principal's job is to support and
facilitate this involvement.

—*Robert Dunbar & Gwen Schroth, 2005*

Objectives

1. Define gifted and talented
2. Discuss equitable identification processes
3. Overview various program approaches for providing services
4. Discuss G/T parent involvement

[1]This chapter was adapted from Dunbar, R., & Schroth, G. (2005). Programs for gifted and talented students. In Pankake, A., Schroth, G., & Littleton, M. (Eds.), *Administration and Supervision of Special Programs in Education* (2nd ed., pp. 131–143). Dubuque, IA: Kendall Hunt.

Introduction

Students in every school, grade level, and classroom vary in their abilities and achievement. It is incumbent on school personnel to identify students with exceptional abilities and address these appropriately. Students' exceptional abilities range from physical, emotional, and cognitive challenges to *greater than expected performance* in one or more of these areas. Students on the greater than expected performance of the exceptional abilities range are the focus of this chapter. Dunbar and Schroth (2005) pointed out that some of these students will experience various types of support to nurture their exceptional abilities while others may languish due to a lack of resources, instructional direction, trained personnel, or supportive adult mentors. They note that "some [of these students] excel; some do not. Some seize opportunities; some fail to recognize them" (Dunbar & Schroth, 2005, p. 132). All of these descriptions apply to students with exceptional abilities identified as gifted or talented. All of these students need instruction and adult relationships that address and nurture their unique educational needs in order to maximize their development.

Unlike Special Education or Title I, there is no federal safety net to guarantee that schools provide services to gifted and talented students. The vast majority of legislation related to these students comes from the states. All but 4 of the 50 states have a definition for high-ability children. Over half of these are defined in legislation while the others were created by state education agencies (Bathon, 2004). In both cases, minimal and essentially immeasurable standards are often set and accountability for schools regarding their delivery of services to gifted and talented students is frequently negligible. If the principal fails to make services to gifted students a priority, the most likely outcome is that these students will simply fail to receive services, resulting in a loss for both the student and society. The last 30 years has seen significant growth in research on the needs and characteristics of gifted learners. Still, there is evidence that in many schools, gifted students fail to receive even the attention that common sense would warrant (Vanderkam, 2003).

The purpose of this chapter is to acquaint readers with various aspects of the group of exceptional abilities students identified as gifted and talented. To do this, we first offer information on the terms themselves. This is followed with an overview of the processes and measures used to identify students as gifted or talented; a particular focus is given to identification of students from underrepresented groups. Designing instruction appropriate for gifted and talented students is given attention in some detail and followed up with information relevant to selecting and supporting personnel to ensure quality delivery of instruction. As with most special instructional programs, a variety of service models exist. These are reviewed regarding their basic components and followed up with sections focused on grouping practices, the ever-present assessment and accountability issues, and the need for the principal's leadership in documenting the provided services for both quality control and accountability purposes. We close with a focus on parents of gifted and talented students and some unique aspects they present to the home-school collaboration effort. Also we provide a section addressing the importance of the school's structure and processes in ensuring an environment that provides enriching experiences for all students.

Gifted or Talented?

The terms *gifted* and *talented* do not always serve to clarify discussion of high-ability students. Different writers often use the terms to describe different kinds of abilities. Some writers simply do not bother to make a distinction and use such descriptors as "gifted and talented," "TAG," and "GT" as if they were one in the same. No Child Left Behind (NCLB, 2002) defines "gifted and talented" as:

> Students, children, or youth who give evidence of high achievement capability in areas such as intellectual, creative, artistic, or leadership capacity, or in specific academic fields, and who need services or activities not ordinarily provided by the school in order to fully develop those capabilities.

States, however, are not bound by this definition. State definitions slightly favor "gifted and talented" over "gifted" (Bathon, 2004). Texas includes artistically gifted, creatively gifted, gifted in leadership, gifted in specific academic fields, and intellectually gifted as part of the definition (TEA, 2009). The National Association for Gifted Children (2004) uses the terms to describe the breadth of students' abilities. In their nomenclature, "gifted" students possess a broad range of exceptional abilities, and are "those who demonstrate outstanding levels of aptitude (defined as an exceptional ability to reason and learn) or competence (documented performance or achievement in the top 10% or rarer) in one or more domains" (NAGC, 2010). "Talented" students possess a more narrow set of abilities or even an exceptional ability in a single area (NAGC, 2004).

GIFTED CHILDREN

Students who are gifted differ from their peers in significant ways and, as a result, require a different curriculum. The gifted curriculum may differ in several ways, including pace, level, and complexity. Students who are gifted, however, are similar to their peers in that each student is a unique combination of strengths and weaknesses. Tannenbaum (1983) suggests that five components make up the attributes of giftedness: general ability, special ability, nonintellective factors (e.g., ego, strength, and dedication), environmental factors, and chance factors.

It is imperative parents, teachers, and administrators understand that these five factors are intertwined with normal physical and emotional growth in students. Often, children identified as gifted are socially awkward. Their giftedness sets them apart from peers while, at the same time, their age and emotional maturity sets them apart from adults so they fit in neither group. Given the diversity of giftedness, a child can shift between conducting a highly academic conversation with a group of adults and throwing a childish temper tantrum over an insignificant event. Unpredictable social behavior often leads to confusion on the part of the child identified as gifted as he or she tries to build upon self-concept. It also creates confusion for the people around the child as they try to react appropriately to the varied behaviors of the gifted individual.

Roedell (1984) identified three vulnerabilities that students who are gifted might be prone to demonstrate. Roedell pointed out that each of these is influenced to some extent by forces in the environment.

> **Uneven development**. Uneven development refers to the gap between intellectual age and emotional age. Students often behave much more maturely when acting in their area of giftedness than at other times. This becomes problematic when adults and other children begin to expect mature behavior at all times. The inconsistency of behavior often leads to frustration and a breakdown of communication. The solution, although not always simple, is for adults interacting with children who are gifted to always expect age-appropriate and not intellectually-appropriate behaviors.

> **Perfectionism.** Part of the makeup of some gifted children is the inherent desire to reach perfection while not having the maturity to understand that perfection is rarely attainable. Students who are gifted need the stabilizing efforts of parents and teachers who set reasonable expectations. Teachers can help by providing detailed instructions and explicit timelines for assignments.

Underachievement. A classic and highly frustrating behavior of some students who are gifted is underachievement. Several reasons contribute to this behavior including problems at home, lack of support, inappropriate educational setting, and peer pressure to not be seen as "smart." Peterson and Colangelo (1996) report students often begin to underachieve in middle school and with appropriate instruction and support can re-engage in schoolwork when they enter high school.

IDENTIFICATION

The identification of truly gifted students is a complex issue with serious cultural and political underpinnings. Traditionally, the most common method of identifying gifted students was standardized aptitude tests such as the Cognitive Abilities Test, and norm-based achievement tests such as the Iowa Test of Basic Skills. Historically, this method of identification resulted in underrepresentation of marginalized populations. Research now suggests the most equitable method for identifying gifted students is a battery of approaches using various criteria including multidimensional, portfolio, dynamic, performance/curriculum-based, observational, and psychometric assessments (Borland, 2008; Clark, 2007; Robinson, Shore, & Enersen, 2007). Such a battery of assessments allows for the inclusion of gifted behaviors not normally valued in the academic arena and helps negate cultural subgroup biases. Cultural subgroups and demographics affecting identification include:

Age. Identification of students age 6 or younger is through individual assessments. Tests to assess younger students usually are scored based on reading readiness and the sophistication and elaboration of student responses to tasks completed at the time of the testing. Early readers and students inclined to embellish a story or picture in detail will score high on these aptitude tests.

Cultural/ethnic diversity. Culturally or ethnically diverse learners remain underrepresented among students identified as gifted. Often the structure of assessments and applications penalize different cultural or ethnic subgroups because their giftedness does not manifest itself in a traditional manner. Clark (2007) suggests giftedness be identified on ability rather than the product of that ability. Using observational and anecdotal records rather than standardized tests allow culturally or ethnically diverse learners to demonstrate abilities such as critical thinking skills, generating original ideas, powerful desire to learn, capacity to retain and retrieve information quickly, and a deeper understanding of concepts in culturally or ethnically appropriate ways.

Language. English language learners comprise another underrepresented cultural group. Multilingual students tend to advance more slowly than their English-only peers, especially through the first few years of school, and then catch up thereafter. Standard measures fail to account for this because they only measure giftedness in English. Alternative methods of identification for ELLs include teacher recommendations, student portfolios, and student performance; all of these help counteract the bias toward English as the only academic language.

Poverty. Children of poverty often enter school lacking the background experiences and skills developed in early childhood by their more affluent peers (Payne, 2005). The identification process for gifted students often overlooks the strengths of low-income promising learners such as resiliency, creative problem solving, tenacity, independence, and the ability to succeed under extremely difficult conditions. Replacing test scores with teacher checklists, anecdotal records, observations of social interactions, creativity, problem-solving behaviors, student portfolios, and provisional placement in gifted programs more equitably evaluates giftedness in low-income learners (Robinson, Shore, & Enersen, 2007).

Gender. Gender differences in gifted students might possibly be the most difficult to identify. It is difficult to ascertain if the gender-based differences found in gifted programs are caused by gender or if they must be attributed to sociocultural learned behavior, in particular stereotype threat. Stereotype threat is defined as fear of negative gender stereotypes that may cause female students to intentionally perform lower on a task. Identification of giftedness in terms of gender requires a risk-free learning environment; it is also important to acknowledge that goals and behaviors differ between the genders and those differences should be valued equally (Plucker & Callahan, 2008).

Twice-exceptionality. Another highly underrepresented group in gifted programs is twice-exceptional students. Twice-exceptional refers to students who are gifted and have an emotional, physical, or cognitive disability. Identification of twice-exceptional students is difficult because gifts and disabilities can mask each other during the identification process. It is important for the evaluation team to be knowledgeable in both behaviors of giftedness and disabilities. The assessment tools used need to be adapted for specific emotional, physical, hearing, and/or cognitive differences. It is appropriate for twice-exceptional student identification to be based, in part, on a comparison of others with similar disabilities (Robinson, Shore, & Enersen, 2007).

DESIGNING INSTRUCTION

Designing instruction for students who are gifted presents unique problems to curriculum writers. Although Van Tassel-Baska (2008) reports it is uncommon to find curriculum specifically designed for the gifted learner, many school districts hire a curriculum director for their gifted program. Regardless of who develops the curriculum, curricular considerations include several factors such as the degree of giftedness; the racial, cultural, and socioeconomic differences of students; gender; area of giftedness; emotional factors; and twice-exceptionalities of students.

Among models currently used by schools are the Autonomous Learner Model, Integrative Education Model, the Integrated Curriculum Model, the Enrichment Triad and Secondary Triad Models, the Enrichment Matrix Model, and the Cognitive-Affective Interaction Model. Each model contains varying proportions of strategy instruction, depth of content instruction, independent study, and interdisciplinary work (Dunbar & Schroth, 2005).

One recent example of a highly evolved model for curriculum and instruction for gifted students is the "parallel curriculum" (Tomlinson, Kaplan, Renzulli, Purcell, Leppien, & Burns, 2002). In this model, the study of each of the core disciplines (English, science, math, social studies, etc.) includes a core curriculum and three additional curricula (connections, practice, and identity) designed to draw students into the discipline in a meaningful way. The core curriculum consists of all of the key facts, concepts, and generalizations that students need to understand the discipline. This emphasizes understanding over rote memorization and must be presented in a careful and coherent manner. The curriculum of connections explores the range of instances throughout and beyond the discipline. It asks students to consider how similar events will vary in different contexts or how they will be viewed from different perspectives. The curriculum of practice emphasizes real-world applications. This curriculum challenges students to think like historians, mathematicians, chemists, and other discipline-based people. Finally, the curriculum of identity requires students to examine their own abilities and interests and then determine what contributions they are prepared to make in the disciplines they are studying. In the parallel curriculum, all four of these curricula must be present in each discipline of study. Over time, perspectives would be visited and revisited like four strands intertwined across the time period of study (Dunbar & Schroth, 2005).

The Integrated Curriculum Model (ICM) was developed to include a balanced emphasis on advanced content, higher level development of process skills and end products, and concept-based learning. The four core disciplines of language arts, science, social studies, and math are included in each unit of study. Van Tassel-Baska (2008) reports that research on the ICM has been ongoing since its initial development and is often used as a curriculum-writing template for advanced learners in a variety of content areas. Curriculum units developed using the ICM framework include such elements as inquiry-based tools, problem-solving learning episodes, and other constructivist strategies for learning. A somewhat unique aspect of ICM is the professional development delivery. While some off-campus traditional training is included in the model, the bulk of the professional development has moved to a more job-embedded or on-the-job model. ICM's on-site ambassadors identify needs through their own observations in classrooms and through talks with the teachers using ICM.

Instruction designed for students identified as gifted needs to allow opportunities to:

Pursue advanced level work.

Be exposed to higher level thinking skills.

Use enrichment centers.

Self-select topics of interest.

Work in groups with students having common interests.

Move to a higher grade for specific subject area instruction.

Work with students of comparable ability across classrooms at the same grade level.

Work on an advanced curriculum unit on a teacher-selected topic.

Participate in competitive programs focusing on thinking skills/problem solving.

Receive concentrated instruction in critical thinking and creative problem solving. (Archambault, Westberg, Brown, Hallmark, Emmons, & Zhang, 1993)

The goal of instruction designed for students identified as gifted is to ensure that all instruction is allowing the students to increase their knowledge base. This can be done either by enriching the content or accelerating the content. Enrichment involves taking the standard curriculum and adding learning opportunities that provide for greater depth and breadth of learning (Reis et al., 1993). Enrichment strategies include self-selected investigations, advanced content, alternative reading assignments, questioning techniques, tiered assignments, individual learning contracts, creative problem-solving activities, and time to produce original and creative products.

Acceleration, on the other hand, allows the student to move through the standard curriculum at an accelerated pace (Reis et al., 1993). Acceleration strategies include cross-grade grouping, ability level content, selected classes with upper grades, high school–college dual enrollment, or promotion on ability rather than age. Although some proponents of acceleration consider students identified as gifted not accelerated are "decelerated" (Elkind, 1988) or victims of "age discrimination" (Kearney, 1996), others urge caution. The decision to choose acceleration instead of enrichment should be made on a case-by-case basis only after considering the emotional, educational, and physical well-being of the student (Smith, 2003).

Studies on accelerated education for gifted students indicate that those receiving acceleration outperform their gifted peers who did not receive acceleration academically (Kulik, 1992). However, the accelerated programs do not always meet the emotional and social needs of the students, thus enrichment programs addressing these areas may be necessary.

STAFFING

Preparing and selecting teachers to work with gifted students requires careful and comprehensive planning. Successful teachers of gifted students possess specific knowledge, skills, and dispositions. Principals needs to look to teachers who have knowledge of the emotional, social, and cognitive needs of the gifted; skill in transferring knowledge into action; and the dispositions for working with highly intelligent, often emotionally and socially challenged young people (NAGC, 1997, 1998; Dvorak, 2007; Robinson, 2008). There is some evidence that teachers with certain personality traits may be more effective in working with gifted students. A study of 1,247 gifted students and 63 teachers reported that the teachers who showed a preference for intuition and thinking on the Myers-Briggs Personality Type Inventory were more likely to be rated highly by high-ability students (Mills, 2003).

There are no federal mandated standards for certification of teachers of the gifted, so each state has the responsibility of developing its own criteria. The executive summary of the State of the Nation in Gifted Education survey reports, of the 47 states that responded to a question on teachers of the gifted preparation, only 5 states required pre-service training (NAGC, 2009). Texas requires teachers to complete 30 hours of training on the nature and needs, identification and assessment, and curriculum and instruction of gifted students. In addition, teachers, administrators, and counselors of the gifted must complete 6 hours of continuing education annually (TEA, 2009). Teachers sent to a workshop or engage in a day of training at school are unlikely to make significant changes in instruction. Instead, there must be application-focused training with equally strong follow-up training. The principal needs to support this training by providing ongoing leadership, modeling, and discussing the strategies with teachers, and provide material resources where necessary. Teachers also need mentoring in the area of personal growth as it applies to teaching. Karnes and Shaunessy (2004) provide a model for supported personal professional growth using a modified Individual Professional Development Plan (Robinson, Shore, & Enersen, 2007) which could be useful to school administrators.

Service Models

The methods of delivering gifted instruction vary greatly. In larger districts that may have gifted coordinators or lead teachers, program organization may be the element of instruction the principal controls least. For reasons often more related to issues of finance, personnel, and facilities than to instruction, districts try to adopt types of services best suited to their particular circumstances.

Integrated classroom support (ICS) also referred to as within-class support is the most common way of delivering service to students who are gifted. This delivery method has the classroom teacher supplementing regular education curriculum with instruction appropriate for gifted students with or without the assistance of a gifted and talented specialist. This type of delivery is popular with schools for several reasons including cost effectiveness by reducing the number of gifted and talented specialists required to serve students (Van Tassel-Baska, 1992), reducing the amount of time spent in transition and increasing the amount of time gifted students receive services (Landrum, 2001), and allowing all students to benefit from gifted curriculum (Tomilinson et al., 2002).

Cluster grouping is another way districts provide service to gifted students. Cluster grouping is an adaptation of integrated classroom support. Similar to ICS, gifted students are taught in the regular education classroom; however, gifted students are ability-grouped together to work on enriched regular education curriculum. The same cost effectiveness as ICS is provided with the use of cluster grouping but a different benefit to regular education students is seen. While all students benefit from gifted instruction in ICS, only the identified gifted students benefit in a cluster group; however, schools using cluster grouping often show an increase in students identified as gifted (Gentry & Owen, 1999).

Pull-out programs are another delivery method for serving students who are gifted. A pull-out program requires a school to have a gifted specialist with a classroom who pulls students from regular education classrooms and teaches an enriched curriculum. Pull-out programs might be daily or weekly and the curriculum might be the regular education curriculum with extensions and enrichments or it might be a curriculum written especially for gifted programs. This type of model can be problematic. The principal is responsible for providing adequate and appropriate classroom space and materials for the pull-out program. Another problem with pull-out programs is students can miss important class content if curriculum is not aligned and pull-out often occurs during non-academic time (art, computer, music) so students miss age-appropriate social activities.

Some districts have opted for special classes for their gifted programs. These classes can be Saturday school; however, most commonly, special classes refers to self-contained classrooms at the elementary level and at the middle and high school level, classes that are either enriched or accelerated such as honors, Advanced Placement (AP), or International Baccalaureate (IB) classes. Special classes have both advantages and disadvantages for students who are gifted.

Occasionally, these special classes are housed in a special school. Special schools are public schools that have been designated for a specific content area. Often called Magnet schools, the faculty on these campuses, while teaching all subjects, will show an inclination toward a specific area like math, science, technology, or performing arts. Districts often make this choice to utilize neighborhood schools with decreasing enrollment or to satisfy integration plans. Magnet students often make up 50% or more of the total campus enrollment.

Concurrent enrollment is a service model where a student is enrolled in one school and is taking classes at another. This happens in a variety of ways. An elementary student highly gifted in math might take most classes at the elementary school and take math at the middle school. Middle school students might spend half a day at the middle school and half a day at the high school. High school students might take a course or two from a local community college or a university. Concurrent enrollment requires diligence at both ends. Principals, supported by the school team, must ensure not only the academic readiness of the student but also the emotional and physical readiness of the student to enroll concurrently. In addition, both student and parents need to have a complete understanding of the requirements to be successful at concurrent enrollment.

Another type of concurrent enrollment available to gifted students is online courses. Many major universities offer online courses for gifted and talented students. The Center for Talent Development offers online programs to supplement enrichment for K-12 students. Online offers students who are gifted the opportunity to personalize their learning by enrolling in programs tailored to their individual interests. These types of programs are usually outside of school time and paid for by parents. Online programs offer the student the ability to connect with other students with similar interests around the country, interact with students and teacher in real-time through videoconferencing or Skype. This type of delivery method is being developed more and more frequently and could be the future of gifted and talented enrichment for students in small or rural school districts.

In a recent survey of students scoring at or above the 95th percentile, 67% of students reported that they received multiple accommodations, the most prevalent of these being pull-out programs, academic competitions, after-school and summer enrichment, and working at a higher grade level in their regular classrooms (Swiatek & Lupkowski-Shoplik, 2003). Schools seem to be using a variety of models to address gifted students' needs. However, of concern in this report was that 12% of the students indicated that they received no accommodations (Dunbar & Schroth, 2005).

A variety of special summer and Saturday programs are available for gifted students who may benefit from intensive accelerated courses, studies on a single subject, mentorships, internships, or on the job shadowing (Olszewski-Kubilius, 2003). Study abroad programs are alternatives for older students. Educational leaders need to be aware of gifted students' participation in such programs since partaking in out-of-school programs may advance or accelerate the students to such an extent that the in-school gifted accommodations that the students receive need to be readjusted and reassessed.

STUDENT GROUPING

Grouping with students who are gifted often leads to controversy. In the course of designing and planning a program for gifted students, decisions about grouping students by ability will be made. The broader definition of the term *ability grouping* includes within-class and cross-grade grouping. The research on ability grouping can be traced back to the early 1900s. There is some confusion among educators and parents as to the effectiveness of ability grouping. An effective campus administrator should understand what the research has to say on this subject, and be cognizant of whether the research on different types of grouping used also describes alterations in the instruction provided. Slavin (1987) cautioned educators of the use of homogeneous student grouping. This caution is warranted in cases where students are homogeneously grouped, but instruction remains the same for all groups (Dunbar & Schroth, 2005). Often times, homogeneous grouping of gifted students is used so that students can receive instruction that is different and more appropriate to their needs than what is done in the general classroom. There is evidence that this type of grouping which includes instruction specialized for the needs of each group is helpful for students of all abilities (Kulik & Kulik, 1990).

It is important that principals understand groupings and be able to articulate how grouping will benefit the students who are gifted. Although cooperative learning is highly successful with some students, research indicates it is often misunderstood when applied to students who are gifted. Principals need to closely monitor student perceptions of unfairness (Clinkenbeard, 1991; Matthews, 1992), and the fear of one student doing all the work (Mulryan, 1992) that often arises from cooperative learning groups. Effective grouping for students who are gifted includes flexible within-class grouping of heterogeneous classrooms and cross-grade grouping within the content areas in which students show giftedness.

Assessment and Accountability

At present, the No Child Left Behind Act aims the nation's attention and resources at ensuring that nonproficient students move systematically toward proficiency. There is little or no incentive for schools to attend to the growth of students once they attain proficiency, or to spur students who are already proficient to greater achievement, and certainly not to inspire those who far exceed proficiency. To provide encouragement—even the impetus—to ensure that schools plan for the growth of every child, thus attending to both equity and excellence, would not require a great deal of work (Tomlinson, 2002).

Each individual state is thus required to develop a state goal for gifted students.

Texas has developed a *Texas State Plan for the Education of Gifted/Talented Students to "to meet the needs of gifted and academically advanced students"* (Texas Education Agency Division of Curriculum, 2012).

Many states are beginning to go beyond norm-referenced test as a way to measure accountability for gifted programs. Texas, for instance, uses The Texas Performance Standards Project (TPSP) which requires students to demonstrate mastery of skills by developing products which show innovation, individuality, and creativity (see http://texaspsp.org/about.php). Used in collaboration with the TPSP, the Gifted and Talented Teachers Toolkit is designed to help teachers, parents, and students understand the skills necessary to successfully negotiate the TPSP, as well as provide an in-depth, rich curriculum for Texas's gifted students.

Students who are gifted are assessed in grades 4, 8, and at exit level using the TPSP project format. Each assessment includes a final product that is deemed to be of professional quality, documentation of extensive research investigation, and an effective presentation and discussion session.

ASSESSMENT

Assessment related to the identification process was previously discussed in the identification section of this chapter with regard to student placement into gifted educational programs. The use of identification procedures and appropriate instruments should stem from research, theory, and best practices, and come from multiple sources—possibly using both qualitative and quantitative measures. As students enroll in gifted education programs, continuous student outcome and program assessments should be implemented in order to develop and advance the students' experiences and abilities. An ongoing, evolving assessment profile of each student in which his or her strengths and needs are described can be useful when planning instruction (National Association for Gifted Children—K-12 standards—principle in Dunbar & Schroth, 2005, p. 138). "In order to meet the unique needs of students with gifts and talents, this program's curriculum must emphasize advanced, conceptually challenging, in-depth, distinctive, and complex content within cognitive, affective, aesthetic, social, and leadership domains" (NAGC-Curriculum Planning and Instruction, retrieved March 2012 from http://www.nagc.org/index.aspx?id=6502).

According to Assouline (2003), "assessment should go beyond placement and should provide information that can assist in educational programming decisions" (p. 129). This is consistent with The National Association for Gifted Children's Gifted Education Programming standard (NAGC, 2009) for assessment that indicates the following:

> Knowledge about all forms of assessment is essential for educators of students with gifts and talents. It is integral to identification, assessing each student's learning progress, and evaluation of programming. Educators' must establish a challenging environment and collect multiple types of assessment information so that all students are able to demonstrate their gifts and talents. Educators' understanding of non-biased, technically adequate, and equitable approaches enables them to identify students who represent diverse backgrounds. They also differentiate their curriculum and instruction by using pre- and post-, performance-based, product-based, and out-of-level assessments. As a result of

each educator's use of ongoing assessments, students with gifts and talents demonstrate advanced and complex learning. Using these student progress data, educators then evaluate services and make adjustments to one or more of the school's programming components so that student performance is improved. (Programming Standard 2: Assessment)

Measuring the effectiveness of an instructional program on any student's performance is extremely difficult, and possibly more so in programs for gifted and talented students. The emphasis on high stakes testing in education across the nation has accentuated the use of criterion referenced tests to determine the mastery of minimum skill levels. On these tests, a "ceiling effect" conceals the total learning of most gifted students. The wealth of knowledge that these gifted students have acquired is thus never assessed, and the gifted and nongifted student may therefore display similar assessment results.

As discussed by Dunbar and Schroth (2005), norm-referenced tests may provide more information about the actual abilities of gifted students since the norm is usually based on a national sample of test-takers. Norm-referenced tests may provide a more accurate view of the gifted child's abilities than criterion-referenced assessment; however, Hagmann-von Arx, Meyer, and Grob (2008) describe several problems that may evolve with their use. For instance, when using norm-referenced tests, average difficulty levels of items are more frequent which causes the test to measure average abilities more accurately than below-or-above average abilities and all cognitive abilities are not assessed in one test which may cause variations if schools or districts are using different instruments; and the instruments may be "normally standardized on average achievers" (p. 172).

A norm-referenced test assigns students to a position on a nationally normed bell curve based on their performance. Data from these tests are better suited to the identification, comparison, and ranking of gifted students. Above-level tests, most commonly college admissions tests used with students at the middle grades or lower, are also used to measure the learning of gifted students. The most common tests for this are the SAT and ACT, but scores from Advanced Placement (AP) tests, College Level Examination Program (CLEP), and International Baccalaureate (IB) tests can also be useful (Hansen, 1992).

ACCOUNTABILITY

In this age of high stakes accountability testing and school report cards, the performance of gifted students is rarely considered. Dunbar and Schroth (2005) state that one explanation for this lack of consideration is the complexity of evaluating the impact of instruction on gifted and talented students' learning. They pose the question whether it is what the student learn in school or engage in on his or her free time that explains the student's performance?

In 1999, the Texas legislature required the Texas Education Agency (TEA) to "develop an assessment system and statewide standards for gifted/talented students at all grade levels" (TEA, Texas Performance Standard Project). In response, TEA created a pilot program known as the Texas Performance Standard Project to develop a set of projects gifted students could complete at their schools to be scored and used to determine the degree to which they had benefited from their enriched instruction. This included a detailed rubric for evaluating student work. At present time, the development and implementation of the standards have not been completed at all grade levels. In fact, only the exit level, eighth-, and fourth-grade standards have been piloted and implemented statewide on a voluntary basis (TEA: Texas Performance Standard Project. Retrieved March 21, 2012 from http://www.texaspsp.org/history.php?prfr=n).

Dunbar and Schroth (2005) predicted that;

. . . [f]or all of this effort, it is likely that, other than the development of some new assessment materials, this project will do little to answer the question the legislature originally asked: How is current funding impacting learning for gifted students? While it can show in great detail where students are in their learning, it cannot show how instruction has affected this. For gifted students, school is just one of many sources of learning that might include summer camps, private tutoring, individual study, peers, siblings, parents, or the internet. Controlling for all of these variables to find the effect of school is problematic in the study of any student, but it is even more difficult with gifted students who are much more likely to receive learning from multiple sources. (p. 138)

As pointed out in the previous edition,

Despite the difficulty of measuring learning for gifted students, advocates of gifted education are quick to point out that the current emphasis on proficiency does little to provide appropriate instruction for our nations' most gifted learners, leaving these students with little attention and few resources. (Dunbar & Schroth, 2005, p. 139)

At present, the No Child Left Behind Act aims the nation's attention and resources at ensuring that nonproficient students move systematically toward proficiency. There is no incentive for schools to attend to the growth of students once they attain proficiency, or to spur students who are already proficient to greater achievement, and certainly not to inspire those who far exceed proficiency. To provide encouragement—even the impetus—to ensure that schools plan for the growth of every child, thus attending to both equity and excellence, would not require a great deal (Tomlinson, 2002).

Despite the difficulty of measuring learning for gifted students, advocates of gifted education are quick to point out that the current emphasis on proficiency does little to provide appropriate instruction for our nations' most gifted learners, leaving these students with little attention and few resources (Dunbar & Schroth, 2005).

Documentation

Along with ensuring that services are delivered, principals must also oversee the documentation of those services so that the campus is prepared for any audit by the district or state that might require these. This includes documentation of specific instructional modifications such as curriculum enrichment, acceleration, or supplemental services as well as documentation of teacher training, particularly that which is required by the district or state.

When a teacher is hired or reassigned to a classroom that will include gifted students, that teacher is often required to complete initial training on the needs and characteristics of gifted learners. (In Texas, this requires 30 clock hours of training.) After this, there may be an annual training requirement of 3–6 clock hours. The principal is responsible for maintaining current records of teacher training (Dunbar & Schroth, 2005).

Parental Involvement

One of the great challenges for school administrators is dealing with parents of students who are gifted. Many times parents accurately identify their child as gifted long before the school does and advocate for their child to receive special program assistance (Robinson, Shore, & Enersen, 2007). The parents of children who are gifted tend to be highly involved in their child's education and the principal's job is to support and facilitate that involvement.

Districts and individual campuses need to have a detailed plan of enrichment ready to share with the parents. The plan needs to detail the type of enrichment to be provided (regular education classroom curricular modifications, pull out programs, etc.), a timeline of delivery, and a demonstration of how modifications and/or curriculum acts as enrichment rather than extra work.

The education of children who are gifted should be seen as a team effort with the team composed of parents, teachers, and administrators. It requires the input of all three different perspectives to create a well-rounded educational plan. The principal can facilitate parental involvement by:

1. providing parents with information about identification measures, resources available locally, assistance in planning enrichment at home, and plans for parents' assistance through classroom involvement;
2. training teachers to use parents in the classroom;
3. encouraging administrators to attend parent/teacher training that includes:
   a. district identification measures,
   b. district philosophy about nature and needs of gifted children,
   c. local resources,
   d. communication skills,
   e. ideas to promote learning at home, and
   f. ideas to incorporate parent assistance in the classroom. (Robinson, Shore, & Enersen, 2007)

Organizational Components for School Enrichment

Joseph Renzulli (1994), reflecting on extensive experience working with schools on improving services to gifted learners, suggests six school components necessary for what he calls the Schoolwide Enrichment Model. These six components are as follows:

1. **Specialist:** Renzulli advocates that a school staff include a full-time nonteaching enrichment specialist who is responsible for providing instructional support for teachers and managing the overall enrichment program. For most schools, budget concerns make this more than difficult, however, with careful planning and staff assignments. But most schools do have the ability to utilize one staff member, teacher, counselor, or administrator, to act in this capacity. Assigning direction of the enrichment program to one individual increases the likelihood that there will be consistency and coherency in the program, and it ensures that teachers will know where to go for help in working with gifted students.
2. **Enrichment team:** An enrichment team, not unlike the more common campus improvement team, consists of teachers, parents, and an administrator who meet periodically with the specialist to review and modify the enrichment program. In a school where a number of committees already exist, this could become the responsibility of one of those existing committees.
3. **Plan for professional development:** Haphazard attempts at teacher training do little to elevate the quality of enrichment. Training is best where it specifically targets the goals of the enrichment team and when it includes opportunities for follow-up and reflection.
4. **Connection to professional organizations:** Renzulli, here, advocates that schools participate in a particular organization developed by him. An equally useful alternative might include active participation in a state affiliate of the National Association for Gifted Children or similar group. These state affiliates often have

annual conventions and produce regular newsletters. They are also often active in monitoring and lobbying state legislatures as advocates for gifted learners.

5. **Parent inclusion:** Many parents of gifted students are already active participants in the education of their children. Renzulli proposes that schools provide structured training for parents to both orient them with the enriched curriculum and equip them to facilitate the learning of their child.

6. **Democratic school management plan:** Renzulli advocates that schools have open management with groups like campus improvement teams comprised of teachers, administrators, support personnel, and parents. Through these democratic structures, Renzulli argues, "policies should be enacted only after considered study, dialogue, and debate, and final policy should be adopted only following experimental or pilot periods during which changes in practice are field tested and evaluated" (p. 291).

In a more recent publication, Reis and Renzulli (2010) present types of enrichment categorized under three types: (1) general exploratory experiences, (2) group training activities, and (3) individual and small group investigations. A more detailed description of the Schoolwide Enrichment Triad Model is available by Reis and Renzulli (2010).

Renzulli's and other researchers' work shows how important the principal's role is in creating an environment where gifted students can flourish. The implementation of the components and enrichment models require direct action and support by the principal. Without this support, none of these could sustain themselves more than a short period of time.

Looking Ahead

Gifted students receive services in a variety of educational settings; the range of delivery designs is almost as great as that among the children themselves. There are gifted and talented magnet schools serving hundreds of high performing children and small, rural schools providing special services to only a few gifted students at a time. In either case, and in all the possible cases in between, it will ultimately fall to the principal to see that students identified as gifted receive instruction that is appropriate to their abilities. The principal must ensure that gifted and talented students are appropriately identified and that their teachers have the necessary skills and knowledge to work with them. (Dunbar & Schroth, 2005, p. 132)

The prospective principal must understand that what is described in this chapter only represents a portion of the current state of education for gifted and talented students. New research suggests that schools may soon be required to reconsider the nature of giftedness and provide increasingly individualized instruction to a larger and more diverse group of gifted learners (Dunbar & Schroth, 2005, p. 141).

The most prevalent forms of intelligence testing and the current nomenclature with which we describe gifted education suggest that students can be arranged along a linear continuum of intelligence and be accurately termed "gifted" at and above a certain point. However, emerging understandings of intelligence indicate that the nature of ability may be more complex than our current interventions can effectively address.

Howard Gardner's (1983) theory of multiple intelligences suggests that there are several components of ability that each person possesses: linguistic, musical, logical-mathematical, spatial, bodily-kinesthetic, interpersonal, and intrapersonal (Dunbar & Schroth, 2005). The implications of this theory for educators are significant. It questions our notions of both assessment and intervention for gifted students. In each case, it calls upon educators to increase the diversity of options and individualize the delivery of services in a manner not unlike what is currently done in special education.

Applying Your Knowledge

Mrs. Smith enrolls her twins, Jeff and Joy, in Greenwood Middle School in January. In a conference with the new principal, Mrs. Smith says that Jeff and Joy were both in the gifted program in their former school and expects that they will both be placed in GMS's middle school gifted program immediately. The principal notices that Joy's scores on the tests administered in her former school are slightly lower than her brother's and is not certain Joy will qualify for GMS's program. Noticing the principal's hesitancy, Mrs. Smith becomes insistent that Joy be included in the gifted program saying, "Joy will be crushed if Jeff makes it and she doesn't. I don't know if she can take it." The principal is aware that the mother is going to be persistent in her request but also knows that the school's gifted program is far from satisfactory. The curriculum is not challenging and the teacher lacks creativity in her teaching practices (Dunbar & Schroth, 2005).

QUESTIONS

1. What will be the impact on the twins if Joy does not qualify for the gifted program at GMS, and should that be a consideration in the placement decision?
2. How does this situation mirror what the authors of this chapter presented regarding the services available for gifted students?
3. As the principal what will be your response to this parent? Explain.
4. What programmatic and community relations consequences may occur if Joy is admitted to the gifted program? What about if she is not admitted?

QUESTIONS FOR THOUGHT

1. How do students qualify for a gifted program in your school district?
2. What is your district's policy for admitting gifted transfer students at the beginning of the year? Do mid-year transfers differ from that?
3. What strategies can a principal use when dealing with parents whose child does not qualify for the gifted program? Should exceptions be made?
4. Should alternatives to a gifted program be made available for students who come close to qualifying but do not?
5. What can this principal do to improve the gifted program in the scenario above?
6. What steps would you take to establish a system that determines the effectiveness of the gifted program in your school?
7. What assessments does your school/district use in order to make sure that English language learners, learning disabled, or poor gifted and talented students have an opportunity to receive the services they would benefit from?
8. How would you as a principal or coordinator of a gifted and talented program ensure that your teachers and support staff have access to adequate training or professional development activities in order to be successful in working with gifted and talented students?

For Additional Information Online

Council for Exceptional Children: www.cec.sped.org

Johns Hopkins University Center for Talented Youth: www.jhu.edu/~gifted/

National Association for Gifted Children: www.nagc.org

The National Foundation for Gifted and Creative Children: www.nfgcc.org

References

Archambault, F. A., Jr., Westberg, K. L., Brown, S. W., Hallmark, B. W., Emmons, C. L., & Zhang, W. (1993). *Regular classroom practices with gifted students: Results of a national survey of classroom teachers* (Research Monograph 93102). Storrs, CT: The National Research Center on the Gifted and Talented, University of Connecticut.

Assouline, S. G. (2003). Psychological and educational assessment of gifted students. In N. Colangelo & G. A. Davis (Eds.), Handbook of gifted education (3rd ed., pp. 124–145). Boston: Allyn and Bacon.

Bathon, J. M. (2004, June). *State gifted and talented definitions.* Education Commission of the States. Retrieved September 11, 2004 from http://www.ecs.org/clearinghouse/52/28/5228.htm

Borland, J. H. (2008). Identification. In J. A. Plucker & C. M. Callahan (Eds.), *Critical issues and practices in gifted education: What the research says.* Waco, TX: Prufrock.

Clark, B. (2007). Issues of identification and underrepresentation. In M. Wayne (Ed.), *Expert approaches to support gifted learners: Professional perspectives, best practices, and positive solutions.* Minneapolis, MN: Free Spirit.

Clinkenbeard, P. R. (1991). Unfair expectations: A pilot study of middle school students' comparison of gifted and regular classes. *Journal for the Education of the Gifted, 15,* 56–63.

Dunbar, R., & Schroth, G. (2005). Programs for gifted and talented students. In Pankake, A., Schroth, G., & Littleton, M. (Eds.), *Administration and supervision of special programs in education* (2nd ed., pp. 131–143). Dubuque, IA: Kendall Hunt.

Dvorak, M. J. (2007). Gifted education teachers: Knowledge, skills, and dispositions in thought and action. (Doctoral Dissertation, University of Kansas). Retrieved from http://proquest.umi.com/pqdlink?vinst=P ROD&attempt=1&fmt=6& startpage=-1&ver=1&vname=PQD&RQT=309&did=1425301711& exp=03-29-2016&scaling=FULL&vtype=PQD&rqt=309&cfc=1&TS=1301598196&clientId=98

Elkind, D. (1988). Mental acceleration. *Journal for the Education of the Gifted, 11*(4), 19–31.

Gardner, H. (1983). *Frames of mind.* New York: Basic Books.

Gentry, M., & Owen, S. V. (1999). An investigation of the effects of total school flexible cluster grouping on identification, achievement, and classroom practices. *Gifted Child Quarterly, 43,* 224–243.

Hagmann-von Arx, P., Meyer, C. S., & Grob, A. (2008). Assessing intellectual giftedness with the WISC-IV and the IDS. *Zeitschrift für Psuchologie/Journal of Psychology, 216*(3), 172–179. DOI: 10.1027/0044-3409.216.3.172

Hansen, J. (1992). Discovering highly gifted students. *Understanding Our Gifted, Open Space Communications, 4*(4).

Karnes, F. A., & Shaunessy, E. (2004). The application of an individual professional development plan to gifted education. *Gifted Child Today, 27*(3), 60–64.

Kearney, K. (1996). Highly gifted children in full inclusion classrooms. *Highly Gifted Children, 12*(4).

Kulik, J. A. (1992). *An analysis of the research on ability grouping: Historical and contemporary perspectives.* Retrieved from ERIC database (ED 350777).

Kulik, J. A., & Kulik, C. C. (1990). Ability grouping and gifted students. In N. Colangelo & G. A. Davis (Eds.), *Handbook of gifted education.* Boston: Allyn & Bacon.

Landrum, M. S. (2001). An evaluation of the catalyst program: Consultation and collaboration in gifted education. *Gifted Child Quarterly, 45,* 139–151.

Matthews, M. (1992). Gifted students talk about cooperative learning. *Educational Leadership, 50*(2), 48–50.

Mills, C. J. (2003). Characteristics of effective teachers of gifted students: Teacher background and personality styles of students. *Gifted Child Quarterly 47*(4), 272–281.

Mulryan, C. M. (1992). Student passivity during cooperative small groups in mathematics. *Journal of Educational Research, 85,* 261–273.

National Association for Gifted Children. (1997). *Preservice teacher education programs.* Retrieved 3, 2011 from http://www.nagc.org/uploadedFiles/PDF/Position_Statement_PDFs/pp_preservice_teacher_preparation.pdf

National Association for Gifted Children. (2004). *Parent information.* Retrieved 11, 2004 from http://www.nagc.org/ParentInfo/index.html#who

National Association for Gifted Children. (2009). *State of the nation in gifted education: How states regulate and support programs and services for gifted and talented students.* Retrieved from http://www.nagc.org/uploadedFiles/Information_and_Resources/State_of_the_States_2008-2009/2008-09%20State%20of%20the%20Nation%20overview.pdf

National Association for Gifted Children. (2010). *Pre-K—Grade 12 gifted programming standards: Curriculum planning and instruction,* Retrieved March 12, 2012 from http://www.nagc.org/index.aspx?id=6502

Olszewski-Kubilius, P. (2003). Special summer and Saturday programs for gifted students. In N. Colangelo and G. A. Davis (Eds.), *Handbook of gifted education* (3rd ed., pp. 268–281). Boston: Allyn and Bacon.

Payne, R. (2005). *A framework for understanding poverty.* Highlands, TX: aha! Process.

Peterson, J. S., & Colangelo, N. (1996). Gifted achievers and underachievers: A comparison of patterns found in school files. *Journal of Counseling and Development, 74,* 339–407.

Plucker, J. A., & Callahan, C. M. (2008). *Critical issues and practices in gifted education.* Waco, TX: Prufrock.

Reis, S. M., & Renzulli, J. S. (2010). Opportunity gaps lead to achievement gaps: Encouragement for talent development and schoolwide enrichment in urban schools. *Journal of Education, 190*(1/2), 43–49.

Reis, S. M., Westberk, K. I., Kulikowich, J., Caillard, F., Herbert, T., Plucket, J., et al. (1993). *Why not let high ability students start school in January?* The Curriculum Compacting Study (Research Monograph No. 93106). Storrs: National Research Center on the Gifted and Talented, University of Connecticut.

Renzulli, J. S. (1994). *Schools for talent development: A practical plan for total school improvement.* Mansfield Center, CT: Creative Learning Press.

Robinson, A. (2008). Teacher characteristics. In J. A. Plucker & C. M. Callahan (Eds.), *Critical issues and practices in gifted education* (pp. 669–680). Waco, TX: Prufrock.

Robinson, A., Shore, B. M., & Enersen, D. L. (2007). *Best practices in gifted education: An evidence-based guide.* Waco, TX: Prufrock.

Roedell, W. (1984). Vulnerabilities of highly gifted children. *Roeper Review, 6*(3), 127–130.

Slavin, R. E. (1987). Ability grouping: A best-evidence synthesis. *Review of Educational Research, 57,* 293–336.

Smith, D. (2003). Acceleration: Is moving ahead the right step? *Monitor on Psychology, 34*(5), 63.

Swiatek, M. A., & Lupkowski-Shoplik, A. (2003). Elementary and middle school student participation in gifted programs: Are gifted students underserved? *Gifted Child Quarterly, 47*(2).

Tannenbaum, A. J. (1983). *Gifted children: Psychological and educational perspectives.* New York: MacMillan.

Texas Education Agency. (2009). *Texas state plan for the education of gifted/talented students.* Retrieved from http://www.tea.state.tx.us/index2.aspx?id=6420

Texas Education Agency. (2012). Curriculum programs: Advanced academics. Retrieved from http://www.tea.state.tx.us/index4.aspx?id=3822

Tomlinson, C. A. (2002, November). Proficiency is not enough: The No Child Left Behind Act fails to balance equity and excellence. *Education Week, 36,* 38.

Tomlinson, C. A., Kaplan, S. N., Renzulli, J. S., Purcell, J., Leppien, J., & Burns, D. (2002). *The parallel curriculum: A design to develop high potential and challenge high-ability learners.* Thousand Oaks, CA: Corwin Press.

U.S. Department of Education. (2002). *The No Child Left Behind Act: Summary of final regulations.* Retrieved February 12, 2004 from http://www.No ChildLeftBehind.gov

Vanderkam, L. (2003, January 20). SAT talent searches lead nowhere for many. USA Today.

Van Tassel-Baska, J. (1992). Educational decision making on acceleration and grouping. *Gifted Child Quarterly, 36,* 68–72.

Van Tassel-Baska, J. (1998). *Excellence in educating gifted and talented learners.* Denver: Love.

Van Tassel-Baska, J. (2008). Curriculum development for gifted learners in science at the primary level. *Revista, Espanola de Pedagogia, 66*(240), 283–296.

Counseling 10
Programs

Reba Criswell
Jerry Trusty
Richard Lampe
Fernando Valle

Responsibilities of school counselors vary, based on the needs of constituencies served and the understandings and expectations of principals who are ultimately responsible for guidance operations in their schools.

—R. Lampe, J. Trusty, and R. Criswell

Objectives

1. Describe the historical and the contemporary scope of school counseling services and the appropriate responsibilities of the school counselor and others in the delivery of up-to-date services
2. Explain current models for the organization, development, implementation, and evaluation of school counseling programs
3. Present legal and ethical considerations of which administrators should be aware and that are related to school counseling
4. Provide outcome research evidence of the effectiveness of comprehensive school counseling programs and suggestions as to how administrators and counselors can promote counseling program effectiveness

Introduction

Of the various services and programs for which educational administrators have responsibility, counseling programs may be one of the least well defined. Some states provide models for organized, comprehensive counseling programs with specified services (Martin, Carey, & DeCoster, 2009; Sink & MacDonald, 1998), and recently, a national model has been published by the American School Counselor Association (ASCA, 2005). In addition, a framework for school counseling programs has been presented by the Education Trust and its National Center for Transforming School Counseling (2011). Models notwithstanding, local administrators have varying dominion over how programs are implemented (Pêrusse, Goodenough, Donegan, & Jones, 2004). Whereas this may at first glance seem desirable for administrators, without research-based guidelines and administrative understanding of how counseling services can be effectively organized and orchestrated, students are less likely to receive the services they need.

Ponec and Brock (2000) described the relationships between school counselors and principals as crucial, yet principals and counselors sometimes see things differently. Summarizing the perspectives of students in counseling and in educational leadership departments at their university, Shoffner and Williamson (2000) wrote that principals-in-training focus on tasks, results, and legal liabilities, while counselors-in-training focus on process, dealing with the dilemma, and the importance of confidentiality. Shoffner and Williamson also described 14 points of conflict between counselors and principals including, for example, formal authority versus shared leadership, discipline, and evaluation of the counselor. Pêrusse et al. (2004) pointed out that the three counselor tasks that were most highly supported by school principals were the same three tasks that were most frequently performed by school counselors. Further, these tasks were listed as *inappropriate* for school counselors in ASCA's National Standards, which the authors reported were endorsed by the National Association of Secondary School Principals and the National Association of Elementary School Principals. Pêrusse et al. expounded that "most school principals continue to believe that appropriate tasks for school counselors include clerical tasks such as registration and scheduling of all new students; administering cognitive, aptitude, and achievement tests; and maintaining student records" (p. 159). Points of conflict such as these may be due to insufficient reciprocal understanding of roles of counselors and principals and the lack of opportunities for each to learn about the responsibilities of the other. Therefore this chapter includes a brief history of school counseling, definitions of related terms, and descriptions of appropriate roles of school counselors. Also presented are contemporary views on how counselors' services can be integrated into an organized guidance program as well as the importance of the use of program standards to meet accountability requirements. Outcome research studies in support of comprehensive school counseling programs are included. In addition, several ethical and legal guidelines related to school counselors are addressed. Finally, suggestions are offered regarding administrators' and counselors' responsibilities for enhancing the counseling program's contributions to overall school effectiveness.

History of School Counseling

Although many pertinent events and conditions occurred earlier, the beginnings of the school counseling movement (or school guidance, as the concept has commonly been called) are often said to have taken place in the early 1900s (Gysbers & Henderson, 2006; Picchioni & Bonk, 1983). Societal changes during and following the Industrial

Revolution, such as immigration to urban areas, resulted in concentrations of populations in urban industrial centers and negative by-products such as slums, ghettos, inattention to individual rights, and masses of unskilled laborers (Schmidt, 2008; Picchioni & Bonk, 1983). With the increasing availability of public education to students from varying economic backgrounds, the resulting student population's needs expanded well beyond preparation for professional positions in areas such as law, medicine, and the ministry (Smith & Gideon, 1929). Subsequently, several schools began to provide guidance in areas of concern such as moral development and vocational choice.

Because of the expanding needs of students and the broadening expectations placed on public schools, guidance outgrew its vocational focus to include a broader range of services such as interpreting standardized tests and counseling students with personal/social and educational problems. Today, counselors provide an even wider range of services. For example, these include consultation with parents and teachers, coordination of various activities, referral for specialized assistance, and teaching age-appropriate guidance curriculum to foster the personal/social, educational, and career development of all students. Ideally, counselors operate as part of the educational team in an early childhood through 12th-grade counseling program that is planned and organized to meet the diverse needs of all students.

Recent developments and initiatives in school counseling such as the American School Counselor Association National Model (ASCA, 2005) and the National Center for Transforming School Counseling (NCTSC) of the Education Trust (Education Trust, 2011) support this *new vision* of school counseling and school counselor roles. These endeavors are committed to the educational development of all students from early-childhood through college and to closing achievement gaps, opportunity gaps, and in-structional gaps among socioeconomic and racial-ethnic groups. These efforts promote school counselors' involvement in the process of raising standards and implementing accountability systems. Both the ASCA National Model and the one from the Education Trust focus on leadership, advocacy, and collaboration roles of school counselors. In short, the frameworks offered by these new efforts seek to align school counselors more closely with the academic missions of schools.

Historically, school counselors have often been perceived by school administrators, parents, and laypersons as providing services that are ancillary to the academic missions of schools; and school counselors are often relegated to these ancillary roles. School counselors themselves have experienced role confusion over the last few decades (see Baker & Gerler, 2004; Brown & Trusty, 2005), and school counselors themselves may seek ancillary responsibilities.

Educating and serving all children in cognitive and affective domains is the collective responsibility of educational stakeholders. The continued disconnect of school counselor roles and data-driven school improvement efforts is a missed opportunity for counselors and administrators alike. The counselor-related terms, organization of services, program standards, and case presented in this chapter is a continued effort to generate synergistic relationships between counselors and administrators in our quest for school improvement.

Definitions of Related Terms

Guidance is sometimes used as the "umbrella" term that encompasses all of the services that counselors and others provide to promote student development. These services collectively are organized into *guidance programs* (albeit, some more organized than others). In current terminology, *counseling program* is sometimes used instead of *guidance program* (cf. ASCA, 2005; Gysbers & Henderson, 2006). It is also popular to use the term *guidance curriculum* to refer to age-appropriate and planned goals, objectives, and activities related to personal/social, educational, and career development that counselors (and sometimes teachers) provide, often in the classroom. *Counseling* in schools historically has denoted a process involving a special relationship in which a trained professional (the counselor) directly assists students with personal problems and concerns. *Therapy* (also *psychotherapy*) is usually differentiated from school counseling in that therapy is more often associated with treatment of deep-rooted, long-standing psychological problems of clients or patients in clinical or medical settings (Myrick, 2003). In non-school settings (in community agencies and hospitals, for example), distinctions between counseling and psychotherapy are less delineated.

Counselor Responsibilities

Duties of school counselors vary according to grade-level assignment, student and community needs, expectations of school administrators, and governmental regulations; however, there are several broad categories of activities and services that describe appropriate counselor responsibilities. These characteristically include, but are not limited to, counseling, consultation, coordination, assessment, large group guidance, and program management—each of which will be summarized in this section. How these different yet interdependent roles can be incorporated into an organized program will be presented in the subsequent section.

COUNSELING

When used in school settings to describe a specific activity (as opposed to a "counseling" program or to the "counseling" profession) *counseling* refers to a process that involves helping students deal with problems of a personal/social, academic, or career development nature (ASCA, 2005; Starr, 1996). Counseling is provided to students on an individual or small group basis. If provided on a small group basis, the group is small enough to allow the counselor to monitor and incorporate the interactions of the group members. Whether on an individual or group basis, counseling usually relates to each student's problems and goals. Involving a relationship between the student and the counselor and theory-based techniques, counseling is not equated with advising or providing information.

Definitions of counseling vary, sometimes extending the domain of counseling beyond developmental and situational concerns into the area of addressing pathology as well. For school children, treatment of pathology, if necessary, is preferably provided by specialists other than the school counselor, possibly through a referral to a resource such as a psychologist, psychiatrist, or community mental health agency counselor (see ASCA, 2005).

CONSULTATION

Although school counselors sometimes use consultants to secure information or to discuss options for dealing with certain situations (perhaps the counselor needs the assistance of a qualified professional regarding how to proceed in an unusual case, how to address an ethical or legal concern, etc.), counselors also provide consultation as a service. In the role of consultant (as opposed to using a consultant), the school counselor provides service to the student indirectly—usually through direct contact with teachers, parents and families, community resources, and/or school administrators (Starr, 1996;

Trusty, Mellin, & Herbert, 2008). For example, a teacher (called the consultee) who is having difficulty with a student might contact the school counselor (the consultant) for assistance. In their interactions, the counselor and teacher share information, discuss options, and perhaps jointly generate a plan of action for the teacher to implement (Myrick, 2003). Parsons and Kahn (2005) emphasized the collaborative nature of consultation, and that consultation is much more than advice giving.

In consultation, although the direct contact interaction is between the counselor and the consultee, the focus of their interaction is on the student—on how the consultee might interact directly with the student for the benefit of the student. In providing consultation, the counselor should guard against focusing on resolution of a personal problem the consultee might introduce. For example, the parent may seek assistance from the counselor for his/her alcoholism. Although this parent would probably benefit from personal counseling, provision of such for the parent is generally not within the role of the school counselor (ASCA, 2010).

The counselor sometimes provides consultation on a group basis. For example, the counselor could work with a group of parents regarding parenting techniques, or the counselor could conduct professional development activities for teachers regarding interpretation of test results. In both examples, the ultimate beneficiaries are the students.

COORDINATION

As a counselor intervention, Myrick (2003) defined coordination as "the process of managing different indirect guidance services to students, including special events and general procedures" (p. 345). In providing this service, counselors are called upon to collect and disseminate information and to develop and maintain positive working relationships with other school professionals and outside resources in the community (Texas Counseling Association [TCA], 2004). As a coordinator, the counselor may also plan and arrange meetings, develop and operate special programs, supervise others, and provide leadership (ASCA, 2005; Myrick, 2003). Examples of specific activities that counselors sometimes coordinate include career day, financial aid workshops, referrals of students to outside community agencies or practitioners, peer helper programs, orientation, scholarships, and so forth.

It is possible for coordination to become a "catch-all" for quasi-administrative duties that are assigned to the counselor, leaving insufficient time and resources for the counselor to adequately serve students in ways more aligned with the counselor's professional qualifications. Coordination of the school's testing program is one example. Although often done by a school counselor, coordinating testing involves a large amount of time securing, counting, packaging, and administering tests—activities not requiring the qualifications of a professional counselor yet limiting the counselor's availability to provide more direct services (Burnham & Jackson, 2000).

ASSESSMENT

Assessment (sometimes called appraisal) refers to collecting and interpreting data to facilitate more-informed decisions. Assessment of students is accomplished by using standardized instruments (usually measuring achievement, aptitude, interest, or personality) and by less standardized techniques such as interviews, surveys, and observations. School counselors may also participate in the assessment of various environments affecting students such as school climate, home environment, and peer groups (Drummond & Jones, 2010).

In schools, assessment results are commonly used for purposes of student description (achievement level, educational diagnosis), placement (courses, special programs), prediction (educational or career planning), or to provide information for the school (curriculum planning, program effectiveness). To serve these purposes, school counselors interpret assessment results as needed to students, parents, teachers, and school administrators. Administration and interpretation of specialized assessments may require the services of the school diagnostician, school psychologist, or school psychometrist.

LARGE GROUP GUIDANCE

Counselors can provide information for and lead discussions with large groups of students. Often referred to as classroom guidance, the focus of this activity is involving students as a group with information designed to meet their developmental needs. Commonly, large group guidance has instructional objectives related to personal and social skills, educational development, and career planning. Although instructional in nature, delivery of large group guidance is not restricted to a lecture format—discussions, multimedia, panels, guest speakers, and other means of involving students in learning are frequently involved. As described, large group guidance is differentiated from group counseling, wherein a smaller and more cohesive group of students interact with each other and a counselor "for more intense and private assistance" (Myrick, 2003, p. 253).

A planned sequence of large group guidance objectives is often outlined in a *guidance curriculum,* with age-appropriate content and delivery methods. A school's guidance curriculum should be planned with the overall needs of the students in mind. Some states provide guidance curriculum guidelines that can be useful in forming an individual school's (or district's) plan. In a recent examination, Martin et al. (2009) reported that 17 of 44 states reviewed provided guidance curriculum models, with more states having models being developed. At the national level, the ASCA National Model (ASCA, 2005) offers tools for gauging the scope and sequence of the guidance curriculum. In the National Model, the guidance curriculum is organized around *student competencies and indicators* from which learning objectives for guidance lessons and units can be developed.

Large group guidance is often delivered by the school counselor, although classroom teachers also teach guidance-related curriculum. In such cases, counselors can assist teachers with planning and resource materials (TCA, 2004). Counselors and teachers also work together to evaluate students' meeting of the guidance learning objectives (Brown & Trusty, 2005). For example, a school counselor and teacher may work together in delivering guidance lessons on time-management skills to fourth graders; and the teacher evaluates students' time-management competencies in academic classes. According to Starr (1996) and supported by ASCA (2005), the guidance curriculum and guidance program should not be seen as ancillary to the school curriculum and school activities. Rather, it should be viewed as an integral component of the total curriculum and school.

PROGRAM MANAGEMENT

Whether viewed from the perspective of a lone counselor trying to serve all students in a rural area, or of a group of counselors serving a particular school, or of a central-office director of guidance for an entire district in a large city, the counselor should be involved at some level in management of the guidance program. Program management responsibilities include planning, implementing, evaluating, and advocating for a comprehensive guidance program. Program management involves organizing personnel, resources, and activities (related to assessed needs and in accordance with carefully developed goals and objectives) in order to better serve students (TCA, 2004). The ASCA National Model (ASCA, 2005) provides valuable direction and tools in developing and managing comprehensive school counseling programs.

Organization of Services

Although the responsibilities described in the preceding section include many of the services provided by counselors, an effective guidance program is more than a loosely connected, unplanned, or hit-or-miss collection of counselors' efforts. Gysbers, Lapan, and Jones (2000) described a contemporary approach to guidance programming as involving the counselor in an "organized, sequential, structured, district-wide program of guidance and counseling K-12" (p. 349). Several resources (e.g., ASCA, 2005; Gysbers & Henderson, 2006; Myrick, 2003; Starr, 1996) have included a description of how effective programs could be organized.

This section summarizes the Gysbers and Henderson (2000, 2006) comprehensive program model. This model is largely the basis for the ASCA National Model (ASCA, 2005). The Gysbers and Henderson model interrelates three broad elements: (1) content, which outlines what students should be able to do, or competencies, as a result of experiencing the guidance program; (2) organizational framework, that addresses the what, why, and assumptions underlying the program as well as the program's major components; and (3) the resources needed to effectuate the program.

CONTENT

According to Gysbers and Henderson (2000, 2006), an organized comprehensive guidance program specifies student competencies that are distinct and developmentally appropriate for different grade levels. These age-appropriate competencies are grouped into domains such as academic development, interpersonal skills, responsible choices, and knowledge of self and others; and it is common to use the same list of domains for all grade levels. Several resources are available for administrators and counselors to assist with the identification of age-appropriate competencies and with grouping these into domains, including models from the American School Counselor Association (ASCA, 2005), the state of Missouri (Gysbers, Starr, & Magnuson, 1998), the state of Texas (Texas Education Agency [TEA], 2004), and the state of New Hampshire (Carr & Hayslip, 1989).

ORGANIZATIONAL FRAMEWORK

Gysbers and Henderson (2000, 2006) delineated the organizational framework of a guidance program through identification of four major program components. These components, briefly introduced here, include guidance curriculum, responsive services, individual planning, and system support.

Guidance Curriculum.

Earlier in this chapter, guidance curriculum was described as referring to age-appropriate and planned goals, objectives, and activities related to personal/social, educational, and career development. The guidance curriculum, one of the four guidance program components, is often implemented through classroom units taught by counselors, by counselors and teachers on a team basis, or by teachers with counselor support and consultation. Other vehicles for implementing the guidance curriculum involve larger group activities such as career days, college/technical school nights, financial aid workshops, and orientations of students to a new school level. Through the guidance curriculum, many desired student competencies are addressed. Examples of age-appropriate curricular goals, objectives, and activities related to guidance are available in the literature (e.g., ASCA, 2005; Gysbers & Henderson, 2000, 2006), but these are samples only, to provide a starting place for the evolution of a locally appropriate guidance curriculum.

Responsive Services.

Whereas the guidance curriculum component provides guidance-related content to all students for everyday life skills, the responsive services component is designed to provide prevention and/or intervention related to immediate concerns of a smaller number of students (TEA, 2004). That is, this component targets students' immediate needs (ASCA, 2005). According to Starr (1996), these services should be available to (but not needed by) all students, and students often initiate services in this component. These students are in situations where (a) preventive action is called for because of threats to healthy development or (b) remedial intervention is necessary to resolve a problem that is already interfering in a student's life. Counselors' responses to either of these situations often involve the earlier described roles of consultation, counseling (including crisis counseling), and/or referral (Brown & Trusty, 2005).

Individual Planning.

A third component of a comprehensive guidance program is individual planning (Gysbers & Henderson, 2000, 2006). This component focuses on helping each individual understand self-development and formulate and monitor plans that are goal oriented. Planning courses to be taken in high school to reach one's goals is an example (see Trusty & Niles, 2003). In assisting students with their individual planning, counselors attempt to help students understand and maneuver through viable alternatives and to help students avoid premature and irrevocable decisions. Although plans regarding personal/social development are included, much of the individual planning component is related to educational and career domains. Even though titled "individual planning," a portion of this component is accomplished through group guidance—particularly with regard to awareness and exploration of educational and career opportunities (Niles, Trusty, & Mitchell, 2004). An individual's plan that is made in secondary school is grounded in developmental guidance curriculum activities carried out in elementary school.

System Support.

The fourth guidance program component, system support, is necessary to sustain the other three. System support activities include, for example, conducting research regarding program effectiveness, providing for continuing professional development of counselors, promoting the program through public relations, organizing and managing the program, educating parents, and consulting with teachers (Gysbers & Henderson, 2000, 2006). Because the guidance program is an integral part of the larger school program, counselor activities that support the school as a system, such as serving on academic curriculum committees, serving on community committees and boards, and assessing student needs also provide relevant system support (ASCA, 2005). Many system support activities are carried out through the earlier mentioned counselor roles of consultation and program management. The school, as a system, also exists within the larger system of the community, and school counselors are appropriate leaders in promoting positive school-family-community relationships and joint efforts (Trusty et al., 2008).

Component Balance.

The four guidance components described above are integrated in different proportions based on the needs of the students. This is particularly evident as one compares and contrasts time spent in each component at elementary, middle, and high school levels. In general, counselors and administrators should expect more emphasis on guidance curriculum than other components at the elementary level, and this focus usually decreases at the upper grade levels. On the other hand, individual planning usually involves less time in the program at the elementary level, but it increases significantly in high school programs. Responsive services maintain a steady and significant portion of the time balance at all three levels. The fourth component, system support, also maintains a fairly steady emphasis through all levels, generally involving less time than the other components throughout (e.g., Gysbers & Henderson, 2000, 2006; TEA, 2004). These typical component ratios are not rigid, however, and should be adjusted as student needs change.

RESOURCES NEEDED

An organized counseling program requires a commitment to providing adequate resources. Some of these resources include adequate counseling department staff, involved parents, staff development opportunities, community resources, materials, supplies, equipment, and facilities. If these are not already in place, funds need to be earmarked for required resources (TEA, 2004).

Counseling Program Standards and Accountability

It is fundamental for school administrators to understand the breadth and depth of the role school counselors play in our schools. School systems, state departments of education, and organizations that have an interest in the work of school counselors continue to seek evidence that school counseling programs are accountable, promote student achievement, and address an advocacy agenda for equity in educational opportunities (Stone & Dahir, 2004). TEA and TCA collaborated on such work and created the 2004 Texas Comprehensive, Developmental Guidance and Counseling Program guide to assist districts in complying with Texas Education Code (TEC) §§33.005-33.007. Texas Education Code, Section 33.005 Developmental Guidance and Counseling Programs states a counselor shall "work with the school faculty and staff, students, parents, and the community to plan, implement, and evaluate a developmental guidance and counseling program" (TEA, 2004, p. 117). The code further instructs counselors to design programs that include the previously addressed components: guidance curriculum, responsive services, individual planning, and system support (TEA).

The principal purpose and basis for the Texas Comprehensive, Developmental Guidance and Counseling Program guide is to offer quality program standards and implement high-quality comprehensive, developmental guidance and counseling program benefits to the various populations involved in the program (TEA, 2004). The guide also serves as a method for tailoring the counseling program model to meet the needs of the vast array of Texas public schools. It focuses on quality counseling programming and on awareness for stakeholders. For parents, it helps them understand, contribute, and support a quality guidance and counseling program in order to effectively guide their children's development; for teachers, it helps them understand the goals of the guidance program so the teacher-counselor partnership can work to the maximum benefit of students; for counselors, it helps them establish, implement, and manage programs which will benefit all of their students; and for principals, it helps them collaborate with counselors to design and deliver a quality guidance program (TEA, 2004).

Counseling standards and developed guides serve as frameworks for counselors and administrators to implement their pressing school concerns that are important to internal and external stakeholders while serving the needs of students. Being cognizant of the counseling standards and policies public schools utilize to align state, district, and campus programming efforts is essential for educational leaders. The overwhelming accountability demands placed on schools can easily consume the existence of most programs. As the executive leadership team of a campus, principals and counselors must continually communicate and collaborate and bring the school mission and vision to life. Counselors and principals are the school's experienced leaders in creating spaces for accountability conversations. They must be the driving force behind a professional learning community where accountability efforts can be discussed, validated with data collection, and acted upon. It is advisable for principals and counselors alike to utilize their combined accountability insights and efforts to be proactive in addressing the opportunities and challenges a counseling program will face in the future.

As school needs are assessed and counseling programs experience updates and revisions, data collected from this implementation and growth are valuable for school improvement efforts. A program audit is an example of a mechanism that can provide both quantitative and qualitative data and divulge the percentage of time counselors invest addressing program standards and time spent in ancillary roles. An audit can delineate the time invested responding to student and parent issues; implementing curriculum; working with communities and agencies; providing individual and group counseling; covering, lunch, game, and bus duties; and administering national and state tests.

To further align counseling program initiatives with school accountability efforts, Stone and Dahir (2011) utilize a six-step accountability process tool they name MEASURE: Mission, Element, Analyze, Stakeholders-Unite, Results, and Educate. A process created for school counselors to align their work with the accountability requirements of state and national standards, such as No Child Left Behind. By communicating and upholding programming standards, counselors and principals can join forces to discern programmatic data and reveal quantifiable successes.

The mission of a school counselor centers on assisting students with achievement of their academic, career, and personal/social potential and working daily with parents, educators, and principals to meet the needs of those being served. The MEASURE action research model is an intersection of theory and practice and according to Stone and Dahir (2011), serves as a framework to guide the design and implementation of accountable counseling programs. The charge for educational leaders and counselors is not only to sustain the supervision and implementation of program standards, but to analyze, document, and celebrate the programming results that support student achievement and school improvement.

Dimmit and Carey (2007) emphasized that when school counselors focus their programs on the academic achievement of students, they are less likely in need of defending their counseling services and time allocated to meeting student needs. The authors further noted that when teachers and administrators see positive student results in the areas of career, personal/social, and academic functioning, they are more inclined to support and value the work of school counselors.

Outcome Research Supporting School Counseling Programs

As noted throughout this chapter and reported by many authors, school counselors are increasingly required to provide evidence that school counseling programs make a difference in student achievement (e.g., Brigman & Campbell, 2003; House & Martin, 1998; Lapan, 2001; Paisley & Hayes, 2003; Sink, 2009). In this section several outcome research studies are presented that support organized school counseling programs' contributions to student development. For instance, Lapan, Gysbers, and Petroski (2001) found middle school students who attended schools with more fully implemented guidance and counseling programs reported better relationships with teachers, more satisfaction with the quality of education received, feeling safer in school, perceiving their education to be important to their future, earning higher grades, and experiencing fewer problems associated with the physical and interpersonal school environment. These results are consistent with previous comprehensive school counseling program research involving high school students (e.g., Lapan, Gysbers, & Sun, 1997). Similar findings by Nelson and Gardner (1998) revealed high school students in schools with more fully implemented guidance programs achieved higher grades on the ACT examination, took more advanced science and mathematics courses, and perceived a better overall educational experience than students in less implemented programs. In a causal-comparative study, Sink and Stroh (2003) concluded that regardless of socioeconomic status, elementary-age children (grades 3 and 4) who remained in schools with well-established comprehensive school counseling programs performed better on academic achievement tests than their peers in schools without programs in place. A similar comparison by Sink, Akos, Turnbull, and Mvududu (2008) revealed that when statistically controlling for socioeconomic status, significant differences in student achievement emerged for middle school students attending schools with at least 5 years implementation of comprehensive school counseling programs. These results echo the efforts of the ASCA National Model (ASCA, 2005) and the Education Trust (2011) regarding closing the achievement gap among socioeconomic groups. Lapan et al. (1997) pointed out that spending time with students to devote to implementation of comprehensive school counseling programs did not detract from student academic progress. Instead, these efforts appeared to play a positive role in the enhancement of student academic achievement. Other reviews involving school counseling outcome research support the findings of these studies (see Whiston & Quinby, 2011; Whiston & Sexton, 1998, for summaries).

In a survey of school counselors, Gysbers, Lapan, and Blair (1999) found those school counselors who rated their programs as more fully implemented reported higher levels of engagement with students, teachers, and parents; more visibility in the school and community; and more time delivering counseling services and less time on clerical duties. Sink and Yillik-Downer (2001) suggested that perhaps the more highly invested school counselors are in the development and implementation of the counseling program, the greater the likelihood that they will assume an increased "ownership" of the program and recognize its value in relation to overall student success.

Developing, Implementing, and Evaluating the Program

School counseling literature provides several models for developing a program (e.g., ASCA, 2005; Gysbers & Henderson, 2006; Schmidt, 2008; TEA, 2004). Among these, various authors have chosen different labels for the steps in the program development process, and some variations exist in the order of proposed actions to be taken. However, similarities are more common than differences, and in many program development models: an assessment is made of the current program, organizing for change occurs, needs are assessed, planning and designing the new or revised program is done, the program is implemented, and the implemented program is evaluated. Also, using a committee (steering committee, guidance committee, advisory committee) is commonly recommended to facilitate the process throughout its steps (e.g., Gysbers & Henderson, 2006; Myrick, 2003; Schmidt, 2008).

ASSESSING THE CURRENT PROGRAM

Assuming that some form of counseling or guidance activities exists, an informal determination that the current counseling program is not as effective as it could or should be is often the spur for change. Once change is being considered, a more formalized assessment of the current program is in order. This assessment might begin with a review of the current written program plan with regard to adequacy and extent of implementation. Potential indicators of the level of program adequacy could include reviews of counselor logs; program budgets; student records; job descriptions and actual involvement of counselors and other personnel; feedback from students, parents, teachers, and administrators; and adequacy of facilities, materials, and equipment (Schmidt, 2008; TEA, 2004).

ORGANIZING THE SUPPORT NEEDED FOR CHANGE

Moving a school from the situation of having guidance as a bare collection of services to having a comprehensive and organized counseling program involves a level of change that often raises anxiety and sometimes evokes resistance. Having commitment from all staff, including administrators, is important. The process of change itself should not overwhelm staff, and time and budget must be set aside for assessing, organizing, planning, implementing, and evaluating the program. Mitchell and Gysbers (as cited in Gysbers & Henderson, 2006) emphasized that an effective organized change process is incremental rather than abrupt.

Appropriate leadership for the change process should be identified. Gysbers and Henderson (2006) proposed (a) that a steering committee be formed to manage the overall change process and (b) that a school-community advisory committee be formed to provide recommendations and advice as a liaison between the school and community. The advisory committee does not form policy or make decisions. The steering committee must be small enough to manage its charge and large enough to be representative of counselors, administrators, teachers, parents, special school personnel (such as the special education coordinator and the school nurse), and perhaps community leaders. The steering committee in this stage would work with the administration and meet with the school board to inform and to seek support and authorization to proceed with the change process.

ASSESSING NEEDS

Gibson, Mitchell, and Higgins (1983) and Niles et al. (2004) described needs assessment as the foundation of program development. They describe processes for assessing the needs of the community, the school, and the target populations (primarily students, but also teachers and parents). A variety of techniques is available ranging from surveys, interviews, focus groups, and Delphi studies to examination of school and public records. Russo and Kassera (1989) described a comprehensive needs-assessment package effectively used in a large high school. In addition to providing a useful needs-assessment model, they pointed out that needs may vary depending on subgroupings in the student population (such as grade level, gender, ability group, racial, and ethnic differences), and that this lack of homogeneity suggests that needs particular to certain groups must not fall victim to pressures to identify only overall needs.

DESIGNING THE PROGRAM

A general program model (such as the model described above consisting of guidance curriculum, responsive services, individual planning, and system support) is adopted and studied thoroughly by the steering committee. The content areas to be infused in the comprehensive guidance curriculum are determined. In designing the program, the assessed needs should be considered on the bases of both frequency and intensity before they are prioritized to form the basis for overall program goals, particular curriculum content areas, program balance, and specific program objectives. Gysbers and Henderson (2006) have suggested an alternative that the formal needs assessment (see preceding section) be conducted *after* the program is designed in order to use desired student competencies established in the program designing stage as items in the formal needs assessment.

IMPLEMENTING THE PROGRAM

Implementing the program involves carrying out the designed improvements and using the school counselors in accordance with job descriptions that properly utilize counselors' competencies. Carefully designed and prioritized activities, provision of staff development for counselors and others involved in the program, and acceptance of a fitting model for the evaluation of school counselor performance facilitate implementation (TEA, 2004).

EVALUATING THE PROGRAM

Broadly defined, evaluating the counseling program involves gathering data about the program and using the data to draw conclusions about the value of the program. As such, evaluation forms the basis for changing a program to increase its effectiveness, for demonstrating accountability (i.e., responsiveness) to needs, and for counselors' professional development and growth. Proper program evaluation requires clearly stated goals that are agreed upon by those involved in the evaluation procedure. As one would find in many fields, program evaluation is a continuous process, not an outcome goal itself. Subsequent to evaluation, requirements for change are recognized, and the cycle of organizing, assessing, designing, and implementing becomes continual.

Evaluating the counseling program entails using data about (a) the *delivery of services* and (b) the *outcomes* related to those served. Schmidt (2008) clarified that *delivery of services* can be evaluated by reporting how many times the services were provided, how many people received the services, and how much time was spent delivering the services. Services-oriented evaluations may also focus, for example, on the balance of time allocated to the different program components, availability of the counselors, timely delivery of services, and relationships between counselors and other school personnel. Program evaluation may also be approached by assessing *outcomes*. This aspect of evaluation centers on assessing the development and/or improvement of competencies in areas such as study skills, decision-making strategies, academic grades, career awareness, and school attendance—either on a schoolwide basis or as needed on an individual student basis. For example, if the counseling program is patterned after the ASCA Competencies and Indicators (ASCA, 2005), the degree to which students meet the Competencies and Indicators are salient evaluation data. If such assessments are limited to schoolwide data, the program runs the risk of not addressing the needs of individual students or of small groups of students (Schmidt, 2008). Also, using schoolwide achievement or behavior data for evaluation purposes can be problematic because so many variables are related to students' achievement and behavior (Brown & Trusty, 2005). With increased emphasis on school reform and student outcomes, Martin and Robinson (2011) asserted that school counselors must transform their work "to create concrete, measurable outcomes for students" (p. 12).

Inherent in program effectiveness is the effectiveness of the counselors in performing their roles. Therefore, an effective means of evaluating individual counselor performance should be incorporated into program evaluation (TEA, 2004). Regardless of the evaluative procedures or databases used, evaluation of individual counselor performance should be based on the job description that the counselor is expected to follow. The procedures should be understood by the evaluator and counselor in advance, and the model should be flexible enough to reflect variations agreed upon by the counselor and evaluator. ASCA (2005), TCA (2004), and Schmidt (2008) provided models for counselor performance evaluation. Evaluations are based on data gathered through a variety of means such as observations (live or taped), interviews, self-reports, input from those receiving services, products developed by counselors, records of activities, and outside expert review. If observations of counselors performing activities are being used as a database, guidelines regarding such observations should be agreed upon. Several resources (e.g., Gysbers & Henderson, 2006; Henderson & Lampe, 1992; TCA, 2004) are available to assist with developing guidelines for using observation as a database in counselor performance evaluation.

Ethical and Legal Guidelines

Ethical and legal considerations affect principals and counselors daily. School counselors have two major sources of ethical guidelines: (1) the *Ethical Standards for School Counselors* (ASCA, 2010) and (2) the *ACA Code of Ethics and Standards of Practice* (American Counseling Association, 2005). In order for the administrator to better understand the counselor's role and decisions, it is important for school administrators to be aware of several ethical issues addressed in these codes. Although ethical standards are not in themselves laws, they often relate to legal issues. Administrators must be familiar with federal and state laws that affect education and counseling in particular. These issues include the release of records, discrimination, documentation, academic requirements, testing, staffing, reporting child abuse, credentials, and special populations. Two general ethical issues drawn from the *Ethical Standards for School Counselors*, both with possible legal ramifications, are presented in the following paragraphs.

Ethically, the school counselor's primary obligation is to the counselee, and information obtained by the counselor is kept confidential unless there is clear and imminent danger to the counselee or others or legal requirements for disclosure. In clear and imminent danger situations, the counselor is ethically called upon to inform appropriate authorities. An ethical dilemma is presented to the counselor when an administrator demands confidential information that does not fall into the above categories. Confidentiality also applies to counseling records, which are to be released only according to prescribed laws and school policies (ASCA, 2010).

Another ethical issue that school counselors and administrators sometimes see differently involves dual relationships, wherein the counselor and the client have a relationship outside of counseling that might impair the counselor's impartiality and/or the willingness of the student to participate in counseling. Obvious examples include sexual contact with clients, counseling family members, and counseling one's own students if the counselor is also a teacher of record. A dual relationship problem occurs when the counselor is called upon to administer or witness punishment or is placed in a potentially disciplinary "spotlight" such as hall monitor. In small communities, some dual relationships are impossible to avoid (e.g., children of family, children of friends, or members of the same church), and the ethical standards provide guidelines for reducing the potential for harm if dual relationships are unavoidable (ASCA, 2010).

Counselor Roles in Promoting Counseling Program Effectiveness

In addition to effectively carrying out the counselor roles described earlier in this chapter, the counselor has responsibility for doing so in a professional manner (ASCA, 2005; TCA, 2004). This requires a commitment to following ethical standards, carrying one's load, being timely and available, maintaining collegiality, advocating for all students, and modeling service. The counselor should demonstrate and promote teamwork among school professionals and keep administrators informed (within ethical limits of confidentiality). The school counselor is also obligated to engage in professional development to stay knowledgeable of current social conditions, techniques, ethical standards, and laws.

Administrator Roles in Promoting Counseling Program Effectiveness

Administrators' roles in promoting the formation and effectiveness of a comprehensive counseling program are varied. These may differ some by administrative level (e.g., principal and superintendent), but regardless of the level, the roles at different levels often parallel each other. For example, at all levels, the administrator plays an important role in supporting program development/improvement efforts in house (among faculty and staff) and in the community. The professional relationship between counselor and administrator is a powerful dynamic when confronting school and community issues. Formal and informal (and frequent) public relations activities, whether spoken or written, can have substantial school improvement impact.

The administrator must promote a budget that allows for the necessary resources, clerical assistance, facilities, information resources, assessment tools, equipment, and supplies. A well-planned budget offers opportunities to provide direct and indirect services for students and staff alike. Also in the budget, the administrator must address funding for professional development activities to better meet the needs of the district by improving the competencies of the counselors (Gysbers & Henderson, 2006).

The administrator plays an important role in hiring an adequate number of properly qualified professional counselors. This is particularly crucial given the shortages of counselors in some locations and the calls for lowering the ratio of school counselors to students, both of which could force administrators to hire less than qualified counselors (Towner-Larsen, Granello, & Sears, 2000).

Assuming properly qualified counselors are hired, the administrator, particularly the building principal, exercises a central role in determining whether or not counselors are involved in nonguidance activities. Burnham and Jackson (2000) reported that although counselors do perform the functions described in contemporary program models, there are discrepancies and wide variations. They further suggest that assignment of nonguidance duties (e.g., lunch, bus, game, clerical, discipline) to counselors remains a most troublesome practice and that involvement of administrators is vital in determining who best should carry out these nonguidance tasks. Gysbers and Henderson (2006) echoed this problem, arguing that it is necessary to streamline counselor involvement in nonguidance activities. Although nonguidance activities benefit the school as an organization, it is a Catch-22 situation, as the school needs to be run safely and effectively, but it is the students who miss the window of opportunity to be served and counseled during the school day when counselors are overextended in ancillary responsibilities. Myrick (2003) pointed out that coordination, an appropriate role of counselors, can become a "catch all" source of overload, and that coordination of activities should be shared with other personnel to give counselors time for more direct services. Recent research examining principals' perceptions of school counselors' time in delivery service areas delineated by the ASCA National Model (ASCA, 2005) revealed that exposure to information about ASCA's Model had the greatest impact on appropriate time allocations for school counselors (Leuwerke, Walker, & Shi, 2009). The authors further noted that school counselors should be encouraged to engage in close collaboration with principals and to take the lead in advocacy to better inform principals of appropriate roles and responsibilities of school counselors.

If a lead counselor in a school is not available to do so, the principal is often responsible for evaluating the effectiveness of individual counselors. This requires an understanding of the proper roles of counselors, a commitment to using counselors fittingly, and knowledge of suitable standards and databases upon which to base the evaluations (TCA, 2004).

Closely related to evaluation is supervision, or overseeing the work of others to improve performance and professional development (Borders & Brown, 2005). Henderson and Lampe (1992) described an effective model of supervision of counselors in a large school district, with particular emphasis on clinical supervision involving feedback regarding counselor activities observed in progress.

Summary

Responsibilities of school counselors vary based on the needs of constituencies served and the understandings and expectations of principals who are ultimately responsible for guidance operations in their schools. Administrators and counselors often do not perceive the profundity of each other's responsibilities and roles. This chapter described varying responsibilities of counselors; defined commonly used counselor-related terms; explained how counseling and guidance services can be organized, improved, and evaluated; and discussed counseling program standards and accountability requirements. Several outcome research studies supporting the implementation of organized school counseling programs were presented, and some of the ethical situations that counselors and principals might see from different perspectives were addressed. Also, the importance of the counselor and the principal working as a corps for the benefit of students was emphasized. The following case study and questions were constructed to help pull together the information and ideas presented in this chapter.

Applying Your Knowledge

As principal of a school in an urban area, you believe you have a good working relationship with the three veteran counselors employed. There are 2,100 students in your school, and budget constraints will not allow the employment of an additional counselor. However, funding has been approved for the hiring of a clerical assistant.

The school counselors appear to be working together as a team by dividing the work load as best as possible, equally among them. In order to meet students' needs, they assume full responsibility for conducting classroom guidance activities. They also provide academic planning for all students; support special education services; and provide inservice training for teachers on a range of topics covering, for instance, conflict resolutions, at risk students, and English language learners. In addition, they coordinate the school's standardized testing program for all students (without much complaint) as well as actively coordinate other programs and special projects. Even though the school counselors are working hard and are extremely busy, you would like to see more individual and group counseling being conducted. Another area of concern is that very little has been done regarding providing data to prove the effectiveness of the counseling program.

Recently, you attended a seminar concerning current issues in school counseling. This seminar addressed the development of a comprehensive school counseling program. As a result of information gained, you have identified ways in which you think the counseling program in your school could be strengthened. You have scheduled a meeting with the school counselors as a team to develop a plan to work toward improving the counseling program.

QUESTIONS

1. Knowing the three counselors have a full work load with 2,100 students, what is your leadership style and approach for creating buy-in and support in this department as you ask them to take on added responsibilities?
2. What strengths do you identify in the existing school counseling program? What are some of the weaknesses?
3. What would be the first step toward initiating change in the counseling program? Who would you involve in this process?
4. What contributions could students, parents, and community members make toward the operation of a comprehensive counseling program? What could be done to elicit their support?
5. What role could teachers in the school play in changing the counseling program?
6. Do you anticipate a counselor–student ratio of 1:700 students a barrier to the effective implementation of a comprehensive counseling program? If so, what are some suggestions for dealing with these challenges?
7. What could be done to provide data to assess the effectiveness of the counseling program?

QUESTIONS FOR THOUGHT

1. What are the major advantages of a comprehensive counseling program? What might be some disadvantages?
2. When implementing change, what are the benefits of a master plan of action? How do you respond to program challenges and support possible naysayers of the action plan?

3. What is the importance of program evaluation? What is the importance of individual counselor evaluation? How often should these processes occur, and what might be done to lessen the overwhelming task?
4. In what ethical and legal aspects of counselor functioning should an administrator seek professional development?

For Additional Information Online

American Counseling Association: http://www.counseling.org

American School Counselor Association: http://www.schoolcounselor.org

References

American Counseling Association. (2005). *ACA code of ethics and standards of practice.* Alexandria, VA: Author. Retrieved January 3, 2011 from http://www.counseling.org/site/Resources/CodeofEthics/TP/Home/CT2 .aspx

American School Counselor Association. (2005). *The ASCA national model: A framework for school counseling programs* (2nd ed.). Alexandria, VA: Author.

American School Counselor Association. (2010). *Ethical standards for school counselors.* Alexandria, VA: Author. Retrieved January 3, 2011 from http://www.schoolcounselor.org/content.asp?pl=325&sl= 136&contentid=136

Baker, S. B., & Gerler, E. R., Jr. (2004). *School counseling for the twenty-first century* (4th ed.). Upper Saddle River, NJ: Pearson.

Borders, L. D., & Brown, L. L. (2005). *New handbook of counseling supervision.* Mahwah, NJ: Lawrence Erlbaum Associates.

Brigman, G., & Campbell, C. (2003). Helping students improve academic achievement and school success behavior. *Professional School Counseling, 7,* 91–98.

Brown, D., & Trusty, J. (2005). *Designing and implementing comprehensive school counseling programs: Promoting student competence and meeting students' needs.* Pacific Grove, CA: Brooks/Cole.

Burnham, J. J., & Jackson, C. M. (2000). School counselor roles: Discrepancies between actual practice and existing models. *Professional School Counseling, 4,* 41–49.

Carr, J. V., & Hayslip, J. B. (1989). Getting unstuck from the 1970s: New Hampshire style. *The School Counselor, 37,* 41–46.

Dimmitt, C., & Carey, J. (2007). Using the ASCA national model to facilitate school transitions. *Professional School Counseling, 10,* 227–232.

Drummond, R. J., & Jones, K. D. (2010). *Assessment procedures for counselors and helping professionals* (7th ed.). Upper Saddle River, NJ: Pearson.

Education Trust. (2011). National Center for Transforming School Counseling. Retrieved February 3, 2011 from http://www.edtrust.org/dc/tsc. Author.

Gibson, R. L., Mitchell, M. H., & Higgins, R. E. (1983). *Development and management of counseling programs and guidance services.* New York: Macmillan.

Gysbers, N. C., & Henderson, P. (2000). *Developing and managing your school guidance program* (3rd ed.). Alexandria, VA: American Counseling Association.

Gysbers, N. C., & Henderson, P. (2006). *Developing and managing your school guidance program* (4th ed.). Alexandria, VA: American Counseling Association.

Gysbers, N. C., Lapan, R. T., & Blair, M. (1999). Closing in on the statewide implementation of a comprehensive guidance program model. *Professional School Counseling, 2,* 357–366.

Gysbers, N. C., Lapan, R. T., & Jones. B. A. (2000). School board policies for guidance and counseling: A call to action. *Professional School Counseling, 3,* 349–355.

Gysbers, N. C., Starr, M., & Magnuson, C. (1998). *Missouri comprehensive guidance: A model for program development, implementation, and evaluation.* Jefferson City, MO: Missouri Department of Elementary and Secondary Education.

Henderson, P., & Lampe, R. E. (1992). Clinical supervision of school counselors. *The School Counselor, 39,* 151–157.

House, R. M., & Martin, P. J. (1998). Advocating for better futures for all students: A new vision for school counselors. *Education, 119,* 284–291.

Lapan, R. T. (2001). Results-based comprehensive guidance and counseling programs: A framework for planning and evaluation. *Professional School Counseling, 4,* 289–299.

Lapan, R. T., Gysbers, N. C., & Petroski, G. F. (2001). Helping seventh graders be safe and successful: A state-wide study of the impact of comprehensive guidance and counseling programs. *Journal of Counseling & Development, 79*, 320–330.

Lapan, R. T., Gysbers, N. C., & Sun, Y. (1997). The impact of more fully implemented guidance programs on the school experiences of high school students: A statewide evaluation study. *Journal of Counseling & Development, 75*, 292–302.

Leuwerke, W. C., Walker, J., & Shi, Q. (2009). Informing principals: The impact of different types of information on principals' perceptions of professional school counselors. *Professional School Counseling, 12*, 263–271.

Martin, I., Carey, J., & DeCoster, K. (2009). A national study of the current status of state school counseling models. *Professional School Counseling, 12*, 378–386.

Martin, P. J., & Robinson, S. G. (2011). Transforming the school counseling profession. In B. T. Erford (Ed.), *Transforming the school counseling profession* (3rd ed., pp. 1–18). Upper Saddle River, NJ: Pearson.

Myrick, R. D. (2003). *Developmental guidance and counseling: A practical approach* (4th ed.). Minneapolis, MN: Educational Media Corporation.

Nelson, D. E., & Gardner, J. L. (1998). *An evaluation of the comprehensive guidance program in Utah public schools.* Salt Lake City, UT: The Utah State Office of Education.

Niles, S. G., Trusty, J., & Mitchell, N. (2004). Fostering positive career development in children and adolescents. In R. Pérusse & G. E. Goodnough (Eds.), *Leadership, advocacy, and direct services strategies for professional school counselors* (pp. 102–124). Pacific Grove, CA: Brooks/Cole.

Paisley, P. O., & Hayes, R. L. (2003). School counseling in the academic domain: Transformations in preparation and practice. *Professional School Counseling, 6*, 198–204.

Parsons, R. D., & Kahn, W. J. (2005). *The school counselor as consultant: An integrated model for school-based consultation.* Belmont, CA: Thomson Brooks/Cole.

Pérusse, R., Goodenough, G. E., Donegan, J., & Jones, C. (2004). Perceptions of school counselors and school principals about the National Standards for School Counseling Programs and the Transforming School Counseling Initiative. *Professional School Counseling, 7*, 152–161.

Picchioni, A. P., & Bonk, E. C. (1983). *A comprehensive history of guidance in the United States.* Austin, TX: Texas Personnel and Guidance Association.

Ponec, D. L., & Brock, B. L. (2000). Relationships among elementary school counselors and principals: A unique bond. *Professional School Counseling, 3*, 208–217.

Russo, T. J., & Kassera, W. (1989). A comprehensive needs-assessment package for secondary school guidance programs. *The School Counselor, 36*, 265–269.

Schmidt, J. J. (2008). *Counseling in schools: Essential services and comprehensive programs* (5th ed.). Boston: Allyn & Bacon.

Shoffner, M. F., & Williamson, R. D. (2000). Engaging preservice school counselors and principals in dialogue and collaboration. *Counselor Education and Supervision, 40*, 128–140.

Sink, C. A. (2009). School counselors as accountability leaders: Another call for action. *Professional School Counseling, 13*, 68–74.

Sink, C. A., Akos, P., Turnbull, R. J., & Mvududu, N. (2008). An investigation of comprehensive school counseling programs and academic achievement in Washington state middle schools. *Professional School Counseling, 12*, 43–53.

Sink, C. A., & MacDonald, G. (1998). The status of comprehensive guidance and counseling in the United States. *Professional School Counseling, 2*, 88–94.

Sink, C. A., & Stroh, H. R. (2003). Raising achievement test scores of early elementary school students through comprehensive school counseling programs. *Professional School Counseling, 6*, 350–364.

Sink, C. A., & Yillik-Downer, A. (2001). School counselors' perceptions of comprehensive guidance and counseling programs: A national survey. *Professional School Counseling, 4*, 278–288.

Smith, L. W., & Gideon, L. B. (1929). *Planning a career.* New York: American Book Company.

Starr, M. F. (1996). Comprehensive guidance and systematic educational and career planning: Why a K-12 approach? *Journal of Career Development, 23*, 9–22.

Stone, C. B., & Dahir, C. A. (2004). *School counselor accountability: A measure of student success.* Upper Saddle River, NJ: Pearson.

Stone C. B., & Dahir, C. A. (2011). *School counselor accountability: A measure of student success* (3rd ed.) Upper Saddle River, NJ: Pearson.

Texas Counseling Association. (2004). *Texas evaluation model for professional school counselors* (2nd ed.). Austin, TX: Author.

Texas Education Agency. (2004). *A model comprehensive, developmental guidance and counseling program for Texas public schools: A guide for program development pre-K—12th grade.* Austin, TX: Author.

Towner-Larsen, R., Granello, D. H., & Sears, S. J. (2000). Supply and demand for school counselors: Perceptions of public school administrators. *Professional School Counseling, 3,* 270–276.

Trusty, J., Mellin, E. A., & Herbert, J. T. (2008). Closing achievement gaps: Roles and tasks of elementary school counselors. *Elementary School Journal, 108,* 407–421.

Trusty, J., & Niles, S. G. (2003). High-school math courses and completion of the bachelor's degree. *Professional School Counseling, 7,* 99–107.

Whiston, S. C., & Quinby, R. F. (2011). Outcomes research on school counseling interventions and programs. In B. T. Erford (Ed.), *Transforming the school counseling profession* (3rd ed., pp. 58–69). Upper Saddle River, NJ: Pearson.

Whiston, S. C., & Sexton, T. L. (1998). A review of school counseling outcome research: Implications for practice. *Journal of Counseling & Development, 76,* 412–426.

Alternative Education Programs

11

Diana K. Freeman
Casey Graham Brown

An alternative program is an educational program
designed to meet the needs of a targeted
population of students who do not
experience success in the
traditional school setting.

—Diana K. Freeman, 2005

Objectives

1. To learn the history of the modern alternative education movement
2. To learn the most common characteristics of the modern alternative education movement
3. To develop an understanding of the administrator's role in an alternative program

Introduction

Alternative programs within the school setting address a wide variety of educational offerings. Any program that differs from the mainstream traditional school is often dubbed an *alternative program.* This creates a wide array of program variations and causes great difficulty when trying to define exactly what comprises an alternative program or what falls under the umbrella of alternative education. One concise definition of an alternative program is:

> an educational program that embraces subject matter and/or methodology that is not generally offered to students of the same age or grade level in traditional school settings, which offers a range of educational options and includes the students as an integral part of the planning team. (New Jersey Department of Education, as cited in Katsiyannis & Williams, 1998, p. 276)

The U.S. Department of Education (USDE) defined an alternative school as:

> a public elementary/secondary school that: 1) addresses needs of students that typically cannot be met in a regular school; 2) provides nontraditional education; 3) serves as an adjunct to a regular school; and 4) falls outside the categories of regular, special education, or vocational education. (cited in Cable, Plucker, & Spradlin, 2009, p. 3)

Aron's (2006) definition of alternative education encompasses "all educational activities that fall outside the *traditional* K-12 school system (including home schooling, GED preparation programs, special programs for gifted children, charter schools, etc.), although the term is often used to describe programs serving vulnerable youth who are no longer in traditional schools" (p. 3). For the purpose of this chapter, a broad definition of alternative programs will be used. The definition of an alternative program in this work is any educational program offered to students that provides a nontraditional curriculum, a nontraditional setting, or both.

Alternative programs can be found as freestanding independent schools operating as a part of a local education unit, a private school, or a charter school. An alternative program may also function as a school-within-a-school. Still other alternative programs are offered as support programs for certain qualifying students within the traditional school setting (Knight & Kneese, 1999). An alternative program may also include non-educational support services such as health services or social services.

As indicated in the definitions above, the method of instructional delivery is one definitive factor of alternative education. Alternative programs embrace nontraditional teaching techniques and either expand or compress the strict timeframe associated with course work in the traditional school to meet the needs of the student. Often, traditional pencil-and-paper work is exchanged for project-driven assignments. Other instructional variations may include vocational experience being honored as progress toward completion of graduation requirements, and business and community members acting as teachers and mentors. While any of these methodologies can be found in traditional schools, their existence there is considered innovative; in alternative programs, however, such methods are considered commonplace (Guerin & Denti, 1999; Knight & Kneese, 1999).

Another common determinant of what is considered an alternative program is the target population. Generally, alternative education is designed to benefit students who are not successful in a traditional school setting, students who are considered at risk of dropping out of school (Lange & Sletten, 2002). A subgroup of at-risk students is made up of those who have committed some type of rule violation or crime that places them within a class of students removed from the traditional campus. A third group of students identified as candidates for alternative programs are those students qualified for special education services according to the Individuals with Disabilities Education Act (IDEA). Some alternative programs are designed specifically to address juvenile offenders while other programs address at-risk students in general. Some programs exclude students with a qualifying condition under IDEA while others include them and still others are offered exclusively to students with an Individual Education Plan (IEP) as defined by IDEA (Lange & Sletten). Each alternative program defines for itself the target population.

The lack of a cohesive, common definition has made the process of studying alternative programs difficult. The number of studies concerning alternative education is limited, and those that do exist generally are limited to describing only the program characteristics. Even fewer studies have been conducted concerning the effectiveness of the alternative program. The majority of the articles addressing alternative education provide information about a single program and tout the specific design of that particular program. If individuals are interested in an overarching view of alternative programs, they must gather and synthesize the material themselves.

History of Alternative Education

Educational opportunities designed to meet the needs of differing groups of students have been a part of the American educational system since its inception. The first schools in the United States widely dubbed alternative schools were schools created in the mid-1800s by Archbishop John Hughes of New York when the government would not appropriate funds for the education of Catholic students. The schools Hughes created were designed to educate students of the Catholic faith who chose not to attend the publicly supported schools that taught Protestant values (Cable et al., 2009). The alternative education movement now present in this country began during the civil rights movement of the 1960s (Lange & Sletten, 2002). The Elementary and Secondary Education Act (ESEA) of 1965 focused attention on the public schools as a major weapon in the war on poverty, and a key in the fight against social injustice. The ESEA provided funding from the federal government to support new educational programs designed to battle these social enemies (Lange & Sletten).

The alternative programs of the 1960s focused on equity. The public schools were viewed as discriminatory institutions organized in such a way that the individuality of the learner was ignored. Success was measured by academic progress in terms that failed to recognize the growth and advancement of many students. The alternative school provided a different school structure tailored to meet the needs of the students who were not successful in the traditional school structures (Raywid, 1998). By the end of the 1960s, these newly structured schools were being called alternative schools (Neumann, 1994).

Near the end of the 1960s, the alternative education movement split into two distinct categories: those inside public education and those outside public education. The alternative programs outside public education had two forms. The first form was categorized as Freedom Schools. They were developed to provide minority students access to a high-quality education that was not perceived as available in the public schools. The Freedom Schools had a community focus and appeared in settings ranging from storefronts to church basements (Lange & Sletten, 2002). In a different vein, the Free School movement focused on the fulfillment and achievement of the individual; the traditional school was seen as confining and limiting. Students were free to define what they would or would not learn. The only rule taught was that each individual had the right to determine what was correct for one's own self (Lange & Sletten, 2002).

The popularity of alternative programs available outside public schools influenced public school educators to develop similar options within the public school system.

One broad category of public school alternative programs was the Open School. "These schools were characterized by parent, student and teacher choice; autonomy in learning and pace, non-competitive evaluation; and a child-centered approach" (Lange & Sletten, 2002, p. 4). The Open School movement is credited with instigating the many different alternative programs that grew within the public schools during the 1970s. Raywid (1998) classified the alternative programs of this era according to the school's focus for change: the student, the school, or the educational setting.

The back-to-basics emphasis of the 1980s and the increasing number of students identified as functioning below average achievement levels also influenced alternative schools. Options available to students began to narrow and the focus was remedial. The organization of these schools was formal and hierarchical; the curriculum was conventional and featured drill and practice (Neumann, 1994). Student and teacher choice was no longer a defining characteristic of alternative programs during this time.

Another focus of the 1980s was the development of alternative programs to educate disruptive students (Lange & Sletten, 2002). This was an outgrowth of the focus on what was perceived as the failure of public schools. Juvenile crime statistics were often cited as either a cause or a result of the deficits of the public school system. One strategy to correct the deficits was to provide a specific educational environment for students who were behaviorally disruptive. By removing the student offenders, the other students could focus on learning; and the removed students could benefit from a setting that allowed them to avoid expulsion and thus continue their education (de los Santos & Lowe, 2001).

The 1990s saw a growth in the number of alternative schools. Once again, student and teacher choice returned as a key characteristic of alternative programs; also, the rise in reports of violent acts committed on school campuses supported continuation and growth of alternative programs designed to house disruptive and adjudicated youth (Kleiner, Porch, & Farris, 2002). Raywid (1994) classified the schools of this decade into three types. The Type I alternative schools were schools of choice designed to create a fulfilling environment for the students and adults associated with the program. Type II alternative schools were last-chance programs designed to provide students one final chance before expulsion; the students in Type II schools did not attend by choice. Type II alternative schools were designed to serve students who had been removed from the traditional school due to behavioral infractions. Type III alternative schools had a remedial focus. The students were viewed as needing either academic or social-emotional rehabilitation or both. The presumption was that with the remediation, the student would be able to return to a traditional school environment. Though Raywid (1994) presented these as *pure* types, any single alternative school could include characteristics of any or all of the three types.

The current emphasis on accountability and the use of standardized tests as measures of student achievement will undoubtedly influence alternative programs as they do traditional programs. According to Martin and Brand (2006):

> Non-traditional schools . . . are pushing up against the accountability requirements, causing them to change some of their instructional strategies. While the focus on improved academics in alternative education is needed, the shift to testing-based accountability, rather than performance or competency-based accountability, may ironically change the profile of many alternative education programs to look more like the traditional schools students left. (p. 6)

The direction the alternative programs will take is not yet clear. The alternative schools in existence now, in the early part of the 21st century, continue the patterns begun in the 1990s. Aron and Zweig (2003) attempted to create a typology for alternative schools. They cited heavily Raywid's (1994) classification of Types I, II, and III alternative schools, and used her framework as the basis for moving forward. They concluded that alternative schools could be classified by the characteristics of the program. They determined that more information was needed concerning alternative education programs before any further classification system could be standardized.

Characteristics of Alternative Programs

Ambiguity surrounds alternative programs. No single factor applies to all alternative programs. In a survey conducted in 2002 for the National Center for Educational Statistics Fast Response Survey System entitled *Public Alternative Schools and Programs for Students At Risk of Education Failure: 2000-2001*, Kleiner and colleagues provided a fairly broad compilation of characteristics of alternative programs. That particular survey was updated in 2007-08 and provides a more current picture of alternative education in the United States. Prior to those efforts, Raywid led a national survey published in 1982 with a more narrow focus in which she surveyed the personnel of secondary alternative schools of choice that she had identified as Type I. Other prominent alternative education researchers, Fashola and Slavin (1997, 1998), completed descriptions and evaluations of various commercial programs designed to benefit at-risk students. Various other practicing educators and researchers have developed lists of common characteristics found among alternative programs (for example, see Aron & Zweig, 2003; Knight & Kneese, 1999; Rutter & Margelofsky, 1997). The following is a compilation of the characteristics identified in these works.

CHOICE

Choice is recognized as one of the key factors present in alternative programs. Choice in this instance indicates the student's freedom to choose whether or not to become a member of a particular alternative program or school. This freedom of choice is considered critical to the student's commitment to the program ("Alternative Schools for Disruptive Youth," 1991; Neumann, 1994; Raywid, 1982, 1994). This choice is important because a sense of commitment or community is linked to school and student success (Leone & Drakeford, 1999).

The school must create an environment that has a sense of community. This allows the students and the staff to work together in creating meaningful goals for learning. The change in the learning structure fosters the continuation of the sense of community that, in turn, maintains the cooperative spirit of the program. This cycle is a prominent feature in alternative programs of choice (Leone & Drakeford, 1999; Raywid, 1994).

Raywid (1994) found that Type I schools, alternative schools of choice, have greater and longer lasting positive effects than either Type II or Type III schools. The students create a connection with the program and achieve more than at any point in their enrollment in a traditional school. "Students who had never engaged with school, or rarely succeeded at it, are sometimes transformed as to attitude, behavior, and accomplishment" (Raywid, 1994, p. 28). Anecdotal evidence from these schools supports this position; however, very little empirical evidence exists concerning the effectiveness of alternative schools ("Alternative Schools for Disruptive Youth," 1991; Aron & Zweig, 2003; Lange & Sletten, 2002).

The concept of choice also applies to the faculty of the alternative school or program. The true sense of community will not develop if the teachers do not also form a personal commitment to the program. Murdock (1999) identified the student's perception of the teacher's long-term expectations as the greatest influence over student engagement and discipline. Knight and Kneese (1999) also identified a respectful, trusting student–teacher relationship as a common strategy among alternative programs. Gold (1995) stated that "giving students warm, interpersonal support" (p. 8) is a key component for successful schools.

Some school districts facilitate alternative schools that serve as correctional institutions in order to serve students who have not adjusted well to traditional schools (Thomas & Thomas, 2008). Discipline alternative education programs do not employ choice as a key characteristic. Students are placed in the alternative schools based on actions taken that violate the published rules and codes of the traditional schools. Discipline schools do not generally strive to create a sense of community or belonging. Students attend for a specified length of time and then are expected to return to their traditional campuses. Although discipline placements can be quite lengthy, up to a full calendar year, the expectation of the discipline alternative education programs is that the students will complete the assigned term and then exit the programs.

SIZE

Closely related to the ability to create a sense of community and belonging for both students and teachers is the size of the alternative program. In fact, a decreased school size is identified quite frequently as a defining factor of an alternative program (Duke & Griesdorn, 1999; Neumann, 1994). Size in this case does not refer to the square footage of the facility but rather to the number of students and teachers served by the program. When students were asked to identify the factors of traditional schools most inhibitive to success, they listed large group instruction as one of the two most deterring factors (Rutter & Margelofsky, 1997). The alternative program strives to overcome this by limiting class size. This particular restriction has caused some alternative programs to turn away prospective students or to place these students on a waiting list (Carver & Lewis, 2010; Kleiner et al., 2002). Alternative education settings that embrace "sustained, family-like support systems of peers and caring adults . . . develop an 'opportunity structure' by setting rigorous standards and high expectations for students" (Wisconsin Department of Public Instruction, 2009, p. 1).

METHOD OF INSTRUCTIONAL DELIVERY

There are a variety of types of alternative schools and just as many delivery methods within the various school types. Some alternative schools facilitate partnerships between the campus and the community; others introduce vocational components in order to add a dynamic that "focuses on making school meaningful while preparing students for the workforce" (Indiana Department of Education, n. d., para. 3). Instructional practices considered innovative in the traditional school have long been practiced in alternative settings. The underlying premise of the flexibility in teaching methodology is that students must be provided the opportunity to succeed. A myriad of methods are thus employed, including "open enrollment, year-round programming, compressed or expanded programs, credit-recovery courses, evening schedules, hands-on career-related courses and internships, GED preparation courses with expanded content to encourage students' further education, dual-enrollment, and credit for competency" (Martin & Brand, 2006, p. 14).

The alternative school is rooted in the idea that the structure of the traditional school does not fit or benefit all learners; therefore, the school must change so that it more closely matches the student. Some traditional school attempts to address the varied needs of the learner such as tracking, ability grouping, or labeling are noticeably missing in the alternative program (Neumann, 1994).

Delivery Practices

Common instructional practices within various alternative education programs include thematic units, high-interest topics, portfolios and other alternative assessments, technology, affective education, and transition skills (Guerin & Denti, 1999). Secondary level alternative programs frequently include a vocational component so that a student can earn a wage and credit toward graduation at the same time (Fashola & Slavin, 1998). Clear, concise goals developed by teacher and student collaboration are also prominent characteristics (Knight & Kneese, 1999). The students who attend alternative programs generally have a background of academic failure, so the structure of the program itself must include added academic supports and the opportunity to learn how to learn ("Alternative Schools for Disruptive Youth," 1991). Slavin (1996) went so far as to state that no improvement in student achievement would be realized until the day-to-day instructional practices change to support that improvement.

Technology Integration

The widespread availability of technology that supports education is also found in alternative school environments. Seventeen percent of the school districts with students enrolled in district-administered alternative schools and at-risk programs utilize distance education as a delivery method (Carver & Lewis, 2010). Some schools facilitate instruction entirely through Internet-based delivery. Watson, Winograd, and Kalmon (2004) identified five categories of virtual schools: statewide supplemental programs, district-level supplemental programs, single-district cyber schools, multidistrict cyber schools, and cyber charters.

Many alternative programs rely heavily on curriculum and educational support materials provided through computers or tablet devices. The widespread availability of divergent content allows relatively few teachers to provide a large variety of material. The schools that use technology report that special consideration must be given to those needs of the students that cannot be met by machines. Care must be exercised to provide opportunities for students to develop a sense of community and to measure progress in nontraditional methods (Archambault et al., 2010).

Virtual education programs are typically of two types—that is, either supplemental or full-time schools (Holstead, Spradlin, & Plucker, 2008). Supplemental programs are identified as those that primarily provide students with the opportunity to take courses beyond the "classroom curriculum offered by the students' schools" (p. 2). Full-time schools provide the majority of coursework to students online (Holstead et al.).

Virtual schools can be useful to particular student populations whose needs are unable to be met in the traditional educational setting (Holstead et al., 2008; Roblyer, 2006). The purpose of virtual schools is to provide students with access to programs and opportunities that may be unavailable on traditional campuses (Holstead et al., 2008). West Virginia, for example, provides flexible, online scheduling to allow students to retake coursework. The state reported that roughly 25% of its approximately 1,500 students who attended the state's virtual school participated in order to retake a failed course (Southern Regional Education Board, 2005).

There are numerous benefits to virtual learning including providing individual instruction to meet specific needs, flexibility in scheduling and location, additional opportunities for students who are not physically able to attend a traditional school, increased motivation, and an allowance for educational choice (Berge & Clark, 2005; Kellogg & Politoski, 2002). The most often mentioned benefit of virtual learning is the expansion of educational access (Berge & Clark). Virtual learning programs can potentially allow school districts the opportunity to offer students courses that were previously unavailable due to financial constraints or physical location.

Due to the unique sizes and scopes of online learning programs, financial variables pertaining to virtual learning should be carefully deliberated (Holstead et al., 2008). Often the development of virtual learning programs encumbers districts with hidden expenses. Technology-based programs are inherently more costly than traditional classrooms due to the expense of the equipment required to operate them.

It is important to provide thorough training and skill development for faculty who are teaching students in virtual settings (Holstead et al., 2008; Roblyer, 2006). Roblyer recommended that professional development for teachers be scheduled virtually and face-to-face in order for teachers to acquaint themselves with the learning platform and have the occasion to collaborate with fellow online educators.

Some virtual campuses fail to meet programmatic goals and objectives (DiPietro, Ferdig, Black, & Preston, 2008; Roblyer, 2006); however, those that do succeed often have the following five components: They (1) prepare students for success; (2) prepare teachers for success; (3) facilitate interactive, flexible course designs; (4) monitor and support teachers; and (5) monitor and support students (Roblyer).

Online programs should develop measures that ensure quality courses meet state guidelines (Holstead et al., 2008). Quality virtual courses should be able to be used to acquire high school credit and be accepted by colleges and universities.

TARGET POPULATION

The most frequently identified population targeted by alternative programs is students at risk of educational failure. Generally, an at-risk student is one who is not expected to complete the traditional course of public school education, grades kindergarten through 12, in 13 years. Individual state or local agencies may include more specific criteria in the definition of at-risk students. Many factors contribute to a student being at risk, and no single factor or group of factors is an absolute predictor of a student's tendency to not succeed in school. Some of the more commonly identified at-risk factors include having a low socioeconomic level, performing below standard on standardized and local assessments, repeating a grade level, having an original language different from the language of instruction, and engaging in criminal activity (Freeman, 2002).

Students at Risk for Dropping Out

For The Pew Partnership for Civic Change, Melville (2006) reported that the approximately 1 million students who drop out of school each year greatly impact their futures and conditions in their respective communities. The students "have only a slim chance of succeeding, earning a decent wage, or achieving a stable and productive life" (p. 7). The effect on the nation of the reduced productivity and taxes results in an annual loss of more than $200 billion, and "that does not take into account the fact that more than two-thirds of the inmates in state prisons are school dropouts" (p. 1). Melville posited that the states in the Midwest have the highest high school graduation rates, compared to the South's highest dropout rates. Racial and socioeconomic differences were also found: "rates for white and Asian students are higher than the national average, with completion rates of the two groups at 75 and 77 percent respectively" while "the dropout problem is most serious among blacks, Hispanics, and American-Indian students, barely half of whom graduate from high school" (p. 6).

Common Characteristics of Alternative School Students

Guerin and Denti (1999) identified an extensive list of characteristics common among students in alternative settings. This list includes low socioeconomic status, limited English proficiency, ethnic minority status, poor literary and academic skills, inadequate social-emotional-behavioral skills, impulsivity and poor judgment, limited or unavailable family support, and lack of positive adult role models. One criticism of alternative schools is that they serve as a dumping ground for unwanted students from minority cultures and low socioeconomic situations (Sagor, 1999). Studies of alternative schools have not indicated this to be entirely true. The ethnic percentages within the alternative programs basically mirror the surrounding communities and schools. These same studies do, however, indicate an overrepresentation of economically disadvantaged students (Freeman, 2002; Kleiner et al., 2002).

Adjudicated Youth

One target population receiving more attention in the current alternative education environment is disruptive or adjudicated youth. Many researchers have cited an increase in juvenile crime and violent acts reported on school campuses (Ferrara, 1993; Sprague & Walker, 2000; Vann, Schubert, & Rogers, 2000). One response has been the creation of alternative schools designed specifically to address that group of students. Raywid (1994) identified these settings as Type II alternative schools or last chance schools. The schools received this designation because they are quite often the student's last chance to avoid expulsion. Interestingly, one of the most effective behavioral intervention strategies available to schools is an engaging academic program. Some last chance schools have recorded instances of student achievement and behavioral improvement; however, to do so the schools have usually incorporated many of the structures more common to the Type I schools or alternative schools of choice (Raywid, 1994; Vann et al.).

STUDENT FAMILY

Because students in alternative programs and at-risk students in general have limited or unavailable family support and lack positive adult role models, alternative programs often include a component designed to bolster the student's family. Fashola and Slavin (1998) identify recognition of the importance of family as a common theme of effective alternative programs. Parent involvement is linked to student improvement and success particularly for at-risk students, potential dropouts, and students with poor social skills. Quite often, schools find themselves unable to create behavioral changes in the students without an increase in parent support (Buroker, Messner, & Leonard, 1993).

Parents of at-risk students who participated in a parent education program in the Lima City School District of Lima, Ohio, indicated several positive outcomes. The parents were pleased with their participation in the program and found it to be both important and necessary for parents of students in an alternative education program. The parents also indicated an increased ability to use positive parenting behaviors and extinguish negative parenting behaviors. The parents increased their involvement with their child's education. Another benefit of the parenting program was the formation of a support group of parents with students facing similar issues (Buroker et al., 1993). Based on this study, a parent education component is recommended for parents of at-risk students. Other studies have also reported positive student gains from mandatory parent and student counseling ("Alternative Schools for Disruptive Youth," 1991).

COMMUNITY AGENCIES

Quite often the alternative program students' needs are greater than the scope of the actual program. Walker and Hackman (1999) advocated collaboration between the school and various community agencies to most effectively meet these needs. In reality, many alternative schools do cooperate with various social and community agencies. The alternative schools most often work in conjunction with the juvenile justice system. Carver and Lewis (2010) indicated that 80% of public school districts with a district-administered alternative school collaborate with the criminal justice system. A clear majority of alternative schools and programs also collaborate with community mental health agencies, police or sheriff's departments, child protective service, health and human services, crisis intervention centers, and drug and/or alcohol clinics. A lesser percentage of alternative programs reported collaboration with family planning/child care/child placement agencies, job placement centers, and parks and recreation departments (Carver & Lewis). A policy statement from the American Academy of Pediatrics (2003) entitled "Out-of-School Suspension and Expulsion" made another plea for cooperation between schools and health agencies. In this particular statement the academy argued that schools should provide services to rule out a mental or physical impairment or illness as the cause of the misbehavior. In order to do this a school has to collaborate with a physician or health clinic.

Alternative Programs in the United States

The number of alternative programs available to students within the United States continues to increase (Carver & Lewis, 2010; Katsiyannis & Williams, 1998; Kleiner et al., 2002; Raywid, 1982). In 1982, Raywid located 2,500 secondary alternative schools of choice. By the 2010-11 school year, there were 6,197 alternative education schools (Keaton, 2012). According to Carver and Lewis (2010), 64% of school districts reported that they had at least one alternative school program active during the 2007-08 academic year. There were 646,500 public school district students enrolled in alternative programs and schools and 87,200 who attended programs that were administered by a nonschool entity (Carver & Lewis). Several federal agencies oversee funds for support services that can be utilized by alternative education programs such as the No Child Left Behind Act (NCLB) of 2001, the Carl D. Perkins Vocational and Applied Technology Education Act, and the Individuals with Disabilities Education Act (Martin & Brand, 2006).

In a survey of alternative schools and programs, Kleiner and others (2002) indicated that 39% of the public school districts in the country offered at least one alternative school or program, and overall 10,900 public alternative schools or programs were in existence during the 2000-01 school year. National Center for Educational Statistics data indicated that in 2007-08, 64% of schools districts had at least one alternative school or program for at-risk students (Carver & Lewis, 2010). The survey authors concluded there were 10,300 district-administered alternative education programs in the United States (Carver & Lewis). They also determined that there were "646,500 students enrolled in public school districts attending alternative schools and programs for at-risk students . . . with 558,300 students attending district-administered alternative schools and programs and 87,200 students attending alternative schools and programs administered by another entity" (Carver & Lewis, p. 3).

Alternative programs for secondary students outnumbered those offered for elementary students. In fact, 88-96% of the districts that offered an alternative program served students in grades 9-12, while only 8-18% of the districts that provided an alternative education program reported serving students in grades 1 through 5. One-third of the districts that provided an alternative program indicated that at some point demand for enrollment exceeded the capacity. The enrollment size and metropolitan status of districts also correlated with the provision of alternative schools or programs. Urban districts were more likely to provide an alternative school or program than suburban districts; suburban districts were more likely to offer an alternative program than rural districts. Large districts (10,000 students or more) were more likely to administer an alternative program than mid-size districts (2,500–9,999 students); mid-size districts were more likely to administer an alternative program than small districts (less than 2,500 students). Interestingly, districts in the southeast region of the country were more likely than those in the northeastern, central, and western regions to provide an alternative school or program (Carver & Lewis, 2010).

The provision of alternative schools was also investigated in relation to the percentage of minority enrollment and poverty concentration within the school district. Districts with greater than 50% minority enrollment were more likely to provide an alternative program. The percentage of districts offering an alternative program decreased as the percentage of minority enrollment decreased. Additionally, districts with a poverty concentration greater than 20% were slightly more likely to administer an alternative program than districts with a poverty concentration of 11-20%, and those districts were more likely to offer an alternative program than districts with a poverty concentration of 10% or less (Carver & Lewis, 2010).

One very specific type of alternative school is housed within a juvenile detention center. Incarcerated youth must also attend school. These schools can be administered by the school district in which the detention facility is housed or by an outside agency. Of all districts reporting a district-administered alternative program, 4% indicated provision of a program within a juvenile detention center (Carver & Lewis, 2010).

These statistics pose no surprises when the target population and purpose of alternative schools and programs are considered. At-risk students have a greater tendency to be from a minority culture and have a low socioeconomic status. Urban areas, by virtue of the size of the population, have larger school districts and a greater number of minority citizens and citizens living in poverty concentration.

Administrator's Role in Alternative Programs

The flexible and nontraditional structure associated with alternative programs does create some differences in the role of the administrator. Quite often in an alternative program, the teachers take on additional responsibilities traditionally assigned to the administrator. The small size of many alternative programs often limits the number of administrators assigned; in fact, some small alternative programs do not have an administrator but are managed exclusively by the teaching staff (Neumann, 1994).

Principals of alternative education programs are called upon to lead in countless unusual and unplanned situations. One role specific to the alternative school principal is that of liaison with those outside the alternative school. This includes the traditional schools from which the students are sent, community agencies, juvenile law enforcement, and the general public.

The alternative school coexists with the traditional campus. Quite often tensions arise between the two schools regarding many different items including rigor of instruction, adherence to school policies, instructional practices, student information accounting procedures, and student enrollment. The alternative education program administrator is the individual who must be an ambassador for the alternative program and present the program in such as way that these tensions can be reduced or, hopefully, resolved.

Particularly in alternative schools designed to serve students placed for disciplinary infractions, the administrator must cooperate with law enforcement officers and probation officers. When students break the laws of the municipality or state, law enforcement personnel are involved. The alternative school administrator must cultivate a positive working relationship with these individuals and form a team to support the change of the student's behavior while at the same time promoting the student's school success. Juvenile probation officers can be powerful partners in providing the structures some students need to refrain from law breaking and focus on completing school. In many instances the administrator of a disciplinary alternative education program is an enforcer of standards and rules. At times this role overshadows any opportunity the administrator might have to be nurturing and supportive.

At-risk students served in alternative education programs can arrive at school with many problems that are beyond the service scope of the school. In those cases, community agencies can partner with the school to provide support for the needy student and the administrator is the individual who works with the community agencies to coordinate services and provide appropriate access to students. Because at-risk students may not be aware of the helps available, the personnel in the alternative education program can provide the connection between the student and the support services.

School leaders should ensure that their alternative programs "focus on developing and transforming the whole person by demonstrating respect for individual intelligence and the ability to contribute to the community" (Wisconsin Department of Public Instruction, 2009, p. 1). Teens need to be a part of settings that nurture, teach, and support them. Successful youth development, according to The Pew Partnership for Civic Change (2001), should "strengthen aspects of a young person's sense of identity and ability to contribute to the larger world" (p. 21).

The administrator in an alternative education program must be a cheerleader for the alternative program within the community. The public view of an alternative school can be negative. Alternative school students do not always behave in ways that create positive connections within the community. The administrator is key in promoting a positive image of the program and in leading students to behave appropriately. Alternative school administrators should seek out opportunities to be visible in community groups and present the many positive stories that arise within alternative education programs. These efforts to be visible are essential because "young people who are connected to people and the community in a positive way achieve more academically and make better decisions" (The Pew Partnership for Civic Change, 2001, p. 22).

The repertoire of instructional strategies required of teachers in alternative schools demands a highly supportive staff development program. The administrator does not have to be the individual who teaches all of the staff development, but the administrator must support the provision of continuous learning opportunities. The administrator is also the faculty member with the greatest responsibility for locating and evaluating programs and methods that will benefit the students and the alternative program generally (Fashola & Slavin, 1997; Griffin, 1993; Slavin, 1996).

Wong (1994) suggested that the principal must create a climate of participation within the school. The alternative school works to include the family of the students with the teachers and the administrator; the principal's responsibility is to create a culture in which all stakeholders work together for the betterment of the students. Wong also stated that the teachers are responsible for creating innovative classrooms, and the parents are responsible for providing input and even securing the financial resources necessary for the school to offer a quality program.

Griffin (1993) used the secondary level School Attitudinal Survey to determine current alternative students' feelings regarding their traditional campus and their alternative campus. Each student responded to the survey twice, once in September in regard to the traditional campus and once in January in regard to the alternative campus. The results of the survey were then used to provide guidance to administrators. Griffin (1993) discovered that the students viewed the teachers in the alternative school as more genuinely concerned about them and less authoritarian and less likely to show favoritism. The students felt that they had more input in decision making. The students also viewed the alternative teachers as more enthusiastic about their job. Overall, the students were more satisfied with the alternative school than the traditional school.

From these findings, Griffin (1993) concluded that the administrator should model and advance equitable treatment of all students. For example, the principal needs to develop a caring, nonthreatening school environment; demonstrate enthusiasm for her job and promote a culture that embraces enthusiasm; and provide an opportunity for students to express their desires and opinions. The principal sets the tone of the program and the standard to be met by all participants.

In 2002, existing alternative school principals gave the following advice to administrators beginning an alternative program (Freeman, 2002, p. 65):

- Decide on the mission and philosophy of the school. This should align with the vision of the district.
- Visit other alternative campuses to help develop a discussion of core values.
- Choose faculty well.
- Treat students with love and respect and they will respect you; they are still kids and need to be taken care of.
- Be flexible and patient.
- Work with the traditional school principals to find out students' needs.

Very few formal programs of study or individual classes exist to prepare educators to work in alternative programs although the structure of the alternative programs demand a more robust knowledge of teaching methods and behavior management strategies (Prater & Sileo, 2000). Teachers and administrator are quite often left on their own to develop the expanded body of knowledge and intrapersonal skills needed to function successfully in an alternative program setting. The administrator is the member of the school team who sets the standard for the teachers, students, and parents (Griffin, 1993; Wong, 1994).

Summary

According to Aron (2006), because alternative schools are "often associated with students who were unsuccessful in the past, many . . . are thought to be of much poorer quality than the traditional K-12 school system, and yet because they are challenged to motivate and educate disengaged students many alternative educational programs are highly valued for their innovation and creativity" (p. 3). An alternative program is an educational program designed to meet the needs of a targeted population of students who do not experience success in the traditional school setting. The alternative program is generally smaller in size than the traditional school and provides a nontraditional method of instructional delivery. The civil rights movement of the 1960s gave rise to the current educational alternative programs, and the number of such programs continues to increase. Alternative programs are available in the majority of geographic areas of the United States and in local school districts of varying sizes and characteristics. However, large, urban districts with a high percentage of minority cultures and low socioeconomic students have a greater tendency to offer an alternative program. Quite often the teachers in the alternative program have an expanded role in the administration of the program. Administrators of alternative programs must establish a caring, supportive environment in which all students take ownership.

Applying Your Knowledge

You are the principal of a high school (grades 9–12) in a suburban school district of 25,000 students. The demographics of the district are changing. The minority population is growing and the number of second language learners is also increasing. The superintendent has asked you to chair a committee to create a plan for your school district to meet the needs of the growing population of at-risk students and to increase the number of students who graduate from high school.

QUESTIONS

1. Who do you want to serve with you on this committee?
2. What are the first five decisions that must be made by the committee?
3. Describe the type of program the committee creates.
4. Change the demographics of the district to be (a) an urban district of 100,000 students, and then (b) a rural district of 1,000 students. How does this change your answers to the first three questions? Explain.

QUESTIONS FOR THOUGHT

1. How have the political and social events of history influenced alternative education?
2. Which of the general characteristics of alternative programs do you feel is most important? Why?
3. Develop a proposal for an alternative program to meet the needs of your student population. Explain your choices.
4. What alternative programs do you have in your district or community? What purpose(s) do they serve? Are the programs successful in achieving their purpose(s)? How do you know?
5. Are the administrative responsibilities in an alternative program different from those in a regular program? How? Why?
6. If you could design a preparation program for teachers in alternative programs, what topics would you include and what skills would you emphasize? Be ready to justify your choices.

For Additional Information

Three authors stand out as critical references and authorities on the subject of alternative education: Robert Slavin, Gary Wehlage, and Mary Anne Raywid. Slavin has focused his efforts on evaluation and creation of programs designed specifically for students placed at risk. Wehlage and Raywid have both studied the structures of alternative schools and programs and their defining characteristics. Raywid has been particularly helpful with her classification of alternative schools. She has also worked diligently to identify existing alternative schools.

When one undertakes a study of alternative education, the process itself can become daunting. The body of work pertaining to alternative education can be found in three broad categories: at-risk students, alternative education, and special education. All three areas must be investigated to find a complete picture. Even then, little information is available. Many of the works published concerning alternative education are simply commercials for a particular existing program. The information in these articles can be useful; however, one must take care to not accept everything said as applicable across all settings. A recent dynamic impacting alternative education is the creation of charter schools; this will be of particular interest to watch and investigate as their numbers increase.

Opportunities for research abound in the field of alternative education. The information currently available is only the groundwork for future studies. The student population is continuing to diversify, and schools must adapt to meet the needs of the variety of learners. The alternative program is designed to meet those needs. Reliable data will be needed so decisions can be made to benefit the students.

Online resources to explore:

Association for High School Innovation: www.ahsi.org

Alternative Schools Network—Creating Futures Everyday: asnchicago.org

National Alternative Education Association (NAEA): www.the-naea.com

National Center on Secondary Education and Transition: www.ncset.org

Texas Association for Alternative Education - TAAE: www.taae.org

References

Alternative schools for disruptive youth. (1991). *School Safety*, 8–11.

American Academy of Pediatrics. (2003). Out-of-school suspension and expulsion. *Pediatrics, 112*(5), 1206–1209.

Archambault, L., Diamond, D., Coffey, M., Foures-Aalbu, D., Richardson, J., Zygouris-Coe, V., & Brown, C. (2010, April). An exploration of at-risk learners and online education (Issue Brief). Vienna, VA: International Association for K-12 Online Learning. Retrieved from www.inacol.org/research/reports.php

Aron, L. Y. (2006). *An overview of alternative education*. Retrieved from http://urbaninstitute.org/Uploaded-PDF/411283_alternative_education.pdf

Aron, L. Y., & Zweig, J. M. (2003). *Educational alternative for vulnerable youth: Student needs, program types, and research directions*. Washington, DC: Urban Institute.

Berge, Z. L., & Clark T. (2005). *Virtual schools: Planning for success*. New York: Teachers College Press.

Buroker, C. D, Messner, P. E., & Leonard, B. C. (1993). Parent education: Key to successful alternative education programs. *Journal of School Leadership, 3*(6), 635–645.

Cable, K. E., Plucker, J. A., & Spradlin, T. E. (2009). *Alternative schools: What's in a name?* (Education Policy Brief). Bloomington, IN: Center for Evaluation and Education Policy. (ERIC Document Reproduction Service No. ED510969).

Carver, P. R., & Lewis, L. (2010). *Alternative schools and programs for public school students at risk of educational failure: 2007–08* (NCES 2010–026). U.S. Department of Education, National Center for Education Statistics. Washington, DC: Government Printing Office.

de los Santos, M., & Lowe, J. M. (2005). Programs for adjudicated youth. In A. Pankake, M. Littleton, & G. Schroth (Eds.), *The administration and supervision of special programs in education* (pp. 175–183). Dubuque, IA: Kendall/Hunt Publishing Company.

DiPietro, M., Ferdig, R. E., Black, E. W., & Preston, M. (2008). Best practices in teaching K-12 online: Lessons learned from Michigan Virtual School teachers. *Journal of Interactive Online Learning, 7*(1), 10–35.

Duke, D., & Griesdorn, J. (1999). Consideration in the design of alternative schools. *The Clearing House, 73*(2), 89–92.

Fashola, O., & Slavin, R. (1997). Promising programs for elementary and middle schools: Evidence of effectiveness and replicability. *Journal of Education for Students Placed At Risk, 2*(3), 251–307.

Fashola O., & Slavin, R. (1998). Effective dropout prevention and college attendance programs for students placed at risk. *Journal of Education for Students Placed At Risk, 3*(2), 159–183.

Ferrara, M. M. (1993). Strategies and solutions: Alternative campuses for disruptive students. *Schools in the Middle, 2*(3), 14–17.

Freeman, D. K. (2002). *A descriptive study of elementary alternative schools for at risk students in Texas* (Doctoral Dissertation, Texas A & M University-Commerce, 2002).

Gold, M. (1995). Charting a course: Promise and prospects for alternative schools. *Journal of Emotional and Behavioral Problems, 3*(4), 8–11.

Griffin, B. L. (1993). Administrators can use alternative schools to meet student needs. *Journal of School Leadership, 3*(4), 416–420.

Guerin, G., & Denti, L. (1999). Alternative education support for youth at risk. *The Clearing House, 73*(2), 76–78.

Holstead, M. S., Spradlin, T. E., & Plucker, J. A. (2008). Promises and pitfalls of virtual education in the United States and Indiana. *Education Policy Brief, 6*(6). Bloomington, IN: Center for Evaluation and Education Policy.

Indiana Department of Education. (n. d.). *Alternative education programs.* Retrieved from http://www.doe.in.gov/alted/altedlinkpg.html

Katsiyannis, A., & Williams, B. (1998). A national survey of state initiatives on alternative education. *Remedial and Special Education, 19*(5), 276–284.

Keaton, P. (2012). *Numbers and types of public elementary and secondary schools from the common core of data: School year 2010–11* (NCES 2012-325). U.S. Department of Education. Washington, DC: National Center for Education Statistics. Retrieved from http://nces.ed.gov/pubsearch

Kellogg, L., & Politoski, K. (2002). *Virtual schools across America: Trends in K-12 online education.* Los Angeles, CA: Peak Group Research Corporation.

Kleiner, B., Porch, R., & Farris, E. (2002). *Public alternative schools and programs for students at risk of education failure: 2000-01* (NCES 2002-004). U.S. Department of Education. Washington, DC: National Center for Education Statistics.

Knight, S., & Kneese, C. (1999). Examining student perceptions in four instructional programs for students at risk. *Teaching and Change, 7*(1), 17–32.

Lange, C. M., & Sletten, S. J. (2002). *Alternative education: A brief history and research synthesis.* Alexandria, VA: National Association of State Directors of Special Education.

Leone, P. E., & Drakeford, W. (1999). Alternative education: From a "last chance" to a proactive model. *The Clearing House, 73*(2), 86–88.

Martin, N., & Brand, B. (2006). Federal, state, and local roles supporting alternative education. Washington, DC: American Youth Policy Forum. Retrieved from www.ncee.org/wp-content/uploads/2010/04/GovrolesAltEd.pdf

Melville, K. (2006). *The school drop out crisis.* Richmond, VA: University of Richmond Pew Partnership for Civic Change. Retrieved from http://www.pewpartnership.org/resources/dropout_crisis.html

Murdock, T. (1999). The social context of risk: Status and motivational predictors of alienation in middle school. *Journal of Educational Psychology, 9*(1), 62–75.

Neumann, R. (1994). A report from the 2nd annual conference on alternative education. *Phi Delta Kappan, 75*(7), 547–549.

The Pew Partnership for Civic Change. (2001). *What we know works.* Retrieved from http://www.pewpartnership.org/resources/whats_works.html

Prater, M. A., & Sileo, T. W. (2000). Preparing educators and related school personnel to work with at-risk students. *Teacher Education and Special Education, 23*(1), 51–64.

Raywid, M. A. (1982). *The current status of schools of choice in public secondary education: Alternative, options, magnets.* Washington, DC: National Institute of Education. (ERIC Document Reproduction Service No. ED 242055).

Raywid, M. A. (1994). Alternative schools: The state of the art. *Educational Leadership, 52*(1), 26–31.

Raywid, M. A. (1998). The journey of the alternative school movement: Where it's been and where it's going. *High School Magazine, 6*(2), 10–14.

Roblyer, M. D. (2006). Virtually successful: Defeating the dropout problem through online school programs. *Phi Delta Kappan, 88*(1), 31–36.

Rutter, R., & Margelofsky, M. (1997). How school structures inhibit students at risk. *The Journal of At Risk Issues, 3*(2), 3–12.

Sagor, R. (1999). Equity and excellence in public schools: The role of the alternative school. *The Clearing House, 73*(2), 72–75.

Slavin, R. (1996). Reforming state and federal policies to support adoption of proven practices. *Educational Researcher, 25*(9), 4–5.

Southern Regional Education Board. (2005). *Getting serious about high school graduation.* Atlanta, GA: Author.

Sprague, J. R., & Walker, H. M. (2000). Early identification and intervention for youth with anti-social and violent behavior. *Exceptional Children, 66*(3), 367–370.

Thomas, R. G., & Thomas, R. M. (2008). *Effective teaching in correctional settings: Prisons, jails, juvenile centers, and alternative schools.* Springfield, IL: Charles C. Thomas Publisher, Limited.

Vann, M., Schubert, S. R., & Rogers, D. (2000). The Big Bayou Associations: An alternative education program for middle-school, at-risk juveniles. *Preventing School Failure, 45*(1), 31–36.

Walker, J., & Hackman, D. (1999). Full service schools: Forming alliances to meet the needs of students and families. *NASSP Bulletin, 83*(611), 28–37.

Watson, J. F., Winograd, K., & Kalmon, S. (2004). *Keeping pace with K-12 online learning: A snapshot of state-level policy and practice.* Naperville, IL: Learning Point Associates.

Wisconsin Department of Public Instruction. (2009). *Alternative education programs.* Retrieved from http://docs.google.com/viewer?a=v&q=cache:0yKB-Rs49w0J:dpi.state.wi.us/alternativeed/pdf/alted_qa.pdf+characteristics+of+alternative+education+programs&hl=en&gl=us&pid=bl&srcid=ADGEESgKjFm-cT-_QEyP6a1JuLNpFgbHn7FMoOQo0UDXmtFOhQc5ViZI49iwvbKfMzdK_pZgraDNETkXFQib1CV4LDJoKhCvHBeFWZJ2X2hIAIF4Gq3vKNTbSFMagH59ZEQYdco34R8_&sig=AHIEtbQrll3x6i36qdcwNtrogNwehbwViQ

Wong, K. (1994). Linking governance reforms to schooling opportunities for the disadvantaged. *Educational Administration Quarterly, 30*(2), 153–177.

Teacher Leaders[1] **12**

Shirley J. Mills

If we want teacher leadership to result in improved
student learning, then the focus of the leadership
must target teacher learning.

—*Moller and Pankake (2006, p. 12)*

Objectives

1. Define shared leadership and teacher leadership
2. Describe the principal's role in supporting teacher collaboration
3. Identify barriers and supports to teachers leading in collaboration

---

[1]Adapted from Moller, G. (2005). Teacher leaders. In Pankake, A., Schroth, G., & Littleton, M. (Eds.),
Administration and Supervision of Special Programs in Education (2nd ed.). Dubuque, IA:
Kendall Hunt.

Introduction

With the passing of No Child Left Behind (2001), the world of education changed. Linda Darling-Hammond (2010) noted that the world is flat and the "new mission of schools is to prepare students to work at jobs that do not yet exist, creating ideas and solutions for products and problems that have not yet been identified, using technologies that have not yet been invented" (p. 2). Meeting these challenges requires a new leadership venue that does not focus solely on statewide assessment results. Instead school must focus on challenging all students to become the best they can be and to empower teachers to create classroom experiences that explore innovations and new ideas with their students. Indeed with today's "flat world," school leadership is facing challenging times. No longer can the principal ride in on the white horse and save the school singlehandedly.

Successful principals are meeting the challenges of public scrutiny by empowering their teachers to give voice to their ideas for reform and improvement. These new teacher leaders are collaborating with other teachers to form leadership teams that effectively deal with significant problems in their schools, thus assisting their principals with the leadership of the school to create successful learning for students. These teacher leaders are supporting the principals in directing their school with good teaching and successful learning for both teachers and student. Teachers, if given the opportunity, are stepping in to share in the decision making that affects their classrooms and their students. Taking into account the potential for this leadership is known by many names—distributed leadership (Spillane, Halverson, & Diamond, 2001; Murphy, Smylie, Mayrowetz, & Seashore Louis, 2009), intentional leadership (Moller & Pankake, 2006), shared leadership (Pearce & Conger, 2003), among others. Principals who take these actions are self-assured enough to "give away" power to effect positive changes in their schools. Katzenmeyer and Moller (2001) noted, "within every school there is a sleeping giant of teacher leadership, which can be a strong catalyst for making change" (p. 2).

Teacher leadership exists in schools whether or not the principal supports its development. To be effective, principals must be intentional in developing positive teacher leadership that results in improved student learning. These teachers must be viewed by their peers as competent, credible, and approachable. These effective teacher leaders not only influence others, but also are accountable for the results of their efforts (Moller & Pankake, 2006). Teacher leadership roles are varied.

Traditionally, people think of teacher leaders as department chairpersons or team leaders. These roles would be defined as formal teacher leadership roles. There are a variety of such formal teacher leadership roles such as interventionist, teacher coach, coordinator, literacy coach, or staff developer. These formal roles hold certain expectations established by the school or the school system and come with their own set of rules and regulations. Perhaps more powerful and influential are the informal teacher leadership roles such as when a teacher sees a need, feels passionately about the issue, and takes action. This informal leadership may result in new initiatives such as increased student activities, more parent involvement, or increased collaboration with the community. Informal teacher leadership affects the entire school, instead of simply meeting the needs of the school (Harrison & Lembeck, 1996). Whether through formal or informal leadership roles, these teachers are proactive in finding ways to help the school and, most importantly, the students.

Building leadership capacity (Lambert, 2003, 2005) is the principal's primary responsibility. Capacity building is a task that requires purposeful learning that creates participation across the community. Lambert (2005) called this highest form of leadership as "leadership for all, learning for all, and success for all" (p. 38). Capacity building is a task that cannot be fully delegated, even though other administrators and teacher leaders can promote this mission. Until there is a different structure in schools, teachers look to the principal for authentic support of their leadership efforts. Occasionally, there will be groups of teachers who subversively provide this type of leadership, in spite of the principal, but normally teachers will resist taking on additional responsibility if the principal gives only token attention to the process.

Effective leadership is the key piece to achieving school improvement (Harris, 2002; Fullan, 2001). This type of leader has a vision for the school and is able to recognize how important teacher leaders are in supporting the vision. This leadership allows for others to be empowered in making and supporting decisions affecting the well-being of the school. School leaders and teacher leaders share values and school goals that empower everyone to take action to help in solving problems within the school.

Leaders must examine their belief systems. Before making a commitment to promote teacher leadership, the principal should examine the benefits to the students, the school community, and the administrative team. For some principals this is a transformation in their understanding of who is the leader. Regardless of the principal's perspective, the decision to support this model requires more than adopting a "program." This is a way of doing business in schools and requires the principal's ongoing support and dedication of energy and attention.

DEFINING TEACHER LEADERSHIP

Though the term *teacher leadership* has been used by many scholars, the definition seems murky. Definitions of formal versus informal teacher leadership are hazy at best. York-Barr and Duke (2005) defined teacher leadership as "the process by which teachers, individually or collectively, influence their colleagues, principals, and other members of the school communities to improve teaching and learning practices with the aim of increased student learning and achievement. Such team leadership work involves three intentional development foci: individual development, collaboration or team development, and organizational development" (pp. 287–288). Katzenmeyer and Moller (2001) saw teacher leadership as having three main facets: leadership of students or other teachers, leadership of operational tasks, and leadership through decision making or partnerships. Lambert (1988) defined teacher leadership for school capacity building as being broad-based with skillful involvement in the work of leadership. Day and Harris (2003) suggested that teacher leadership translated into the principles of school improvement into the practices of individual classrooms and participated in the work of leaders with their expertise and created a mutual learning among the teaching staff.

It is clear that teacher leaders are first and foremost expert teachers themselves. Ash and Persall (2000) noted that the majority of the teacher leaders take on different leadership roles at different times. These teacher leaders work in both formal and informal ways. They exert their leadership when it affects the academic achievement of students or professional development of teachers.

Informal Teacher Leadership

Katzenmeyer and Moller (2001) defined informal teacher leadership as the "sleeping giant" within the ranks of teachers; York-Barr and Duke (2004) defined it as the process where teachers influence their colleagues, principals, and other members of the school community to improve teaching and learning (pp. 287–288); and Moller and Pankake (2006) defined informal teacher leaders as those individuals who step up to the needed leadership roles in diverse situations when they see and issue in their school that needs attention. These informal teacher leaders want to create successful learning environments in their schools for all students and are willing to do what is necessary to make it happen. In the process, they become learners themselves. They search for new strategies and use new instructional models that they believe will assist in creating student achievement for all students' needs. And to that end, they are willing to share their new ideas with their fellow teachers. Teacher leadership encompasses the assumption that the work of teachers is not limited to their individual classroom. They believe that teachers are part of learning community working together to improve students' learning. This sharing of the responsibility and accountability is inherent to the teaching-learning process. Lieberman and Miller (2004) believed it was all about our classrooms, not my classroom. These informal definitions of teacher leadership indicate a powerful tool for principals to use to impact student learning and the culture and climate of their schools (Watt, Mills, & Huerta, 2010). These are the teachers who ask the important questions at teacher meetings and make the important connections between individual and group thinking that foster student learning.

Formal Leadership

This form of teacher leadership is driven by the appointment to a designated leadership position by the principal to fix a problem that exists in the school. This leadership is usually defined within the school and all teachers understand that this leader is no longer part of the school teaching ranks or a member of the leadership team (Mills & Schall, 2012). They are sandwiched between being teacher leaders with very little power given to them except to carry out the leadership's request. These leaders might be teacher coaches, interventionist, or teacher who have subject-area instructional expertise. They work specifically with the teaching and learning processes rather than completing managerial tasks. The formal teacher leader is a clearly defined position with defined leadership responsibilities. Creating a collaborative relationship is the key to the effectiveness of these leaders.

These formal teacher leadership positions are often impacted with the "crab bucket culture" because teachers in the rank and file, like crabs, seek to hold others back rather than allow them to flourish for the benefit of all (York-Barr & Duke, 2004). This mentality can be very detrimental to the formal teacher leaders as they many times find themselves isolated with few colleagues in the teaching ranks or in the leadership ranks.

Despite all of the literature on teacher leadership, it is still all about learning together and constructing meaning and knowledge collectively and collaboratively to impact student achievement in a positive manner.

Benefits of Teacher Leadership

Faced with demands from a multitude of sources, the principal must make choices in his or her leadership style. One option is for principals to pretend that they have the answers to everyone's concerns. This top-down paradigm is no longer an option in improving student learning because there are so many mandates; it is impossible for one person to do it all. Another alternative is for principals to ignore the important issues and focus on procedural infractions. Hopefully, principals can see beyond these options and seek help from teachers in addressing the upsurge in problems facing schools. The emerging multifaceted nature of schools, the public's higher-level expectations for results, and the increasingly diverse student population force principals to abandon the "hero" stance and to build the capacity of teachers to take on leadership roles in order to address substantive challenges. Barth (2001) called for "good principals (who) are more hero-makers than heroes" (p. 448). Undeniably, the new principal is steering schools and their teachers into a new understanding of what school leadership and school learning is all about in the 21st century.

The idea that teacher leadership can be effective in school reform initiatives is an important one (Foster, 2004; Lieberman & Miller, 2004). In the past, teachers worked in isolation with no ability to influence the workings of the larger school body. They worked in isolation with no capability to influence the operations of the school. This is obsolete in our world today (Craig, 2006). Under the old regime, principals were the experts in charge of fixing any problems that arose and teachers were the workhorses that were voiceless in controlling the destiny of their students.

One of the benefits of teacher leaders is found in special instructional programs. These teachers may arrive at the school with skills that are different than the general education teachers. Many of these skills are leadership skills. Here are examples of the leadership skills many teachers in special instructional programs acquire:

- supervising paraprofessionals in their work with special needs students,
- developing action plans that require accountability,
- assuming consultative role with general education teachers,
- managing cases,
- brokering resources, and
- serving as liaison with parents and community leaders.

Another reason for promoting teacher leadership is to retain quality teachers. Darling-Hammond (2010) noted "high achieving nations are also more steady and more focused on critical elements of the system: the quality of teachers and teaching, the development of curriculum and assessments that encourage ambitious learning by both students and teachers, and the design of schools as learning organizations that support continuous reflection and improvement" (p. 8). High-quality teachers are mandated in today's schools and some of these teacher leaders are able to use their own higher order thinking skills to solve student and curriculum problems in their school. They are the ones that principals ask to lead task forces for solving specific problems. Louis and Wahlstom (2011) noted that changing the image of leadership from the principal as the hero to the culture of distributed leadership created major improvements in student achievement. Clearly teacher leadership is emerging as an important step to improving student achievement.

Special education teachers often are not prepared to step into the leadership role that is required of their job. It is estimated that as many as half of all new special educations leave the field within the first three years as a result of poor administrative support, poor preparation, complex job responsibilities, and overwhelming paperwork requirements. In their research Ingersoll and Smith (2003) reported that although salary is cited as a decision to quit, even more teachers shared that working conditions influenced them to leave the profession. Four specific areas of concern were: ". . . student discipline problems; lack of support from the school administration; poor student motivation; and lack of teacher influence over school wide and classroom decision making" (p. 14). Talented teachers with specialized training were walking out of the schools to find jobs in which they were treated as adults and given benefits beyond just an increase in salary. Principals do not have much control over salaries for teachers, but they can influence the working conditions in the school.

The increasing student diversity demands multiple perspectives from teacher leaders and others to meet their needs. This diversity is espoused to be a value, whereas, in reality, people may view this as a problem. As principals face the demand to meet higher standards for all students, principals must take advantage of the different talents teachers can bring in order to build an inclusive professional community. If principals claim to support inclusion and differentiated instruction in classrooms, then how can they deny that this is how the adults should function in the school? No matter how successful a school is perceived, there are always more concerns, issues and problems than there are leaders.

Teacher leadership can result in expanded collaboration and professional learning among the professional staff. There appears to be significant support for the building of professional learning communities in schools (Hord, 2004; Hipp, Huffman, Pankake, & Olivier, 2008; Gabriel, 2005; Harris, 2003; Louis, Marks, & Kruse, 1996) as a means of increasing teacher leadership. Teacher leaders must recruit fellow teachers based on their expertise. Danielson (2007) identified several benefits of teacher leadership. She noted that the teaching responsibility of a veteran teacher is much the same as a brand new teacher and if the veteran teacher can create greater influence in their schools by exercising more responsibility in meeting challenges in their schools, they feel more fulfilled. Additionally, teachers remain longer in their positions than principals and often are the custodians of the school's culture. Furthermore a single principal cannot in all practicality meet all of the tasks laid out for him or her by state and federal law. Teacher leaders are essential in moving the school improvement plan forward. Finally, many principals have lost their instructional expertise and must depend on teacher leaders to sustain the research based best instructional practices needed to create academic achievement for all students.

Marginalized in the School Culture

Teachers in special instructional programs often face exclusion from the mainstream of school life. University undergraduate and graduate programs design course requirements keep students in separate tracks. Students in general education and special instructional programs do not have an opportunity to learn about each other's roles and responsibilities or to examine their opinions on how students learn (Shoffner & Briggs, 2001). The itinerant nature of a number of special instructional programs and the lack of time for collaboration contribute even more to these feelings of separateness. Louis and Wahlstrom (2011) noted, "neither organizational learning nor professional community can endure without trust between teachers and administrators, among teachers, and between teachers and parents" (p. 53). If there is not a concerted effort by the school leadership to build an inclusive professional community, then this sense of isolation will almost certainly continue to exist.

The principal's role is to build an inclusive school culture so that all teachers can contribute to the leadership in the ways that match their talents and interests. DuFour (2011) stated, "we cannot waste another quarter century inviting or encouraging educators to collaborate" (p. 57). We must collaborate now. Tapping into both the general education and special program teachers' gifts can result in a school culture that promotes positive teacher leadership. Within this isolation dilemma rest two tracks of separateness. One is between the general education teachers and those of other educators in the school who share instructional responsibilities for the same students. The other track includes those teachers whose work parallels the general education teachers' work, but who seldom share instructional responsibilities.

SHARED INSTRUCTIONAL RESPONSIBILITIES

There are teachers who share instructional responsibilities and are most likely the people who must work together for these students. The counselors, special education teachers, teachers of the gifted and talented, and teachers of English as a second language (ESL) students work with the same students as the general education teachers regarding overlapping instructional responsibilities. Strategies are evolving to bring these special program teachers together with the general education teachers to collaborate rather than working separately. An example of this relationship is teacher leaders, who work with students exhibiting behavior/emotional disorders, and her attempts to build relationships with her counterparts in general education. Dismayed by the expectations the general education teachers had for the students she taught, this teacher collaborated with one general education teacher who, she believed, would be open to a new discipline approach. As a result, this teacher expanded her influence beyond her classroom to resolve an issue that concerned her.

The adult-to-adult relationships are especially relevant in attempts to build inclusive classrooms for special needs students. Ferguson, Ralph, and Sampson (2002) suggested that current roles for special education teachers reflect ". . . less about working with students and more about working with grownups" (p. 145). These teachers are advocates for the students they serve, but they must develop relationships with other teachers in order to execute the students' educational plans. DuFour (2011) promotes professional learning teams across the disciplines to encourage and promote collaboration. He stated, "Professional doesn't mean autonomous" (p. 58). The new classrooms should be filled with professionals working side by side to help all students, regardless of their special needs, perform to the best of their abilities.

PARALLEL INSTRUCTIONAL RESPONSIBILITIES

In contrast, other teachers in special programs work with the same students as general education teachers, but there are few opportunities for these teachers to come together. For example, vocational education, art, music and physical education teachers work with the same students as general education teachers, but unless there is an effort to integrate curriculum, the teachers work separately. These teachers are especially isolated from the professional conversations in this era of academic testing. So much of teachers' and principals' attention is focused on high stakes testing that any subject not tested tends to fade into the background of conversation and activity in the school.

Even further removed from collaboration with general education teachers are the special programs teachers who are located outside the physical school plant, for example, alternative education teachers and those who teach in criminal justice facilities. Articulation between the faculties of "regular" schools and teachers in programs for disenfranchised youth is virtually nonexistent. One principal of an alternative school program set as a goal to communicate with leaders in the schools where the students were originally assigned to attend. He hoped to influence the teachers' perspectives regarding the students in the alternative program. Sharing must begin as a model and time provided for teachers to collaborate. Budig (2011) noted in his research that the public "wants students to learn in environments that reflect the world in which they live," and that supports collaboration between the parallel activities that occur in schools today.

Teachers in special instructional programs are parallel to the general education teachers. They are often left to their own devices to develop collaborative relationships among themselves. One vocational education teacher leader designed an open house for general education teachers to visit the special program classrooms. Another art teacher developed relationships with the fifth-grade teachers so that she could integrate what they were teaching into her classes. In these examples of teacher leadership, the principals approved the teachers' plans, but had little involvement in advocating or even attending the events. An opportunity to promote teacher leadership was not only lost but the model for collaboration was not endorsed.

The principal cannot ignore the complexity of teacher relationships. Mills and Schall (2012) stated that teacher leadership has evolved from teacher leaders who were in the formal, managerial roles to instructional leaders to participation in important changes to curriculum and the school culture. Teacher leadership in many districts are somewhere on the continuum of managerial to effect real second order change in the culture of the schools. After understanding the different types of isolation those teachers in special instructional programs face, the principal needs to examine the barriers to building teacher leadership.

Barriers to Teacher Leadership

There are many reasons why teachers find it difficult to lead and to collaborate together. Principals' reluctance to share leadership, too little scheduled time, lack of quality professional development, and physical isolation are challenging barriers, but they can be overcome. The more difficult barriers involve relationship. Teachers resistant to changes, subgroups of teachers who can sabotage change, and educators' reluctance to value conflict are barriers that demand skillful leadership. Johnson and Donaldson (2008) found in their research that many teachers who are enthused about becoming a teacher leader discover that the school cultures have not really changed. Classroom boundaries still exist and the same professional isolationist attitudes exist. Watt, Mills, and Huerta (2010) surveyed over 1,300 administrators and found that administrators thought teacher leadership attributes, such as mentoring and conducting professional development, were important but when they chose the AVID teacher leaders, they ignored those attributes they thought were important. Clearly, leadership must learn to walk their talk.

THE NEED FOR PRINCIPAL LEADERSHIP

Regardless of the relationships between general education and teachers in special instructional programs, the potential for tapping into these teachers' talents is often overlooked. Many principals may be unaware of this talent pool due to their distraction by the multitude of responsibilities or they may be unwilling to acknowledge that all teachers, even these teachers in special instructional programs who travel on the periphery of school life, can contribute to the school's leadership. Lambert (2003) called this type of top-down leadership archaic and outdated. Donaldson (2009) noted that it is the leadership practices that inspire teachers to grow into leaders that focus on the problems of the school.

TIME

There is never enough time in schools to meet the needs of all the students or for teachers to discuss how to work together to determine how to address these needs. When asked about the greatest obstacle to working with other teachers, inevitably teachers report the lack of time (Kinney, 2007). The structure of American schools offers teachers' minimal time for the deep conversation that is necessary to build relationships for collaboration. Snippets of time are grabbed in hallways and parking lots, but the luxury of meeting in a comfortable setting for an extended period of time is rare. What many organizations in the private sector take for granted, teachers rarely experience. Donaldson (2009) stated, "Extended blocks of time during the school day are the most productive structure for learning communities worthy of the name" (p.23). Having stated that, we all know it is easier said than done.

PROFESSIONAL LEARNING

However, many schools are making the time to provide teachers an opportunity to collaborate. Early outs, late starts, and designated blocks of time are assigned to teachers to get together and create meaningful instruction and assessment. Principals are finding the time within the day because they know that teachers are tired at the end of the day.

They are recognizing the need for professional learning within their buildings. Darling-Hammond and Richardson (2009) noted that high-quality professional development must be integrated within the school improvement plan. Their research suggested that any professional development opportunity that lasted 14 hours or less showed no effects on learning. Innovative ideas suggest using the five professional development days allowed each school year to allocating those hours throughout the school year in compliance with the research points that support job-embedded, collaborative professional development.

Teacher leadership and professional learning are tightly linked. In many school districts, professional learning still consists of fragmented workshops unrelated to a focus on a school's students and their learning. As teachers collaborate, attention must be paid to the professional learning of all teachers. Collective learning is occurring more in the form of professional learning teams. Chappuis, Chappuis, and Stiggins (2009) suggested that teachers must not only commit to their learning team but also commit to working together between the team meetings. Educators who participate in these teams are committed to working collaboratively to achieve better results for the students they serve. The key to improved learning for students appears to be continuous, job-embedded learning for educators (DuFour, DuFour, Eaker, & Many, 2006).

PHYSICAL LOCATION

Teachers in special instructional programs are often placed in classrooms that are far removed from the main classrooms. With minimal time away from student responsibilities, there are few opportunities for teachers to interact in a meaningful way and still be present when the students return to the classroom. Teachers in vocational education programs may be placed in facilities that house unique equipment and it is not possible for their classrooms to be near the general education classrooms. Similar situations often occur for music/band teachers, art specialists, physical education teachers and others.

RESISTANCE TO COLLABORATION

Teacher leadership and, in turn, teacher collaboration are alien in the majority of schools or only found in pockets of teachers within a department or a grade level. Educators are socialized to be isolated even during their student teacher experiences (De Lima, 2003). In addition, teachers value autonomy in their work with students, and collaboration threatens this (Little and Bartlett, 2002). America's society values individual accomplishments. The resistance to an inclusive professional community reflects these values. Educators experience minimal contact with other adults except during lunch or at the mailboxes. In addition, the current structure of schooling presents barriers to efforts at collaboration. Johnson and Donaldson (2009) noted that the "egg-crate" structures of schools discourage teachers incorporating collaboration.

However, there is a revolution of teacher-led schools that are spreading across the nation. Williams (2007) discussed these new institutions as being totally cooperative venture that teachers make all of the decisions on work assignments and assessment methods for students. While they are not in the majority, they are moving out into the mainstream.

SCHOOL CULTURES

A fully developed inclusive professional community is rare in schools. Even if there were plenty of time and physical facilities that promoted communication, collaboration focused on student learning is countercultural in teaching. School cultures can be dangerous territories. Walk into a teachers' lounge in such a school and a person immediately feels excluded. Even in schools that are viewed as high performing, there may exist subcultures of teachers who can cause concern for even the most experienced principal. Reminiscent of the high school cliques that keep certain people on the fringe of the action, this teacher leadership can take on a negative quality.

CONFLICT AVOIDANCE

Educators enter the profession with a desire to help others. They strive to build harmony so that they can survive in the classroom while caring for their students. Conflict is discouraged and avoided by most educators. Many teachers do not like to be called "teacher leaders," because they believe that it will harm their relationships with their colleagues. Indeed, some of these teacher leaders are caught in the middle. They are shunned by their fellow teachers because they have a "label" that creates distrust. They are no longer "one of us." However, these same teacher leaders are not accepted to participate in the leadership teams of the school. They cannot meet during the school day when the leadership teams typically meet and often are not even considered for attendance. Many teacher leaders resign from these assignments just to have a "place" in their school (Mills & Schall, 2012).

Conflict is healthy in professional communities (Achinstein, 2002). If educators truly value the diversity of their students, then the challenge is to accept and honor the differences in their own colleagues. The prevalent focus on consensus building may be a detriment to community building.

Fortunately, there are efforts to build support systems for teacher leaders and to encourage teachers to collaborate and overcome these barriers. There are schools across the country where principals and teachers are learning together to improve student achievement together as a team.

Principals' Roles in Building Teaching Leadership

Once principals decide they will be purposeful in the promotion of teacher leadership, there are beliefs, skills, and leadership strategies that are essential (Moller & Pankake, 2006). Foremost, it is the principal's belief regarding teacher leadership and how all teachers must contribute within an inclusive professional community that is essential for building trust. Then there is the need for principals to provide supportive conditions to build and sustain teacher leadership. Finally, teacher leadership does not grow in a vacuum and the principal must facilitate collaboration.

BELIEFS

Few people are fooled when a principal states a personal belief, but acts in ways that do not support that belief. The principal must be clear about his or her beliefs about teacher leadership in an inclusive professional community and how this is vital to the success of the school. This demands more than a printed vision statement in the office. Effective principals facilitate the development of a shared vision, articulate the vision, make decisions based on the vision, and help others to support the vision. If the principal does not believe in promoting teacher leadership within a professional community, it will not happen.

A good strategy for principals in their exploration of their beliefs about teacher leadership is to examine their personal experiences as a teacher. Most principals were teacher leaders and can remember which administrators truly supported their growth and development. In contrast, there will be memories of principals who did not value teacher leadership and established obstacles to what teachers hope to accomplish.

A principal's belief system is the key to promoting teacher leadership and building an inclusive professional community. As the person with the formal power over resources, the principal must believe it is possible and beneficial to work collaboratively with teachers in shared leadership roles. Even if teacher leadership is possible, unless the principal wants it, it is unlikely to be pursued. There are principals who do not desire, or perhaps even fear, sharing school leadership with others.

Not only must the principal believe teacher leadership is possible, the teachers must be included in developing a shared vision of how the adults will work together. Changed relationship is one of the most difficult challenges, and resistance should be expected. Not everyone will adopt the shared vision, but principals can move forward with the people who are ready and willing with the expectation that others will "get on board" as things develop.

The use of time provides an example of how a shared vision is a prerequisite to teacher leadership and collaboration. Before the issue of time can be addressed, the faculty, staff, and, especially the principal must believe that collaboration is essential to the school's improvement. With the physical structure of schools contributing to the isolation of teachers and the socialization of teachers to work alone, collaboration is not the norm. Many faculty members will claim that their school "is like a family," but few school faculties move beyond this collegiality. Once the faculty and staff members believe that collaboration is beneficial, then the time structures will be used for the purpose of professional conversations toward the improvement of teacher.

With all the attention on the value of professional learning communities, many principals jump on the bandwagon so that they can claim that their school reflects this model. With good intentions, these principals work with the teachers' schedules to build time for teachers to "dialogue." The teachers are told to meet and talk with each other about their profession. After initial confusion about these assignments, teachers soon find ways to subvert these efforts. Meanwhile, many principals are distracted with other duties or new projects and the time for professional collaboration becomes imperceptible as teachers take the lead to use this precious time for their individual responsibilities to the school and their students.

An alternative approach is for the principal to personally engage teachers in discussion regarding collaboration and the use of time. Arrangements for visits to other schools where mature professional learning communities exist can help teachers understand the value of working together and see how it can be accomplished. Principals can invite teachers to work on creative schedules to build time into the school day. (See Schroth, Beaty, & Dunbar [2003] for scheduling options.)

Once the school leaders are committed to teacher leadership and collaboration, then the focus must be placed on how to support the teachers. Only when people, especially the principal, believe in this structure will the supportive conditions that are put into place serve a purpose.

SUPPORTIVE CONDITIONS

If the principal and the faculty members are clear about their beliefs about teacher leadership, the school's resources can be aligned to these beliefs. Fiscal resources, human resources, and structures to support teacher leaders are critical to the school's success. Underlying each decision regarding resources should be these two questions:

1. How does this decision promote improved teaching and learning for students in our school?
2. How will this decision support teacher development that serves to improve teaching and learning for students in our school?

After personnel costs are removed from a school's budget, there are relatively few discretionary dollars to use within a school. Yet the decisions regarding the use of these diminishing funds can reflect how the principal views professional collaboration. Too often these decisions are made easy by allocating the same amount of money to each teacher regardless of the need. As teacher leaders take the risk to assume additional responsibilities, decisions about funds may be distributed differently. The students' needs and the school's attempts to meet those needs must determine where the money is spent.

In addition personnel decisions should be based on these same two questions. As principals conduct the most important task of their role—the selection of teacher staff—they must consider these consequences. Here is where the principal can exhibit a belief in teacher leadership. If the selection of faculty and staff are crucial to all programs, teachers should be involved in this process. Teachers are in a position to know what the students' needs are. Before inviting teachers to participate in the selection process, the principal must make it clear what their roles will be. If the principal is not ready to turn the hiring of teachers over to a consensus decision-making method, the teachers must know that they will advise the principal but the final decision will be made by the principal. On the other hand, if the teachers are going to be equal members in an interview team and the decision will be made by the teachers, the teachers should know that as well (Bateman & Bateman, 2006).

Once quality teachers are selected, the hard work begins. The strategies that the school uses to orient new teachers, whether experienced or beginning teachers, can make a difference in the retention of these teachers. Practices such as assigning mentors, buddy-teachers and other induction approaches are essential to help new teachers understand the school's cultures and to adopt the belief that teacher leadership in inclusive professional communities in the norm; leaving induction to chance can result in "war stories" that quickly tell the new faculty member that it is best to stay isolated within the classroom.

Also, new teachers need mentors with similar content knowledge to help them. This may require creative ways to link with teachers from other schools who teach in the same areas. Many beginning teachers lament the lack of contact with other teachers in their fields. Although a teacher in another field can help a teacher learn the school's culture, they are unable to help the new teacher with content pedagogy. The following quote was shared by a beginning special education teacher:

> Even when you have one [a mentor], [he/she] had no idea of what my job description was.
> It would be nice to have a mentor in the county with your same degree.

Learning to work together demands professional development. Understanding the value of quality, results-driven professional development is a knowledge base that every principal and teacher leader must acquire. Developing a substantive plan for professional learning is critical to building teacher leadership and encouraging collaboration. There are leadership skills, as well as instructional skills, that every teacher needs to learn in order to be an effective member of the school community. The principal's role is to be a co-learner with the teachers and then reinforce the use of the skills.

Providing supportive conditions relies on building positive relationships with the teachers. Littrell and Billingsley (1994) examined general and special education teachers and the relationships between their job satisfaction and principal support. Both groups of teachers reported that emotional support was the most important type of support that administrators can provide. Principals' actions that build a climate of collaboration, rather than competition, influence a higher level of commitment from teachers. Donaldson (2007) identified the assets that teacher leaders bring to a school: (1) They build relationships among the staff; (2) they maintain a sense of purpose amongst the staff; and (3) they improve instructional practice by modeling and sharing instructional ideas. These are valuable assets for any school. Principals walking around the school and finding opportunities to positively interact with teachers can help provide them the social support they need.

FACILITATING COLLABORATION

Principals have a responsibility to teachers of special instructional programs to facilitate their collaboration with each other and with the general education teachers. Hiring a teacher and then leaving that person alone to build relationships is risky. Even though teachers like to claim that there is an egalitarian ethic in their profession there is a social structure in teaching roles. There often is no logic to this structure because it depends on the unique power bases of teachers. In some schools, the teachers with power are the teachers of those subjects or grade levels where there is accountability testing. In another school, it will be the teachers of advanced placement courses. Other examples of sources of power are the teachers who go fishing or attend some outside organization, such as church, together. The reason for the power is not as important as how to encourage teachers to work together.

TEACHERS WITH SHARED INSTRUCTIONAL RESPONSIBILITIES

With the busyness of school life, teachers find it difficult to collaborate even with people who are closest to them. The quick planning over a short lunch or an infrequent conversation in the hallway is usually the only times available for people with common schedules to see each other. Often these are teachers whose classrooms are in proximity to each other. Teachers in special instructional programs may be near each other for collaboration; however, special instructional programs are often housed in areas of the school building, away from the general classroom teachers with whom they are to collaborate.

For teachers who must share instructional responsibilities, the decisions about who will work together are crucial. Taking time to assess the faculty members' relationships to each other can help develop teams that are compatible. Placing a new special education teacher with a teacher who does not value the inclusion of special needs students can place the new teacher at risk. Instead principals can draw on the positive teacher leaders when selecting the best team configurations.

"A . . . web of relationship spanning the school [that] must be created and nurtured" (York-Barr & Vandercook, 2003). Finding ways to facilitate these interactions is a challenge for any leader, but may be an opportunity to tap into teacher leadership talent. If the faculty has a shared vision for an inclusive community, the first step is to have conversations with teachers about the difficulty of collaboration among general education teachers and teachers of special instructional programs. Teacher leaders might facilitate these conversations. At first, the reasons for collaborating or not that will merge will be superficial, such as the physical proximity and conflicting schedules. As conversations get to the root causes, the reasons that emerge may be represented by statements such as these:

General Education Teacher	*Special Programs Teacher*
I feel uncomfortable with her in the classroom and don't know how to assign her tasks.	I feel like a helper in her classroom, rather than a professional.
He promises to come to my classroom every day at 2 o'clock, and there are	The principal told me to be accessible for parents and sometimes they come into the

too many times that he doesn't show up. I can't depend on him.	school when I am supposed to be in her classroom.
She acts like she knows everything about Susan (the student). I've taught her for 3 months and I have some ideas about her needs.	I have a master's degree and expertise to share about Susan (the student) and she won't listen.

These are the deep-rooted reasons that block effective communication between the general education teachers and teachers in special instructional programs. To move beyond reasons revealed on the surface demands leadership beyond the principal. Teachers, who are credible with others, can help other teachers get to these issues. The principal's role is to be an advocate for teacher leaders who are willing to build an inclusive professional community based on an understanding of the real obstacles to collaboration. The principals' involvement does not stop with encouraging these conversations. At times, the principal should be a contributor to the conversation. On the other hand, the principal must be attuned to know when the conversation should be among only the teachers.

TEACHERS WITH PARALLEL INSTRUCTIONAL RESPONSIBILITIES

Carroll (2009) noted that teaming up teachers to work together creates a power learning team that can make use of skill and expertise to "diagnose, treat, and provide care" for students who are in peril of not being successful" (p. 10). Knowing that the team approach is most successful with students, teachers who work in special instructional programs are still isolated in many instances. They do not intersect with the general education teachers to support students with their expertise. This provides another type of challenge in achieving collaboration amongst teachers. Although many of the students may be shared between these teachers and the general education teachers, both groups of teachers may believe there are few areas in which they have to collaborate for instruction. For example, vocation education teachers teach students who are also in general education classes, but the goals of both programs may not be viewed as integrated. In addition, there may be teachers of special programs for which none of the students interact with general education teachers. Examples of this type of fragmentation are widespread at all levels of schooling. Even at faculty meetings, teachers tend to sit together with friends and conversations focus on anything other than instruction. The few attempts at integrating curriculum are often abandoned due to the energy it takes to do this effectively. Learning teams may be the key to changing this grim picture of special program integration.

Moller and Pankake (2006) suggested that this collective learning begin with the principals. Principals can approach this problem with their own solutions or they can bring the problem to the teachers to see who would be willing to find solutions. Often just bringing problems out in the open for discussion can reveal how it violates the school's shared vision of an inclusive professional community. The initial plans may be small, but any attempt to bring all faculty members together for collaboration to solve the school's universal problems can result in significant changes. It works but not without vision, dedication, and trust built from within the schools themselves.

At first, strategies may be contrived. For example, seating at the faculty meeting could be prearranged by the principal or set of teachers seeking to build consensus. Once the initial resistance to not being able to sit with friends subsides, the teachers will find that they have common instructional concerns if they are led through a process to explore their similarities. Dedicated principals and teachers determined to implement a new paradigm can make the difference. Teachers will find ways to build more communication across the grade levels, special instructional programs, and content areas if they begin to work in teams dedicated to solving the problems of the classrooms.

Principals face the responsibility of supporting these decisions. This may involve physical relocation of classrooms, blocks of quality time for collaboration, or additional adult coverage in the classroom to allow teachers time to share. Teachers watch to see if principals will follow through on their commitments. Fiscal resources, human resources, and other supportive conditions should be allocated to support the teachers' decisions that focus on the improvement of student learning. Not every decision can be supported, but the decisions that are feasible must move forward. This support is another measure of the principal's belief in teacher leadership in an inclusive professional community. In addition, the teachers' commitment to leadership responsibility needs to be monitored. This does not mean that teachers will be placed in a threatening position, but the principal can help teachers establish benchmarks for accountability. These benchmarks are assessed as teacher leaders move toward their goals.

Finally, no other person sends as strong a message as the principal about what is important and what is not of value. Co-learning with teachers, turning faculty meetings over to teacher leaders for professional development, and frequent conversations in the hallways about teaching and learning are ways that a principal can let the staff know that their work is vital. To do this demands finding ways to deal with other administrative responsibilities. There is a temptation to focus on paperwork, parent complaints, discipline issues, and other managerial duties rather than moving into the teachers' world. Retaining good teachers and supporting the novice teachers with expertise from the veteran teachers with the use of learning teams can be a powerful means for the principal to build commitment to teacher development and improved student achievement.

Summary

Eklund (2011) noted, "Teachers subject to burnout are those who are involved, devoted, and conscientious" (p. 27). To improve retention of quality teachers, working conditions make the difference in teacher job satisfaction and, therefore, the retention of teachers. Teachers in special instructional programs are, by the nature of their work, isolated from the general education teachers. It is the work of the principal to build a network of support to improve working conditions. The principal is the leader of promoting teacher leadership within an inclusive professional community. Teachers are adults and they want to work in a school where they are respected and supported. The lack of attention to these factors will results in unhealthy attrition and possible emergence of negative teacher leadership.

Beyond retention of teachers, the principal and school will benefit from positive teacher leadership, possibly even reducing personal stress. Teachers in special instructional programs bring leadership skills that can contribute to building an inclusive professional community. With increased student diversity, schools must capitalize on diverse teacher perspectives to address the students' needs. Through teacher leadership and teacher collaboration the professional community will move toward collective learning. Finally, an inclusive professional community models for students how adults can work together effectively in a democracy.

Barriers prevent the development of teacher leadership and can hinder student achievement. If the principal does not believe in sharing leadership, he or she will be unwilling to provide time, physical proximity, or quality professional development to achieve the goal of improved learning of both teachers and students. Also, the teaching culture often works against teacher leadership by causing staff members to resist change. Even when the change is positive, the force from negative subgroups can be powerful.

Teachers as a whole try to avoid conflict even if it is considered productive. Going with the flow seems easier. Principals are powerful deterrents to this type of behavior.

If the principal has a shared vision for teacher leadership within an inclusive professional community, supportive conditions must be in place to realize this goal. Supportive conditions include fiscal resources, human resources and structural systems, and the small things like sharing information, celebrating successes, and providing feedback that is specific to the task. In addition, the principal must facilitate teacher collaborations by providing the time resources and incentives for collaborating about instructional issues.

Until there is a different leadership structure in schools, the principal is the person who must take responsibility for building healthy workplaces. With all the other demands on administrators, personal survival may depend on developing teacher leaders. Teacher will take on the roles if there is authentic support from the principal. Principals sometimes assume that teachers want only to teach and not accept other forms of leadership responsibilities in the school. Generally this is not the case; in fact, many teachers are looking for opportunities to exercise more influence in the schools. Schools need many people leaders; no one person or small group of people can solve all the problems in the school. The goal is to build a critical mass of teacher leaders so that leadership is viewed as an assumed part of the culture of the teaching staff solving problems within and allowing the principal to be a visionary and strategic leader.

Applying Your Knowledge

Miss Della Rosa attended a regional conference and heard a speaker talk about the value of collaboration. She was excited and wondered if her school could develop learning teams to improve student achievement. She wanted to talk to her principal but she was just a teacher. Should she trust her instincts? This might be a wonderful way to meet her student needs and fulfill her own needs for improving her instructional strategies.

QUESTIONS

1. What recommendations would you make to Miss Della Rosa as she approaches her principal and fellow teachers?
2. What barriers to collaboration do you expect Miss Della Rosa to meet? What could you suggest to help her?
3. How will the current culture and climate of her school affect the outcome of her collaborative initiative?

QUESTIONS FOR THOUGHT

1. What are some ways to reduce the barriers to collaboration in schools?
2. What are the characteristics of a teacher leader? Do these characteristics differ between the special programs and general education teachers?
3. How would a principal's job change if shared leadership was the norm in the school? What about teachers?
4. If money was not an issue, what actions would you take to create a culture of collaboration in your school?
5. How could you create a positive experience for collaboration for all fellow members of the faculty in your school?
6. What should be done if some teachers in a school are not interested in or willing to collaborate?

Additional Information Online

Teacher Leaders Network: Center for Teaching Quality: http://www.teacherleaders .org/

Association for Supervision and Curriculum Development: http://www.ascd.org

National Staff Development Council: http://www.nsdc.org

Phi Delta Kappa: http://www.pdk.org

References

Achinstein, B. (2002). *Conflict amid community: The micropolitics of teacher collaboration.* TC Record. Retrieved from http://www.tcrecord.org/Content.asp?ContentID=10846

Ash, R. C., & Persall, J. M. (2000, May). The principal as chief learning officer: Developing teacher leaders. *NASSP Bulletin, 84*(616), 15–22.

Barth, R. (2001). *The teacher leader.* Providence, RI: The Rhode Island Foundation.

Bateman, D., & Bateman, C. F. (2006). *A principal's guide to special education* (2nd ed.). Arlington, VA: Council for Exceptional Children.

Budig, G. A. (2011). Thoughtful change. *Educational Leadership, (92)*5, 76–77.

Bush, G. W. (2001). No Child Left Behind Act. Retrieved from http://www2.ed.gov/policy/elsec/leg/esea02/107-110.pdf

Carroll, T. (2009). The next generation of learning teams. *Phi Delta Kappa, 91*(2), 8–13.

Danielson, C. (2007, September). The many faces of leadership. *Educational Leadership 65*(1), 14–19.

Darling-Hammond, L. (2010). *The flat world and education: How America's commitment to equity will determine our future.* New York: Teachers College Press.

Day, C., & Harris, A. (2003). Teacher leadership, reflective practice and school improvement. In K. Leithwood & P. Hallinger (Eds.), *Second International Handbook of Educational Leadership and Administration.* Dordrecht: Kluwer Academic.

De Lima, J. A. V. (2003, November). Trained for isolation: The impact of departmental cultures on student teachers' views and practices of collaboration. *Journal of Education for Teaching: International Research and Pedagogy 29*(3), 197–217.

DePalola, M. F., & WaltherThomas, C. (2003, February). Principals and special education: The critical role of school leaders. Retrieved from http://scholar.google.com/scholar?q=DiPaola+%26+Walther+Thomas+%282003%29+special+educators&hl=en&as_sdt=0&as_vis=1&oi=scholart

Donaldson, G. A., Jr. (2007). What do teachers bring to leadership? *Educational Leadership 65*(1), 26–29.

DuFour, R. (2011). Work together: But only if you want to. *Phi Delta Kappa, 92*(5), 57–61.

DuFour, R., DuFour, R., Eaker, R., & Many, T. (2006). *Learning by doing: A handbook for professional learning communities at work.* Bloomington, IN: Solution Tree.

Eklund, N. (2009). Sustainable workplaces, retainable teachers. *Phi Delta Kappa, 91*(2), 25–27.

Ferguson, D. L., Ralph, G., & Sampson, N. K. (2002). From "special" educators to educators: The case for mixed ability group of teachers in restructured school. In W. Sailon (Ed.), *Whole school success and inclusive education: Building achievements and accountability.* New York: Teachers College Press.

Fullan, M. (2001). *Leading in a culture of change.* San Francisco, CA: Jossey-Bass.

Gabriel, J. B. (2005). *How to thrive as a teacher leader.* Alexandria, VA: ASCD.

Harris, A. (2002). *School improvement: What's in it for schools?* London: Falmer Press.

Harris, A. (2003, August). Teacher leadership as distributed leadership: Heresy, fantasy or possibility? *School Leadership & Management, 23*(3), 313–324.

Harrison, J. W., & Lembeck, E. (1996). *Emergent teacher leaders.* In G. Moller & M. Katzenmeyer (Eds.), *Every teacher is a leader: Realizing the potential of teacher leadership.* San Francisco, CA: Jossey-Bass.

Hipp, K. A., Huffman, J. B., Pankake, A., & Olivier, D. (2008). Sustaining professional learning communities: Case studies. *Journal of Educational Change, 9*, 173–195.

Hord, S. M. (2004). *Learning together, leading together.* New York: Teachers College Press.

Kinney, K. (2007). *Enhancing learning through the scholarship of teaching and learning: The challenges and joys of juggling.* Boston: Ankar Publishing Company, Inc.

Ingersoll, R. M., & Smith, T. M. (2003, May). The wrong solution to the teacher shortage. *Educational Leadership, 60*(3), 30–33.

Johnson, S. M., & Donaldson, M. L. (2007). Overcoming the obstacles to leadership. *Educational Leadership, 65*(1), 8–13.

Johnson, S. M., & Donaldson, M. L. (2008, Summer). Overcoming the obstacles to leadership. *Educational Leadership, 65,* 8–13.

Katzenmeyer, M., & Moller, G. (2001). *Awakening the sleeping giant: Helping teachers develop as leaders.* Thousand Oaks, CA: Corwin Press.

Lambert, L. (2003, November). Leadership redefined: An evocative context for teacher leadership. *School Leadership and Management, 23*(4), 421–430.

Lambert, L. (2005). What does leadership capacity really mean? *Journal of Staff Development, 26*(2), 38–40.

Lieberman, A., & Miller, L. (2004). *Teacher leadership.* San Francisco, CA: Jossey-Bass

Little, J. W., & Bartlett, L. (2002). Career and commitment in the context of comprehensive school reform. *Teachers and Teaching: Theory and Practice, 8*(3), 345–354.

Littrell, P. C., & Billingsley, B. S. (1994). The effects of principal support on special and general educators' stress, job satisfaction, school commitment, health, and intent to stay in teaching. *Journal of Remedial & Special Education 15*(5), 1–19.

Louis, K. S., & Wahlstrom, K. (2011, February). Principals as cultural leaders. *Phi Delta Kappan, 92*(5), 52–56.

Louis, K. S., Marks, H. M., & Kruse, S. D. (1996). Teachers' professional community in restructuring schools. *American Educational Research Journal, 33*(4).

Mills, S. J., & Schall, J. C. (2012). Barriers and marginalization in female teacher leadership. (pp. 117-139). In E. Murakami-Ramalho & A. McCoskey Pankake (Eds.), *Educational Leaders Encouraging the Intellectual and Professional Capacity of Others—A Social Justice Agenda.* Charlotte, NC: IAP.

Moller, G., & Pankake, A. (2006). *Lead with me: A principal's guide to teacher leadership.* Larchmont, NY: Eye on Education.

Murphy, J., Smylie, M., Mayrowetz, D., & Louis, K. S. (2009, April). The role of the principal in fostering the development of distributed leadership. *School Leadership and Management, 29*(2), 181–214.

Pearce, C. L., & Conger, J. A. (2002). *Shared leadership: Reframing the hows and whys of leadership.* London, United Kingdom: Sage Publishing.

Schroth, G., Beaty, D., & Dunbar, R. (2002). *School scheduling strategies: New ways of finding time or students and staff.* Lancaster, PA: Proactive Publications.

Shoffner, M. F., & Briggs, M. K. (2001). An interactive approach for developing inter-professional collaboration: preparing school counselors. *Counselor Education and Supervision, 40*(3), 193–202.

Spillane, J. P., Halverson, R., & Diamond, J. B. (2001, April). Investigating school leadership practice: A distributed perspective. *Educational Researcher, 30*(3), 23–28.

Steel, C., & Craig, E. (2006). Reworking industrial models, exploring contemporary ideas, and fostering teacher leadership. *Phi Delta Kappan, 87*(9), 676–680.

Watt, K. M., Huerta, J., & Mills, S. J. (2010). Advancement via individual determination (AVID) professional development as a predictor of teacher leadership in the United States. International Professional Development Association. *Professional Development in Education, 36*(3), 1–16.

Watt, K. M., Mills, S. J., & Huerta, J. (2010). Identifying attributes of teacher leaders within the advancement via individual determination program: A survey of school principals. *Journal of School Leadership 20*(3), 352–368.

Williams, J. (2007, November). Revolution from the faculty lounge: The emergence of teacher-led schools and cooperatives. *Phi Delta Kappan, 89*(3), 204–216.

York-Barr, J., & Duke, K. (2004). What do we know about teacher leadership? Findings from two decades of scholarship. *Review of Educational Research, 74*(3), 255–316.

York-Barr, J., & Vandercook, T. (2003). Lesson learned on the way toward inclusion. *Minnesota School Boards Association Journal, 54*(6), 12–14.

Accessing Central Office Resources 13

Ava J. Muñoz

Anita Pankake

Administering special programs in a school is one among many areas for which principals and teachers need the help and support of central administration. Taking full advantage of the resources (human and nonhuman) that exist at district's central office is a responsibility as well as an opportunity for school leaders.

—Anita Pankake

Objectives

1. Provide an understanding of the role of central office staff in regard to schools
2. Present a model that promotes collaboration and cooperation between the school and central office staff members
3. Demonstrate how school leaders can best access the persons and resources available in central administration

Introduction

Central office administrators work to facilitate the seamless operation of school districts. Their job responsibilities are, for the most part, vast in nature. "Superintendents depend on their (central office staffs) expert knowledge and capability to implement policy initiatives and visions promulgated by states and local boards of education" (Björk, 2001, p. 206). Central office administrators are expected to support and assist in the implementation of instructional improvement.

"As school districts grow in size and complexity, it becomes necessary to develop specialized functions, and the central office staff comes into being" (Rebore, 2007, p. 9). Almost every special program in a school district is accompanied by one or more specialists, consultants, directors, coordinators, or assistant superintendents who function externally to the classroom delivery of that program. Often, though not always, the individuals who occupy these positions are located at the school district's central office. According to the National Center for Educational Statistics, in the fall of 2008, over 73,457 positions comprise some aspect of central office operations other than the superintendent (http://nces.ed.gov/programs/digest/d10/tables/dt10_085.asp). More recent statistics from the U.S. Department of Education (August 2010) show that the number of central office positions have more than doubled over the past 10 years. Current data identifies 80,553 positions under the category of "Instructional Coordinators and Supervisors."

Traditionally, the purposes of such positions have been to monitor and control decisions and resources related to specific programs and administrative functions. Additionally, responsibility for support, assistance, and coordination of program efforts for the district as a whole often appear in the formal job descriptions for such positions. Unfortunately, these central office positions have not always been viewed as particularly helpful by the intended audience (i.e., individuals at the school). The perspective of principals and teachers regarding the responsibilities and practices of these various administrators is often less than positive. Rather than seeing the superintendent and the central office administrators as individuals whose roles are to serve and support, the individuals operating at the delivery points of these programs (principals and teachers) see people in these positions as creators of complications, confusion, and massive paperwork. A particularly poignant description of such perceptions is offered by Sarason (1996, p. 163):

> The dominant impression one gains is that school personnel believe that there is a system, that it is run by somebody or bodies in some central place, that it tends to operate as a never ending source of obstacles to those within the system, that a major goal of the individual is to protect against the baleful influences of the system, and that any one individual has and can have no effect on the system qua system. . . ."

Although total quality management (TQM) postulates that individuals regularly work at their highest capacity and that it is their organization's responsibility to maintain this level of excellence by continuously bringing about positive improvements to the multifaceted layers of this organization (Deming, 1982), Whitaker and Moses (1994) point out that within the TQM philosophy proffered by Deming the most important job of leaders is to find and remove barriers in the organization that might be preventing people from being successful. Whitaker and Moses, then, transfer this perspective to the school superintendent by stating that, "It is up to the superintendent to remove the hurdles faced by principals and teachers as they initiate change. Central office personnel must begin to view themselves not as regulators, but as leaders who help initiate improvement efforts and involve others in those efforts" (p. 166). They go on to assert, "One thing is certain, school level changes are near impossible without the help and support of central administration" (Whitaker & Moses, 1994, p. 166).

Presently, in the structure of a school organization, it is commonplace to include the concept of site-based management (SBM). SBM was introduced as a means of refocusing management back to student, teaching and learning outcomes. It has now been widely recognized that special program decisions as a category of decisions are better made or influenced in part by professionals at the school site, especially teachers and principals. "It is believed that shared decision making results in a number of benefits over individual decision making, including increased decision quality, creativity, acceptance, understanding, judgment, and accuracy" (Lunenburg & Ornstein, 2008, p. 365). But, alas, not all concepts are implemented, uniformly. Although SBM has its defenders as well as its foes, "some school districts, mostly moderate-size suburban districts, have implemented on-site management to good effect" (Owens & Valesky, 2011, p. 333). Consequently, some of the larger urban school districts appear to be experiencing difficulties putting their SBMs to proper use. Furthermore, Owens and Valesky state that "school boards and central office bureaucracies are reluctant to cede their powers to schools" (2011, p. 333), unfortunately, initiating a 'lame duck' SBM committee with little to no power" (Owens & Valesky, 2011).

Teacher empowerment is considered one of the most significant reforms within the education profession and as a concept for facilitating effective school leadership has become synonymous with site-based decision management. Advocates of this leadership concept agree that site-based decision making is a potentially powerful mechanism for achieving teacher empowerment resulting in a campus leadership team that is better able to respond to the unique needs of the individual school. The central office administrator-principal relationship has become a key point of review and importance in an educational environment of high stakes accountability. Principals are now held accountable for program and educational outcomes and so it follows that authority for some measure of program and educational program decision making must be delegated to the campus.

Consistent with this point of view, Ray, Hack, and Candoli (2001) suggest that effective organizations should create planning cadres that address the planning function. This team would undertake all planning activities for the campus, including the establishment of educational goals, the development of educational programs reflecting the goals, the identification of resources needed to implement programs, the allocation of physical and human resources for implementation, and an evaluation process which supports a continued plan development.

Since program implementation responsibility has not yet become completely the role of the principal, it makes sense that the principals and staff must maintain an effective relationship and lines of communication with central office program administrators. A close relationship between campus staff and central office special program staff is essential in facilitating the achievement of student performance goals of a campus. Central office special program staff will continue to exercise the monitoring and control functions under site-based management. This function becomes even more critical to the overall organization since many new centers of activity are created at each campus and so must be controlled and monitored.

Administering special programs in a school is one among many areas for which principals and teachers need the help and support of central administration. Taking full advantage of the resources (human and nonhuman) that exist as district's central office is a responsibility as well as an opportunity for school leaders. Central office, no matter how large and complex or small and overworked, can provide information, technical assistance, legal advice, networking with programs in other districts and regions, clerical support, and myriad other essentials for the quality operations of special programs at the building level. This chapter will give an overview of central office in terms of definition and design and some information regarding significant changes that are being initiated and/or being thrust upon central office administrative operations because of efforts to decentralize and increase site-based decision making for school improvement efforts. The last section offers some specific ways in which school leaders can access and utilize central office services and support. A tone of advocacy is evident throughout the chapter. Neglect of or inappropriate use of the resources available to school leaders—in this case, those at central office—result in missed opportunities to do our best for the children to be served.

A Brief Overview Central Office

Today, the fact that there is a central office staff in a school district is taken for granted. Now and then there may be some grinching about the organization being "top heavy" or "having too many people 'over there,'" but, according to English (1992), administrative roles other than the principal and superintendent have become a fixed part of our thinking regarding school district administration. The general development of central office is described by Knezevich (1984). He marks the beginning of central office administration with what he refers to as the "one-person-office-of-the superintendent." During this time an individual in the position of superintendent often taught one or two classes, coached, and/or did the district's clerical work. Other duties at the central office were formed as assists to the initial administrative position of school superintendent. Knezevich (1984) divides the development of central office into three phases:

1. Phase one began when superintendents were relieved of nonadministrative functions such as teaching and coaching.
2. Phase two occurred when personnel were hired to assume the clerical and non-professional administrative responsibilities of the school district.
3. Phase three was initiated when enrollments in elementary and secondary units became large enough to merit their own full-time administrators.

As might be expected, large districts were the first to move through these phases and actually develop a central office team. As various federal and state initiatives have been implemented, new and different needs for specialized administrative positions have developed. Many larger districts have one or more central office administrative or supervisory positions devoted each to special education, guidance and counseling program, migrant education, bilingual and ESL programs, programs for the gifted and talents, career and technology education, and myriad others. The number and focus of specialized management positions at the district level varies between and among school districts and can change with any federal or state legislation or state department initiative.

Orlosky, McCleary, Shapiro, and Webb (1984, p. 50) claim that

> To understand the configuration of administrative and supervisory positions of a district central office, one can subdivide the responsibilities of the superintendent as required by the number, complexity and size of tasks into a range of positions occupied by specialists. This configuration is referred to as the superintendency.

Central office management for the district is created when a function or set of functions is divided into specific tasks and delegated to a specialist. Depending on the nature of the tasks delegated, the administration will be structured into levels with assistant superintendents in charge of one or more functions. Major tasks under the responsibility of an assistant superintendent may be assigned to directors. Although titles may differ, two- and three-level hierarchies of administrative specialists are not uncommon.

Little uniformity exists in titles and the commensurate responsibilities of central office positions from one district to another. Such variation in these positions exists to the extent that a study by Association for Supervision and Curriculum Development completed in the 1980s concluded that the roles of central office supervisors were so unique from one district to another that they were "non-comparable" (Snyder, Giella, & Fitzgerald, 1994). Knezevich (1984) demonstrates this vividly in the following statements, "Members of the administrative team include personnel with such diverse titles as deputy, associate or assistant superintendent; director; supervisor; administrative assistant; coordinator; and consultant, all of whom are attached to the office of the superintendent of schools." However, the distinguishing characteristic of central office administrators is that they

> are charged with responsibilities that are system-wide in scope but limited in range within the institutions. Thus, the supervisor of music's functions are system-wide in scope but confined to music; the assistant superintendent in charge of elementary education is responsible for elementary education only, but in all parts of the system. (p. 312)

An important distinction to be made between and among central office administrators is related to knowing the hierarchical power and authority of their roles. English (1992) differentiates the two types of positions: "line" and "staff." He defines line positions as those "directly concerned with implementation" and staff positions as "those who support, but do not directly deliver instructional programs" (p. 147). Perhaps even more important for our purposes in this chapter is the contrast between the two types of positions offered by Wiles and Bondi (1983). They describe line personnel as the "formal leadership" in the schools and school districts and staff personnel as those "who advise and consult others of the organization, formally and informally, but have no authority" (pp. 113–114). Position titles sometimes help in revealing the line or staff authority of central office administrative positions, but they are no guarantee.

Central office administrators working with special programs or in other areas may also differ in the focus of their positions responsibilities—that is, "generalists" or "specialists" (Campbell, Cunningham, Nystrand, & Usdan, 1985, p. 226). Generalists, such as superintendents and principals, have a wide range of responsibilities encompassed in their positions. Individuals in positions that have a focus on one area or single group of functions are specialists. Some of these positions are advisory (i.e., staff) positions, others have line authority. School districts need both kinds of positions to operate; generalists need advice and information from a variety of specialists to make good decisions and someone needs to see the "big picture" of the school system operation which goes beyond any one specialty area.

An understanding of the traditional perspectives helps one to appreciate the monumental changes being proposed (and in some places implemented) regarding the purpose and practice of central office administration (Pankake & Boyter, 1998). Whitaker and Moses (1994, p. 166) state:

> Historically, the superintendent and central administration have assumed the roles of primary decision makers and enforcers of school board policies. Although the roles of central administration still include being accountable for decisions, they are gradually changing from enforcing ones to supporting ones.

These changes provide important opportunities for school leaders to use and even help develop central office resources as supports for, rather than barriers, in the administration and delivery of special programs.

Major reform and restructuring efforts have influenced the roles and responsibilities of central office personnel as well as the individuals in the school sites. A shift from the traditional control and monitoring roles toward roles more focused on services and supports that assist with improved student performance generally in the school is occurring in varying degrees in districts across the nation (Hord & Smith, 1993). "Central staff are no longer the sole authority figures, distributing directives and monitoring compliance" (Hord & Smith, 1993, p. 23). Rather, in the "new central office staff members must learn to operate without the crutch of hierarchy and have only themselves to rely on" (Hanna, 1988, cited in Tewel, 1995, p. 66). Accordingly, Tewel (1995) admonished that

". . . success [in central office positions] now depends on figuring out whose collaboration is needed to act on good ideas. In short, the new work implies very different ways of obtaining and using power and influence" (p. 66). School systems, like businesses and government agencies, are trying to create flatter organizations, or as Tewel (1995) described it—a need to "become leaner, less bureaucratic, and more entrepreneurial" (p. 65). Certainly some school districts' central office administration would fit perfectly in one or more of the traditional schemes described earlier. Others, however, are in the midst of trying to implement the new roles, relationships, and responsibilities that accompany the system restructuring. As with any system, making a change in one area of the system results in associated changes in other areas of the system. Consequently, as changes occur in the structure and operations at central office, changes will be enabled and required in response at the school level.

Proposed changes in central office administrative operations are numerous. They include more channels for action created, cross-department projects, interagency ventures, and collaboration with various professional associations; and the creation of "more potential centers of power" to provide "the opportunity for greater flexibility" (Tewel, 1995, p. 66). To accomplish these changes, central office administrators and supervisors must (a) shift to being facilitators and sources of technical expertise to help the school in their efforts to change (Hord & Smith, 1993), (b) begin sharing and in some instances relinquishing decision-making authority in many areas of school operations (Hord & Smith, 1993), and (c) start thinking cross-functional and building multiple networks (Tewel, 1995, p. 67). According to Tewel (1995), survival and thriving for central office administrators will depend on finding knowledge and services of value to individuals at the building sites. This will happen only if these individuals spend more time working across boundaries with peers and other staff members over whom they have no direct control but need to use their interpersonal and negotiating skills. Power will evolve from personal strengths of the individuals, not from organizational structure (Tewel, 1995).

An important point made by Tewel (1995), and one to be kept in mind as these various concepts of the traditional and contemporary operations regarding central office administration are linked, is that, "While the old organization no longer exists on paper, . . . it continues to haunt the minds, habits, and performance of staff." (p. 76). School leaders need to assess the situation in their district and take advantage of both the old and/or the new in terms of leadership opportunities. Obviously not all districts will have made the transition from the traditional, more centralized structure to the more decentralized, autonomous site operations. Being able to analyze how a district actually is operating (whether or not that is what's described in the organizational chart and/or the operational philosophy) will be important in taking advantages of the resources available.

Accessing and Using What Is Available

As the new ways of operating become embedded in the central office, school leaders will need to respond appropriately. In order to take full advantage of the collaborative, facilitative, shared decision making, support, and assistance perspective developing at the central office, similar perspectives need to be developed at the school site. Sarason (1996, p. 180) points out,

> More than any other single position in the American School hierarchy, the principalship represents the pivotal exchange point, the most important point of connection between teachers, students, and parents on the one hand and the educational policy-making structure—superintendent, school board, and taxpayer—on the other. Through the principal's office pass both the needs, problems, and issues of the local community and the problems and issues that accompany the implementation of policies flowing downward from the top of the school bureaucracy.

This statement emphasizes the importance of the school leadership in making use of all resources that may improve the quality of programs. Following are some ideas on how school leaders can take advantage of the new opportunities developing as the restructuring at central office occurs or how to take better advantage of the existing opportunities if restructuring of central office is yet to be initiated in the current situation.

It was not uncommon, during earlier central office reform efforts, for personnel and other program resources to be decentralized and located at the school rather than at central office. The concept of moving the resources as close to the point of instructional impact for students as possible was a driving force of central office restructuring. According to Delehant (1990), "The traditional, centralized district organization is being replaced with a structure that directs all resources that bear upon student performance to be the work of the schools. The responsibility and accountability for decisions that affect student performance are shifting from central management to the schools" (p. 17). This reallocation is an effort to assist improved student performance in the school generally not just in the specific special programs. Locating human and nonhuman resources where the programs are happening allows some authentic on-site technical assistance to be afforded to students, teachers, and building administrators alike.

Presently, dissimilar from the previous reforms, "large, urban districts have tended to expand their centralized staff and activities over recent years in order to administer court-ordered policies and state and federal guidelines, programs, and funds and to cope with union-style teacher associations" (Lunenburg & Ornstein, 2008, p. 303). One very important and highly positive aspect of school districts with highly specialized staff and centralized leadership is that they are more efficient in their decision making (Lunenburg & Ornstein, 2008).

The following suggestions are offered to principals and teachers as strategies that will improve their relationships with central office administrators and help assure that the resources and services available are accessed for the benefit of students:

Knowing your priorities. As central office administrators offer support and assistance, they will need to know what your priorities are in order to make the best use of their time, knowledge, and skills in addressing the needs at the various school sites. Central office resources will be limited. To get the best service and assistance school leaders need to be clear about what they need, when, and how they perceived it might best be delivered.

Offering feedback on the quality of services and assistance. As Hunter (1982) noted, everybody likes to have an answer to the question, "How am I doing?" In fact, it is necessary to have some sense of this in order to know how to adjust to improve the quality of services. The only ones who have the information on how well those at central office are meeting needs will be individuals at each building site. Therefore it is incumbent on the building leadership to set up various means of collecting feedback on the services and assistance provided and convey this information to those at central office. Without such information, whether or not activities are truly resulting in quality services will be a best guess on the part of the central office personnel (Pankake, 1998).

Getting information about who can do what for whom. Depending on the size and complexity of the central office staff, there may be several sources of information available. Knowing who has the information and services that you need will increase the efficiency and accuracy with which central office can respond to any request. Representatives from the school site may find it helpful to both themselves and their central office administrators and supervisors to spend some time learning about who knows what and who can do what regarding the various special programs operating in the building. This may well be a point at which knowing who are the generalists and who are the specialists in the central office will become quite useful. It will also be helpful for the school leadership to understand the line and staff divisions at central office. This will prevent them from asking for a decision from someone who does not have the authority to make it, and will lead to asking for advice from those who truly have the expertise in that particular area.

Some of the resources available at central office may not be encompassed in personnel specifically allocated to the administration of special programs. For example, the central office unit dealing with staff development may be of great assist in a variety of areas. While they may not have specific information about a particular program they may well be able to locate who does. If there is a particular knowledge base needed by the school staff to implement new strategies, the staff development personnel can find, organize its presentation, and maybe even fund it.

Another central office unit that may be helpful to school leaders as they look to make quality improvements are the administrators in the central office who work with personnel matters. Generally these people are experts in certification requirements and can be most helpful in identifying applicants that meet the paper requirements as well as the practice requirements. Personnel office administrators and staff may also be involved in the allocation of time for individuals who serve more than one school—that is, the "traveling teachers" or "shared personnel." Staying informed about who makes these assignments and, in turn, keeping those individuals informed about the school's needs for the services of these staff members will make it more likely that staff allocations are based on needs, not just numbers.

Another opportunity for building level access to central office resources that is presenting itself more frequently is participation in district level planning. Many districts are implementing vertical teams in their planning processes to ensure that a variety of perspectives are being considered at the planning stages of all operations and of any new initiatives. School leaders need to have personnel ready and willing to take part in these activities as the opportunities arise. Full participation in these opportunities requires that school leaders know the interests, skills, and talents of their staff members. School leaders would do well to get acquainted with everyone in their organization to discover what talents and areas of expertise exist (Pankake, 1998). Knowing who has had special training in a particular area, who may be bilingual but not working in the bilingual program, who has some community connections and involvement that might assist on a school or district project, who is looking to pursue a school administration career, and who is looking to accept some leadership responsibilities but does not wish to leave their classroom assignment can help assure that when central office extends an invitation to participate, your school is ready to respond.

"Specialists" at central office can be a wealth of information regarding the rules, regulations, and reports that seem to be part and parcel of every special program. The role of school leader is much more of a generalist than a specialist. "Generalists" have a wide range of responsibilities included in their jobs, while "specialists" usually have their responsibilities focused on one area or group of functions operationally or programmatically (Campbell et al., 1985). Individuals with specialized information related to various school and district programs are often located at the district level. However, their specialized knowledge is only a phone call, e-mail, or office visit away. They know the latest in their area. School leaders who access this specialized knowledge can help ensure quality programming for students and help avoid complaints and litigation situations for everyone.

Specialists may also have established contacts and working relationships with individuals in external agencies that provide needed services and support to students and/ or their families. School leaders can work through the central office specialists to move more quickly and effectively in accessing personnel and information located in these external agencies. Taking advantage of the bridges and communication networks already in place through central office specialists can facilitate interagency cooperation in providing services for students and reduce bureaucratic frustrations for everyone.

Closing Comments

"With a decades-long drive to push reform to the school level, central office has too frequently become the bad guy in these efforts. The accusations of central office 'interference' in reform are many ..." (Richardson, 2000, p. 1). It is time to end the traditional blame game of "them" and "us" when considering school reform with a focus on quality programming for all students. Schools and school systems won't improve with leaders spending their time waiting for each other to change. If the oft-used term "systemic change" has any real meaning for quality education, surely it is that all levels and all individuals working at those levels in the educational system have some responsibilities for making changes. Leaders at both central office and school sites have important roles to play in the school improvement process and the implementation of special programs. Central office efforts to become less bureaucratic and dominating and more service and support oriented are taking hold in many systems throughout the country; other systems are likely to follow. However, when the efforts to change toward this decentralized service and support structure are initiated, school leaders must simultaneously reciprocate by recognizing this and taking action to access the information and services offered. This can be done in myriad ways, only a few of which have been offered here.

Applying Your Knowledge

The new superintendent has expressed a desire for some major changes in the roles, relationships, and responsibilities for all leadership personnel throughout the district. She has asked that you and three of your colleagues from other schools serve as members of a restructuring task force (RTF). Other members of the task force are the Director of Staff Development, the Assistant Superintendent for Noninstructional Support Services, one of the Bilingual Instructional Facilitators, the Early Childhood Education Services Coordinator, the Director of Social, Psychological, and Psychometric Services, the Administrative Assistant for Business and Purchasing, two parents, and a Program Administrator for the Educational Service Center for the region.

To get things underway, the superintendent has hosted a continental breakfast and now everyone is seated at the conference table. The superintendent calls the meeting to order and repeats her desire for the RTF to explore some of the major issues that may be preventing quality delivery of instructional and support services to the children enrolled in the district. She reinforces that it is her intent to determine ways in which positions, procedures, and resources can be reallocated and restructured to increase the quantity and quality of services for all children. She has provided two individuals from her office to serve as scribes for the meeting. Her goal for this session is to have everyone offer ideas on what they perceive to be problems or issues that should be explored by the RTF.

You are feeling optimistic about this effort and the leadership of the superintendent. In a variety of informal meetings with your school leadership colleagues, you have been openly critical of operations at central office, especially as they related to services for special needs students and the quality and relevance of teacher in-service offerings. Suddenly you are jogged from your satisfied reflection when you realize that the superintendent has just spoken your name. All eyes at the conference table are on you and the scribes have their markers in hand as the superintendent says to you, " … let's have you start us out. Have you experienced any difficulties in securing the assistance you need from those of us at central office?"

QUESTIONS

1. How will you respond to the superintendent's questions with honesty, but in such a way that it keep the discussion positive and open?
2. What do you think about the makeup of the task force membership? Is there anyone you believe should be added to the group? Anyone currently on the group that you believe probably shouldn't be? Explain.
3. Will you share information about the work of the RTF with others in your school? Will you seek their input? Why? How?

QUESTIONS FOR THOUGHT

1. How might knowing which central office administrators are in "line" positions and which are in "staff" positions impact building leaders in their work with special programs?
2. Give a brief history of the development of the central office. Discuss what you believe will be the future of the central office given the current climate.
3. What are some professional development issues related to the delivery of quality special programming that the central office might support? What forms would this support take?
4. If a decision were made to reallocate the resources and responsibilities of one central office position to your building, what position would you request? Why? How would you put the resources to work? What responsibilities would you give the person in this position?

For Additional Information Online

American Association of School Administrators (AASA): www.aasa.org

National Center for Education Statistics (NCES): www.nces.ed.gov

National Staff Development Council (NSDC): www.nsdc.org

Association for Supervision and Curriculum Development (ASCD): www.ascd.org

Education Week: www.edweek.org

Also, many universities and private agencies have policy analysis units that could be helpful. Each of these organizations has affiliate organizations in most states. State affiliates could be sources of information more specific to the unique information requirements of a particular area.

References

Björk, L. G. (2001). Institutional barriers to educational reform: A superintendents' role in district decentralization. In Brunner, C. C. & Björk, L. G. (Eds.), *The new superintendency* (pp. 205–228). New York: Elseiver Science, Ltd.

Campbell, R. F., Cunningham, L. L., Nystrand, R. O., & Usdan, M. D. (1985). *The organization and control of American schools* (5th edition). Columbus, OH: Charles E. Merrill.

Delehant, A. M. (1990). A central office view: Charting a course when pulled in all directions. *The School Administrator, 47*(8), 14, 17–19.

Deming, W. E. (1982). *Out of the crisis.* Cambridge, MA: Massachusetts Institute of Technology, Center for Advanced Engineering Study.

English, F. W. (1992). *Educational administration: The human science.* New York: HarperCollins.

Hord, S., & Smith, A. (1993). Will the phones go dead? *Insight* (Winter), 23–26.

Hunter, M. (1982). *Mastery teaching.* El Segundo, CA: TIP Publications.

Knezevich, S. J. (1984). *Administration of public education: A sourcebook for the leadership and management of educational institutions* (4th edition). New York: Harper & Row.

Lunenburg, F.C., & Ornstein, A. C. (2008). *Educational administration: Concepts and practices* (5th ed.). Belmont, CA: Thomson Higher Education.

National Center for Educational Statistics. (Fall, 2008). *Institute of Education Sciences.* U.S. Department of Education, Washington, DC. Available at http://nces.ed.gov/programs/digest/d10/tables/dt10_085.asp

Orlosky, D. E., McCleary, L. E., Shapiro, A., & Webb, L. D. (1984). *Educational administration today.* Columbus, OH: Charles E. Merrill.

Owens, R. G., & Valesky, T. C. (2011). *Organizational behavior in education: Leadership and school reform* (10th ed.). New York: Allyn and Bacon/Pearson.

Pankake, A. M. (1998). *Implementation: Making things happen.* Larchmont, NY: Eye on Education.

Pankake, A. M., & Boyter, G. A. (1998). Central office career choices for women. In B. J. Irby & G. Brown (Eds.), *Women Leaders: Structuring Success,* (pp. 168–179). Dubuque, IA: Kendall/Hunt Publishing Co.

Parsley, J. F. (1991). Reshaping student learning. *The School Administrator, 48*(7), 9, 11, 13, 14.

Ray, J., Hack, W. G., & Candoli, L. C. (2001). *School Business Administration: A planning approach.* Needham Heights, MA: Allyn & Bacon.

Rebore, R. W. (2007). *Human resources administration in education: A management approach.* Boston: Pearson Education, Inc.

Richardson, J. (2000, October). Central office guidance strengthens the whole district. *NSDC Results* (October), 1, 6.

Sarason, S. B. (1996). *Revisiting "The culture of the school and the problem of change."* New York: Teachers College Press.

Snyder, K. J., Giella, M., & Fitzgerald, J. H. (1994). The changing role of central office supervisors in district restructuring. *The Journal of Staff Development, 15*(2), 30–34.

Tewel, K. J. (1995). Despair at the central office. *Educational Leadership, 52*(7), 65–68.

Whitaker, K. S., & Moses, M. C. (1994). *The restructuring handbook: A guide to school revitalization.* Boston: Allyn and Bacon.

Wiles, J., & Bondi, J. (1983). *Principles of school administration: The real world of leadership in schools.* Columbus, OH: Charles E. Merrill.

Student 14
Activities

Jennifer T. Butcher

Schools that foster positive interactions among
students and between students and teachers are more
likely to have engaged, high-performing students.

—*Jennifer Butcher*

Objectives

1. Discuss the definition and history of student activities
2. Discuss the importance of student activities
3. Explain the role of the University Interscholastic League in Texas schools
4. Discuss intramural activities and other student activities available to students
5. Discuss legal implications pertaining to student activities
6. Discuss the administrative responsibilities and role in supporting student activities

Introduction and Background

Student activities provide opportunities for students to enhance social skills and learn character-building lessons they can apply to their study habits and their lives. Student activities may contribute to students staying in school and finding personal meaning during their school years (Stearns & Glennie, 2010; Olszewski-Kubilius & Lee, 2004). A principal's active involvement helps create a positive climate and reassures teachers that activities are important extensions of the educational and social programs already present in the school.

Athletic exercises date back to educational fundamentals in Persia, Sparta, Athens, and Rome. Olympic games and other activities that occurred from the eighth century B.C. to the fourth century A.D. gave opportunities for youth to compete in sports music, dancing, and poetry. The long history of student activities extends from classical Greece to the present (Frederick, 1959).

In 1918, the Commission on the Reorganization of Secondary Education proclaimed seven aims of education. The seven aims of education included health, command of fundamental processes, worthy home membership, vocation, citizenship, worthy leisure, and ethical character. The commission believed that these aims could be achieved through the combination of an academic curriculum and an activities curriculum. The student activities were an especially important means of accomplishing the goals of health, citizenship, and worthy use of leisure time (Kleese, 2004).

Several terms have been applied to designate the variety of activities engaged in by students in the educational environment. The most common term used is *extracurricular activities*. According to Frederick (1959), extracurricular activities can be defined as programs and events, carrying no academic credit, sponsored and organized by students, student organizations, or by the educational institution designed to entertain, instruct, and provide for areas of interests and abilities. Another common term used is student activities. Student activities are those school activities voluntarily engaged in by students, which have the approval of and are sponsored by the faculty but do not carry credit toward promotion or graduation (Frederick, 1959). Other terms that have been used include allied activities, informal school activities, the third curriculum, nonacademic activities, extraeducational, extraclass, and cocurricular activities.

Importance of Student Activities

Schools that foster positive interactions among students and between students and teachers are more likely to have engaged, high-performing students. One strategy that can make a strong impact on school success is the cultivation of a relationship between a caring school climate and student engagement. Schools can involve students and build spirit in a variety ways. School activities recognize each student as a member of the school community (Kleese, 2004).

Based on a study by Hollrah (n.d.), students involved in extracurricular activities receive better grades by teaching them character-building lessons and lifelong skills, saving some at-risk students who would possibly drop out of school, and helping students develop social skills. Students learn character-building lessons that they can apply to their study habits and to their lives, and students learn life skills that benefit their studies. Not only do extracurricular activities help students that are already successful in school, they also help at-risk students to further excel. Similar findings were reported by Stearns and Glennie (2010). Stearns and Glennie found that student who participated in activities had a greater commitment to school; additionally, they found that students' being active in sports and vocational activities was associated with keeping potential dropouts in schools.

The student's nonclassroom activities are of real and immediate importance (Frederick, 1965). Extracurricular activities allow students to meet and interact with peers. The activities also help to enhance social skills and teach lessons not learned in a classroom. Extracurricular activities may contribute to students staying in school and finding personal meaning during their school years. Students involved in the activities are better able to extend and enrich cognitive skills learned in the classroom through competitions and real-world experiences (Kleese, 2004; Stearns & Glennie, 2010).

University Interscholastic League (UIL)

Schools are governed by the rules and regulations of their state's interscholastic association. This chapter will focus on the University Interscholastic League (UIL), which is the statewide organization for public elementary and secondary interschool competition in Texas. The University Interscholastic League was created by the University of Texas at Austin to provide leadership and guidance to public school debate and athletic teachers. Since 1909, the UIL has grown into the largest interschool organization of its kind. The University Interscholastic League operates under the auspices of The University of Texas System. The UIL provides educational extracurricular academic, athletic, and music contests. A public school district or open enrollment charter school in Texas that is subject to accreditation by the Texas Education Agency may become a member of the UIL.

The objectives of the UIL are:

- to enhance students' educational experience;
- to prepare them for citizenship by providing interschool competition among the public elementary and secondary schools of Texas; and
- to establish rules and procedures for sanctioning and conducting interscholastic competition, including rules providing penalties for rules violations by school district personnel, which are consistent with rules of the State Board of Education. (About the UIL, n.d.)

The UIL places emphasis on the following:

- providing students with educational experiences through competition,
- promoting good sportsmanship and cooperation among member schools,
- working to prevent exploitation of students by special interest groups,
- seeking to safeguard the health and welfare of students by requiring physical examinations for participants in athletics, and
- sponsoring district, regional, and state tournaments or meets in athletic, music, drama, and academic contests. (About the UIL, n.d.)

The Music Program of the UIL is designed to support and enrich the teaching of music as an integral component of the public school curriculum in the state of Texas. The UIL-sponsored music programs are concert band, choir, marching band, music (medium ensemble performance), music (memory), music (solo-small ensemble performance), and music theory (Music–UIL, n.d.).

The UIL provides services to its member schools in the organization and administration of regional and state championship in 14 sports. The UIL-sponsored sports are baseball, basketball, cross country, football, golf, soccer, swimming, tennis, track and field, volleyball, and wrestling (Athletics–UIL, n.d.).

The UIL offers the most comprehensive literary and academic competitive program in the nation. The programs include theatre, journalism, speech and debate,

A+ academics (grades 2–8), and high school academics (grades 9–12). The UIL offers more than any other UIL division in terms of activities, with 22 high school and 18 elementary and junior high contests. More than a half million students participate in UIL academic contests.

These activities, which exist to complement the academic curriculum, are designed to motivate students as they acquire higher levels of knowledge, to challenge students to confront issues of importance, and to provide students with the opportunity to demonstrate mastery of specific skills (see http://www.uiltexas.org/files/constitution/uil-ccr-subchapter-m.pdf).

A student is eligible to participate in a UIL varsity contest as a representative of a participating school if the student:

- is not high a school graduate,
- is a full-time student,
- has attended classes since the sixth day of class of the present school year or has enrolled and been in regular attendance for 15 or more calendar days before the contest,
- is eligible under no-pass, no-play,
- has the required number of credits for eligibility,
- is enrolled in a 4-year program of high school courses,
- was initially enrolled in the ninth-grade not more than 4 years ago, or in the 10th grade not more than 3 years ago,
- was not recruited, and
- is not in violation of Awards Rules (Academic Eligibility Basics–UIL, n.d.).

Interscholastic competition is an excellent way to encourage students to enrich their education and expand their horizons. Leadership and citizenship experiences through interschool activities help prepare students for a more useful and wholesome life. Teamwork is an important component of student activities. Participation teaches that it is a privilege and an honor to represent one's school and students learn to win and to lose—to take as well as to give. From the beginning, administrators from across Texas have served on UIL committees and helped write and establish rules and administrative guidelines (About the UIL, n.d.).

Intramural Activities

The term *intramural* simply means "within the walls." Traditionally, this term refers to team and dual/individual activities, tournaments, meets, and/or special events that are limited to participants and teams from within a specific school or institutional setting. Intramural activities are intended to be voluntary—that is, the students have a choice of participating in activities. Every student is given an equal opportunity to participate in intramural activities regardless of physical ability. Students have the opportunity to be involved in the planning, organizing, and administering of intramural programs. Such involvement should be age-appropriate and under supervision and guidance of a qualified adult (National Association for Sport and Physical Education, 2001).

The goals of an intramural program include the following:

- provide an opportunity to participate in sport and physical activities without regard for high performance skill or ability;
- provide activities in a safe and professionally supervised environment;
- nurture healthy competition, enjoyment, fair play, and teamwork;

- establish a student-centered program that considers the needs and interests of all students;
- enhance social interaction and reduce student conflict;
- provide opportunity for co-ed physical activity participation;
- provide opportunities for students to experience a variety of physical activities that will contribute to an active lifestyle and enhance their leisure time. (National Association for Sport and Physical Education, 2001)

Intramurals should be considered an enhancement of the school's physical education curriculum. Schools should provide for physical activity opportunities for students outside the physical education program. Intramural programming does not replace a physical education curriculum, but provides an outlet for learning achieved in physical education classes. Intramurals should be directed by professional educators, have access to adequate facilities and equipment, ensure safety of participants, and be adequately funded. A student leadership program should provide input into selection of activities and policy development and enforcement. Grouping of students during activities should be based on age-appropriate activities as well as considerations of skill and maturity level (National Association for Sport and Physical Education, 2001).

Intramural activities should include competitions in various sports, clubs, self-directed activities, open gym, special events, and instructional and practice opportunities. The guidelines should provide opportunities for inclusion of males, females, and co-educational participation through organization that facilitates full participation for all students in all activities. The activities should meet the needs of all skill levels and physical abilities, including students with disabilities.

Modification of activities should be appropriate to the age, physical development, and skill levels of individual participants. Leagues may need to be established based upon low, moderate, and high skill levels. Specific rules and regulations should be established that assure equal opportunity, fair play, and safe participation. Activities should reflect student interest and provide challenge, enjoyment and moderate to vigorous activity for all participants (National Association for Sport and Physical Education, 2001).

Health and safety guidelines should be followed for intramural activities. All activities should be structured to ensure that safety requirements are met including consideration of each participant's readiness for the activity based upon age, skill, and physical condition. All participants should have a medical clearance to participate, and should be reaffirmed on a periodic basis. Medical problems that may affect participation should be communicated to the program leader. Locker rooms should be supervised with clear rules for student behavior. Parents must provide informed consent for student participation. Written policies should outline procedures for accident prevention, management of injury situations, reporting, and notification of parents/guardians in the event of an emergency. Immediate first aid must be available from trained providers any time the program is in progress. First aid equipment and communication mechanisms must be available on-site and ready should an emergency situation develop. It is imperative that students participating in intramural activities be supervised at all times (National Association for Sport and Physical Education, 2001).

Other School Activities and Organizations

Cheerleading and drill team are two organizations in many middle and high schools. The organizations allow students to participate and display school spirit. Students participating in the organizations must adhere to guidelines established by the school or affiliated association.

The American Association of Cheerleading Coaches and Administrators (AACCA)is a nonprofit educational association for the over 70,000 cheerleading coaches across the United States. The association's membership includes junior high school coaches, and high school coaches and advisors. AACCA has the following guidelines:

1. Cheerleading squads should be placed under the direction of a qualified and knowledgeable advisor or coach.
2. All practice sessions should be supervised by the coach and held in a location suitable for the activities of cheerleaders.
3. Advisors/coaches should recognize a squad's particular ability level and should limit the squad's activities accordingly.
4. All cheerleaders should receive proper training before attempting any form of cheerleading gymnastics.
5. Professional training in proper spotting techniques should be mandatory for all squads.
6. All cheerleading squads should adopt a comprehensive conditioning and strength building program.
7. All jewelry is prohibited during participation. **Religious medals and medical medals are not considered to be jewelry. A religious medal without a chain must be taped and worn under the uniform. A medical alert medal must be taped and may be visible.**
8. An appropriate warm-up routine should precede all cheerleading activities.
9. Prior to the performance of any skill, the immediate environment for the activity should be taken into consideration including but not limited to proximity of non-squad personnel, performance surface, lighting, and/or precipitation. Technical skills should not be performed on concrete, asphalt, wet or uneven surfaces, or surfaces with obstructions.
10. As a general rule, all programs should qualify cheerleaders according to accepted teaching progressions. Appropriate spotting should be used until all performers demonstrate mastery of the skill.
11. Supports, braces, etc., which are hard and unyielding or have rough edges or surfaces must be appropriately covered. A participant wearing a cast (excluding a properly covered air cast) shall not be involved in stunts, pyramids, tosses, or tumbling.
12. Squad members must wear athletic shoes.
13. When discarding props (signs, etc.) that are made of solid material or have sharp edges/corners, team members must gently toss or place the props so that they are under control (AACCA, n.d.).

Cheerleading coaches and advisors also use the AACCA guidelines pertaining to partner students, pyramids, tosses, tumbling, jumps, and restrictions for elementary, junior high, and middle schools.

The list of student clubs and organizations are extensive. Administrative approval is required before implementing new organizations. Other student related activities include the following:

INTEREST ACTIVITIES

- C.H.I.C.K.E.N. (Cool, Honest, Intelligent, Clear-headed, Keen, Energetic, and Not Interested in Drugs) Club
- D.A.R.E. (Drug Abuse Resistance Education) Program
- S.A.D.D. (Students Against Destructive Decisions/Students Against Driving Drunk)
- Fellowship of Christian Athletics

HONORARY ACTIVITIES

- National Honor Society
- Beta Club

COCURRICULAR ACTIVITIES

- Future Teachers of America
- Future Farmers of America
- Spanish Club
- French Club

Legal Implications

The liability and legality of interscholastic associations at local, state, and regional levels has become a focal point of extensive litigation. Liability of schools, administrators, and advisors is a major concern in school districts. Administrators can avoid possible court cases if they are informed about legal issues including court opinions, governing board policies, agency regulations, and coaches' rules (Strope, 1984). Administrators are not required to be law scholars; however ignorance of the law is not an excuse.

Among the most important legal issues about which administrators need to know in relationship to student activities is negligence. Negligence is part of a broad context of laws called torts, which are wrongful acts, not including a breach of contract or trust, which results in injury to another's person, property, reputation, or the like, and for which the injured party is entitled to compensation. Torts can be intentional (e.g., forcing a student to do something that is likely to cause injury), but these are rare in litigation against an administrator. The most common tort action sought against an administrator is an allegation of *unintentional negligence*. Negligence has a number of definitions. The most common definition is the failure to exercise that degree of care which, under the circumstances, the law requires for the protection of other persons (Permuth & Permuth, 2000).

It is essential for administrators to recognize that a successful negligence suit can arise out of an act of omission (not doing something you should do) or commission (doing something you are not supposed to do). To take legal action successfully against an administrator, a person must establish evidence in four separate areas: recognizable legal duty, breach of a recognizable duty, proximate cause, and injury. Lack of evidence in any one of these areas will result in a claim's dismissal. For administrators the prevention of a successful negligence suit lies in their understanding of these elements and how they apply to the administrators' direct responsibilities regarding student activities (Strope, 1984). *Frances Barrett v. Unified School District* (2001), Robert Alexander Barrett, a 12th-grade high school student at Southeast High School in Wichita, collapsed on the practice field after participating in the first mandatory football practice of the 1998 season. He died in the hospital the next day. His death is alleged to have resulted from negligent supervision. The court determined that the recreational use exception found in K.S.A. 75-6104(o) applies in this case, which eliminates any liability of the defendants for ordinary negligence.

Another legal concern involving legal implications in the realm of education is random drug testing. According to Kallio (2007), based on data from 2007, few schools (close to 1,000) had enacted random drug testing programs. Several states have passed legislation mandating random drug testing for high school athletes. *Vernonia School District 47J v. Acton* (1995), the Court upheld suspicionless drug testing of students participating in athletic programs. The Court declared that the Fourth Amendment imposes no irreducible requirement of individualized suspicion, reasoning that the school district's custodial responsibility for the welfare of children entitles school personnel to more control than would be allowed in other settings. The Court also recognized the important government interest of deterring drug use among school children, especially among athletes,where drug use poses a significant risk of harm to others. The Court noted that the students' privacy interests are negligible given the element of communal undress inherent in athletic participation.

The Supreme Court of Colorado struck down a program calling for suspicionless drug testing of students participating in extracurricular activities, including band members who took instrumental music classes for credit. The court concluded that band participation was not a discretionary extracurricular activity and furthermore found no evidence of drug use among band members. The court reasoned that the suspicionless drug-testing program for all sixth through twelfth grade students participating in extracurricular activities was not justified by safety concerns and other considerations that the Supreme Court recognized when it upheld the drug-testing program (*Trinidad v. Lopez,* 1998).

The Supreme Court ruled in *Board of Education of the Independent School District of Pottawatomie County v. Earls* (2002). In this case, the school district, in an effort to prevent and deter drug use, instituted a policy that required all students who engaged in competitive extracurricular activities (unlike Vernonia who only tested athletes) to consent to random drug testing. The Supreme Court acknowledged that drug use has reached epidemic proportions in the United States and, therefore, has determined that school districts are not required to prove that their campuses have substantial drug problems before implementing drug policies. The Court has also decided that collecting urine samples under conditions similar to those experienced by persons in public restrooms is not overly intrusive. In essence, the Court maintains that the government's concern regarding the nation's abuse of drugs takes precedence over students' right to privacy, that random drug testing of students involved in competitive extracurricular activities is a justifiable means to attempt to deter student drug use, and that random drug testing is reasonable in scope. With this background, the Supreme Court may in the near future be asked to decide whether it is constitutional for schools to test all members of the student body for drugs. It's likely that the Court's decision will further discuss whether the searches can be random or whether the school district must make its decision based on individualized suspicion.

Administrative Responsibilities

If principals are not supportive of student activities, the teachers will not display support either. Teachers should see the principal in the trenches of student activities. Their active role will help reinforce the importance of the student programs. Principals can demonstrate support for the activities program by (1) being visible to students and teachers, and (2) continuing to create new clubs and activities. It is important that teachers see the principal in the trenches of student activities. Students and parents are delighted when they see their principal at sporting events, theater productions, band concerts, and other activities. Faculty members who volunteer their time feel supported when they see their principal in attendance at student activities (Hirsch, 2000).

Another area of administrative responsibility in student activities is safety and security. Administrators should give due diligence to planning for security at extracurricular activities throughout the school year by considering and acting on the following recommendations:

- Make sure a clear and structured chain of command for supervision should be in place.
- Ensure that supervisory staff members have adequate training and understand the expectations for making decisions.
- Call a pre-event meeting of assigned staff members prior to the start of an activity making decisions.
- Identify, verify, and post in clear view at all entrances and exits the evacuation routes and in-place sheltering locations.
- Announce certain safety information before the event begins, especially at big events or when the noise level may be a serious factor in communicating with the crowd.
- Require supervisory staff members, ushers, or others who are designated to assist or oversee an event to wear attire that is easily recognizable.
- Equip staff members with essential equipment and supplies, such as flashlights and cell phones.
- Designate locations for first-aid supplies and crisis kits to be placed in the area where an event is being held.
- Alert local law enforcement agencies when large crowds are anticipated at extracurricular activities and events.
- Provide scenario-based training to members of the crisis management team and others who may be called upon to supervise extracurricular activities. (Brunner & Lewis, 2005)

Conclusion

There are numerous benefits of student activities in schools. These activities allow students to explore their physical, creative, social, political, and career interests with their peers. Students also have the opportunity to collaborate with classmates who share their interest. Research has shown that students involved in extracurricular activities receive better grades because activities teach them character-building lessons and lifelong skills, saving some at-risk students who would possibly drop out of school, and helping other students develop social skills. Administrators can demonstrate support of student activities by being visible and creating new clubs and activities.

Applying Your Knowledge

You are the principal of a high school with limited student organizations. A group of students meet with you and discuss their interest in organizing a Gay-Straight Alliance Club. The students mention the Fellowship of Christian Athletes, which has permission to meet on campus. They express their rights to be offered an equal opportunity to form a club. The students express their awareness of the Equal Access Act of 1984. If permission is not granted, this would be in violation of the Equal Access Act, a law mandating that federally funded schools provide access to extracurricular activities.

QUESTIONS

1. What steps will you take to address the issue of forming the Gay-Straight Alliance?
2. What factors will you consider before making a final decision?
3. If the group is denied to form the Gay-Straight Alliance, will the Fellowship of Christian Athletes be allowed to continue meeting on campus?

QUESTIONS FOR THOUGHT

1. What is the significance of student activities in schools?
2. Compare and contrast the goals of the UIL and the intramural program.
3. What is a tort action? Explain and provide an example as it relates to student activities.
4. Can schools conduct suspicionless drug testing for students participating in extracurricular activities? Why or why not?
5. What are the recommendations for administrators in planning for security at extracurricular activities throughout the school year?

References

About the UIL. (n.d.). Retrieved December 20, 2010 from http://www.uiltexas.org/about

Academic eligibility basics–UIL. (n.d). Retrieved December 20, 2010 from http://www.uiltexas.org/academics/resources/eligibility

American Association of Cheerleading Coaches and Administrators (AACCA) School Cheerleading Rules for 2010-2011. (n.d.). Retrieved March 15, 2011 from http://www.aacca.org/content.aspx?item=Safety/20111_School_Cheer_Rules.xml

Athletics–UIL. (n.d). Retrieved December 20, 2010 from http://www.uiltexas.org/athletics

Board of Education of Independent School District No. 92 of Pottawatomie County v. Earls, 536 U.S. 822 (2002).

Brunner, J., & Lewis, D. (September 2005). A safety game plan for extracurricular events. *Principal Leadership*, 73–74.

Frances Barrett 86022 v. Unified School District No. 259 (2001).

Frederick, R. W. (1959). *The third curriculum.* New York: Appelton-Century Crofts-Inc.

Frederick, R. W. (1965). *Student activities in American education.* New York: The Center for Applied Research in Education, Inc.

Hirsch, M. (October 2000). Student activities snapshot. *Principal Leadership*, 34–37.

Hollrah, R.(n.d.). Extracurricular activities. Retrieved December 20, 2010 from http://www.public.iastate.edu/~rhetoric/105H17/rhollrah/cof.html

Kallio, B. (Fall 2007). Random drug searches in schools. *National Association of Secondary Principals, 8*(1), 1–6.

Klesse, E. J. (2004). *Student activities in today's schools: Essential learning for all youth.* Lanham, MD: Scarecrow Education.

Music–UIL. (n.d.). Retrieved December 20, 2010 from http://www.uiltexas.org/music

National Association for Sport and Physical Education. (2001). Guidelines for after school physical activity and intramural sport programs. Retrieved January 3, 2011 from: www.aahperd.org/naspe/standards/upload/Guidelines-for-AfterSchool-PA-Intramural-Sport-Programs-2001.pdf

Olszewski-Kubilius, P., & Less, S-Y. (2004). The role of participation in in-school and outside-of-school activities in the talent development of gifted students. *Journal of Secondary Gifted Education, XV*(3), 107–123.

Permuth, S., & Permuth, R. S. (October 2000). Legal dimensions of school activities. *Principal Leadership*, 38–41.

Stearns, E., & Glennie, E. J. (2010). Opportunities to participate: Extracurricular activities' distribution across and academic correlates in high schools. *Social Science Research, 39*, 296–309.

Strope, J. L. (1984). *School activities and the law.* VA: National Association of Secondary School Principals.

Trinidad School District No. 1 v. Lopez, 963 P.2d 1095 (Colo. 1998).

University Interscholastic League. (n.d.). Constitution, Subchapter M. Eligibility, Section 400: Student's Eligibility for all UIL Contests. http://www.uiltexas.org/files/constitution/uil-ccr-subchapter-m.pdf

Vernonia School District 47J v. Acton, 515 U. S. 646 (1995).

Response to Intervention: A School Improvement Model

15

Jesus "Chuey" Abrego
Michelle H. Abrego

> In differentiated classrooms, teachers begin where students
> are, not the front of a curriculum guide . . . teachers provide
> specific ways for each individual to learn as deeply as possible
> and as quickly as possible, without assuming one student's
> road map for learning is identical to anyone else's.
>
> —*Tomlinson, 1999, p. 2*

Objectives

1. Discuss the history and legislation related to response to intervention (RTI)
2. Identify the different tiers, essential elements, and principles and models of response to intervention
3. Discuss the implementation of response to intervention
4. Explain the links between RTI and Professional Learning Communities
5. Identify the role of the campus administrator in leading and managing RTI at the school building level

Introduction

A Nation at Risk was published in 1983. Since that time, local and state education agencies, and the federal government, have been focused on how to improve schools and increase student achievement. Over the last three decades, schools have been focused on high stakes testing and a number of programs and initiatives for at-risk youth have been implemented; however, schools and their initiatives have failed to address the academic and behavioral needs of students. On the other hand, during this same time period, educators have learned more about assessment, evaluation, and the use of scientifically based instructional practices (Wedl, 2005).

With that in mind, the Individuals with Disabilities Education Act was reauthorized in 2004 and renamed the Individuals with Disabilities Education Improvement Act (IDEIA). The new law allowed districts to adopt alternative models such as the Response to Intervention (RTI) model.

Response to Intervention has been referred to as a process with the aim of encouraging schools to help students who are struggling academically and behaviorally. In essence, RTI encourages school personnel to determine if the problems children are having may be due to inadequacies in instruction or in the curriculum rather than as the result of a disability (National Dissemination Center for Children with Disabilities, 2011). Response To Intervention (RTI) is a school improvement model that is designed to prevent school failure for all students.

This chapter will focus on response to intervention (RTI), provide a brief historical and legislative context of RTI, and discuss the tiers, essential elements, and models of RTI. Additionally, the link between RTI and Professional Learning Communities (PLCs) will be explored, and finally, an explanation of the campus administrator's role in implementing, monitoring and sustaining response to intervention is offered.

Historical and Legislative Perspective

On December 3, 2004, President George W. Bush signed the Individuals with Disabilities Education Improvement Act (IDEIA, 2004) into law. The reauthorization "allowed changes to the mandates of the IDEA, modified requirements and introduced an alternative means of identifying a disability, known as responsiveness to intervention, or RTI" (Buffum, Mattos, & Weber, 2009, p. 2). In clarifying their interpretation of RTI, Fuchs and Fuchs (2006, p. 1) described the revised law in the following manner:

> Whereas practitioners were previously encouraged to use IQ-achievement discrepancy to identify children with learning disabilities (LD), they now may use "Response to Intervention," or RTI, a new, alternative method. It is also a means of providing early intervention to all children at risk for school failure.

Furthermore, Burns and Gibbons (2008, pp. 1–2) comment on the effect of the changes due to the law and also mention other issues that have contributed to the push for implementing RTI:

> . . . this simple sentence [excerpt from IDEA] is the basis for a great deal of change but other issues such as the role of the federal government in funding special education, dissatisfaction with special education, increased knowledge of learning and academic interventions, and the accountability movement in this country have contributed to RTI's development and popularity.

Together, IDEIA and The No Child Left Behind Act of 2001 (NCLB) have created an environment in which RTI has been identified as a plausible approach to special education eligibility and overall school improvement; furthermore, IDEIA includes specific language on the use of RTI procedures and is described as "a process that determines if the child responds to scientific research-based intervention as a part of the evaluation procedures [Public Law (P. L.) 108-446 § 614 [b][6][A]; § 614 [b][2 & 3])" (Cummings, Atkins, Allison, & Cole, 2008, p. 24). Thus, IDEIA and NCLB clearly lay the groundwork for the implementation of RTI at the campus and district levels for all students.

The Different Tiers of Response to Intervention

WHAT IS RTI?

RTI is a model of instruction and is often perceived as a multitiered model or system that focuses on early intervention to prevent school failure. According to Burn and Gibbons (2008), RTI should be perceived as a general education initiative that brings the campus together for students. The following definition, stated by Austin Buffum, Mike Mattos, and Chris Weber in their 2009 book, *Pyramid Response to Intervention: RTI, Professional Learning Communities, and How to Respond When Kids Don't Learn*, applies to how RTI **should** be viewed:

> In the new model, the effect on student learning and the response of students in both general and special education to interventions are as important as following procedures. RTI provides a unified system of studying student difficulties and providing early intervention prior to referral for formal evaluation for special education or allowing such evaluation only as a last resort. The ultimate decision to qualify a child for special education should be made by a team of stakeholders only after high-quality interventions have been attempted and frequently monitored. (pp. 18–19)

THE TIERS OF RTI

As mentioned earlier, RTI is often characterized by as either a three- or a four-tier model. The multitier models are used to help structure the type of intervention as well as the intensity of that intervention. (See Figure 15-1.) Progress monitoring, usually with short assessments, is used to determine whether a student is responding to the interventions, or lessons (Duffy, 2008). The tiered model design can be used as a guide or blueprint to provide early intervention to prevent school failure.

The **first** or "universal" tier is intended to represent instruction and services available to all students. Students not successful within the first tier are referred to the next one. The **second** tier uses targeted, short-term instruction for [about 15%] students who need more help to master a subject and or specific content. The **third** tier represents the most intensive level of instruction [for about 5%]. A student who does not respond to the intensive intervention at this third level may need more intensive help via special education services.

The assessments used in the third tier can be used in combination with "discrepancy model" methods that use severe discrepancies between a student's IQ [intellectual ability] and academic achievement level to identify learning disabilities (Duran, Hughes, & Bradley, 2011; Duffy, 2008; Hall, 2008; Fuchs & Fuchs, 2005; RTI Action Network, 2011). Application of the model is guided by a core set of elements or characteristics.

According to Sailor (2009, p. 21), all forms of RTI have certain common features and characteristics:

> . . . that includes the three levels of educational support, or interventions: primary (universal), secondary (targeted group), and tertiary (individual). The process begins with early screening for academic and behavioral risk factors that may impede learning due

Figure 15-1   **Multitier triangle of interventions. National Association of State Directors of Special Education (NASDSE) and the Council of Administrators of Special Education (CASE) at the Council for Exceptional Children. (2006, May). Response to intervention: NASDSE and CASE white paper on rti. Retrieved June 21, 2012, from http://www.nasdse.org/Portals/0/Documents/Download%20Publications/RtIAnAdministratorsPerspective1-06.pdf**

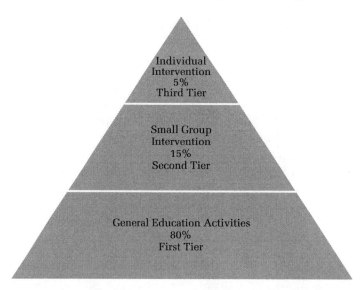

Individual
Intervention
5%
Third Tier

Small Group
Intervention
15%
Second Tier

General Education Activities
80%
First Tier

to the presence of disability or other factors. Students determined to be at risk undergo monitoring to determine if increased levels of support are merited, if the student is responding to interventions, and if more intensive levels of support can be withdrawn. Data from both screening and progress monitoring assessments must emerge from the use of measurement tools with strong psychometric properties.

Sailor's synopsis helps to clearly delineate the anatomy of a typical RTI model and its essential elements. In turn, these common elements help to define the end product for a campus implementing RTI.

Common Essential Elements and Principles of RTI

Numerous researchers and national organizations have identified that essential elements can be found in the RTI process. These essential elements, which range from measuring outcomes and encourage progress monitoring to the use of research-based interventions, help to create an "implementation" road map for school leaders. What follows is a brief overview of different perspectives on the essential elements as described by various experts and researchers in the field.

According to Ehren, Ehren and Proly (2009, p. 7), RTI has both essential and common elements. The common elements are:

- student outcome measures,
- high-quality (scientifically based) instruction/intervention,
- progress monitoring/formative assessment,
- data-based decision making,

- educational decision making based on responsiveness to instruction/intervention,
- instruction/intervention intensity changes based on performance,
- other common elements such as universal screening to identify struggling learners, and
- use of tiers as an infrastructure to organize levels of intensity.

Mellard and Johnson (2008, pp. 5–6) elaborate on the common and essential elements and provide additional details explaining that the "core requirements of a strong RTI model" include:

- high-quality, research-based classroom instruction. All students receive high-quality instruction in the general education setting. General education instruction is research based; general education teachers assume an active role in students' assessment in the classroom curriculum.
- universal screening. School staff including the classroom teachers conducts universal screening of academics and behavior. Specific criteria for judging the achievement of all students are applied in determining which students need closer monitoring or intervention.
- progress monitoring at all tiers. Progress monitoring is essential. In Tier 1, progress monitoring allows teachers to readily identify those learners who are not meeting expected standards. In Tiers 2 and 3, progress monitoring enables teachers to determine the interventions' effectiveness and to make changes as needed.
- research-based interventions at Tier 2 and Tier 3. When a student's screening or progress monitoring results indicate a deficit, an appropriate instructional intervention is implemented. School staff implements specific, research-based interventions to address the student's difficulties.
- fidelity measures. The fidelity with which instruction and interventions are implemented is systematically assessed and linked to continuing professional development to increase the effectiveness of the RTI process.

Because progress monitoring plays a critical role in RTI it is important to elaborate on the concept. According to Stecker, Lembke, and Foegen (2008, p. 48),

> progress monitoring is the application of curriculum-based measurement [CBM] as a research-validated practice [assessment method] for monitoring student academic achievement and eventually raising learning outcomes. Thus, teachers and school leaders use progress monitoring data to focus on students who are not performing adequately and to track their academic growth during the various stages of research-based instructional interventions.

Weishaar and Weishaar (2012) further support the critical role of the elements when they claim that RTI is based on the premise that all students can learn. They reference the National Association of State Directors of Special Education (NASDSE) as having clearly outlined the "core principles of RTI":

1. All children can be taught and can learn.
2. Intervention must occur early.
3. Services are best delivered in several different "tiers."
4. For children to move from one tier to another, employing a problem-solving method is useful.
5. To the greatest extent possible, teachers should use evidence- or research-based instruction and interventions.
6. Student progress should be monitored and used to adjust instruction.
7. Data from student progress (and other sources) should be used to make decisions.

8. Assessments are typically used for three different purposes:
    a. screening for all students to identify those who are not progressing as expected,
    b. conducting diagnostic or more in-depth assessment to determine what students can and cannot do in academic and behavior areas, and
    c. monitoring progress of students to determine if they are learning at expected rates. (p. 3)

These elements and principles provide a blueprint of essential steps that a campus should follow when implementing and sustaining RTI. Everyone referenced here regarding these elements and principles stressed the importance of instructional interventions for both behavior and academics at each of the three levels of RTI (Sailor, 2009).

MODELS OF RESPONSE TO INTERVENTION

As the definitions and essential elements of RTI have evolved over the past years, so too have the models of RTI. Currently, there are three RTI models: (1) standard protocol RTI, (2) problem-solving RTI, and (3) schoolwide RTI. What follows is an explanation on each model.

The first, **standard protocol RTI,** involves an approach that, according to Sailor (2009), defines "intervention strategies connected to psychological test data as a basis for diagnosing LD and determining eligibility for services" (p. 20). Another perspective on the standard protocol by Mellard and Johnson (2008) describes the approach as "interventions that are not accommodations to existing curriculum but rather are instructional programs aimed at remediating a student's specific skill deficit (e.g., phonological processing, math computations, and reading comprehension)" (p. 85). Furthermore, Ehren, Ehren, and Proly (2009) note that standard protocol RTI is "often used because of its more specific design"; they reaffirm what is already known about the model by further sharing that in "this approach, there are more specific and prescriptive interventions within a treatment category" (p. 27).

The second model is called **problem-solving RTI**. Ehren, Ehren, and Proly (2009) share that "the problem-solving approach is essentially a collaborative effort" (p. 27). According to Sailor (2009) this model, "is not particularly concerned with eligibility determination for special education. Rather, it is directed more to matching school resources with identified need on the basis of ongoing assessments" (p. 21). Mellard and Johnson (2008) further define and describe this model as a form of RTI in which, "the student's performance data are collected, analyzed, and used to develop hypotheses about the cause of the student's problem and the appropriate evidence-based strategies to remedy them" (p. 84).

The last model that evolved thus far is the **schoolwide RTI**. This model is recognized as a combination of the standard protocol and problem-solving RTI models (Sailor, 2009). Burns and Gibbons (2008) assert that in order for the RTI process to work effectively, it requires an approach that is,

> integrated into the overall system of communication and decision making in the school (Kameenui & Simmons, 1998) . . . schools that have successfully implemented RTI systems typically engage in three broad practices. First, they collect data regularly on all students to screen for difficulty. Data are collected more regularly for students who are at risk to determine if they are responding to well-designed instructional programs. Second, schools use empirically validated interventions and instructional practices within a multitiered service delivery model. Finally schools are organized to ensure the most effective instruction possible for each student. Without a school-level system of implementation, it is nearly impossible for assessment-and-instruction best practices to be put into place effectively. The school as the "host environment" must be organized to ensure

that research-based practices can thrive and be sustained (Coyne, Kameenui, & Simmons, 2001). (p. 51).

In summary, though different in some ways, the models of RTI also have certain common features. Numerous researchers (Fuchs & Fuchs, 1998; Gresham, 2002; Kame'enui, 2007; National Research Center on Learning Disabilities, 2007) agree that the "proposed models of RTI involve two critical components: implementation of evidence based instruction/intervention and ongoing assessment to monitor student progress or response" (Richards, Pavri, Golez, Canges, & Murphy, 2007, p. 56).

RESEARCH ON THE EFFECTIVENESS OF RTI

In an invited commentary in the *School Psychology Review*, Kovaleski (2007) argues, "there is a sufficient evidence base regarding many of the components of a comprehensive, multitier system to warrant adoption of the procedures at a local level" (p. 644). Additionally, a recent report by the Regional Educational Laboratory [REL Southeast] by Sawyer, Holland, and Detgen (2008) describes the efforts of several state and local education agencies in implementing RTI. The laboratory's research was encouraged, in part, by promising studies conducted pertaining to the implementation, effectiveness, and benefits of response to intervention (Compton, Fuchs, Fuchs, & Bryant, 2006; McMaster, Fuchs, Fuchs, & Compton, 2005; Speece & Case, 2001).

Mellard and Johnson (2008) shares that one of the major research findings "is that the components and procedures used within the RTI framework have allowed for better understanding of instructional quality and informed decision-making" (p. 7). They also claim that the RTI framework also provided accurate information in terms of peer group ranking and the campus curriculum. Finally Mellard and Johnson notes that research on the effectiveness of RTI demonstrates that students indicating at-risk behavior and learning difficulties can be identified and receive appropriate intervention.

Additionally, a study conducted by Hoover, Baca, Wexler-Love, and Saenz (2008) presents a national perspective on RTI. The group conducted a study investigating the level of emphasis of current and projected statewide efforts for implementing RTI from the point of view of special education state program department directors in all 50 states. They had an 86% response rate; and every state indicated some emphasis on RTI. Furthermore, training efforts in 90% of the states studied were focused on emphasizing RTI, specifically the progress monitoring and data-driven decision-making components. Survey responses indicated that at least one-third of the states that responded planned to use RTI.

IMPLEMENTATION OF RTI

Implementation means making things happen (Pankake, 1998). How it is done plays a critical role in the success of any initiative or project. The following are some suggestions for successful implementation of RTI for campus leaders.

An important first step for school leaders requires that they help their staff learn more about RTI by helping them understand the premise for RTI. Once that is accomplished, it is important to have the campus select an appropriate RTI model that meets the needs of students and the culture/climate of the school. Note that the principal should be directly involved in creating 'buy-in' throughout the whole process. Consequently, the principal is engaged in shared and supportive leadership activities that keep teachers informed and involved in the decision making related to the implementation process.

Another key area is providing professional development training for all staff directly involved in delivering RTI interventions and assessments. It is critical that staff know how to connect the interventions to research-based curriculum. In addition, since RTI is systemic, it is necessary to develop appropriate assessment and data collection proce-dures/systems. Key staff should be responsible for collecting and analyzing all student assessment data. Finally, the campus leader and teams should establish a realistic mul-tiyear timeline for implementing and assessing RTI as a program initiative across time and the campus (Kimmel, 2009).

Implementation is about understanding change and changing behavior. Hall and Hord (2006) offered certain change principles that are applicable to the implementa-tion of RTI; one of those is that, "an organization does not change until the individuals within it change and interventions are the actions and events that are key to the success of the change process" (p. 4). These aspects of the change process should be clearly understood by campus principals when attempting to implement initiatives. Success with RTI at the campus level requires a paradigm shift, in other words, a different way of thinking about what and how staff should be involved when it comes to planning, implementing and delivering instructional and programmatic changes.

THE BENEFITS OF IMPLEMENTATION OF RTI

Researchers such as Klingner and colleagues (2005) believe that RTI has the potential to reduce the disproportionate representation of culturally and linguistically diverse students in special education. Ultimately the aim of Response to Intervention is to raise the academic achievement of all students—special and general. In addition, the RTI framework is designed to ensure that students are properly identified which in turn may result in a reduction in special education referrals.

Since the approach to RTI is systemic, it has the potential to significantly change how academic needs and services are identified and delivered to students across any campus. Another important distinction involves the ongoing monitoring of the academic success/process instead of waiting for children to fail at the end of year; thus, with RTI the overall climate and culture at the campus targets assistance to those students who need academic and behavior support. The nature of RTI, "demands a cultural shift within the schools to ensure that all staff members demonstrate a collective responsibil-ity to help all students learn" (Buffman, Mattos, & Weber, 2009, p. 5). Thus an obvious benefit of RTI is its promotion of collaboration and shared responsibility among all cam-pus educators, administrators, and the community members served.

RTI AND PROFESSIONAL LEARNING COMMUNITIES

As shared earlier, numerous researchers document the integral role leadership plays in the successful implementation of RTI. In addition, during this time of high-stakes test-ing and accountability, how a leader manages and leads change as well as the tools and structures a leader uses to sustain efforts over time is a major determinant to whether a school level framework such as RTI succeeds or falls by the wayside. But more impor-tantly, it is the shared leadership between the team of stakeholders—the general and special education teachers, administrators, diagnosticians, paraprofessionals, reading specialists, speech-language pathologists, school psychologists, guidance counselor, social workers and parents—that seems to play a critical role in whether RTI is success-fully implemented and sustained over time. That shared leadership can be found within the structural concept of a professional learning community.

Buffman, Mattos, and Weber (2009), "make the case that the most promising and research-supported way to implement response to intervention is to operate as a profes-sional learning community" (p. 10). They stress that "RTI should be embedded within the PLC structure" (p. 23). While there are several models of PLCs, most contain similar concepts though the terminology differs. According to Hord (1996, 1997); Hipp and Huffman (2010); and Abrego and Pankake (2011), the structure of the professional learning community (PLC) consists of five dimensions; when these are appropriately implemented they influence student achievement and build the capacity of the organization. The five dimensions are:

1. shared and supportive leadership,
2. shared values and goals,
3. collective learning and application of that learning,
4. supportive conditions, meaning relationships and structures, and
5. shared personal practice.

Numerous approaches to sustaining school reform efforts across districts have failed to work. However, one promising strategy according to Schmoker (2005a) is to build professional learning communities. DuFour and Eaker (1998) noted the initiation and implementation of PLCs as, "The most promising strategy for sustained, substantive school improvement is developing the ability of school personnel to function as professional learning communities" (p. xi). The issue of sustainability is found in the following from Pankake, Huffman, and Moller (2004):

. . . professional learning communities (PLCs) are not only a school-based reform but, their establishment creates a structure helpful for sustaining other initiatives intended to foster school improvement. Consequently, professional learning communities are increasingly identified as critical to the success of school reform efforts. (Louis, Marks, & Kruse, 1996; Newmann & Wehlage, 1995; Bryk, et al., 1994; McLaughlin, 1993, p. 2).

In terms of providing a supportive structure, the dimensions of a professional learning community (PLC) seem to lay the groundwork for supporting the implementation and sustainability of any of the RTI models. Furthermore, the PLC structure supports collaboration and a systemic approach to interventions. According to Buffman, Mattos, and Weber (2009, p. 8):

A PLC relies upon frequent, timely, common formative assessment data to determine which students need additional time and support, not last year's summative assessment data. The RTI emphasis on progress monitoring will not be effective, however, if educators have not first collaborated to identify common instructional goals.

According to Cummings, Atkins, Allison, and Cole (2008, p. 30), "the RTI process is about more than special education eligibility; it is ultimately a focus on school improvement to build effective systems of service delivery."

THE PRINCIPAL'S ROLE

Any initiative or effort to improve schools requires the direct involvement of the campus administrator. However, a school leader will find it challenging to implement best practices and lead change without supportive structures and conditions in place; in other words, the implementation of new structures and leading organizational change requires the creative support of a team of educators including, but not limited to the campus principal. Given this the question becomes how does a leader go about creating those new structures and conditions that empower teachers and other members of the school community to implement and support RTI?

Leithwood and Riehl (2003) believe that leaders serve specific functions that help enhance the effectiveness of the organization. Thus an effective leader provides two main functions: providing direction and exercising influence. Leithwood and Riehl go on to state that leaders at all levels mobilize and work with others to achieve shared goals. This definition has several important implications:

- Leaders work with others to create a shared sense of purpose and direction.
- Leaders primarily work through and with other people. They also help to establish the conditions that enable others to be effective.
- Leadership is a function more than a role. Although leadership is often invested in—or expected of—persons in positions of formal authority, leadership encompasses a set of functions that may be performed by many different persons in different roles throughout a school. (p. 2)

The implication, of course, is that the key to successful implementation and sustainability of RTI is through shared leadership and decision making. According to Kowalski (2010), "principals functioning as leaders make decisions about *what* needs to be done to improve schools" (p. 23). But this expectation doesn't diminish the fact that collaboration between the principal and teachers is a main ingredient in the RTI process (IRA Commission on RTI).

So what specific role should a principal play in promoting and sustaining RTI? The process should begin by having the principal ask direct questions about instruction at the campus level (NEA, 2010; NASDSE, 2008). These questions should center on such issues as:

- whether or not effective instruction is taking place in every classroom;
- is differentiating instruction based on students' talents and needs and not deficit thinking;
- is the school working from the perspective that one size fits all; and
- is the campus providing tiered or increasingly intense interventions for students who, based on different forms of data from across the campus, show they need more strategic and intensive academic and behavioral instruction?

One valid solution is to use the following recommendations from the International Reading Association Commission on RTI (IRA, 2009). The principal should carefully consider implementing the following aspects:

- create school-level decision-making teams (intervention teams, problem solving teams, RTI teams)
- determine who will provide leadership (i.e., IRA recommends that reading specialists/literacy coaches provide leadership in every aspect of the RTI process—planning, assessments, provisions of more intensified instruction and support, and making decisions about next steps);
- establish congruence between core instruction and interventions (collaboration should increase this congruence) which requires a shared vision and common goals;
- involve parents;
- create scheduling, which requires reworking a student's time to receive interventions when the rest of the class isn't learning a new lessons;
- observe classroom to verify that quality instruction is occurring as expected;
- establish systemic and comprehensive programs:
  - Administrators must ensure adequate resources and provide support for appropriate scheduling along with ample time for all professionals to collaborate.
  - Administrators must provide ongoing and job embedded professional development. (p. 1)

By this point, it should be obvious that the implementation of an RTI framework requires a great deal of coordination and sustained effort across the campus. The principal must help the school community recognize that RTI is a systemic process. According to

Elliot (2009), the most effective way of implementing RTI is through a systemic process. A variety of decisions by the principal and academic teams need to be made about both instruction and progress monitoring [assessment] practices before schools implement an RTI framework. For example, schools need to decide on what scientifically based comprehensive core curriculum and which instructional delivery practices should be used in a general education setting. Fidelity [reliability] of instructional practices along with the provision for coaching or teacher support are also important considerations as the implementation of RTI moves forward.

Keeping in mind that teachers deal daily with a variety of issues and classroom responsibilities, the main challenge with RTI is ensuring that staff, especially general education teachers, understand how it works and how to manage the tiered interventions collaboratively. Thus, a well-organized and collaborative faculty, clearly structured campus schedule, targeted resources, and job-embedded professional development are needed to successfully accommodate RTI.

Applying Your Knowledge

You are the principal of a struggling middle school that has a diverse student population. The campus has performed poorly over the past several years. You and your staff have attempted several different initiatives to help increase student performance, but the campus continues to struggle to meet academic goals. The district has made a decision to use Response to Intervention (RTI) to help its campuses increase student achievement.

QUESTIONS

1. What first steps would you take to encourage your staff to use RTI?
2. What types of data would you gather and use for more effective and efficient intervention planning?
3. How would you structure communication efforts within your campus to better meet the RTI needs of your faculty?
4. How would you go about monitoring progress of RTI at your campus?

QUESTIONS FOR THOUGHT

1. What is RTI and what are some advantages to implementing RTI at the campus level?
2. What are some specific steps a principal might take to introduce the concept of RTI?
3. What are the essential elements of RTI?
4. Describe the role of the principal in sustaining RTI at the campus level?
5. What role does a professional learning community play when implementing RTI?
6. What are the different dimensions of a professional learning community?

References

Abrego, C., & Pankake, A. M. (2011). The district-wide sustainability of a professional learning community during leadership changes at the superintendency level. *Administrative Issues Journal: Education, Practice, and Research, 1*(1).

Bryk, A. S., Eason, J. Q., Kerbow, D., Rollow, S. G., & Sebring, P. A. (1994). The state of Chicago school reform. *Phi Delta Kappan, 76*(1), 74–78.

Buffman, A., Mattos, M., & Weber, C. (2009). *Pyramid response to intervention: RTI, professional learning communities, and how to respond when kids don't learn.* Bloomington, IN: Solution Tree.

Burns, M. K., & Gibbons, K. A. (2008). *Implementing response-to-intervention in elementary and secondary schools: Procedures to assure scientific-based practices.* New York: Routledge.

Compton, D. L., Fuchs, D., Fuchs, L. S., & Bryant, J. D. (2006). Selecting at-risk readers in first grade for early intervention: A two-year longitudinal study of decision rules and procedures. *Journal of Educational Psychology, 2,* 394–409.

Coyne, M. D., Kameenui, E. J., & Simmons, D. C. (2001). Prevention and intervention in beginning reading: Two complex systems. *Learning Disabilities Research and Practice, 16*(2), 62–73.

Cummings, K. D., Atkins, T., Allison, R., & Cole, C. (2008). Response to intervention: Investigating the new role of special educators. *Teaching Exceptional Children, 40*(4), 24–31.

Duffy, H. (2008). *Meeting the needs of significantly struggling learners in high school: A look at approaches to tiered intervention.* National High School Center at the American Institutes for Research.

DuFour, R., & Eaker, R. (1998). *Professional learning communities at work: Best practices for enhancing student achievement.* Bloomington, IN: National Educational Service.

Duran, G. Z., Hughes, E. M., & Bradley, R. (2011). Progress monitoring: Support and practice implementation from the federal level. In E. S. Shapiro, N. Zigmond, T. Wallace, & D. Marston (Eds.), *Models for implementing response to intervention: Tools, outcomes, and implications* (pp. 1–7). New York: The Guilford Press.

East, B. (2006). *Myths about response to intervention (rti) implementation.* Retrieved October 7, 2011 from http://www.rtinetwork.org/learn/what/mythsaboutrti

Ehren, B. J., Ehren, T. C., & Proly, J. L. (2009). *Response to intervention: An action guide for school leaders.* Alexandria, VA: Educational Research Service.

Elliott, J. (2009). *What does rti mean for the classroom?* Education Week Teacher PD Sourcebook. Retrieved October 7, 2011 from http://www.edweek.org/tsb/articles/2009/03/01/02rtichat.h02.html

Fuchs, D., & Fuchs, L. S. (2005). *Responsiveness-to-intervention: A blueprint for practitioners, policymakers, and parents.* Retrieved September 12, 2011 from http://www.advocacyinstitute.org/resources/TEC_RtIblueprint.pdf

Fuchs, D., & Fuchs, L. S. (2006). Introduction to response to intervention: What, why, and how valid is it? *Reading Research Quarterly, 41*(1), 93–100. doi:10.1598/RRQ.42.2.4

Fuchs, L. S., & Fuchs, D. (1998). Treatment validity: A unifying concept for reconceptualizing the identification of learning disabilities. *Learning Disabilities Research & Practice, 13,* 204–219.

Gresham, F. (2002). Responsiveness to intervention: An alternative approach to the identification of learning disabilities. In R. Bradley, L. Danielson, & D. Hallahan (Eds.), *Identification of learning disabilities: Research to practice.* Mahwah, NJ: Lawrence Earlbaum Associates.

Hall, G. E., & Hord, S. M. (2006). *Implementing change: Patterns, principles, and potholes* (2nd ed.). Boston: Pearson Education, Inc.

Hall, S. L. (2008). *A principal's guide: Implementing response to intervention.* Thousand Oaks, CA: Corwin Press.

Hipp, K. K., & Huffman, J. B. (2010). *Demystifying professional learning communities: School leadership at its best.* Lanham, MD: Rowman & Littlefield Education.

Hoover, J., Baca, L., Wexler-Love, E., & Saenz, L. (2008). *National implementation of response to intervention (RTI): Research summary.* Retrieved September 15, 2011 from http://www.spannj.org/pti/NationalImplementationofRTI-ResearchSummary.pdf

Hord, S. M. (1996). *School professional staff as learning community.* Austin, TX: Southwest Educational Development Laboratory.

Hord, S. M. (1997). *Professional learning communities: Communities of continuous inquiry and improvement.* Austin, TX: Southwest Educational Development Laboratory. Retrieved September 15, 2011 from http://www.sedl.org/pubs/change34/welcome.html

Individuals With Disabilities Education Improvement Act of 2004, P. L. 108-466.

International Reading Association. (2009). IRA commission on rti: Working draft of guiding principles. *Reading Today, 26*(4), 1.

International Reading Association. (2010). *Response to intervention: Guiding principles for educators from the international reading association.* Retrieved October 7, 2011 from http://www.reading.org/Libraries/Resources/RTI_brochure_web.pdf

Johnson, E., Mellard, D. F., Fuchs, D., & McKnight, M. A. (2006). *Responsiveness to intervention (rti): How to do it.* Lawrence, KS: National Research Center on Learning Disabilities. Retrieved September 21, 2011 from http://www.nrcld.org/rti_manual/index.html

Kame'enui, E. (2007). A new paradigm: Responsiveness to intervention. *Teaching Exceptional Children, 39*, 6–8.

Kemeenui, E. J., & Simmons, D. C. (1998). Beyond effective practice to schools as host environments: Building and sustaining a schoolwide intervention model in beginning reading. *Oregon School Study Council, 41*(3), 3–16.

Kimmel, M. (2009). *The successes and challenges of response to intervention: A case study of the impact of rti implementation.* Paper presented at the Annual Meeting of the American Educational Research Association, San Diego, April 13–17, 2009.

Klingner, J. K., Artiles, A. J., Kozleski, E., Harry, B., Zion, S., Tate, W., Durán, G. Z., & Riley, D. (2005). Addressing the disproportionate representation of culturally and linguistically diverse students in special education through culturally responsive educational systems. *Education Policy Analysis Archives, 13*(38). Retrieved December 28, 2011 from http://epaa.asu.edu/epaa/v13n38/

Kovaleski, J. F. (2007). Response to intervention: Considerations for research and systems change. *School Psychology Review, 36*(4), 638–646.

Kowalski, T. J. (2010). *The school principal: Visionary leadership and competent management.* New York: Routledge.

Leithwood, K., & Riehl, C. (2003). *What we know about successful school leadership.* Retrieved on September 15, 2011 from http://www.cepa.gse.rutgers.edu/whatweknow.pdf

Louis, K. S., Marks, H. M., & Kruse, S. (1996). Teacher's professional community in restructuring schools. *American Educational Research Journal, 33*(4), 757–798.

McLaughlin, M. W. (1993). What matters most in teachers' workplace context? In J. W. Little & M. W. McLaughlin (Eds.), *Teachers' Work.* New York: Teachers College Press.

McMaster, K. L., Fuchs, D., Fuchs, L. S., & Compton, D. L. (2005). Responding to nonresponders: An experimental field trial of identification and intervention methods. *Exceptional Children, 71*, 445–463.

Mellard, D. F., & Johnson, E. (2008). *RTI: A practitioner's guide to implementing response to intervention.* Thousand Oaks, CA: Corwin Press.

National Association of State Directors of Special Education (NASDSE). (2008). Response to intervention: Blueprints for implementation. Retrieved on June 20, 2012 from http://www.nasdse.org/Portals/0/DISTRICT.pdf

National Association of State Directors of Special Education (NASDSE) and the Council of Administrators of Special Education (CASE) at the Council for Exceptional Children. (2006, May). Response to intervention: NASDSE and CASE white paper on rti. Retrieved June 21, 2012, from http://www.nasdse.org/Portals/0/Documents/Download%20Publications/RtIAnAdministratorsPerspective1-06.pdf

National Education Association. (2010). An NEA Policy Brief. Response to intervention: A transformational approach. Retrieved on June 20, 2012 from http://www.nea.org/assets/docs/HE/PB27_Responseto Intervention.pdf

National Dissemination Center for Children with Disabilities. (2011). Response to intervention. Retrieved on September 20, 2011 from http://nichcy.org/schools-administrators/rti

National Research Center on Learning Disabilities (2007). *Core concepts of RTI.* Retrieved on September 25, 2011 from http://www.nrcld.org/about/research/rti/concepts.html

Newmann, F., & Wehlage, G. (1995). *Successful school restructuring.* Madison, WI: Center on Organization and Restructuring of Schools. No Child Left Behind Act of 2001, P. L. 107-110.

Pankake, A. M. (1998). *Implementation: Making things happen.* Larchmont, NY: Eye on Education.

Pankake, A. M., Huffman, J. B., & Moller, G. (2004, February). *Professional learning communities: A synthesis of findings–A foundation for the future.* Paper presented at the Annual Meeting of the Southwest Educational Research Association, Dallas, TX.

Richards, C., Pavri, S., Golez, F., & Canges, R. (2007). Response to intervention: Building the capacity of teachers to serve students with learning difficulties. *Issues in Teacher Education, 16*(2), 55–64.

RTI Action Network. (2011). *Universal screening within a response-to-intervention model.* Retrieved December 27, 2011 from http://www.rtinetwork.org/learn/research/universal-screening-within-a-rti-model

Sailor, W. (2009*). Making rti work: How smart schools are reforming education through schoolwide response-to-intervention.* San Francisco, CA: Jossey-Bass.

Sawyer, R., Holland, D., & Detgen, A. (2008). State policies and procedures and selected local implementation practices in response to intervention in the six southeast region states (Issues & Answers Report, REL 2008-No. 63). Washington, DC: U.S. Department of Education, Institute of Education Sciences, National Center for Education Evaluation and Regional Assistance, Regional Educational Laboratory Southeast. Retrieved September 12, 2011 from http://ies.ed.gov/ncee/edlabs

Schmoker, M. (2005a). No turning back: The ironclad case for professional learning communities. In R. DuFour, R. Eaker, & R. DuFour (Eds.), *On common ground: The power of professional learning communities* (pp. 135–153). Bloomington, IN: Solution Tree.

Speece, D. L., & Case, L. P. (2001). Classification in context: An alternative approach to identifying early reading disability. *Journal of Educational Psychology, 93*(4), 735–749.

Stecker, P. M., Lembke, E. S., & Foegen, A. (2008). Using progress-monitoring data to improve instructional decision making. *Prevent School Failure, 52*(2), 48–58.

Tomlinson, C. (1999). *The differentiated classroom: Responding to the needs of all learners.* Alexandria, VA: Association for Supervision and Curriculum Development.

Wedl, R. J. (2005, July). Response to intervention: An alternative to traditional eligibility criteria for students with disabilities. Retrieved September 12, 2011 from Education/Evolving Web site: http://www.educationevolving.org/pdf/Response_to_Intervention.pdf.

Weishaar, P. M., & Weishaar, M. K. (2012). *Implementing response to intervention in reading within the elementary classroom* (pp. 65–72). Boston: Pearson.

Index